The J
of
Arthur Griffith

Colum Kenny is Professor Emeritus at Dublin City University. A barrister, journalist and historian, he has written widely on culture and society. His books include *An Irish-American Odyssey* (2014) and *Moments that Changed Us: Ireland after 1973* (2005). An honorary bencher of King's Inns, he has been awarded the gold medal of the Irish Legal History Society and the DCU President's Award for Research. A founding board member of the E.U. Media Desk in Ireland, he served on the Broadcasting Commission of Ireland.

The Enigma
of
Arthur Griffith

'Father of Us All'

COLUM KENNY

MERRION
PRESS

First published in 2020 by
Merrion Press
10 George's Street
Newbridge
Co. Kildare
Ireland
www.merrionpress.ie

9781785373145 (Paper)
978178537-3152 (Kindle)
9781785373169 (Epub)
9781785373176 (PDF)

British Library Cataloguing in Publication Data
An entry can be found on request

Library of Congress Cataloging in Publication Data
An entry can be found on request

Typeset in Minion Pro 11.5/15 pt

Cover front: *New York Times* supplement, January 1922.
Cover back: Griffith and Collins in Sligo, spring 1922 (NLI, INDH400A).

A father, Stephen said, battling against hopelessness,
is a necessary evil.

– from *Ulysses*
by James Joyce (1922).

You had the prose of logic and of scorn,
And words to sledge an iron argument,
And yet you could draw down the outland birds
To perch beside the ravens of your thought –
The dreams whereby a people challenges
Its dooms, its bounds. You were the one who knew
What sacred resistance is to men
That are almost broken; how, from resistance used,
A strength is born, a stormy, bright-eyed strength
Like Homer's Iris, messenger of the gods,
Coming before the ships the enemy
Has flung the fire upon. Our own, our native strength
You mustered up.

– from 'Odysseus: In Memory of Arthur Griffith'
by Padraic Colum (1923).

CONTENTS

I

Griffith and Mother Ireland

Arthur Griffith was 'an enigma', mysterious or difficult to understand, wrote his contemporary James Stephens. He was 'the father and the founder' of Sinn Féin, John Dillon MP informed the House of Commons in 1916.[1]

A photograph of Griffith taken in London during the treaty talks in late 1921, but published by *The New York Times* in 1922 above the caption 'Head of the Irish Free State' is a reminder of his resilience (Plate 1), – until civil war finally undid him.

Harry Boland, who fought against Griffith's side in that civil war and who died just eleven days before him, is purported to have said of Griffith to a friend, 'Damn it, Pat, hasn't he made us all?'[2] The first prime minister of the Irish Free State, W.T. Cosgrave, declared in 1925 that Michael Collins could but say 'Griffith was the greatest man of his age, the father of us all.'[3]

Griffith was a politician and thinker, a cultural and economic analyst. Yet when the French journalist Simone Téry met him in Dublin in the summer of 1921, she remarked: 'With his broad-shoulders, square fists and square face, Arthur Griffith looks more like a manual worker than an intellectual.'[4]

He was one of the founding fathers of the Irish state, if not indeed *the* founding father. It took courage and judgement for him to sign the articles of agreement for an Anglo-Irish Treaty in 1921. Doing so after him, Michael Collins said that he had signed his own death warrant. Assessing Griffith – warts and all – tells us something about ourselves. For, like him or not, he shaped the political framework of modern Ireland. When he died, his devastated and loving widow Mollie bitterly described him as having been 'a fool giving his all, others having the benefit.'[5]

James Joyce sought his advice when trying to get *Dubliners* published, and Griffith gave W.B. Yeats both paternal guidance and what John Hutchinson has described in his study of the Gaelic Revival as 'invaluable' aid.[6] Joyce and Yeats had complex relationships with their own fathers, who were not very practical.[7] Griffith's helpful dealings with these men merit closer attention than they have received to date, and they are explored in this volume. Yeats has a reputation that sometimes seems to depend on diminishing Griffith, and Joyce cannot be fully appreciated if his interest in Griffith's politics and his respect for Griffith's journalism overall is discounted.

In the Dublin societies to which he belonged when young, Griffith's friends loved him. They went rambling and cycling in the country. They swam naked at 'The Forty Foot' in Sandycove, sun-bathing nearby on the hidden roof of an old Martello Tower. James Joyce also visited that tower and located there the opening scene of his novel *Ulysses* (Plate 6). The era of Joyce's *Ulysses*, set in 1904 but not published until 1922, was also that of Griffith. What is it about this shy, hard-working nationalist, who enjoyed a quiet glass of stout with his friends and delighted in street songs, that irks some people and can find him begrudged a generous mention on commemorative occasions?

This book will take a fresh look at Griffith's life from its humble beginnings to its sudden end, and in the context of his relations with Maud Gonne, James Connolly, Éamon de Valera, James Joyce and W.B. Yeats, among others. His creation of Sinn Féin, his leadership of the treaty negotiations in London and his presidency of Dáil Éireann are traced through exciting and disturbing developments of his day. But we also see Griffith the man, father and father figure, who whistled and sang ballads and arias; who was an influential journalist and a loyal friend and husband. Darker issues are also addressed, including Irish anti-Semitism and racism.

Politic Words

One morning recently, in the hushed surrounds of Ireland's National Library where Griffith liked to read, I met someone suspicious of Griffith even yet. The man was struggling with a microfilm and requested

Griffith arrives at Earlsfort Terrace for Dáil Éireann's treaty debate in December 1921 (National Library of Ireland (INDH386]).

my help. He informed me, in a strong Ulster accent, that he was trying to access back issues of *The Freeman's Journal*. He asked me what I was researching and I told him. 'Ah', he said, giving me a certain look. 'Some people didn't like Griffith'. Then, 'He signed The Treaty' and 'he wasn't a republican'. I did not ask my neighbour to define 'republican'.

'Arthur Griffith, as the world knows, was the father of Sinn Féin,' said Griffith's acquaintance Kevin O'Shiel.[8] Yet the notion that Griffith somehow let down a victorious struggle of which he disapproved, or that the treaty that he signed was to blame for partition, gained traction following his sudden death in 1922. This is despite the fact that partition was already a reality when negotiations for a treaty began. The parliament of Northern Ireland had opened. It was axiomatic that the Irish went to London to make concessions in return for concessions. An unbending demand for the political unity of the island of Ireland as a republic would not succeed where military action had already failed. It was not partition itself, nor the continuing use of some Irish ports by the British navy, but the form of oath prescribed for members of the new Dáil and the nature of the new state's future relationship with the Crown that finally led to civil war.

In the early 1900s, Griffith laid out a constructive and principled path to independence and, within twenty years, he and his team agreed treaty terms in London that created the Irish Free State. The signing of those terms in Downing Street was an act of compromise and statesmanship by which they acknowledged that, with independence, came responsibilities. They were subsequently backed by a majority of representatives in Dáil Éireann, and thereafter by a majority of voters in a general election who chose candidates supportive of the treaty. Griffith told the people that the treaty was the basis for further developments: 'It has no more finality than we are the final generation on the face of the earth.'[9]

Griffith and his treaty delegation in London engaged in real politics with a United Kingdom government that was itself vulnerable to its own domestic pressures. The emotive and shifting nature of such constitutional negotiations has been clearly evident again during the recent Brexit debates in Britain. Brexit has been a reminder of the great challenges involved in reconciling very different perspectives, both cultural and political. Irish people, then and since, might too easily overlook the difficulties on the British side in 1921. And de Valera's refusal to attend the crucial negotiations with Prime Minister David Lloyd George from October to December 1921, no matter what his rationale, greatly complicated the challenges involved.

Griffith, like any revolutionary or politician, had both strengths and weaknesses. This book is a critical assessment, not the hagiography of a saint. It will contextualise his occasionally problematic attitudes but not seek to excuse them. Was he 'narrow' as some detractors allege? Overall, his voluminous journalism suggests otherwise. However, given how much he wrote and that he did so usually to a tight deadline, it is unsurprising to find that Griffith sometimes penned or printed regrettable statements. He was no perfect Marvel-comic hero. He was a small, limping, lower-middle-class politician with poor eyesight, an unglamourous wife, an aversion to dramatising violence and a tendency to sharp comments. Yet his leadership inspired a generation.

Was Griffith also among those who regarded art or literature ultimately as 'the scullery maid of politics'? W.B. Yeats used that term dismissively about people whom he distinguished from 'the men [*sic*] of letters' and from those 'who love literature for her own sake' (whatever that might mean). It is true that Griffith believed literature should serve purposes other than those of mere entertainment or even speculation. Yet for him the priority of Irish independence by no means precluded art from providing pleasure or enlightenment. While he was strongly critical of *The Playboy of the Western World*, his antipathy to John Millington Synge has been somewhat exaggerated, and the weekly papers that he edited for twenty years bear eloquent witness to the fact that he was no philistine. In any event, literature is never entirely free of ideological, social or political implications.

Griffith is an awkward father figure, the one who cannot be denied but whose actions and foibles risk exposing characteristics and contradictions in ourselves that we would rather not see. In the case of Yeats, it is instructive to recall the period when that poet was a member of the Irish Republican Brotherhood (IRB), and when Griffith boosted Yeats' career. Yeats later wished to put behind him his former IRB membership but it possibly helped him to win a seat in the senate of the new Irish Free State.[10] When considering the dynamics of the relationship between Griffith and Yeats it should be remembered too that both men were closely involved with the dazzling Maud Gonne, a fact that the patrician Yeats turned to his reputational advantage even as the paternal Griffith did not.

Born in the heart of Dublin, Griffith was a hard-working artisan who married late due to his poverty, who then had two children whom he deeply loved. He was ready to compromise, including with unionists, but firm in his resolve that independence was Ireland's right and that the Irish Free State was a stepping-stone towards greater things. 'How time has justified the Irish Treaty,' wrote the ambassador Michael MacWhite to W.T. Cosgrave as the Irish Free State became a republic in 1949. 'We know now what Griffith meant when he wanted freedom to achieve freedom,' he added.[11] The fact of partition was already a reality when Griffith signed the agreement for a treaty and, contrary to a widespread misunderstanding, was not the immediate cause of de

Valera's resignation as president of a Dáil that then voted to accept the document that Griffith and Collins had signed in London.

Mother Ireland

A constellation of defeat, dependency, despondency and martyrdom – in the face of sometimes brutal imperialism – gave strength over centuries to the myth of Mother Ireland as a poor woman reduced to demanding the self-sacrifice of her sons for an almost hopeless cause. That woman, known as 'My Dark Rosaleen', 'Kathleen Ni Houlihan', 'Shan Van Vocht', 'Éire/Erin' etc., was both an object of desire and a pietà, whose beloved children's blood watered a tree symbolising national regeneration or resurrection. For James Joyce's Stephen, Ireland was 'the old sow that eats her farrow'.[12] Griffith himself invoked regeneration by using the word 'resurrection' in the title of his key 1904 tract on the constitutional and economic salvation of Ireland (*The Resurrection of Hungary*), while the weekend that rebels chose for the 'rising' in 1916 was significantly that of the festival of Christ's resurrection. In 1917 Yeats wrote of Ireland that 'There's nothing but our own red blood can make a right Rose Tree,' while also expressing dismay that 'a breath of politic words has withered our Rose Tree'. He was still singing in 1938, as he flirted with fascist ideas:

> And yet who knows what's yet to come?
> For Patrick Pearse had said
> That in every generation
> Must Ireland's blood be shed.

Griffith preferred 'politic words' to bloodshed, regarding them as an art and a democratic necessity rather than a withering disease. Yet, he was no pacifist, for he advocated defensive force and even countenanced attack where it was necessary. In 1914 he attended a key private meeting with Patrick Pearse and other future signatories of the 1916 proclamation and, as will be seen, agreed a broad strategy with them. He participated in the Howth gun-running of 1914 and later drilled dutifully with the rifle that he got there, although he was not at the barricades on Easter Monday 1916. He subsequently became acting president of the provisional government during the War of Independence, when de Valera went to America for eighteen months.

Griffith informed and guided the political consciousness of a cultural revival that had floated on an ocean of sentimental affection for the idea of Mother Ireland, or 'Erin' – that poor old woman worn down, but destined to come into her queenly inheritance and be rejuvenated: 'There was much Kathleen Ni Houlihan, Dark Rosaleen poetry written,' Mary Colum later remarked somewhat sarcastically of the period.[13] Griffith himself was not adverse to idealising Ireland and Irish women when articulating his vision of an Ireland that he hoped would be self-sufficient, while also being less materialistic than England. However, his unifying emphasis was ultimately modern and pragmatic.

In an effort to explain the significance of Sinn Féin's sensational victory at the polls in 1918, the Anglo-Irish anarchist Jack White offered a psychological interpretation inspired by the 'subliminal uprush' idea of pioneering psychologist Frederic H. Myers, who also influenced W.B. Yeats. White saw Sinn Féin's function as one of 're-introducing pure emotion as a factor in Western world-politics', which could only be prevented from 'lapsing into hysteria' by the restraints and objectives of organised labour. White's well-intended theory ran the risk of once more casting 'the Irish race' (as he called it) as essentially the wild and 'intuitive' type.[14] Griffith's plan was not 'pure emotion' but was to harness national consciousness within national political structures such as existed elsewhere in Europe, taking advantage of an expanding electorate with its broader social base and with some women enfranchised for the first time in 1918. He wanted voters to accept the need for and benefit of self-reliant institutions rather than just venting their anger or lapsing into reliance on favours from the Westminster parliament. He wished to see people develop independently and, in that respect, attempted to exercise on a national level that which Carl Jung has represented as the centrally organising psychic function of a father.

In July 1922, as Ireland faced into civil war, the distinguished Welsh psychoanalyst Ernest Jones also addressed non-political factors that might throw light on the political roots of the English–Irish conflict. He recognised the particularly rich variety of female names used by the

Irish for Ireland, remarking that 'the customary one of Erin … would content most countries'. The tradition of the Gaelic 'aisling' or dream poetry had fostered such variety. Jones wrote that 'The complexes to which the idea of an island home tends to become attached are those relating to the idea of woman'. He suggested that history might have been different had England 'instead of ravishing Ireland as though she were a harlot, wooed her with the offer of an honorable alliance'.[15] He also discerned Oedipal implications in the strong identification of the homeland as 'mother', and these are relevant to a consideration of the fate and reputation of anyone cast in the national role of 'father of us all'.

In a gloss on Jones' commentary, one Irish analyst in 1998 cautioned against seeing the dominance of the myth of Mother Ireland as some kind of deterministic or primary given. Cormac Gallagher related the myth to what he saw as a singular lack of Irish father figures. Instead, there are 'sons and brothers who have been willing to lay down their lives to defend the honour of their mother'. He asked, with an eye perhaps to Freud's key text on the biblical patriarch, 'Where do we find an Irish Moses?'[16] In doing so, he echoed the lament of Gaelic poets who identified Ireland's plight with that of Israel.

For years after King William routed King James at the battle of the Boyne in 1690, many Irish regarded the possible return of a Jacobite king or prince as their best hope of salvation. The impoverished poet James Clarence Mangan, who died in 1849 and who intrigued not only Griffith but also Yeats and Joyce, ended his rendering of an old Jacobite song by praying that 'He who stood by Moses, when his foes were fierce and strong' might 'show forth his might in saving Kathleen-Ni-Houlahan [i.e. Ireland]'. Gradually, Irish writers identified possible Irish versions of the biblical patriarch who had led the Jews out of captivity in Egypt. Charles Stewart Parnell in particular but also Michael Davitt by Fanny Parnell were cast in this fantasy role.[17] Another candidate was 'Griffith', albeit as Moses in the shape of a leader for an industrialised and democratic age, or even as a modern version of the Irish patriarch St Patrick, determined to drive out all snakes of faction and convert his people from UK parliamentarianism to Irish independence.

However, in Yeats' influential play *Kathleen Ni Houlihan*, written with assistance from Lady Gregory and even ostensibly with some help

Supplement gratis with the WEEKLY NATIONAL PRESS, 24th OCTOBER, 1891.   PRICE ONE PENNY.

Ireland grapples with the serpent 'Faction' following the death of Parnell in October 1891 (*Weekly National Press*, 24 October 1891).

from Griffith as will be seen, it was not sustained paternal leadership but the blood sacrifice of her children that was seen to redeem Mother Ireland. Indeed, relative to certain 'typical examples' of 'innumerable' identifications of Ireland as a woman that he cited (and for the selection of which he thanked one Violet Fitzgerald), Ernest Jones found the final scene of Yeats' *Kathleen Ni Houlihan* to be for him 'the most moving description of all'.[18] Yeats himself later wondered if his words were responsible for sending men out to die in the Rising.

Following that bloody revolt of 1916, Éamon de Valera stepped into the sandals of Moses but then delegated to Griffith the task of crossing the Irish Sea to negotiate a treaty. Although in 1923 a former IRB man George Lyons described Griffith as 'the Moses who led his benighted people out of the shadows into the light', Griffith never satisfied de Valera. Was de Valera, whose own father and mother were absent from most of his childhood,[19] unconsciously taking revenge by sending the man then known as the 'father of Sinn Féin' to London instead of going himself? De Valera was 'president' or first minister of the new Dáil Éireann and might reasonably have been expected to sit opposite Prime Minister Lloyd George during those negotiations. His absence was critical.

Griffith long encouraged people to assert their independence (*sinn féin, sinn féin amháin*: we ourselves alone) rather than wait impassively to be washed clean by the blood of martyrs or yearn impotently and submissively for that salvation from abroad that Gaelic poetry long invoked. Yet anyone who thought that he might have earned for himself the eternal gratitude of all those whom he led to the promised land of an Irish state had not reckoned with the kind of patricidal or Oedipal undercurrents that are as much a feature of nations as of families.

During a bitter parliamentary debate on 27 April 1922, Griffith claimed that when he agreed the previous October to lead a delegation to negotiate a treaty, de Valera said to him, 'There may have to be scapegoats.' He told the Dáil that he replied to de Valera that he was 'willing to be a scapegoat to save him from some of his present supporters' criticism'. And Griffith was to become something of a scapegoat, not just in respect to the treaty but also as regards Irish anti-Semitism. His reputation as well as his life fell victim to the civil war, during which he collapsed and died in August 1922.

Patriotic verses that Yeats wrote in 1891 mourning Parnell as Moses were reprinted in 1922 to mourn Griffith in the same terms. Since then, some politicians have used his name to bolster their arguments, but others have opted not to speak of him at all. That may be easier than admitting that he was an Irishman who perhaps represented the emerging consensus of an increasingly inclusive electoral franchise more accurately than did his more violent friends and acquaintances. To this day remembering Griffith disturbs our national psyche. If we drop a bucket into his pond we draw up a mix as real but less heady than the blood of which Yeats sang so gloriously. We may unconsciously yearn for the intoxication of heroic daydreams.

It is true that twenty-six of the thirty-two counties of Ireland might not have achieved what level of independence they did in 1922 without the shock of the rebellion and executions of 1916 or the plotting of the IRB and the Volunteers. However, it was the constant commitment and steady hard work of Arthur Griffith and a few others that created and sustained the Sinn Féin movement, giving context and shape to the emotional desire for freedom and eventually enshrining that ambition in a viable constitutional compromise that was pragmatic rather than fanciful. Griffith risked his life, but saw no good reason to throw it away. His way was fatherly, at times paternalistic. His friends and critics alike frequently used epithets to describe him that were characteristic of positive and negative aspects of the father archetype.

The Ireland of the European Union, of the United Nations, of the Good Friday Agreement is the kind of everyday Ireland for which Griffith worked. The state's foundation in 1922 should not be recalled in 2022 without generously recognising his crucial role in its conception and birth.

The Name of the Father

Arthur Griffith was born at 61 Upper Dominick Street, Dublin, on 31 March 1871. His widow later said that Dublin was 'where his grandfather or great-grandfather had come to from Redhills in Cavan, having been thrown out by his Presbyterian family because he had become Catholic'.[1]

Arthur Griffith's father, who was also named Arthur, was a printer. He was of the Dublin artisan class that comprised the backbone of the Fenian movement. Among Fenians who had been 'out' in the troubled year 1867 was another printer, the present author's great-grandfather, Michael Kenny. In 1898 Michael took out of its frame an old printed oleograph sketch of 'The Death of Ireland's Liberator' (namely Daniel O'Connell) that his own father had earlier framed in 1849. The sketch clearly meant something to Michael, for he carefully cleaned and reframed it.[2]

Young Arthur Griffith was known by his family, friends and future wife as 'Dan'. Some believe that he got this name 'because of his boundless capacity for debate and his consummate absorption with the cause of national independence. To his associates he was another Daniel O'Connell.'[3] If so, the nickname identified Griffith with a political leader whose peaceful parliamentary campaign to repeal the union of Ireland and Britain had failed, and on whom in his younger days Griffith used to 'pour unlimited scorn'.[4] He preferred the writings and songs of the revolutionary movement that superseded O'Connell in the 1840s, looking up to the Young Ireland leaders Thomas Davis, John Mitchell and James Fintan Lalor. Scattered throughout the papers of which he became editor are many extracts from their works. Ironically, given such views, 'Dan' would later develop into a democratic constitutionalist, defending the nascent Irish state against those whom his colleague Kevin O'Higgins described as 'wild men screaming through the keyholes'.[5]

Griffith's nickname 'Dan' also hints at fatherly warmth, with its last consonant lenthening the first two letters that spell the most common Dublin term of endearment for a father, 'Da'. One of his friends later wrote 'that name, I think, gave his likeableness and his humour'.[6]

In 1899, Griffith delivered a public talk in the Workingmen's Club on 'The Songs of our Fathers', including patriotic songs that reflected Young Ireland and Fenian values. This was probably the same Griffith lecture 'on the ballad poetry of the Young Ireland period' that a future president of Ireland, Seán T. O'Kelly (also Ó Ceallaigh), attended that year.[7] In Griffith's own life, the Young Irelander and veteran Fenian leader John O'Leary (1830–1907) became an occasional fatherly mentor or advisor.

Griffith's Creed

In an editorial in the first issue of his *United Irishman*, on 4 March 1899, Griffith wrote:

Lest there be a doubt in any mind, we will say that we accept the [revolutionary] Nationalism of [17]98, [18]48 and [18]67 as the true Nationalism; and Grattan's cry 'Live Ireland – Perish the Empire!' as the watchword of patriotism.

Two years later he repeated that sentiment. He also then described three movements as 'tending to build up and brace the Nation for the final struggle for independence', these being movements for the development of the Irish language, literature and industry. He regarded every objective as ultimately subsidiary to the achievement of independence itself:

A fatter Gaelic-speaking Ireland kissing its chains would be perhaps more contemptible than even a pauperized, English-tongued Ireland fighting with its mouth against the Government which believes in preaching to the weak from the 'holy text of pike and gun'. What we wrote in the first issue of the *United Irishman* [4 March 1899, quoted above] we reaffirm as our creed.[8]

To understand Griffith, to fathom his methodology and motives, it is crucial to recognise his single-mindedness. James Owen Hannay, a Church of Ireland clergyman who penned popular novels as 'George A. Birmingham', wrote of Griffith that 'He was more idea-possessed than any one I have ever met and the idea which possessed him to the exclusion of every other was that of an Ireland free to lead her own life and manage her own affairs.'[9] Helena Molony, secretary of Inghinidhe na hÉireann between 1907 and 1914, admired his capacity to inspire people to overlook differences of opinion and work together.[10]

Five factors in particular shaped Griffith's character and outlook, and he cannot be understood without appreciating the importance of each of them. Their burning significance for him may not be self-evident today when Irish people live in a very different Ireland, as he always hoped we would:

- His poverty and that of his city
- The Parnell affair and its lasting trauma
- The role of the Catholic Church
- Catastrophic and continuing emigration
- British economic and political repression

His Poverty and that of his City

Griffith was raised in the heart of a city teeming with poverty. The slums of Dublin were amongst the worst in Europe, with many of its Georgian houses that had been home to prosperous middle-class families before the Act of Union of 1800 now reduced to tenements.[11] Dublin's population had increased as people deserted rural Ireland, not least during the Great Famine, putting great pressure on its infrastructure. Political union with Britain after 1800 had not benefited Ireland, and both Dublin and Cork 'saw the manufacturing share of their workforce halved between the famine and the early twentieth century'.[12] Diseases such as tuberculosis and typhoid were rampant. Griffith's own father suffered from bad health for years and the Griffiths moved a number of times, always renting rooms in central Dublin in an arc around Summerhill. It was an area blighted by decline.

Griffith's parents Arthur and Mary had been married at Dublin's pro-cathedral on 14 May 1860 and had five children.[13] Their son Frank, born in 1874, said that his father 'often' spoke of having been in Richmond, Virginia, at some point during the US civil war of 1861–5, and of having worked as a printer on the popular *Illustrated London News* in England before settling back in Ireland.[14] Frank himself sometimes helped to run the *United Irishman* office and was an usher in the Gaiety Theatre.[15] Frank's brother Billy was born in Dublin in 1865. Billy, 'upright and conscientious', became a hairdresser and, as registrar of the hairdressers' trade union, found jobs for unemployed barbers. He died of pneumonia in 1924.[16] Their sister Marcella was a machinist who, in 1900, died of an ulcerous disease of the larynx of a tubercular nature.[17] Their other sister, Frances (known as 'Fanny'), joined the women's nationalist group Inghinidhe na hÉireann, and lived until 1949.[18]

In 1897 Arthur Griffith bid farewell to his parents and went to South Africa, working there at a small newspaper and in mining administration. He returned by September the following year 'as poor as when leaving Ireland' his widow later wrote. She added 'Poor Dan never could make money.'[19] His father died in 1904, aged 66.[20] Griffith was still unmarried, and during the first decade of the twentieth century continued to reside in the family's rented rooms at 83 Summerhill (today the site of a modern block). He supported his widowed mother and surviving sister Frances. A fellow tenant in that house later said that 'The Griffiths lived a very quiet life.' The house belonged to the widow of a seaman who had been drowned.[21]

The Griffiths moved in the shadow of 'Monto', a notorious district centred on Montgomery Street and known for prostitution. James Joyce memorialised it as 'Nighttown' in *Ulysses*. A description of the adjacent Gardiner Street about 1900 is graphic:

Fifty years ago this street was inhabited by professional people and other rich residents, and every house had its carriage, its coachman and its butler. To-day this imposing stretch of street has sunk to the condition of a street of tenement houses, inhabited not alone by the lowest class of society but by the tramp and vagrant, and mendicant classes. The area around it ... constitutes, perhaps, the greatest blot upon the social life of Dublin and of Ireland. There is no such area in London, or in any other town of Great Britain, that I ever saw or heard of. Within this area the trade of prostitution and immorality is carried on as openly as any branch of legitimate business is carried on in the other portions of Dublin.[22]

Many impoverished Dubliners joined the army. Molly Bloom in Joyce's *Ulysses* lies in bed musing on the attraction of a lost soldier, recalling one she liked who was killed on the British side in the Boer War: 'he was a lovely fellow in khaki and just the right height over me ... he was pale with excitement about going away ... and I so hot as I never felt'.

Griffith and other contributors to his papers sometimes idealised Irish women and protested against certain theatrical depictions of them. There is a curious mixture of respect and chauvinism in his admonition to young Irishmen: 'Do not talk lightly of women. To do so is to be English.'[23] His attitude was partly informed by the degradation and exploitation that he saw before his eyes. When he conducted a campaign against Irish girls walking out with soldiers on Dublin's main thoroughfare, he was not simply being priggish. His principal objective was to discourage recruitment, but he also saw the effects of economic deprivation on people's options and of prevalent venereal disease on their health. In 1918 Francis Hackett wrote of those who followed James Connolly in rebellion that 'They knew that incest and prostitution and syphilis accompanied that slum life, a life of indecencies so unmentionable that no one can fully quote the government reports [e.g. of 1914].'[24] Unlike some of the clients of 'Nighttown', people who lived near it had not fragrant homes in the suburbs to which to retreat.

When he became an editor, Griffith liked to meet friends over a glass or two of stout, but he never grew rich and was widely believed to have refused better-remunerated journalism in Dublin and abroad in order to continue working on his advanced nationalist papers. Chrissie Doyle, an activist, later said that he was 'awfully badly off ... The story is true of his working in his office in stockinged feet while his shoes, the only pair he had, were being repaired at the shoemakers. He was the most simple of men … he would eat anything served to him'.[25] Dan McCarthy, who helped Griffith to produce the *United Irishman*, described him as 'poverty-stricken', and McCarthy and others commented on his worn clothing.[26]

Sinn Féin, 13 November 1909. By Austin Molloy ('Maolmhuaidh').
Dirty streets added to the threat of diseases such as TB and typhoid.

James Joyce appreciated Griffith's efforts to improve the lot of his people. In 1906, in Italy, he wrote that

> as far as my knowledge of Irish affairs goes, he was the first person in Ireland to revive the separatist idea on modern lines nine years ago. He wants the creation of an Irish consular service abroad and of an Irish bank at home ... He said in one of his articles that it cost a Danish merchant less to send butter to Christiania and then by sea to London than it costs an Irish merchant to send his from Mullingar to Dublin. A great deal of his programme perhaps is absurd but at least it tries to inaugurate some commercial life for Ireland and to tell you the truth once or twice in Trieste I felt myself humiliated when I heard the little Galatti girl sneering at my impoverished country. You may remember that on my arrival in Trieste I actually 'took some steps' to secure an agency for Foxford Tweeds there.[27]

The Parnell Affair

The political divisions that marked Parnell's downfall were deeply felt by Griffith. There was a pervasive bitterness such as Joyce encapsulated in his *Portrait of the Artist as a Young Man* when a row over Christmas dinner in Bray ends with an angry but gleeful cry: 'At the door Dante turned round violently and shouted down the room, her cheeks flushed and quivering with rage: – Devil out of hell! We won! We crushed him to death! Fiend! The door slammed behind her.'

When Parnell fell in disgrace for having an affair, and died soon afterwards, the door slammed shut for years on the prospect of Ireland winning back a measure of political independence through 'Home Rule', which Irish parliamentarians at Westminster had been seeking. Griffith as a young man emotionally defended Parnell, although he was not an enthusiast for Parnell's parliamentarianism. He regarded Parnell's downfall as an example of the factional distractions that destroy political movements, and to the end of his days insisted on the primacy of the fight for political independence over all else. This is the key to understanding his loss of interest in artists when they diverged on an individualistic or subjective track.

Similarly, he drew a clear distinction between private and public life when this suited his objectives. During the Parnell split certain leading English politicians and some members of the Irish Catholic hierarchy and of the Irish Parliamentary Party responded to news of Parnell's relationship with Katharine O'Shea by turning on the leader. But Griffith articulated in the *United Irishman* a general principle that 'A man can be a good patriot without being virtuous in his private life.'[28] This was not the later sentiment of an anonymous writer of a Sinn Féin pamphlet in September 1917 who declared 'The only way to be a patriotic Irishman is to do your best to become a perfect man.'[29] Griffith in 1900 contrasted the example of an Arab leader who unwisely appointed 'a notorious libertine' to be keeper of the harem with one who appointed such a man as the State Treasurer:

> I do not see, unless the libertine were also a rogue, why he should not prove himself a faithful public servant. I do not believe that a political leader should be deposed for any save a political offence. I believe the Irish people made themselves ridiculous by their treatment of Charles Stewart Parnell. He had committed no political crime. He had not sinned against *them*.

This led to debate in his paper between himself and a regular contributor, the nationalist priest Fr Patrick Fidelis Kavanagh.[30] Griffith's position was consistent when it came to the scandalous Oscar Wilde and his homosexuality, a sexual orientation into which Griffith may have had some personal insight due to the warmth of his devotion to his close friend William Rooney who died young:

> Last week one of the most brilliant Irishmen of the century, Oscar Wilde, died. Our highly moral Dublin newspapers printed the announcement in their back columns. The *Evening Herald* timidly referred to the passing of Wilde in order to bring in a compliment to Mr John Redmond. For it appears that Mr Redmond had the moral courage, once upon a time, to quote some lines of Wilde's poetry to the British House of Commons ... It was not because Wilde was a sinner that our cowardly journals kept silence – it was because they feared to shock the fetid conscience of pharisaical England.[31]

And when reviewing *A Treasury of Irish Poetry in the English Tongue*, edited by S.A. Brooke and T.W. Rolleston, Griffith complained of Wilde's omission: 'We have not Wilde. 'Twould have offended the virtuous Englishman to have included him.'[32] That Griffith thus distinguished between Wilde's public and private lives may surprise some who assume that his criticism of Synge's *Playboy* was merely prudish.

Griffith's inclusiveness meant that he wished the cause of Irish nationalism to encompass all who desired to embrace it. He made this clear in the first issue of his *United Irishman*, and repeated and endorsed that position in the issue of 18 May 1901 when wrapping up what had become a somewhat bitter exchange in the paper as to whether 'there is no Irishman but the Gael' (or 'the Irish are now a composite race'). Of this proposition he wrote:

> That the very same test which is the hall-mark of the American citizen ought to be the test of the Irishman, that he accept the doctrine of an Irish nation, Irish in its language, Irish in its policy, Irish in every outlook of its national life; and that to forswear all allegiance to every other nation in the world ... be he Gael or Cromwellian, French-Huguenot or Spanish-Irish, the man who swears to an Irish Nation and he only is an Irishman.[33]

To this list he was explicitly to add Jewish people, as will be seen. In his *United Irishman* on 15 February 1902 he stated: 'Ireland is our mother whichever father begot us.' In 1927, when the minister for external affairs Desmond FitzGerald referred at a public meeting to Tom Johnson, the English-born leader of the Irish Labour Party, a heckler cried 'He is an Englishman.' FitzGerald retorted 'Long ago Arthur Griffith said an Irishman was a man who was prepared to work for the Irish people, and in the Black and Tan days Tom Johnson did his part in the job.'[34]

The Parnell affair clearly demonstrated the threat of divisivness to Irish political ambitions, but Griffith himself was under no illusions about his own shortcomings as a possible unifying national leader. In *Ulysses*, James Joyce has a character declare that Griffith 'has no go in him for the mob'. Griffith readily placed his hopes in others. At the same time, his acquaintance Padraic Colum understood that the downfall of Parnell had taught Griffith the dangers of relying on just one man:

> In Arthur Griffith's mind there were contradictions. He was to devote his maturity to the formation of an order in which Parnellism or O'Connellism would have no part. And yet, more than any other man, he believed in the avatar. He saw Parnell as an avatar. He was to see Éamon de Valera as an avatar. Parnellism had been a tremendous force – he had felt it – but was it right that a country should put its whole trust in one man? And there was O'Connellism which, too, had left the country at a dead end. But here was one who would lead the country – William Rooney [his friend who died young].[35]

The Role of the Catholic Church

The vast majority of Irish nationalists were observant members of the Catholic Church, but Griffith was not afraid to question its authorities and pointed out that it was legitimate for a Roman Catholic to do so.[36] His *United Irishman* contextualised Irish hierarchical power by noting a condemnation of anti-English Boers that was published in *L'Osservatore Romano*, the Vatican newspaper, and recalling when 'Bishop Moriarty condemned the Fenians.'[37] One correspondent soon complained that 'The *United Irishman* lends its pages to writers who slander the Catholic Church.'[38]

The fact that Griffith came partly of Ulster Protestant stock may have given him a particular insight into religion, with one of his ancestors leaving his church for the love of a Catholic woman. Griffith looked around at Ireland's rapidly shrinking population and advised young men 'if you can do nothing else for your country, get married'. He thought that Catholic priests were infected by a 'gloomy Presbyterian spirit':

> Lack of employment and grinding poverty are largely responsible for the ever-continuing and increasing emigration. If the Irish people support their own industries they can mitigate those evils. But there is another and a potent cause in the drab dullness of Irish rural life.

With the priests of Ireland the remedy lies; with good intentions, but bad judgement they frowned down upon the merrymaking, the ceilidh and roadside dance, which gave colour and joy to the lives of the poor. Irish men and women cannot live merely to work and eat and sleep, and thousands of those who flee yearly from the land do so to escape the dreary monotony of life in a country where the gloomy Presbyterian spirit seems to have infected so many of the Catholic clergy. The Gaelic League has done much to bring a little joy into the people's life. The three thousand priests of Ireland, by being true to their own Irish nature, could do much ...[39]

A week later, he pointed out that the proportion of Protestants in Ireland was rising relative to Catholics (and thus was Anglo-Irish culture spreading), demanding to know what the Catholic hierarchy would do to resist the trend.[40] There were also sharp exchanges in his paper following its publication of a negative review of Canon Sheehan's novel *My New Curate*.[41] And a nationalist priest in sympathy with Griffith's political aims nevertheless attacked a letter in the *United Irishman* written by the socialist Fred Ryan. The priest condemned its 'heresy' in ridiculing the doctrine of eternal hell in the context of a discussion of Chinese news, and demanded to know if the paper would 'be used in future for disseminating such un-Christian and un-Catholic doctrines'. Griffith as editor blandly replied underneath 'we are not responsible for the opinions of our correspondents'.[42]

Griffith favoured the provision of non-denominational higher education and published criticism of a 'sycophantic speech' about a Catholic university made to a gathering of Englishmen by the Jesuit intellectual Fr Thomas Finlay (with whom James Connolly also had a disagreement). Griffith's objections to Finlay's idea were as much socio-economic as secular, it being 'proposed to tax the workers for the education of the sons of landowners and retired commercials'.[43] Such critical views in his paper, including one outright reference by a letter writer to 'the spirit of opportunism, full-fledged in the Irish Catholic Church',[44] cannot have endeared Griffith to its bishops. Those views may even have contributed to a perception of him as 'un-Irish', or not 'typically' Irish, that will be considered later. In the end, indeed, it was a defamation action by a priest that forced the *United Irishman* out of business.

W.B. Yeats described Griffith in his thirties as 'an enthusiastic anti-cleric',[45] but the editor did not like being boxed in by definitions. Celebrating the survival of his first paper on its second anniversary, Griffith wrote 'they accused us of being madmen, notoriety-seekers, socialists, bigots, cranks, anti-clericals, anti-Parnellites and Parnellites. We were none of these things. We were Irishmen, speaking straight to the people'.[46]

Straight talking got him into some trouble with a prominent churchman at a tense moment in October 1921. With the treaty talks due to begin in London, the Dáil's cabinet was making detailed preparations. Nasty rumours about de Valera and his ministers were circulating, and the Irish republican delegation's office in Rome informed Griffith that the rumours had reached the ears of John Hagan, rector of the Irish College there. Ministers suspected 'enemy work', and a brief note was dashed off on behalf of Griffith as minister for foreign affairs requesting Hagan to name whoever had spread the rumours in Rome. Hagan, who was sympathetic to republicans and was de Valera's personal confessor for a period, took great umbrage at this innocuous note, claiming that it was 'almost insulting in tone and written as from a superior to an inferior'. Margaret Gavan Duffy at the Irish office in Rome immediately contacted de Valera seeking his intervention, and the latter promptly wrote to the rector to explain, if not to apologise, that

> the apparent curtness was due to the fact that it was dictated by the minister in charge in a moment's interval in a Cabinet discussion on a reply which we were about to send to Lloyd George. The pressure of work here is very great and there is little time to give to our letters that polish and finish which we desire.

Emigration from Ireland

In 1918 Francis Hackett, the Irish-born founding editor of the influential left-wing *New Republic* journal in New York, pointed out that the population of Ireland halved between 1851 and 1914.[48]

The impact and scale of Irish migration in the nineteenth century and beyond can scarcely be exaggerated. Many who left went with a feeling of being wrenched away. The 1841 census of the United Kingdom, which is considered to be the first modern UK census, revealed that then, before the Great Famine, the population of Ireland (8.2m) was more than half that of England and Wales combined (15.9m). By 1901, it was about one-seventh, with just 4.5m inhabitants left on the island of Ireland but 32.5m people living in England and Wales. The *United Irishman* noted on 12 April 1900 that, on one day alone, 'The extraordinary number of Irish people fleeing to the United States resulted in the frightful exodus of 1,100 on Easter Sunday, with "wild Irish howls", as our friends say.'

In August 1900, it was reported that a rumour that French troops had landed in the west of Ireland swept through Irish migrant labourers in Lancashire and that up to a thousand of these workers fled home in panic to the west of Ireland.[49] In September 1900 Griffith devoted two and a half columns to the trauma of emigration, within the context of addressing Franco–Irish relations. He evoked the memory of the

In ten years to 1891 the population fell by half a million. From *United Ireland*, 11 April 1891.

French force under General Jean Joseph Humbert that had landed in Co. Mayo in 1798:

> The mountain men of Connaught and Ulster, whose grandfathers marched after the banner of France and Humbert to Castlebar, still anxiously ask the sympathetic travelers when the French will come again … And France will not despise their simple faith. If fifty years ago, when nine millions of our people dwelt within our four seas, the tide of hope bounded fiercely through our veins and the lessons of self-reliance appealed strongly to us, it is not so today. We are a dwindling, sickly people, dwindling to extinction, and the blast of the war-bugles of France across our land is needed to rouse us from this death-sleep that is creeping upon us to save us from the Antichrist of Nations who e'er he destroys us, would fain mark us with the Mark of the Beast.[50]

On 15 December 1900 the *United Irishman* noted the death of Michael G. Mulhall (1836–1900), a fellow of the Royal Statistical Society, whose dictionary of international statistics was widely read. Mulhall had made the point that, during the reign of Victoria, 1,225,000 Irish people had died of famine, 4,186,000 emigrated and 3,668,000 were evicted: 'The only European country which has suffered depopulation in the present century is Ireland …. The marriage-rate and birth-rate are the lowest in the world.'[51] Yet Griffith, a contrarian editor, also published a lengthy piece by Edward McVey advocating emigration as the best option for young Irish people.[52]

From time to time in Ireland, including in the *United Irishman* on 15 June 1901, it was claimed bitterly that the editor of the London *Times* wrote during the Great Famine: 'A Catholic Celt will be as rare in Ireland as a Red Indian on the shores of Manhattan.' The currency of the claim, regarded as symptomatic of British disdain, is reflected in a reference to it in Joyce's *Ulysses*. The renowned Stanley Morison for *The Times* later suggested that the quotation had not appeared in a leading article, but conceded in respect to the Celts of Ireland 'going and going with a vengeance' that some such words 'may have appeared' in a letter or telegram that was published.[53]

British Economic and Political Repression

Griffith's analysis of the actual causes of economic disadvantage in Ireland was detailed. Britain had long restricted Irish trade to its own advantage, and the Irish had little control of taxation or investment in their own country. Hackett thought that, for Griffith, 'The economics of Ireland were secondary to his hatred of England, stones of wrath in a Ulysses battle against the Manchester Cyclops.'[54] Kelly suggests 'It is easy to be sceptical about Griffith's constitutional theories, his economic projections, and his statistics.'[55] But were Griffith's arguments not at least as evidence-based as those of his opponents?

Griffith's papers included much information on agriculture and banking and many other areas of Irish life. He condemned restrictions on Irish trade as well as the dearth of local capital for investment in Irish business, something that Catholics in particular felt keenly. He articulated their suspicion that they were discriminated against by Protestant bankers and investors in favour of Protestant and even Jewish businessmen, the latter being free to join the Freemasons while the Catholic Church forbid its members to do so. He pointed out that Ireland payed a disproportionately high share of taxation while enjoying a low share of the United Kingdom's capital investment. On 23 March 1901, for example, the *United Irishman* indicated that invested capital in Ireland was one-forty-fourth of that available throughout the United Kingdom while taxation revenue was one-twelfth of the whole. Griffith also published pamphlets, with James Joyce buying his tract on *The Finance of the Home Rule Bill*, for example.[56]

Griffith's Sinn Féin movement forefronted industrial development. He and other party members and supporters were closely involved in the Industrial Development Association (IDA), a voluntary precursor of the future state's Industrial Development Authority. According to Seán T. O'Kelly, writing when he later became the president of Ireland, 'Mrs. Wyse Power, afterwards Senator; Ryan who was afterwards the first Secretary of the I.D.A. and Kevin J. Kenny [grandfather of the present author], were the principal promoters of the I.D.A. in Dublin.'[57] Jennie Wyse Power, nationalist and suffragette, ran the Irish Farm and Produce Company. At its shop and restaurant at 21 Henry St, Dublin, in the months before the 1916 Rising, O'Kelly frequently lunched with Griffith, Seán Mac Diarmada (MacDermott) and other activists. A plaque on the site now commemorates the signing of the 1916 proclamation there.

With Wyse Power, Mac Diarmada, Kevin J. Kenny, Bulmer Hobson, Helena Molony and others, Griffith in 1907 formed the first Aonach committee. The annual Aonach, or industrial fair, held under Sinn Féin auspices between 1908 and 1914, served to popularise that political movement amongst Dublin businesses and to emphasise its importance.[58] When Griffith's weekly *Sinn Féin* paper went daily for a period he subtitled it 'The Daily National Industrial Journal'. From 1908 Griffith also published, through Sinn Féin, the innovative *Leabhar na hÉireann: The Irish Year Book,* which was a digest of information intended to boost Irish manufacturing. When he reorganised it for 1910, he stated that 'the business side of the book has been entrusted to the capable hands of Mr Kevin J. Kenny', who founded Ireland's first full-service advertising agency. This commercial relationship did not stop Griffith later from publishing criticism of Kenny when the latter's agency was hired to promote military recruitment.[59] *The Irish Year Book* of 1910 included an article contending with certain prejudices among established Irish companies against advertising, a commercial practice that some saw as 'undignified' and ineffective.[60]

During 1910, Griffith described the *Year Book* and the Aonach, along with the Sinn Féin Co-operative People's Bank Ltd which he had also founded (Plate 10), as three institutions Sinn Féin established that 'could claim to be successful from the first'.[61] If such innovative activities make Griffith a capitalist, they also place him in the mainstream of Irish economic ambitions before and after independence. His disinterest in taking on capitalism as a system in addition to taking on imperialism has irked some observers. Not least because of this, as Davis noticed, 'Socialists and radicals naturally lost few opportunities for attacking Griffith.'[62]

During 1919 a brilliant young journalist and future renowned London theatre critic came to Ireland. The editor of *The Guardian*, C.P. Scott, had dispatched Ivor Brown to meet Sinn Féiners who were then on the run or expecting arrest. Brown wrote that the

Most powerful and clear-headed of these was Arthur Griffith. For a leader of rebellion in a romantic country he was totally unromantic. I met him in a clandestine way in a grubby little office where he sat with a bowler hat on one side looking like a grocer in his back room … But, he had, below his fanaticism, a Fabian capacity for handling facts and figures as well as ideas …[63]

Michael Laffan, in a recent entry for Griffith in the *Dictionary of Irish Biography*, writes of him as 'inundating his readers with demographic, financial, and other statistics'. That he frequently presented cogent evidence-based arguments in support of his contention that Ireland was inequitably treated by Britain, both socially and economically, is not always clearly recognised. Welcoming the first annual report on the agricultural statistics of Ireland, issued by the government's new department of agriculture and technical instruction, he thought 'Politics or no politics we must have the *facts*, and the better and more widely these facts are known, the sooner we shall get rid of talking and theorizing, and get down to work to lift the country out of its present beggarly condition.'[64] He believed that Ireland's fundamental economic problem was its exploitation by Britain. Interned in an English jail when the rebel parliament, Dáil Éireann, first met on 21 January 1919, he wrote 'England in her propaganda pointed to the Dublin slums as proof of Irish incapacity and corruption. The tables should be turned on her … Dublin slumdom is the creation of English robbery.'[65] While he frequently berated Dublin Corporation and took aim at Irish traders and other locals whom he felt had selfish objectives, he never lost sight of the underlying problem caused by the extraction of resources from Ireland and by oppressive restrictions on his country's trade and growth. In the late twentieth century, the leading economist Patrick Lynch acknowledged Griffith's grasp of economic and financial realities.[66]

3

1871–1901: Hard-Working Men

'It is tiresome being a boy. To relieve the ennui of my youth I had taken to having convictions. My first conviction was that the English were a detestable race, my last that my compatriots were an exceedingly foolish but highly admirable people.' So wrote Arthur Griffith.[1] Educated by the Christian Brothers, he was said by a fellow pupil to be 'dilatory and unresponsive to the master's strap'.[2] Griffith believed that only the school system of the Christian Brothers properly recognised Ireland. In schools controlled by government nominees, he wrote: 'The pupil was not taught as he is in every system elsewhere, to look out upon the world from his own country.'[3]

By the age of fourteen at the latest, Griffith left school to become apprenticed to a Protestant printer. About that time, his family later said, he wrote a piece that an English magazine (*Old and Young*) published.[4] He also joined the Young Ireland Society. In 1885 its president John O'Leary, the Fenian veteran, presented him with books at the annual prize-giving of this 'neo-Fenian' organisation. Another member of the society was W.B. Yeats, with whom O'Leary shared his personal library.[5] O'Leary, who was something of a mentor to Griffith and Yeats, once stated that no account of his own life as an ardent nationalist and journalist could be complete without mentioning his devotion to books.[6]

The Leinster

By the age of eighteen Griffith was also one of the most enthusiastic members of a group that styled itself variously as the Leinster Debating Club/Society or the Leinster Literary Club/Society. Its members met in a room at 87 Marlborough Street, where they kept a small lending library.[7] Significantly, the bitter split in Irish politics occasioned by the downfall of Parnell led to the demise of the Leinster in 1892, and Griffith was to be the instrument of its destruction.

Meetings of the Leinster started by reading and discussing papers written by its members, and ended in poetry and sing-songs that included both 'classical and patriotic' ballads. Those 'beautiful little concerts made the evenings enjoyable', wrote one member.[8] At St Patrick's Day and Christmas there were special celebrations. All this happened in the centre of a city that was dirty and decaying. At Griffith's suggestion in 1889, members organised long, healthy walks together in the country on Sundays, and reported back on sites of interest visited by them.[9] In 1891 James Moran joined the club. He later fondly recalled these young men out together in the Dublin hills. Another acquaintance wrote of Griffith that 'he was a splendid man to be with on tramps', for 'he could go on for hours with a deliberate gait, talking in a rather low voice about people and places. He knew everything about the local history of Dublin and the places adjoining'.[10] Even when in London for treaty negotiations in 1921, Griffith led members of his delegation's staff on rambles through that city.

Some of the young men also cycled together on Saturdays during the 1890s. Griffith got himself an old second-hand bike and named it 'the humming-bird', on account of the noise it made before it even came into sight.[11] Later, he and some friends peddled 140 kilometers to a Gaelic League festival in Wexford.[12] Such outings benefited him in 1916 when he had to ride his bicycle on a long circuitous route by the outskirts of Dublin for a secret meeting across town with Eoin MacNeill.

Minutes of the Leinster society survive for the years 1888–92,[13] as does a bound volume of some contributions to the first seven issues of its occasional handwritten journal *Eblana*. 'Eblana' was a name that the Greek geographer Ptolemy once gave to an Irish settlement on or near the site of Dublin.[14] Each issue of this journal that survives appears from the minutes to have been read aloud and discussed at meetings. The surviving volume, from 1889, includes an emphatic preface addressed by *Eblana's* first editor, Robert Flood, to anyone whose property it might become in the future:

Our society was composed of hard-working young men of humble circumstances who formed a society for their mutual improvement … Therefore, Oh stranger, toss not your head in scorn when you peruse their maiden efforts in literature. Sneer not if colons, semi-colons, and full periods, are less numerous than they would be if our society boasted of M. [A.] and B.A … [It was] written by youths, to fortune and fame unknown.[15]

As if to underline this point, Flood had to be replaced as editor later in 1889 when he emigrated. He had been its main contributor, with Griffith the other main writer.[16] In the fashion of the time contributors adopted pen names, with Griffith already using 'Shanganagh', with which he would become closely associated through the pages of the *United Irishman*. All pen names are identified at the start of the *Eblana* volume. Out of forty-nine contributions listed for the period of the extant volume, ten were by Flood and nine by Griffith. Shortly before Flood left, he contributed an essay on the 'Social Condition of the Working Classes' in which he praised a principle that became Griffith's political philosophy, writing about 'that all important factor … the principle of Self Reliance [underlined on the manuscript]'. He reported that his paper had given rise to 'a most interesting debate'.[17] Flood was followed as editor, successively, by Edward Whelan, John Doyle and William Rooney. No issue that any of these three edited appears to have survived.

Griffith spent a night alone in Glasnevin Cemetery, writing for the *Eblana* about doing so.[18] His friend Ed Whelan wrote on 'Strikes: Their Remedy'. The minutes show that 'Whelan advocated a system of state socialism or the owning of all sources of trade and industry by the state', and that his paper was favourably received by Griffith and other members.[19]

There appear to have been about twenty active members of the club, writing about and discussing a range of literary and other matters from Longfellow and Tennyson, through socialism and religion and on to Irish poetesses. All its members were male, although an explicit late effort by John R. Whelan to have the exclusion of women written into the club's rules as a requirement, was defeated on the casting vote of the meeting's chairman, Arthur Griffith.[20] Griffith was president of the club from 3 October 1890 until 11 December 1891.

Papers read by Griffith to members included 'The Irish Writers of the Sixteenth, Seventeenth and Eighteenth Centuries' ('loudly applauded'), 'The Elizabethan Poets', and 'Thomas Parnell and His Contemporaries'. The latter 'exhaustive paper' was unfortunately interrupted from time to time by 'the uproariousness of a dance club in the room beneath us'.[21] During the delivery of his paper on Elizabethans on 5 February 1892, Griffith 'contended that Marlowe and Massinger have not been accorded the position among the poets of their time which their words entitled them to, and that the abilities of Ben Jonson were much over-rated'. This he delivered to a club of hard-working men like himself who had left school early and who were trying to make a living by day.

There were also formal debates. Griffith argued in the affirmative on a question 'Is the Church opposed to civilization', and 'also spoke in favour of republicanism' on a heavily defeated motion 'That monarchial is a better form of government'.[22] In a paper on 'Grattan and Flood', who were leading lights of the pre-1800 independently minded Protestant Irish parliament, Griffith said of Grattan 'Had he not played the generous fool prating of Ireland's trust in English generosity the misery of the last ninety years would have been impossible … Had Henry Flood's advice been taken by his rival, Ireland, in all human probability would to-day be a free and prosperous nation.' This paper was read on the evening that his younger friend William Rooney joined the club in 1891.[23] Griffith's contributions to *Eblana* also included essays on Irish street ballads, James Clarence Mangan, the Gracchi and Sir Richard Steele. The editor commended Griffith for his essay on Irish street ballads, including 'the simplicity of language and humourous descriptions', and said of the eighteen-year-old who was already using what became his best-known pen name 'We expect much from "Shanganagh"'. In the spirit of the club he also criticised some of Griffith's other work.[24]

Griffith's humourous contributions to *Eblana* included some lyrical lines devoted to 'Ye Maide Without a Name'. These resemble in tone verses that he would later dedicate to 'Mollie' (Mary/Maud Sheehan) in the 1890s. In this way he responded to the editor's appeal for a lighter approach than that which he and other earnest young men had taken on 'very heavy subjects' when first invited to write for *Eblana*.[25] Griffith also showed his sense of humour in a piece about printers, such as he and his father were. He wrote for *Eblana* of 'the unfortunate being' who misreading the line 'I kissed her under the kitchen stairs' rendered it as 'I kicked her under the kitchen stairs'.[26] As MP for the Coombe in a moot parliament held by the club he wittily opposed a bill proposing Home Rule for Ringsend on the paradoxical grounds that he was 'following the dictates of his own conscience and the instructions of his constituents', only to abstain on the vote.[27]

Griffith and others 'succeeded in contributing much to make the evening a very bright and happy one' when members organised a 'smoking-concert' one dismal November day. On another occasion a meeting 'resolved itself into a bohemian choral society'. Apparently members sometimes drank 'gooseberry wine champagne', as at their St Patrick's Annual Banquet, held in the room where they usually met. At Christmas 1891, Griffith recited 'The Courtship of Tarlagh Mulligan', while his friend William Rooney sang 'A Nation Once Again' and 'Carolan's Cup'.[28]

Tensions and Charles Stewart Parnell

Contributions to the *Eblana* were sternly criticised at meetings, and also in writing by its editor. This was believed to encourage success in the tradition of Young Ireland.[29] Its range and tone prefigured the ethos of Griffith's *United Irishman*. The club's minutes also show that, as might be expected of any group of young Irishmen debating politics and society, there were occasional tensions and disagreements. However, reading its minutes, one is unprepared for the eruption that destroyed the club in 1892 and that saw Griffith and his friend Rooney express different opinions. It was an example of the damaging divisiveness caused by 'the Parnell split' in Irish politics, a split that Griffith would long seek to avoid replicating by his single-minded demand for national independence and his determination that all other considerations, whether personal, cultural or social, be subsidiary to that.

Griffith at this point even tried his hand at Parnellite verse, more successfully than James Joyce's alter ego would in the latter's *Portrait of the Artist as a Young Man*, where Stephen Dedalus 'saw himself sitting at his table in Bray the morning after the discussion at the Christmas dinner table, trying to write a poem about Parnell on the back of one of his father's second moiety notices. But his brain had then refused to grapple with the theme'. On 8 March 1889, Griffith included in his contributions to the first run of *Eblana* some verses entitled 'The Crimes of *The Times*'.[30] It was just two weeks since the Pigott forgeries published in the London *Times* had been exposed, having been used to implicate Parnell falsely in the Phoenix Park murders. It was nine months before Katharine O'Shea's husband filed for divorce. Griffith's lines included these:

> Our great and glorious Parnell's victorious
> The forgers scattered far and near
> And the wicked crimes of the blaguard *Times*
> Will soon be punished I have no fear.

However, by the following winter events finally overtook the Irish leader. On 25 November 1890 Prime Minister William Gladstone's letter urging Parnell's resignation was published. Later that week Griffith proposed a very strong and detailed motion of support for Parnell, and persuaded members of the Leinster 'comprising all shades of public opinion' to agree with it unanimously: 'Mr Griffith spoke as one who never was a supporter of Mr Parnell but was an independent nationalist.' The club agreed to inform Parnell that 'To us it matter not whether ecclesiastical domination on the one side, or Dublin Castle influence on the other prevail, our duty is imperative. The path of independence is before us.'[31] Griffith and a friend are said to have tried but failed to persuade Timothy Harrington, a Parnellite MP, to give up his seat in Dublin so that Parnell might be elected there instead.[32] The Leinster also canvassed the voters of North Kilkenny in a vital by-election, with Griffith as club president using then on its notices his pen name J.P. Ruhart (an anagram of 'Arthur').[33]

In 1891 Griffith went to support Parnell at Broadstone Station in Dublin when Parnell left for Creggs, Co. Galway, to address what was his last election meeting. Parnell told those present that he was going to the west 'contrary to his doctor's orders, as he was suffering from a severe cold'.[34] It was a dismal time, recalled in Griffith's paper twenty years later:

> On a September night, gloomy and cold, Parnell came to the Broadstone on an outside car to journey to his last meeting, accompanied by one faithful friend. Around the station the present writer and fifty or sixty others waited to give him a parting blessing – to cheer him up with the message that the rank-and-file of his followers in Dublin would stand by him to the last, although every man who wore the letters 'M.P.' after his name disappeared from his side. When Mr Parnell arrived at the station, it needed no physician to see that he was ill, and wretchedly ill. His face was livid and haggard, one of his arms bandaged, and the hand I shook had no longer the firm grip I had felt previously … As he descended from the car a woman beside me stretched out her hand to him saying 'God bless you, Mr Parnell – don't go tonight.' He turned towards her, smiled and shook his head. That was the last we saw of Parnell alive.[35]

Joyce's fictional Leopold Bloom had a moment with Parnell too: 'He saw him once on the auspicious occasion when they broke up the type in the *Insuppressible* or was it *United Ireland*, a privilege he keenly appreciated, and, in point of fact, handed him his silk hat when it was knocked off and he [Parnell] said *Thank you*'. When Parnell died, Griffith and Rooney and other members of the Leinster marched as a group in the funeral procession on Sunday, 11 October 1891.[36]

Parnell's downfall poisoned and dulled Irish politics for more than a decade, its venom evident at a meeting of the Leinster Debating Club, when one of that society's occasional visitors, James McCluskey, scoffed at members and claimed that they would be anti-Parnellites if they lived down in Mallow, Co. Cork. Nevertheless, Rooney and others in the club proposed McCloskey for membership a fortnight later. Griffith spoke strongly against McCloskey's admission but was defeated. He and some others immediately resigned.[37] During a lively discussion one week afterwards, Rooney explained that he had supported McCloskey on the assumption that the man had spoken originally in the heat of the moment and would pull back. But the damage was done, and on 9 December 1892, the remaining members of the Leinster Debating Club wound up their society.

Girls and Gas

Girls did not participate in the usual meetings of the Leinster. But Griffith could enjoy female company at the house of his more affluent Whelan cousins, where there were frequent Sunday teas, with a piano and girls singing favourite songs.[38] A printer's apprentice told Padraic Colum that when a group including Griffith paired off with girls, "'Dan" [i.e. Griffith] would begin to spout lines such as "To be or not to be," or "The quality of mercy is not strained" [both by Shakespeare].' Padraic Colum suspected that this display of erudition was as much to cover Griffith's shyness as to make an impression, and one fears that some of the girls were not impressed.[39]

However, if he was not always fascinating, at least Griffith was by no means out of place in the emerging social order for which James Joyce in *Ulysses* outlined alternative qualifications:

> You must have a certain fascination: Parnell. Arthur Griffith is a squareheaded fellow but he has no go in him for the mob. Or gas about our lovely land. Gammon and spinach. Dublin Bread Company's [DBC] tearoom. Debating societies. That republicanism is the best form of government. That the language question should take precedence of the economic question. Have your daughters inveigling them to your house.

Griffith and Rooney could certainly, and did 'gas about our lovely land'. Why would they not when others trumpeted the glories of empire? Griffith frequented lively debating clubs, when a growing number of small literary societies generated a head of steam about a national revival. Pubs and tearooms such as the DBC provided further venues for discussion with his friends. And at the Leinster he argued that republicanism was the best form of government. Whether or not he was 'inveigled' by Peter Sheehan's daughters into their home on Cook

Street is unknown, but he certainly visited them there, and perhaps later called to the new home that, at the turn of the century, the family acquired on a fashionable street. Griffith might not be convinced that the Irish language question 'should take precedence of the economic question', regretting as he did that there were 'muddled persons who confound language and nationality' and disdaining 'camp-followers of the language movement, shouting raucously their shibboleth "An Gaedheal Thu?"'. But he studied Irish, believing that 'all of us surely can inspire those destined to carve our epitaphs to re-learn it'.[40] Seán T. O'Kelly, when later president of Ireland, wrote that from 1899 'Griffith and Rooney, in the pages of the *United Irishman* gave the Gaelic League all the support that they could'. O'Kelly added:

> Griffith himself practised what he preached, and was a regular attendant at Irish classes which were held every week in the rooms of the Celtic Literary Society. Though I know that he worked hard to learn Irish, and long years after these days I speak of now, I can say Griffith attended regular classes in Irish in Reading Prison, I am afraid his efforts to get a knowledge of the language were never very successful, but he gave the example which was the effective thing at the time.[41]

The turn of the century saw many young men attempting to learn Irish, with James Joyce among those taking lessons.

South Africa

When the Leinster was dissolved, Rooney soon became the founding stalwart of a new Celtic Literary Society. Griffith seems not to have been actively involved at meetings of this new group before going to South Africa in January 1898, although before leaving he attended its Christmas festivities with the woman whom he would one day marry.[42] He had recently lost his job in Dublin, perhaps by quitting in resentment at the response to a practical joke played on him, and this presumably put him under financial pressure. Printing jobs were not easy to find at the time.[43] He was not alone or first among his friends in leaving

Ireland. John R. Whelan, 'a capable and energetic secretary' of the Celtic Literary Society and 'a disciple of John Mitchel' had no sooner had his considered appeal to 'the thinking Irishman' on literature and nationalism printed in the advanced nationalist *Shan Van Vocht* in 1897 than he went to South Africa before Griffith. In his case, Dublin Castle suspected that it was for political rather than economic reasons. Griffith was fond of Whelan, and Griffith's humorous poem 'The Thirteenth Lock' was recited at Whelan's farewell drinks.[44] Griffith's son Nevin later said that Whelan wrote from Africa urging his father to go out. Rumours that Whelan was killed there were false, and he later returned to Ireland before emigrating long-term to Scotland.[45]

When Griffith announced that he was leaving Ireland, his friends held a farewell session for him too. At it Rooney paid Griffith a glowing tribute, speaking as someone who knew 'how much the existence of many National organisations have owed to your support, who have watched how well the gospel of Young Ireland has been put into practice by you, who have recognised the reality of your enthusiasm and patriotism by your very modesty and reserve.'[46] Before Griffith went he contributed for the society's journal under his pen name 'J.P. Ruhart' a 'very amusing skit' about the adventures of an Irish philosopher.[47]

Griffith may have emigrated simply in search of better-paid employment. But there is also a hint of threatened tuberculosis, a disease that was common in Dublin. It has even been suggested that he deliberately went to South Africa to 'make friends for Ireland'.[48] Perhaps he went as part of a general strategy on the part of the IRB, when it was hoped that the Boers might beat the British in an imminent war. He was certainly politically active there, along with John MacBride.

So much did Griffith's friends admire his skills that months after he left they took the unusual step of devoting a special session of the Celtic Literary Society to his writings. These consisted 'in a great measure of local stories, sketches, and songs, dealing with life in the Liberties and other ancient parts of our city'. It was recorded that 'The character drawing, treatment of dialogue, and general surroundings of the story were recognised and heartily enjoyed by the audience as absolutely true to their models.'[49] Members regretted that Griffith's writings were not better known, 'and trusted that some effort would be made to bring them into greater popularity'. In this way a seed was planted that would grow into Rooney's decision to propose for the position of editor of the planned *United Irishman* his friend Arthur Griffith, who returned to Dublin from South Africa in the autumn of 1898.

Griffith then sometimes made his way to Sandycove, in south Dublin, to swim at the Forty Foot and relax on the sheltered roof of a nearby Martello tower that Oliver St John Gogarty occasionally leased from its owner (Plate 6). Gogarty, like Griffith, was a strong swimmer and the two men ventured far out into Dublin Bay.[50] James Joyce was to set in this tower the opening scene of *Ulysses*, perhaps the most famous novel of the twentieth century. As that century dawned, Arthur Griffith was approaching his thirtieth birthday.

Sackville/O'Connell Street, 1903–8. The Dublin of Griffith and of Joyce's *Ulysses* (National Library of Ireland [L_CAB_06672]).

4

An 'Un-Irish' Personality?

During negotiations for the Anglo-Irish Treaty, Michael Collins was filmed impatiently pacing a back balcony at the Irish delegation's house in Hans Place. Griffith was photographed standing quietly at its front door with his wife, facing a little park on the other side of the building (Plate 15). He was not excitable, being 'one of the calmest appraisers of men', and 'not lavish of his praises'.[1] He reluctantly granted interviews to journalists, and could prove difficult to interview due not least to his falling silent.[2] Yet to shy young people he was fatherly and kind. When the Butler sisters first approached him as teenagers at his 'grimy' office in Fownes Street, for example, 'suddenly his face lit up with a smile that had something paternal in it – though he was quite a young man'.[3]

Patrick Carey said 'I often had a conversation with him, but he was a very silent and retiring man, not pushing. His parents were nice and respectable people. They had no time for gossip. Griffith was a hard-working man and had nothing to give away.' Carey, a crane operator along the Liffey, was a tenant at 83 Summerhill in the early 1900s, when the Griffiths also rented rooms there.[4]

Griffith being a Dubliner of artisan or lower middle-class origins and of low income, his formal education was undistinguished. He left school in his early teens as was common then, but he read widely, buying books cheaply from barrows along the quays. He facilitated, argued with and was surrounded by confident men who had completed secondary school and attended college. They included John O'Leary (Tipperary Grammar School, TCD and QCG), W.B. Yeats (Erasmus Smith High School and the Metropolitan School of Art), James Joyce (Clongowes and Belvedere, UCD), Patrick Pearse (Christian Brothers' School, UCD, Trinity and King's Inns) and Éamon de Valera (Blackrock College, the Royal University of Ireland and lectures at TCD and UCD).

Neither his features nor his temperament marked Griffith as exotic. He did not pose in a studio with a gun, as Constance Markievicz did with her revolver, thus bequeathing future generations an image of her as a dramatic revolutionary icon. Griffith was photographed not as he collected his rifle from a boat at Howth, but bent over a desk at work. 'Griffith's Sinn Féin policy was improving the morale of the people but it was plodding work, not revolution,' wrote Maud Gonne, somewhat dismissively, of the hard grind of everyday politics.[5]

When Michael Lennon was gathering information about Griffith in the early 1950s, a correspondent wrote:

I think the man in any Irish revolutionary movement who is likely to be remembered longest is the one with a romantic sounding name. O'Donovan Rossa is spoken of now when James Stephens [1825–1901] is forgotten – the latter was the more prominent in the Fenian days. De Valera is another instance of this Irish tendency. The name had an irresistible fascination for the crowd.[6]

De Valera's name also evolved, from George de Valero on his New York birth certificate to Edward at his baptism, to Eddie Coll when sent back to live with his mother's people in Ireland, to Éamon (sometimes spelt by him with two letters 'n') de Valera (sometimes spelt by him with an accent/fada). His 'exotic name helped him to stand out in later life', thinks his most recent biographer.[7] And perhaps his birth overseas even strengthened de Valera's appeal at some level in the national psyche, by associating him with that salvation from abroad that Gaelic poets had long anticipated in the form of exiled Irish lords returning with Spanish or French help?

For his part Griffith was a common Dubliner, born and bred in the heart of a city long set apart from Gaelic Ireland. He had no exotic name, no Anglo-Irish sheen of a George Moore or Yeats, and no barrister's wig like Patrick Pearse. Although a city boy, he had not the working-class profile of his socialist friend Connolly or of 'Big Jim'

Larkin. Yet H.E. Kenny ('Sean-ghall') admired his dedication, writing to Alice Stopford Green in 1915 'He has remained voluntarily poor in a venal age' and 'I love him with as rich a love as my nature can yield.'[8]

'Un-Irish'?

Among the papers that Seán Ó Lúing left to the National Library of Ireland are two reports for his publishers that implicitly raise an interesting but disturbing question: was Griffith's artisan and ostensibly Protestant background a factor in how he was assessed by Irish Catholics among others?

One of the reports refers to Ó Lúing's manuscript for his book on Griffith, and the second to his manuscript for an essay subsequently published in a collection edited by the historian F.X. Martin.[9] The first reader, who is unidentified, wrote 'I have heard it said … that Griffith in his early stage flirted with theosophy or neo-Buddhism. The text rightly says he was given to private judgement.'[10] The second reader, identified as F.X. Martin himself, asked 'Was he [Griffith] not intolerant? Un-Irish in character and application? Was he not either vain or rigid so as to be caught by Lloyd George on the point of "honour" in the Treaty negotiations – any typical Irishman would have dismissed Lloyd George's objection.' The question of whether or not Griffith was 'caught' by Lloyd George into *giving* his word will be considered later. What is relevant here is the suggestion that *keeping* one's word (assuming that this was what Griffith actually did) might not be 'typically' Irish.

The two reports raise the spectre of someone suspected of having rather too carefully weighed up moral decisions and then taken them unduly seriously, who relied on a very non-Catholic 'private judgement' rather than follow dogma (nationalist dogma) and who, being given to sipping quietly just a glass or two of Guinness when gathered with voluble friends in a pub, was 'un-Irish' in an ill-defined but communally understood way (being not 'one of the lads' as it were).

Griffith's widow mentioned an ancient relative of Griffith who contacted her and invited her to Cavan.[11] Griffith's Ulster Protestant antecedents were mentioned in broad terms when he was a candidate in Cavan for Sinn Féin, as candidates often accentuate local connections if they can do so at election time. However, biographers have pinned down little or nothing definite about Griffith's ancestors or his father's family outside Dublin. At one point, as files in the National Library show, the district justice Michael Lennon went to considerable lengths searching for that information. Griffith's acquaintance Dan McCarthy told Ó Lúing that Griffith 'was extremely reticent about his family, ancestors, etc.'[12]

Lennon was, for some unknown reason, made aware of the story of one 'Billy Griffith' of Co. Tipperary that had appeared in *Young Ireland*.[13] Attributed to 'Mrs J. Sadlier', this told how a Protestant farmer Billy Griffith had long ago hidden a Catholic priest from men hunting him.'[14] To Irish Catholics of Griffith's day, Arthur's own name and that of his brother Billy (William) would seem more likely to be Protestant than Catholic. Indeed, according to Ó Lúing, when Griffith's son was presented for baptism, a Catholic priest challenged the choice of the name Nevin: 'Huh? What? Naomhán! My goodness, I never heard of it. Was Naomhán a saint?' Griffith reportedly answered simply that he did not know but that 'He was a bishop, anyway', and the priest laughed.[15] His laugh suggests discomfort. Occasional speculation that Griffith's ancestors came from Wales to Ireland as settlers is no more than gossip, but the kind of gossip that might do damage to one's Irish nationalist credentials.

The series of articles about 'notable graves' that Griffith and Rooney wrote for a Dublin newspaper in 1892 included those of Lord Clare and Charles Lucas, two persons who would not occur to many Catholic nationalists to be praiseworthy but whom Griffith respected as independent spirits.[16] He also had kind words for Lord Russell of Killowen on the latter's death.[17] Griffith's advocacy of a system of government for Ireland akin to that which had existed before the Act of Union, including a monarch but now with a Catholic majority in a restored Irish parliament, echoed Douglas Hyde's desire 'to render the present a rational continuation of the past'.[18] It left the door open to northern Protestants to support independence, not least by maintaining a link with the Crown.

Was Fr F.X. Martin unconsciously painting the ostensibly Catholic Griffith as a morally severe Presbyterian who took life too seriously, as even being akin to those Protestants whom some Catholics found 'un-Irish' in their sensibilities and termed 'sourpusses'? Griffith prided himself on basing his arguments rationally on economic and other statistical evidence. However, when the conscience of Catholics was expected to be primarily 'informed' by the hierarchy, 'private judgement' was a fruit of the Reformation that might raise suspicions.

Any suspicion that he was 'un-Irish' may have been coloured too by his being not only a Dubliner but also a trade unionist printer before he became an editor. In 1943 Michael Hayes commented to Seán Milroy, 'Griffith was a remarkable man but he had essentially the outlook of the Dublin skilled worker. It would be interesting to see from his writing whether he had any rural touch at all.'[19] The respective definitions of 'a rural touch' and 'a Dublin skilled worker' might include reference to class, personal attitude and anglicisation among other factors. For implying that someone is not 'one of us' is a way of marginalising that person. Thus, for example, John Devoy described Éamon de Valera as

> the vainest man intellectually that I ever met. He is really a half breed Jew and his mother was a 'Palatine' – that is, of German descent. His temperament is not Irish and no man can get along with him except on the condition of absolute submission to his will … he has not an original mind nor any real grasp of politics.[20]

Such descriptions tell us at least as much about the person making them, and that person's understanding of their community's imagined identity, as they do about the object of their description.

Or was Ó Lúing's reviewer simply acting the part of devil's advocate, taking his cue from Lloyd George's stereotyping? In December 1922 the latter wrote of sitting in Downing Street opposite 'a dark, short, but sturdy figure with the face of a thinker. That was Mr Arthur Griffith, the most un-Irish leader that ever led Ireland, quiet to the point of gentleness, reserved almost to the point of appearing saturnine.'[21]

Allied to Griffith's 'un-Irish' character and moral decisiveness was a certain perceived intolerance or narrowness for which he was criticised by Bulmer Hobson and Patrick Pearse among others. He impatiently filled columns of his papers with articles dismissing humbug and 'sunburstery', a term in use then to denote fine words spouted by those who are elated by their own bright ideas and rhetoric.

Yet, in at least one way, he was quintessentially Irish. For he bristled when facing an English opponent, and the memory of past slights and wrongs was never far from the surface. On 10 January 1922, in Dáil Éireann, he was challenged on a point by Erskine Childers. Born in London and educated in England, Childers had been reared partly by his Barton cousins in Co. Wicklow. Although secretary to the Irish negotiating team in London, he joined the anti-treaty side.[22] Griffith struck the table before responding angrily 'I will not reply to any damned Englishman in this Assembly.' It was an uncharacteristic outburst.

Griffith does not fit neatly into an Irish stereotype. James Owen Hannay, the Church of Ireland clergyman who wrote novels as 'George A. Birmingham' and who also wrote fiction for *Sinn Féin*, became acquainted with him first through the Gaelic League. He found Griffith

> utterly unlike any Irish politician that I knew. He had no gift of private conversation and indeed talked very little. He used to look at me through pince-nez glasses which always seemed on the point of falling off his nose. When he did speak, it was briefly and coldly. Yet, from the first time I met him I was greatly attracted by him. He was a man of absolute honesty and no idea of self-glorification or self-advancement ever seemed to enter his head. He had a very clear intellect and was one of those rare men who never shrink from the logical conclusion of any line of thought or seek to obscure meaning with misty words.

Hannay thought Griffith to be unrelentingly serious: 'I never discovered in him a trace of a sense of humour. Things seemed to him right or wrong, wise or unwise, but they never seemed funny; though that is what most things are.'[23] Others disagreed.

Sense of Humour

Unlike Hannay, other acquaintances discerned in Griffith a keen if sometimes caustic sense of humour. His wife found him 'such fun with friends.'[24] James Joyce took pleasure in Griffith's tilting at the windmills of parliamentary verbiage. For Griffith such humbug was well represented by the standard graphic above the daily editorial column of Dublin's *Freeman's Journal*. This showed the sun shining above the building that had once housed the old pre-Union Irish parliament. Joyce was prompted to write mischievously in *Ulysses*:

> Sunburst on the titlepage. He smiled, pleasing himself. What Arthur Griffith said about the headpiece over the Freeman leader: a homerule sun rising up in the northwest from the laneway behind the bank of Ireland. He prolonged his pleased smile. Ikey [Jewish] touch that: homerule sun rising up in the northwest.[25]

Griffith jokes at his own expense (*Sinn Féin*, 9 April 1910).

Griffith's satirical streak is evident also in certain verses or poems that he wrote, as well as from a witty if lengthy article on the Royal Irish Academy that appeared under his pen name 'Lugh' in 1901, and another on the 'Royal Academy Auf Musicke' that spoke up for Irish compositions that same year. A 'delightful' piece on Professor Atkinson of Trinity College reportedly filled readers with 'great glee'.[26] His ability to quip is also evident in the *United Irishman*. On 16 March 1901 he wrote 'The *Australian Leader* is wrong in supposing that the *United Irishman* would back the devil if that personage attacked England. The *United Irishman* would not interfere in a family quarrel.' He published a cartoon of himself as the devil, to please his detractors.

Liam Ó Briain, a founder member of Taibhdhearc na Gaillimhe, the Irish-language theatre, insisted that Griffith could be delightful company.[27] On one occasion Griffith brought an old acquaintance with him to meet friends. He extracted much amusement from pretending that his companion was a Hungarian baron interested in Griffith's proposal to adapt the Austro-Hungarian constitutional model for Ireland.[28] And for all the economics and politics he read, he sometimes liked to help sleep come by reading a popular romance such as Charles Garvice's *Her Heart's Desire*.[29]

When interned in Reading in 1916, Griffith grew a beard, about which he joked, and kept up the spirits of fellow prisoners by organising games of handball and other activities that included the writing of verses. A fellow prisoner later thought that Griffith was 'never depressed in jail, or never appeared to be depressed'.[30] Even during the tense weeks at 22 Hans Place in London, lodged with his team negotiating an Anglo-Irish treaty in late 1921, his private secretary found evidence of his sense of humour and composure.[31]

Shyness and Obstinacy

Maud Gonne wrote that she got to know Griffith well in 1899: 'He was not an orator, and was at first very shy and inaudible when addressing meetings'.[32] George Lyons too met him then, at a session of the Celtic Literary Society after Griffith's return from South Africa:

Griffith, from his studious and bookish habits and his long spells of solitary companionship with his pen, became somewhat shy and retiring, and to many who knew him but slightly appeared cold and unsocial, but this was not his true nature. He would pass through the streets of Dublin without noticing his associates or even his friends. He would enter a hall or a crowded meeting place and pass through without saluting any one. There were three reasons: firstly, his eyesight was extremely defective … secondly, he was usually preoccupied in his thoughts, but, strongest reason of all was, he really never thought that anyone wanted a nod from him; he really believed himself to be an unknown and an unnoticed man and he was entirely oblivious of the fact when he walked through a crowd that anyone paid the slightest importance [sic] to his actions.[33]

Seán T. O'Kelly, later president of Ireland, was an assistant in the National Library when he first encountered Griffith – whom he said made 'constant' visits and spent many hours researching there in the 1890s. They subsequently worked together in Sinn Féin, and O'Kelly wrote 'He was a very difficult man to know. He was always very reserved. His friends were few – that is, those he took into his intimate confidence. It was some years before I could say I had won his confidence.'[34]

Lyons thought 'In organisation affairs he oft-times failed to check an abuse through his inability to realise that he held any sort of authority, and in no possible circumstances could he ever be conceived in the position of ordering people about their duties.'[35] Griffith wrote in the *United Irishman* of 24 June 1899: 'We have at all times opened our columns to our critics. The want of a free, tolerant, and intelligent public opinion in Ireland is directly traceable to the Irish politicians and their press.' This willingness to permit a range of views to be expressed in his papers, however admirable, allowed people such as F.H. O'Donnell and Oliver Gogarty to indulge their prejudices in a manner that continues to dog Griffith's reputation. Maume believes that 'Like many professional unmaskers, Griffith's scepticism shaded into paranoia, and he was susceptible to demented cranks.'[36]

However, Griffith was also at times stubborn in his interpretation of a question, and this offended some nationalists who failed to change his mind. Tongue-in-cheek, his friend Padraic Colum later wrote:

> People in Dublin said he was intolerant of ideas, and that he preferred to have with him second-rate men who accepted the whole of his doctrine rather than first-rate men who differed from him on a point. I must say that I never knew any of the first-rate men who differed from him on a point offering their services to him.[37]

Colum may have had in mind persons such as Patrick Pearse. Pearse, like de Valera, did not join Sinn Féin before 1916. Indeed, in an open letter that he published as editor of *An Barr Buadh* on 18 May 1912, Pearse admitted 'I have never loved the same child [Sinn Féin].' But this did not deter him from urging Griffith to change before it was too late. As Sinn Féin weakened, Pearse wrote he was 'sorry to see its father being killed.' While he described Griffith as narrow-minded, distrustful and overbearing, he confessed that the latter was also best placed in Ireland to lead the movement, and thought it a great pity that Griffith might fail because nobody else could work under his leadership.

If some found Griffith difficult, others were more sanguine. In 1917 the socialist Cathal O'Shannon told the Irish Labour Party leader Tom Johnson,

> Arthur Griffith of course is narrow and stubborn – always was and I suppose always will be. I, however, have found that I can always get along with him even when we differ. Most of our people on both sides have a way of saying things that might be more effectively said in another way – there is a great deal in the way a thing is said.[38]

Notably, even a number of those who supported the opposing side during the civil war, such as Seán T. O'Kelly and Maud Gonne, later wrote kindly of Griffith.

One of those who disliked Griffith was the writer Sean O'Casey, who opposed the treaty. He mocked Griffith's championing of Thomas Davis, the hero of Young Ireland, and even sneered at Griffith's gait:

Right enough, there was Up Griffith Up Thomas a Davis, hunched close inside his thick dark Irish coat, a dark-green velour hat on his head, a thick slice of leather nailed to his heels to lift him a little nearer the stars, for he was somewhat sensitive about the lowness of his stature. His great protruding jaws were thrust forward like a bull's stretched-out muzzle; jaws that all his admirers spoke of, or wrote about, laying it down as an obvious law that in those magnificent jaws sat the God-given sign of a great man ... As plain as a shut mouth could say, he said he was Erin's strong, silent man. What was he thinking of as he stood there, grim and scornful?[39]

Dan McCarthy, who worked with Griffith, also thought that he put a cork wedge in his boots to make himself higher. Griffith did walk unusually, in footwear made for him by Barry's of Capel Street, perhaps because of a minor disability. In South Africa from 1897 to 1898 he was nicknamed 'Cuguan', an approximation of the sound made by doves and attributed alternatively to his gentleness with black employees who were accustomed to brutality and whippings or to the manner of his walking.[40] He often used 'Cuguan' as one of the pseudonyms on his articles.

James Moran, an early acquaintance of Griffith, described him as 'One of the finest men it was ever my good fortune to meet; modest, sensitive, courageous, clean-minded, with a keen sense of humour, he was utterly selfless, a friend in need, and a boon companion, who could discuss almost any subject without obtruding himself.'[41]

Reading, Swimming and Chess

Throughout his life Griffith treasured time with books. At the National Library, for example, he and a friend spent many nights searching in old papers for poems by James Clarence Mangan that were hard to identify because of the widespread use of pen names then. Mangan greatly appealed to Griffith, as he did to James Joyce who spoke publicly about him in 1902.[42] Mangan's classic poem 'Kathleen-Ni-Houlahan' was a source of inspiration for Yeats' play about that particular personification of Ireland, a play with which (as will be seen) Griffith said he helped Yeats. On Saturday afternoons Griffith also visited booksellers on the quays, and bought many 'twopenny or threepenny bargains': 'In his humble home', wrote one friend, 'he was the despair of his mother – books for breakfast, books for dinner, and books by the light of a halfpenny candle after the rest had gone to bed'.[43] Another friend, James Starkey (the writer 'Seumus O'Sullivan'), visited him when he lived in Summerhill: 'Sometimes I would accompany him to that old house, a strange house with a low wall in front of it, and talk far into the night amidst the chaos of books with which his room was heaped. For he was an omnivorous reader.'[44] Patrick Carey, Griffith's fellow tenant in Summerhill, described him as 'very quiet and hard-working'. He added that Griffith 'used to work till all hours of the night ... in a little front parlour room, facing Buckingham Street. He called it his "den". He had a table and chair in it and did all his research and writing there. He would be up till two and three o'clock in the morning.'[45] But Griffith liked fresh air too. He was a keen swimmer all his life, bathing regularly at Clontarf or the Bull Wall or further afield in Sandycove:

> Although he worked in his office like an insect, although he would round off his day by going into the National Library and reading until ten o'clock, Arthur Griffith was very much an open-air man. Every day, when the water was not absolutely chilling, he swam in the sea; the vigorous constitution that he had and his persistent exercise kept him in good condition: often, however, he showed weariness and strain.[46]

He had 'amazingly strong muscular arms', declared Robert Brennan 'which he attributed to his early gymnastic training and his regular daily swim'. He also had something of a reputation as a boxer, and he surprised Brennan and other fellow inmates interned in England by the ease with which he scaled a ten-foot wall, on which there was apparently no foothold, in order to retrieve a handball.[47]

He enjoyed playing chess, a pastime that suited his reserved demeanour and his reputation for calm, strategic thinking. He wrote to thank friends who, for his thirty-eighth birthday, gave him a 'beautiful chess board and chessmen'. True to type, he feared that it might distract him from his work. He sometimes played with friends in a popular café on O'Connell Street – the 'DBC', later destroyed during the 1916 Rising. One friend with whom he is said to have 'often' played chess was Abraham Briscoe, father of Dublin's first Jewish lord mayor, Robert. Griffith, when interned, also passed time playing or teaching chess. On the train from Holyhead to London with the treaty team in 1921, he produced a portable set and played chess with Desmond FitzGerald.[48]

Lower Sackville/O'Connell St, Dublin, after the 1916 Rising, with Nelson's Pillar and (first on right) the shell of the Dublin Bread Company (DBC). As noted in *Ulysses*, nationalists met for chat and chess in the DBC tearooms, a haunt of Griffith (National Library of Ireland [KE116]).

Nights at The Bailey

Seán T. O'Kelly recalled that 'Griffith, though never a heavy drinker, would take one or two bottles of stout during the course of the night', while friends sat around and discussed literary and political topics.[49] He liked to meet his acquaintances at an establishment just off Grafton Street that Parnell had also frequented, as one of them later wrote:

Griffith made The Bailey his own particular haunt, all the more so since his other rendezvous, Davin's pub, The Ship, in Fleet St., had been destroyed in the Rising ... He generally arrived some time after seven o'clock and made for the smoke room upstairs on the second floor. This was a small room, with two windows looking out on Duke St ... Griffith had his own special seat ... on the leather couch that ran along the inner wall that divided that room from the dining-room, between the fire-place and the window.

Should you enter the smoke room early in the evening, you would be sure to see 'A.G.', as he was always referred to, ensconced in his corner, a cigarette in his mouth, a silver tankard of stout on the table before him, going through a great pile of newspapers and journals. As he scrutinized the printed matter, he would now and again mark, with a blue or red pencil, passages that struck him for reference in his articles ... When the last paper was duly scanned, A.G. would put them aside with a sigh of relief and join in the talk and discussions with his friends ... And of friends he had many and diverse, attracting them from every class and level, high and low, Protestant, Catholic, Jew, atheists. Indeed, their social, religious and political variety was as astonishing as their personal and temperamental differences not to say clashes and contests.

However, having so written, the barrister and land commissioner Kevin O'Shiel noted that 'Griffith's part in those discussions was mainly that of a listener ... speech he only resorted to when he felt he had something to say that was worth saying, and then he said it in the fewest possible words and with a most un-Irish lack of adjectives.' O'Shiel added:

Griffith had two marked habits that one could not fail to notice. One was a habit of blinking his eyes. He was short sighted and always wore pince-nez; but I think the blinking was not due to his sight but to his innate shyness and sensitiveness. The other habit was that of every now and again pulling up his neck-tie. He could never make the usual tie knot, and so had to confine his tie through a gold ring which required constant adjusting.[50]

At closing time Griffith seldom walked alone to O'Connell Street. Usually one of his friends walked with him to Nelson's Pillar where he boarded a tram.[51] Some people who encountered him in public felt ignored. George Lyons wrote 'he often confessed to me that he never knew who a person was until he heard their voice.'[52] One evening, for example, Griffith was with a group when Eddie Lipman, a young doctor on leave from the war in Europe, joined them in uniform. Griffith did not give him a look of recognition. Lipman wanted to chat with Griffith but misunderstood Griffith's demeanour as coolness towards the uniform and left. When Griffith heard of this a moment later he went to find Lipman, and stood talking with him in College Green.[53] However, not everyone who hailed Griffith respected him. His solicitor and 'close friend' Michael Noyk told the Bureau of Military History of an occasion when Griffith was walking home with Seamus O'Sullivan from The Bailey and 'an Irish-Party man, or maybe an A.O.H. man, made some nasty remark as Griffith was passing and pulled his hat. Griffith turned round and gave him a punch, knocking him down, even though Griffith had very bad sight and had to wear glasses.'[54]

James Moran remembered that one day, as he and his friends swam, 'a very powerful shower of rain came down. We made for the dressing boxes for cover, but noticed that Griffith remained in the water, and was swimming in circles. Showing off was a thing he was never known to practise, so we shouted at him to come in.' Immediately Griffith made for them, and they found him exhausted. They helped to dry and dress him before heading off for the nearest pub 'where after a drop of good whiskey he was himself again'. Moran says Griffith explained 'When the shower came down it splashed the water into his eyes, and his sight, always a little weak, became blurred. He couldn't see what direction he was swimming in, but he gave no sign he was in distress. A most remarkable man!'[55]

5

Ballads, Songs and Snatches

Griffith had a musical ear, and it heard not only pleasant harmonies but also the voices of Irish people articulating in song their grief and scorn. He often crossed the Liffey to the Liberties, an old area of the city adjacent to Cook Street where his future wife lived until 1900. He met friends in the convivial surroundings of McCall's 'quaint old tavern' at 25 Patrick Street. There, near St Patrick's Cathedral, he would 'listen to good talk about ballad poetry and old Dublin streets and people'. James Clarence Mangan had once frequented the pub, being a friend of an earlier McCall. At the time that Griffith used to go there 'one could still be shown the actual place once favoured by Mangan, and even occupy his accustomed chair or bench'.[1] Outside during the day, as an old photograph shows, a variety of street traders sold vegetables, shellfish and clothing among other items. Griffith also liked The Brazen Head pub nearby, with its table at which the patriot Robert Emmet was believed to have written. One of his earliest and strongest memories was said to have been of an 'ancient' female relative 'who saw the dogs of Thomas St lap up a martyr's blood [Emmet was executed there in 1803]' singing defiantly 'When Erin First Rose'.[2]

From an early age then Griffith was attuned to street ballads, which were a form of popular culture and a way to get a political message out. One of the first discussions of the Irish Transvaal Committee, when Griffith and Gonne decided to oppose Britain's involvement in the Boer War, concerned 'the practicability of utilising local ballad singers in singing appropriate songs against enlistment'.[3] Griffith himself composed ballads for that purpose, with McCracken noting that, while 'the Boer war did not throw up enduring works of literature, it did

Patrick Street, Dublin, looking north, c.1895. McCall's tavern is on the left (National Library of Ireland [L_ROY_05934]).

produce a rich literary legacy in the form of ephemeral doggerel. Much of this was written by Griffith', some under his pen name Cuguan.[4] He distinguished ballads from what he saw as the commercial vulgarity of music-hall singers with their English airs, complaining 'They [our readers] have seen the old music forsaken for the jingles of Cockneydom, the songs that made men neglected for the things that reduce men to mere animals.'[5]

When he was fourteen, Griffith won copies of two books of Irish songs and ballads. They were awarded for his attendance and performance at Irish history classes of the Young Ireland Society, and were presented to him by the society's president, veteran Fenian John O'Leary. According to a contemporary report, the books were Barry's *Songs of Ireland* and a collection of ballads and poetry by 'Duncathail'.[6] On that day, O'Leary urged the rising generation to seek the ideal of Thomas Davis, whom Griffith was long to champion. It had been intended that Davis would, had he lived longer, edit the volume of ballads that Barry actually edited and that was first published in 1845. Barry, of whose collection Griffith now had a prize copy, informed readers that he 'of course, rejected those songs which were un-Irish in their character or language, and those miserable slang productions, which, representing the Irishman only as a blunderer, a bully, a fortune-hunter, or a drunkard, have done more than anything else to degrade him in the eyes of others, and, far worse to debase him in his own'.[7] Barry, like many other nationalists in the nineteenth century, contended with the stage-Irishman, with 'humourous' or other representations of his countrymen that were not merely a matter for literary critics to address. For, together with some cartoons in *Punch* magazine that represented Irish people as ape-like, such stereotypes served to pander to prejudice and imperialism.

Young Ireland had utilised ballads and song as a means of protesting and of galvanising support, and the Fenians of 1867 did likewise.[8] In 1889 Griffith, aged eighteen, read to the Leinster Debating Club a short but entertaining paper on the topic.[9] One striking feature of it was that the first and oldest ballad he cited was not nationalist in sentiment. He used this to make a point about street ballads generally:

Their influence at times has been remarkable. For instance, a ballad written by a noble lord in James II's reign is said to have contributed not a little to his overthrow [by King William of Orange] – here is a verse:

There was an old prophecy found in a bog
Lillabulera Ballera la!
That Ireland would be ruled by an ass and a dog
Lillabulera Ballera la!
And now this old prophecy has come to pass
Lillabulera Ballera la!
For Talbot's the dog and King James is the ass
Lillabulera Ballera la!

Griffith was quoting a song that became widely known before the Battle of the Boyne in 1690, and that his Ulster Protestant ancestors may well have sung. 'Lillabulera' (also 'Lilliburlero') is thought to have played a significant role in eroding public support for King James II. Its satirical, taunting lyrics were put to an old jig that Henry Purcell arranged and were sung by the supporters of 'King Billy'. Its words were written in 1688 by Thomas Wharton, later a lord lieutenant of Ireland, and they satirised sentiments of the Catholic Irish that were then being voiced by royalist balladeers. Its opening line sets the tone: 'Ho! Broder [brother] Teague, dost hear de decree?' As seen above, the ballad has a sting in the tail for King James and his lord deputy Richard Talbot, earl of Tyrconnell (there was then a breed of dog used for tracking, especially on the battlefield, that was known as a Talbot). The refrain of the song may be an anglicised version of Irish words, perhaps 'Lilly ba léir dó, ba linn an lá' meaning 'Lilly foretold it, this day would come.' William Lilly (1602–81) was an immensely popular English astrologer.[10] The air is played, to this day, by Orange bands, although with different lyrics and known as 'The Protestant Boys'. A version of it also long served as the signature tune of the BBC World Service, despite the poet Robert Graves objecting to it.[11] Such was its significance in Ireland under the Stuarts, that Bagwell equated its effect to that of *The Marriage of Figaro* in France before the French revolution and of John Brown's March in the American civil war.[12] It was said that forty thousand copies were circulated by the end of the 1680s and that the taking of Carrickfergus and the crossing of the Boyne were accompanied by the playing of it.[13] It was not usually sung by nationalists.

As an editor, Griffith promoted the recovery and playing of Irish music and airs. His taste encompassed all sorts of ballads that he picked up on the streets. Any suggestion that Griffith was solely interested in the political content of his papers, while others took care of cultural or literary matters in them, is far too reductionist. Soon after Griffith's death, George Lyons wrote 'Among the most important and most beautiful achievements of Griffith was his "Ballad History of Ireland" which ran through the pages of *The United Irishman* from January 1904 till February 1905.' Griffith's brother Frank claimed that Brown's *Historical Ballad Poetry of Ireland* was a 'piece of piracy' of Griffith's work in the *United Irishman*.[14] Griffith's series was by no means all that he published on the topic of ballads, or on music more generally, and his body of work in that and other respects awaits further attention.[15]

Griffith's friend William Rooney went to great lengths until his early death to find and have sung as many old Irish songs as he could discover, and Griffith kept up a campaign in support of Irish compositions and airs. As always, Griffith's objective was to reinforce national self-esteem and to develop Irish economic and cultural activity. It is evident from reading his pieces in the *United Irishman* that he believed that some ostensibly highly cultured people patronised or scorned what was indigenous, and he would have none of it. On St John's Eve 1910 young nationalist people gathered in Donnycarney near Dublin to celebrate midsummer, consciously adopting what they understood to be traditional customs of the old Irish on such special occasions. These included jumping over bonfires, which was perhaps once a fertilty rite. They also sang popular nationalist songs, including 'God Save Ireland', 'The Memory of the Dead', 'The Green Flag' and 'poor Fear na Muintear's [the late William Rooney's] "Men of the West"'. The *United Irishman* reported 'we thought of the dark days of ten or twelve years ago, when William Rooney and his little band of comrades were sneered and jibed at as foolish dreamers and mad enthusiasts by the "practical men"'.[16] James Joyce remembered a quieter visit to the same district:

> O, it was out by Donnycarney
>> When the bat flew from tree to tree
> My love and I did walk together;
>> And sweet were the words she said to me.[17]

Griffith's private secretary during the treaty negotiations in London wrote that 'Griffith liked good music, and had a sweet, weak singing voice … He liked patriotic love songs such as The Foggy Dew or Maire my Girl'.[18] Interned with him in England, a future minister for finance, Ernest Blythe, discovered that 'Griffith had an extraordinary knowledge of Irish music. No matter what tune was mentioned in any discussion he was able to whistle it. He must have had at least hundreds of tunes in his mind.'[19] Griffith also liked arias from some of the well-known operas that were performed regularly in Dublin, with patrons of different social classes mingling at performances. He could be heard singing them aloud. James Joyce had a better singing voice than Griffith and even came close to winning the tenor competition of the annual Feis Ceoil. He shared with Griffith a taste for the everyday and is said to have known hundreds of songs 'composed by Irish men and women … about wars, battles, patriotism, nature, love, drinking, all in an Irish context … known and sung by the Irish'. They included 'The Memory of the Dead' and some other pieces that featured in the talk about the 'songs of our fathers' that Griffith gave publicly in 1899.[20] Joyce's short, well-known story 'The Dead' poignantly evokes the kind of recreational evening of mixed song, piano accompaniment and recitation that was long a feature of Dublin life, especially at Christmas even into the present author's youth, and that Griffith and his friends enjoyed in their societies.

Imprisoned with Griffith in Gloucester during the Irish War of Independence, Robert Brennan was fascinated by his knowledge of song:

> There was no opera which I had seen, up to that time, which was strange to A.G. Now and again he used to sing snatches from *The Barber of Seville* or *Faust*, but never for an audience. He had rather a poor baritone voice, but he whistled very well. He was a typical Dubliner in his fondness for Wallace and Balfe, and as for drama, he knew his Congreve, Sheridan, and Goldsmith very well. He had a keen appreciation of Shakespeare and Beaumont and Fletcher. He knew and loved every melodrama that had been produced in the Queen's Theatre for a generation.[21]

Later, during the strained weeks in London embroiled in negotiations for an Anglo-Irish Treaty, Griffith took himself off as a respite to the Hammersmith Theatre to enjoy its new production of *The Beggar's Opera*. On 27 October 1921, he did so with Michael Collins and Kitty Kiernan.[22]

Across the table from Griffith at the negotiations in Downing Street sat Winston Churchill, whose father and Arthur Balfour had both featured in a satirical ballad which, in 1889, Griffith had quoted in his paper for the Leinster Debating Club – but he presumably did not sing this to his select audience in Whitehall.[23]

After Griffith died, Piaras Béaslaí edited a pamphlet containing two dozen ballads that Griffith himself had composed. These ranged from the fiercely political 'Twenty Men from Dublin Town', which sings of

United Irishmen who left Dublin after the 1798 insurrection and joined the rebellious Michael Dwyer in the mountains, to his humourous 'Thirteenth Lock'. This features the drunken skipper of a canal barge negotiating Dublin's Grand Canal by Dolphin's Barn and Inchicore. It takes sideswipes along the way at certain Trinity College professors who were hostile to the Irish language.

Visiting Paris, Griffith was impressed by J.B. Duffaud's painting 'Les Anglais en Irlande 1798', referencing the French-backed rebellion in Ireland that year,[24] and a number of times called for Irish artists to paint significant historical scenes. He thought that the Irish also deserved new theatrical works of art that that would be accessible. Referring to those 'known in England as the lower-middle-class and bred on Poe, Cowper and Macaulay', he wanted for their Irish counterparts '[a] few simple farces and ordinary plays on conventional lines, with an Irish flavour … Shapespeare wrote Julius Caesar and his Lucretia for this class, and his Hamlet and his Sonnets for the other'. Griffith warned in fatherly fashion that as regards such Irish people, 'symbolism affrights them as darkness does a child'.[25]

SONGS BALLADS
and
RECITATIONS
by
FAMOUS IRISHMEN

Arthur Griffith

Edited by PIARAS BEASLAI

6ᵈ

PUBLISHED BY:
WALTONS MUSICAL INSTRUMENT GALLERIES
(PUBLICATIONS DEPT.) LTD.
2, 3 & 4 NTH. FREDERICK ST., and 90 LR. CAMDEN ST.
DUBLIN.

Some of Griffith's verses, published after he died. On the cover is the portrait of Griffith by Lily Williams now in Dublin City Gallery/The Hugh Lane.

6

His 'Best Friend' Rooney Dies

A rthur Griffith loved his close friend William Rooney (Liam Ó Maolruanaidh). Rooney's dark hair, good looks and romantic vision thrilled his contemporaries (Plate 5). When Rooney died in his late twenties, Griffith was so devastated that he was admitted to hospital.[1] The following year, Yeats dedicated his signal play *Kathleen Ni Houlihan* to Rooney's memory.[2] Joyce criticised Rooney's poetry but did not forget the man.

Griffith and Rooney both attended the Christian Brothers' school in Strand Street, and together trawled bookstalls for works by Irish poets and activists.[3] As they grew older, they broke into journalism by writing for the *Evening Herald* a series on the graves of notable Irish patriots, hoping to resurrect the spirit of Irish independence. They later launched and edited the new *United Irishman*, which ultimately impelled the foundation of Sinn Féin. Griffith thought Rooney a Thomas Davis for the twentieth century: 'Davis spoke to the soul of the sleeping nation – drunk with the waters of forgetfulness. He sought to unite the whole people. He fought against sectarianism and all the other causes which divided them,' according to Michael Collins.[4]

William Rooney: Thine Own Sweet Tongue

Griffith, when he recovered from the trauma of Rooney's death, published his late friend's poems and ballads.[5] He gave pride of place to 'Ceann Dubh Dílis' ('O Dear Dark Head'). Written in English, it was addressed to Mother Ireland. Hanna Sheehy Skeffington thought it 'embodies in poetic form the story of her [Ireland's] life-long dream for freedom'.[6]

By placing first this poem by Rooney in the collection that he published in 1902, Griffith makes Rooney a promise:

O Dear Dark Head, bowed low in death's black sorrow,
Let not thy heart be tramelled in despair;
Lift, lift thine eyes unto the radiant morrow,
And wait the light that surely shall break there.
What, though the grave hath closed about thy dearest,
All are not gone that love thee, nor all fled;
And though thine own sweet tongue thou seldom hearest,
Yet shall it ring again, O Dear Dark Head.

Both Griffith and Rooney were 'northsiders', with Griffith born in 1871 on Dominick Street and Rooney in 1873 on Mabbot Street. The latter led into the notorious red-light district mentioned in *Ulysses* by Joyce: 'The Mabbot street entrance of nighttown, before which stretches an uncobbled tramsiding set with skeleton tracks, red and green will-o'-the-wisps and danger signals. Rows of grimy houses with gaping doors. Rare lamps with faint rainbow fans.'

Griffith and Rooney left school before the age of fourteen to find work. Griffith became a printer's apprentice and Rooney a solicitor's junior clerk.[7] Where Griffith's father was a printer, Rooney's was a coachbuilder. In 1902 a former schoolfriend recalled that Rooney 'took a hard position as clerk which hardly brought him a comfortable competence. He, the most energetic, the best informed, and the ablest of them all, elected to occupy a humble position in order to work for Ireland.'[8]

We know very little about Rooney's family and personal life. None of his papers appear to survive.[9] About 1888, he and Griffith attended the Irish Fireside Club. Here they learnt some Irish language, and discussed works by Thomas Davis and John Mitchel. Their friendship subsequently grew in the Leinster Literary Club/Society, of which Griffith became president and into which Rooney followed him. In February 1893 Rooney founded the Celtic Literary Society, of which Griffith was president at the time of the former's death. This was a significant cultural forum that by its very name asserted that literature was not the preserve of the English or Anglo-Irish alone. The two friends also supported Douglas Hyde's Gaelic League, founded later in 1893. Rooney played an active role in that league to the end. The intensity of his personality is evident from an incident said to have occurred when he arrived one night at the rooms of the Celtic Literary Society to find some men playing cards: 'He neither remonstrated nor argued, but, with his eyes blazing and his face stern, threw the cards into the fire, kicked over the table, and pointed to the door.'[10]

They were apart for nearly two years when Griffith in 1897 went to South Africa. During that period Rooney published his poem 'An Exile's Shamrock', likely if not actually calculated to make Griffith yearn for home by referring to 'voices of friends beloved of boyhood years' and 'the strong true friendship time nor space can kill'.[11] Maud Gonne said of Griffith that 'home-sickness brought him back to Ireland' in the autumn of 1898.[12] But he had also been offered a job editing the *United Irishman* newspaper, albeit on a very small income. It is said that Rooney had turned down an offer to be its editor, proposing Griffith instead because, as he is said to have put it: 'Dan is not doing well in South Africa.'[13] Griffith on his return to Ireland was enthusiastically elected an honorary member of the Celtic Literary Society.[14] Also admitted to the society was George Clancy, who took lessons in Irish from William Rooney and who himself taught Irish to James Joyce for a period.[15]

Working by now as a clerk with a railway company, Rooney also immersed himself in the writing and production of the *United Irishman* as fully as his other commitments allowed. The 'All Ireland' section on the front page was his in particular.[16] In 1900, he and Griffith founded Cumann na nGaedheal, an organisation intended to unite advanced nationalist and cultural groups, and a forerunner of Sinn Féin.

Boys of The Heather

Rooney like Griffith frequented the National Library of Ireland, 'a haunt loved by us', as H.E. Kenny, Griffith's friend and the future librarian of Dáil Éireann, called it.[17] It was, wrote Maud Gonne, 'a very pleasant place indeed for reading and writing', which Yeats also used then.[18] When her close relationship with the French politician Lucien Millevoye ended in November 1898,[19] Gonne returned to Dublin quite frequently. She left their daughter Iseult in Paris.[20]

In 1898 Rooney was heavily involved with Gonne and Yeats and others in organising celebrations to mark the centenary of the United Irishmen rebellion. He wrote a rousing ballad, 'The Men of the West', to commemorate the men who, in 1798, had supported a force of French soldiers that landed in Co. Mayo and routed the English at a victory known as 'the races of Castlebar':

> Forget not the boys of the heather
> Who rallied their bravest and best
> When Ireland was broken in Wexford
> And looked for revenge to the West.[21]

Rooney's ballad was popular, soon acquiring something of the cachet of a traditional folk song. James Joyce is thought to allude to him and to it in *Ulysses* – 'that minstrel boy of the wild wet west', and 'We are a long time waiting for that day, citizen, says Ned. Since the poor old woman told us that the French were on the sea and landed at Killala.'[22]

Moral Pollution

Rooney promoted the Irish language and Gaelic culture at a time when employees worked six days a week. He frequently finished work on a Saturday, took a train to address a meeting on Sunday, came back to Dublin again by the night mail, and was at his job again on Monday morning.[23] The *Liverpool Mercury* praised him, because 'Working ten hours a day as a railway clerk, he taught classes of men, women and children every evening, produced literature of a lasting kind, and refused a single penny of recompense.'[24] Given the currency of British jingoism then, and the very British syllabi in many Irish schools where Irish history might go untaught, it is not surprising that he tried to persuade young people to read works by Irish authors, both Catholic and Protestant. In explaining his position as early as 1889 in a paper read to the Irish Fireside Club, he had indicated that the Irish writers whom he had in mind included Elizabeth Hamilton, Maria Edgeworth and Lady Wilde.[25]

Griffith and Rooney also helped Maud Gonne and a group of women who founded in 1900 Inghinidhe na hÉireann (Daughters of Ireland), with not only Griffith and Rooney joining them on the initial organising committee but also, as Gonne recalled, 'the sisters of both and Willie Rooney's fianceé, Maire Kil[l]een'.[26] Rooney confessed 'I am not an advocate of the "political woman" or the "woman's rights" specimen, but I think that the best interests of the nation could be benefited if the women of Ireland were educated, as their brothers should be, to the needs and capabilities of the country'.[27] He also wrote for the *Shan Van Vocht* paper edited by Alice Milligan and Anna Johnston.[28]

Rooney's poems are of his time, the era of Rudyard Kipling and others whose particular form of earnestness and chauvinism seem very dated now. In the *United Irishman* Kipling was characterised as 'the Poet of the Empire' and repeatedly mocked.[29] Rooney was the poet of the nation. He could be bluntly priggish, castigating (for example) 'all the drivil and dirt of cockneydom' that was imported from England and that Irish people bought when their own country did not support even one native comic paper. He condemned the Dublin evening papers for retailing 'the doings of American widows or English aristocrats' and lamented 'the immoral and unnatural ideas which underlie' modern society plays.[30] Rooney was, said a contemporary:

> The first public voice raised insistently against the moral pollution of the London music-hall ditties … Indeed, everything which weakened the moral fibre of our people found him its sworn foe … the sheer beauty and simplicity of his character was known to all who had the good fortune to enjoy his friendship … Almost always he was gay in company, but when a scoffer at female goodness, a juggler of words of dubious double meaning … obtruded himself, a solemn and stern rebuke awaited him from the high-minded William Rooney.[31]

In a preface to the collection of Rooney's poems, it was said that 'His aim was to write such verse and prose as would appeal to the average Irish man or woman, and all his work, whether in prose or verse was written with the one object – that of strengthening and perpetuating the feeling of Irish nationhood in its highest form, in the minds and hearts of the people.'[32] In reviewing that collection of poetry, James Joyce thought that Rooney 'might have written well if he had not suffered from one of those big words which make us so unhappy', although Joyce left the word 'patriotism' unsaid.[33] Joyce later echoed himself in *Ulysses*; 'I fear those big words, Stephen said, which make us so unhappy.'

In 1909, in his brief introduction to a separate volume of some of Rooney's prose from the *United Irishman*, Seumas MacManus noted 'These are not the laboriously polished essays of one whose mission was the making of literature, but the outspoken words of a deeply-in-earnest man.'[34]

Typhoid

Rooney fell ill on 2 March 1901 and died two months later at home in North Strand, in his twenty-eighth year and 'to the inexpressible grief of his parents and friends'.[35] To the last his busy brain planned cultural initiatives: 'If I were well,' he said on his deathbed, 'we should surprise everyone … we would teach every singer a song that was never heard in Dublin before. I know where to get airs and words.'[36] The *United Irishman* reported 'as we sat by his bedside, with a wistful smile he told us, quoting from a poem of Denis Florence McCarthy's, that he was weary waiting for the May. And the May brought him death, as he knew it would, although we had hoped and prayed it might bring him health.'[37] A death certificate records the cause of his death on 6 May 1901 as typhoid, a hazard then of the Dublin tenements.[38]

Griffith never doubted Rooney's value to the national movement, and his immediate response to Rooney's death was immensely emotional. He confessed 'I came to build my hopes for Ireland on him, and to regard him as the destined regenerator of his people.' He recalled that Rooney had 'stayed with the peasant in his sheiling [a small, rough structure] and learned from him the old folk-stories and folk-songs which are now becoming known to us'.[39] He added 'As a man and as an Irishman, his life was beautiful.'[40]

If Griffith was in love with Rooney, nothing indicates that his love was other than platonic. Griffith was to describe him as the 'best friend' he ever had.[41] In the next issue of the *United Irishman*, its editor admitted 'we have scarcely looked at our correspondents' letters for the last few days. In the presence of the calamity that has befallen the national cause, we have neither time nor heart to deal with other subjects.' Rooney was 'dead in the spring of life – a martyr to his passionate love of our unhappy country', and 'It seemed impossible to us that he could die.'[42]

When Griffith mourned Rooney's passing he was, as William Murphy notes, 'unstinting (well past the point of hyperbole) in his praise.'[43] The pages of the *United Irishman* were decked out with black mourning borders or rules, as they had been when James Stephens 'the greatest Irishman of the century' died one month earlier.[44] On 21 May 1901, W.B. Yeats wrote to Lady Gregory that the death 'has plunged everybody onto gloom. Griffith has had to go to hospital for a week, so much did it affect him.'[45] Maud Gonne wrote:

> In Boston, I got a cable from Griffith, telling of Willie Rooney's death. It was a great blow … He was Griffith's greatest friend and helper in the paper. His loss was irreparable; I wondered if Griffith would be able to carry on without him … In Philadelphia I got a short, broken-hearted letter from Griffith. Rooney … had a cold and should have stayed in bed, but he had meetings in the West for the weekend and insisted on going. He came back very ill and never recovered. He was engaged to be married to Marie Killeen, one of the executive of *Inghinidhe na hÉireann*, a dark girl who, in our *tableaux vivants*, looked very beautiful as the Dark Rosaleen. He had done a lot to help our women's organisation.[46]

In St Louis she received another letter, Griffith 'begging me not to stay too long in America as I was badly needed in Dublin.'[47] On 26 October 1901, in the *United Irishman*, Griffith wrote of Rooney that '[we] feel every hour of our lives his loss'. Michael Collins, just ten years old when Rooney died, later acknowledged his role in the national movement. As the Irish Free State came into existence in 1922, Collins wrote glowingly of him.[48]

'Those Big Words'

Griffith's *United Irishman* gave publicity to James Joyce's early essay 'The Day of the Rabblement', which warned that 'the artist, though he may employ the crowd, is very careful to isolate himself ... it is strange to see the artist making terms with the rabble.'[49] But Joyce quite liked the rabble, and his review of Rooney's poems and ballads for the Dublin *Daily Express* of 11 December 1902 was not some kind of dramatic break with Ireland or with its people. It was the first of twenty book reviews that he wrote for that Dublin paper.[50] He penned it on his way to Paris, at the age of twenty. He had dropped out of medical school in Dublin and thought that he might instead study medicine in France while also developing a literary career. He had spoken with Lady Gregory who recommended him to the editor as a reviewer, although the Dublin *Daily Express* scarcely reflected his own perspective on society. It had a unionist and conservative reputation, with Karl Marx condemning it in 1858 as 'the Government organ, which day by day treats its readers to false rumours.'[51] Joyce himself, in his short story 'The Dead', later had a character discover that Gabriel Conroy writes for the *Daily Express*. She asks him 'Now, aren't you ashamed of yourself?'

> A look of perplexity appeared on Gabriel's face. It was true that he wrote a literary column every Wednesday in *The Daily Express*, for which he was paid fifteen shillings. But that did not make him a West Briton surely ... He wanted to say that literature was above politics. But they were friends of many years' standing and their careers had been parallel, first at the university and then as teachers: he could not risk a grandiose phrase with her. He continued blinking his eyes and trying to smile and murmured lamely that he saw nothing political in writing reviews of books.[52]

Strikingly, in the launch issues and in some subsequent issues of the *United Irishman* in 1899, Griffith had complimented the *Daily Express*, thanking it for its courtesy in informing its readers about Griffith and Rooney's new paper and describing the *Express* under its then editor as 'the best written and generally best informed, daily paper in Ireland'.

However, in late December 1899, the *United Irishman* claimed that, 'The *Daily Express*, under its new management, has reverted to its old pre-Maunsell policy of lying.'[53]

Joyce's review in the *Daily Express* was unlikely to go unnoticed because, as he stated in its opening sentence: 'These are the verses of a writer lately dead, whom many consider the [Thomas] Davis of the latest national movement ... They are illustrative of the national temper.' He wrote that the volume had 'issued from headquarters', by which he meant the offices of the *United Irishman*, which had also very recently published a play by W.B. Yeats.[54] It may be relevant that Joyce had recently been trying his own hand at poetry but the critic and translator William Archer, to whom he sent verses during 1901, told him that his early efforts were too moody, 'more temperament than anything else'.[55] Joyce now asserted in his review of Rooney that (from an exclusively literary perspective perhaps), 'a man who writes a book cannot be excused by his good intentions, or by his moral character'. He judged that Rooney had 'no care then to create anything according to the art of literature':

> Instead we find in these pages a weary succession of verses ... [that] have no spiritual or living energy, because they come from one in whom the spirit is in a manner dead ... a weary and foolish spirit, speaking of redemption and revenge, blaspheming against tyrants, and going forth, full of tears and curses, upon its infernal labours. Religion and all that is allied thereto can manifestly persuade men to great evil, and by writing these verses, even though they should, as the writers of the prefaces think, enkindle the young men of Ireland to hope and activity, Mr Rooney has been persuaded to great evil.

Joyce excluded from his harsh criticism 'one piece in the book which seems to have come out of a conscious personal life'. It is a translation of 'Impidhe: A Request' by Douglas Hyde, which Griffith published in pride of place on the front page of the *United Irishman* in the week that Rooney died and from which Joyce quoted some verses as translated by Rooney.[56] But the fact that he chided Rooney for spoiling his art by speaking 'those big words which make us so unhappy' irked Griffith. The latter responded smartly by quoting Joyce's phrase without comment in an advertisement for Rooney's book but adding, within that quotation, the single word 'Patriotism' in brackets.[57]

Joyce was harsh not only on Rooney's poetry but also on *Poets and Dreamers* by Lady Gregory. Gregory had been instrumental in getting Joyce commissions from the *Daily Express* and also in persuading Yeats to entertain him for some hours in London on his way to Paris. The editor placed Joyce's initials at the end of the reviews to indicate clearly who had written them, and also urged Joyce in future to write more favourably. Joyce made use of this incident in both *Dubliners* and *Ulysses*, in the former when Gabriel Conroy's initials betray him to Miss Ivors as a reviewer of the poet Robert Browning.[58] In *Ulysses*, Buck Mulligan (Gogarty) exclaims to Stephen 'O you inquisitorial drunken jewjesuit! She gets you a job on the paper and then you go and slate her drivel to Jaysus. Couldn't you do the Yeats touch?'

While Joyce did not renounce his review of Rooney he gave the latter a certain artistic afterlife in his own work and retained his copy of Rooney's poetry until his own death.[59] Joyce had studied Irish under George Clancy, himself a student of Rooney, and Joyce approved of the Sinn Féin independence movement, albeit with reservations.[60] He seemingly references Rooney in both 'The Dead', the best-known short story of Joyce's *Dubliners*, and *Ulysses*. The short story, published in 1914, happens to share its title with an article in Griffith's *Sinn Féin* on 3 April 1909 that recalled Rooney mourning the passing of John Millington Synge, who had died aged just thirty-eight after what the paper described as 'a long period of ill health', and whom the editor thought 'would have become one of the first of modern dramatists'.

The Potent Dead

Alice Milligan, founder and president of the Irish Women's Association and editor of *Shan Van Vocht*, wrote a long poem in Rooney's honour, 'By the Grave-Side', which challenged those who thought that the dead are simply gone. It includes these notable lines:

'Sweet were his songs, his dreams were wild and vain.
He is dead and silent now and shall dream no more.'

They know not Ireland by whom such words are said;
They know not Ireland's heart, they cannot know
More potent than the living are our dead.[61]

In Joyce's short story 'The Dead', one can see the potency of past lives, and aspects of that story are related to the milieu of Griffith and Rooney. One of Joyce's sources for it appears to have been Richard Irvine Best's rendering of an old Irish myth in the pages of the *United Irishman*.[62] 'The Dead' also happens to echo aspects of William Rooney's work. For in 1898, the *Weekly Freeman* newspaper awarded Rooney a prize for the best poem written on an incident in the 1798 rebellion. The title of Rooney's winning entry 'The Priest of Adrigoole', refers to one Fr Conroy who was instrumental in helping the French force that landed in Co. Mayo in 1798 but that was heavily defeated.[63] Gabriel Conroy in 'The Dead' has a brother who is a priest. Moreover, the climax of 'The Dead' posits an Ireland sleeping under snow while Gabriel and his wife in the Gresham Hotel uneasily conjure up the ghost of her long-deceased sweetheart from the west of Ireland, Michael Furey. The story's last paragraph begins 'A few light taps upon the pane made him turn to the window. It had begun to snow again.' Compare this stanza of Rooney's 'Priest of Adrigoole':

There's someone at the window. Tap! tap! tap, anew;
Sharp thro' the silent midnight it speeds the cottage through;
'Some poor soul speeding onward, some sudden call to go
Unshriven on the pathway we all of us must know.'
Thus muses he, that sagart [Irish for 'priest'], as from his couch he
    flies
And opens full the window where wonder-widened eyes
Look into his, and accents with haste all husky spake –
'The French are in Killala – and all the land's awake!'[64]

Here too, as in Rooney's poem 'Men of the West', the poet is haunted by the power of the past glorious failure. Joycean scholars such as Kevin Whelan have seen the defeated rebellion of 1798 as 'a hidden reverberative source' for 'The Dead'.[65] Dialogue with the dead itself is reverberative of an ancient Irish creative tradition.[66]

Joyce did not forget Rooney, for in *Ulysses* he again used the motif of persistent tapping, the tapping being that of a blind man's cane as he sings a ballad about 1798. At one point Joyce drops into this passage the surname Rooney, albeit with the first name Micky (a diminutive of the 'Michael' he had given Furey in *Dubliners*): 'Tap. Tap. Tap. Tap. Tap. Tap. Tap. Tap. Bloom went by Barry's. Wish I could. Wait. That wonderworker if I had ... But for example the chap that wallops the big drum. His vocation: Micky Rooney's band.' Advanced nationalists such as William Rooney were mockingly dubbed 'the Green Hungarian Band', because Griffith's proposal for a dual monarchy for Ireland and Britain was based loosely on the Austro-Hungarian constitution.[67] Also, in 'The Dead', Michael Furey 'was going to study singing only for his health.'[68] As noted already, both Rooney and Griffith were collectors of Irish ballads. We have seen that Rooney was reported publicly to have spoken wistfully in his last days of how he 'would teach every singer a song that was never heard in Dublin before', knowing where 'to get airs and words'.

At the next meeting of the Celtic Literary Society after Rooney's death, with Griffith presiding, they sang and recited songs or poems by his late friend 'and the proceedings were brought to a close by the singing of "The Memory of the Dead" – which on the occasion had a singular and sad appropriateness for those present'. The rousing ballad, written by the poet and economist John Kells Ingram (and not by William Elliott Hudson as once thought), was first published anonymously in Thomas Davis' *The Nation* on 1 April 1843 and was often sung at patriotic events. It is better known today as 'Who Fears to Speak of [17]98'.[69] The currency of the ballad is reflected in a report in Griffith's *United Irishman*, on 3 February 1900, when the editor recalled a summer evening two years earlier in Pretoria. Griffith and others had 'gathered to greet a comrade who had journeyed down from Bechuanaland to drink a toast to the memory of the dead'. They stretched out beside the Apies River

and there under the shadow of the black hills he sang us 'The Memory of the Dead', and we made the kopjes [small hills] re-echo back the chorus. We chorused in many brogues, for we were Leinstermen and Ulstermen, Connaughtmen and Munstermen, and some of us had never seen Ireland at all ... It was midnight ere we quitted his side ... He talked to us long and earnestly of Ireland and her future and his hopes for it ... I see him now as he stood up to sing the parting song – 'The Memory of the Dead.' I hear his voice in memory again as he sang ... but only in memory. Never again shall my eyes behold him or my ears hearken to his voice. For he died for Ireland like the men whose memory he revered. Tied to a post in Mafeking he was riddled by the bullets of Baden-Powell's assassins for being 'an Irish Fenian'. His name was James Quinlan. Let his countrymen be but as true through good and ill to Ireland as he was, and the dream he dreamed will yet be realised.[70]

If Joyce read this evocative report in one of the cuttings from or copies of Griffith's paper sent to him abroad, it may have made a lasting impression on him. At this very time he was certainly impressed by Henrik Ibsen's latest play *When We Dead Awaken*, and intrigued by its lines 'We see the irretrievable only when [*breaks off silent*] ... When we dead awaken.' He wrote a review of the play that he sent to Ibsen who found it 'very benevolent'. [71]

Quinlan, stationmaster at Mafeking, himself rose from the grave. More precisely, reports of his demise turned out to be premature. In 1901, his friends welcomed him home to Ireland, their celebrations ending with the singing of 'The Memory of the Dead'.[72] On one occasion Griffith was outraged to learn that the London Catholic *Universe* had published a version of 'The Memory of the Dead' that compared soldiers of the British Army in South Africa to the men of 1798: 'The fellow who wrote this deserves the horsewhip,' his paper fulminated.[73] When praising a new edition of the poetry of John Kells Ingram, Rooney himself had written 'It may safely be asserted that "The Memory of the Dead" has cheered the heart and cheered the soul of every single man and woman of the Irish National millions at home and abroad.'[74] It was reported that at a Wolfe Tone Memorial Concert the great proportion of an audience rose and left a hall in protest when the event turned out to be 'low music hall entertainments'. They sang 'The Memory of the Dead' as they did so.[75] Griffith publicly lamented the 'oversight' involved when an Oireachtas festival opened without a mention of his late friend Rooney, remarking 'The dead are soon forgotten by some people.'[76] In

1910 Yeats appears to have regarded the song as emblematic.[77]

In Joyce's 'The Dead', Gabriel Conroy, a language teacher like Joyce himself, asks his wife about her dead admirer Michael Furey: 'Who was he?' She replies 'He was [working] in the gasworks.' Gabriel presses her 'And what did he die of so young, Gretta? Consumption was it?' She retorts 'He died for me.'[78] Maud Gonne thought 'Rooney had literally killed himself from over-work'[79] by pursuing his revivalist campaign and writing for the *United Irishman* while also holding down a job in a railway. A less romantic view, akin to Gabriel Conroy's in respect to Michael Furey, is reflected on William Rooney's death certficate. Typhoid and tuberculosis ('consumption') killed many then, albeit aided by bad diet or exhaustion.

Joycean scholars believe that the character of Michael Furey is based primarily on Michael Bodkin who once courted Joyce's wife Nora. Confined by TB to his sickbed in Galway, Bodkin stole out when he learnt that she had resolved to move to Dublin, and sang to her under an apple tree. He died soon afterwards. Nora was first attracted to Joyce, she said, because he resembled Bodkin.[80] But there are parallels too with Rooney's desperate dedication to Ireland and to the memory of '98, as well as with Rooney's early tragic death.

Rooney has faded from the national memory. This cannot be simply because he often spoke in Irish on the platforms that he mounted across Ireland, with many journalists therefore unable to understand what he said.[81] It may be because his prose and poetry were very much of the Victorian era and frankly, as Joyce thought, of limited quality. Their inspiring political significance was greater than their literary merit. Mathews finds it 'astonishing that his writing and influence remain largely occluded' and has argued for Rooney's role around 1900 in creating a national consciousness to be given more weight, particularly by way of contrast to D.P. Moran of *The Leader* in the context of the campaign for an 'Irish-Ireland'.[82]

Women as Comrade and Wife

Griffith welcomed women's participation in the struggle for independence and also in the pages of his papers. Maud Gonne acknowledged his and William Rooney's encouragement.[1] Steele has praised his *United Irishman* itself for disproving 'a familiar feminist criticism of Irish nationalism as a movement of failed potential' and for giving a platform to women writers who were 'avidly discussed as autonomous participants in cultural and political affairs of the day'.[2] In 1901 Griffith published these sentiments of the socialist Fred Ryan:

> Let us face the truth. The old spirit of sham sought to make of woman unthinking dolls, the new spirit must regard them as human beings, as intelligent comrades and helpers in the various concerns of public life, in morals, no stronger and no weaker in the mass than men, and worthy no less than men of the frankest and fullest confidence and trust, and the highest and best education the community can bestow.[3]

Also in 1910 a *United Irishman* writer declared in favour of women lawyers, doctors, soldiers and (as he put it) 'blue-stockings' generally – on the basis of his belief that ancient Ireland had not barred them.[4] Later that year, Griffith himself addressed the rights of women, thinking that 'some thousand years or so ago the Irishman was good enough to reckon the Irishwoman his equal, and until one century ago looked on her as only a trifle his inferior.' He concluded 'if in course of time we in Ireland and the remnant of the earth came to live under a gynocracy, I should not repine. I am weary living in a world ruled by men with mouse-hearts and monkey-brains, and I want a change.'[5] He also recommended that people read an essay on women's equality in education by the male feminist Francis Skeffington that had been rejected elsewhere, observing 'I have always believed that God made woman to be man's comrade, not his toy, not his slave, and therefore I agree with Miss [sic] Skeffington.'[6] Some of his columnists were less progressive and, as always with Griffith, no cause was to deflect him from the goal of achieving an independent Ireland. He was prepared to declare his belief in equal voting rights for women – but just not quite yet.[7] This was similar to the position of the Irish Parliamentary Party in 1912 when it helped to defeat a franchise proposal at Westminster because it was thought that controversy concerning the proposal to give women the vote would delay Home Rule.

Into Griffith's own life stepped two women in particular. 'Mollie' (or Maud) Sheehan and Maud Gonne were very different, but each mattered to him. He fell in love with Sheehan when she was at school, but more than fifteen years passed before he married her. During that time he came under the spell of Maud Gonne. He addressed both as 'queen'. Gonne (Plate 2) was generous to Griffith, and he stayed with her at her apartment when he visited Paris. He was briefly jailed in Dublin for horse-whipping a man who insulted her. William Butler Yeats desired her and, although frustrated by her many refusals, may have had a brief physical affair with her.[8] What if, in common with Yeats and a leading French politician Lucien Millevoye and John MacBride (Plate 3) whom she married, Griffith shared Gonne's bed? She claimed that MacBride suspected as much.[9] She certainly had her secrets, including the birth of two children in France. Would it make Griffith more attractive today if found to have had a fling with Ireland's 'Joan of Arc', as she was sometimes called?

Mollie Sheehan

Arthur Griffith did not marry Mollie Sheehan until November 1910, when he was almost forty years old.[10] Christened 'Mary', she was known in public as 'Maud' but was 'Mollie' to Griffith, as he was 'Dan' to her and his friends. Born at home on 11 October 1874, she was three years younger than him (Plate 4).[11] He invited her out first in the early 1890s, but when he went to South Africa in 1897 she did not accompany him. Maud Gonne later wrote: 'I was often worried about Griffith's finances; I knew he had broken his engagement to a girl who was in the National movement because he saw no prospect of money to marry on.'[12] Among Griffith's few surviving personal papers are four love poems that he addressed to his future wife with the desperation of frustrated youth.

Her parents were Peter Sheehan and his wife Mary Purdue. Their home near Christ Church was at 4 Cook Street, which had earlier become known as 'Coffin Street' due to the number of coffin-makers located there. Her father, a paper, rag and marine merchant, had resided and worked there since at least 1847.[13] Peter appears to have gone bankrupt after the Great Famine,[14] but during the late Victorian era the collection of rags for making paper and of old clothes for resale was a fairly lucrative business.[15] When he died aged eighty-two, on St Patrick's Day 1899, he was worth more than £2,000.[16]

It was here in the heart of old Dublin that Arthur Griffith first came calling for Mollie, who met him when she was fifteen. Having worked the night at the newspaper where he was employed, Griffith took her and her sister for a jaunt in a horse and car through the Phoenix Park, 'getting home for eight o'clock Mass which they attended before going to school'.[17] In an undated poem we find young Griffith describing 'Mollie' thus:

> Her laugh is music sweet and low
> Her heart is gentleness enshrined,
> Her soul is fairer than the snow
> And purity dwells in her mind.
> Sweetest of maidens, truest, best,
> So fair, so pure, so far above me,
> Would with your head upon my breast,
> I once could hear you say you love me.[18]

On 18 January 1894, Griffith formally invited her to a show:

Dear Miss Sheehan, The 'Lily of Killarney' is announced for Saturday night. Do you remember your promise? If you are not better engaged

Where Arthur met Mollie: looking west from Cook Street towards Wormwood Gate, at the corner of Lower Bridge Street, 1888. Griffith's future wife lived on Cook Street (National Library of Ireland [JL11]).

for that evening, I would be delighted to meet you at, say a quarter past seven o'clock at the corner of Winetavern Street and Merchant's Quay [a block from Cook Street]. Sincerely yours, Arthur Griffith.[19]

The 'Lily of Killarney' is based on the Irish playwright Dion Boucicault's *The Colleen Bawn*, a melodrama that was very popular in the late nineteenth century. Its rousing song 'The Moon Hath Raised Her Lamp Above' may have made their hearts flutter. Later that year he wrote more lines, using language that seems quite typical of Victorian popular verse. They imply that kissing and her laying her head on his breast remained then only dreams, but he was thinking of the future:

> To feel your kisses on my face,
> To hear your voice love whisper to me
> To know your heart my resting-place,
> And feel your eye's lovelight pierce thro' me.
> This is my never-changing dream,
> And dare I hope you'll prove it true love,
> And that a-sailing on Life's stream
> My barque will proudly carry you, love?[20]

In a second poem of the same date he proclaimed her 'Queen of a heart that never knew, Till stormed and captured by surprise, What direful ravage love could do'. She was 'Queen of my soul, my love, my pride, Sweet Molly [spelt thus]'.[21] In the last of four surviving poems we find him in August 1895 declaring 'Oh! Queen of mine, my love, my world, my dream, So pure, so fair, so tender, true and sweet, I bend and kiss the dust beneath your feet.'[22] 'Queen' was a usual term of endearment (like '*ma reine*' in French), with Parnell for example constantly using it when addressing Katharine O'Shea in correspondence.[23]

On a list of about fifty people who in 1896 attended a Christmas celebration of the Celtic Literary Society, just weeks before Griffith went to South Africa, we find his and Mollie's name one after the other. Perhaps they attended as a couple. She sang at the event, and was said to have 'often played piano as accompaniment at these Celtic gatherings'.[24] Chrissie Doyle recalled Griffith at ceilidhs but said that he did not dance: 'He just sat quietly and unobtrusively in a corner, and talked to his friends.'[25] When he returned from South Africa the following year it was to throw himself into the editing of a new newspaper advocating advanced nationalism, and into various other political activities. Decades later Sheehan told the Bureau of Military History that Griffith 'never talked to me about politics as I did not want to, having been brought up in a family in which my father was an ardent Parnellite and my mother a follower of William O'Brien, with consequent frequent disputes in political matters'.[26] But Griffith knew a woman who wanted to talk of little else. This was Maud Gonne, an English convert to Irish nationalism.

Maud Gonne

Maud Gonne (Plate 2) wrote that she first met Arthur Griffith when she attended a meeting of the Celtic Literary Society to recite some of Thomas Davis' poems in order to illustrate a lecture by William Rooney:

> He [Griffith] was a fair, shy boy one would hardly notice, but I was at once attracted to him. I hardly knew why, for he did not speak, and I got to know him well only in 1899 when he and Willie Rooney came to me with the first copy of the *United Irishman* [dated 4 March 1899]. They had collected £30 and hoped it would be enough to start the paper, and found they had not even enough for the second number.[27]

She presided at a meeting of the 'Celtic' on 6 October 1899, when Griffith did speak. Its minutes record him seconding a motion in support of the Boers. Gonne discovered that women were not in practice admitted members of the society, but wrote that Griffith and Rooney both disapproved of the exclusion and 'when I did actually start Inghinidhe na h-Éireann in 1900, gave me all the help they could'.[28] The police noted of this organisation ('Daughters of Erin'), which held its first meeting on Easter Sunday 1900 and also on that day provided a nationalist 'Treat' for many children, that it intended to teach the Irish language 'and lecture against enlisting'. Gonne afterwards wrote: 'Disrespectfully and affectionately our friends often called Inghinidhe "the Ninnies"'.[29]

Levenson summed up in conventional terms Gonne's attractiveness to contemporaries, who frequently commented on it:

> Maud Gonne was one of the great English beauties of the Victorian period ... Six feet tall, with a willowy figure, soft hazel eyes, an apple blossom complexion, and hair of burnished bronze, she was the kind of woman whose appearance in a room, at a ball, or on the street caused heads to turn and conversation to cease.[30]

In her romantic but somewhat unreliable autobiography,[31] Gonne unashamedly reproduced a glowing tribute to her physical beauty that the leading British journalist W.T. Stead penned.[32] Even Mary Colum, when writing that physical looks alone could not explain Gonne's impact, still tried to explain her charm without regard to what men may have found most overwhelming about her, her political determination and financial independence:

> there was only a minimum of the conventional enchantress about her. She wore chic clothes carelessly; choosing hats was a bother, so she wound veils around her head, turban fashion. She used, as far as one could see, no cosmetics. Beauty alone could never have won her the lasting devotion of men and women, or the tribute of immortal verse that Yeats has given her ... She had three qualities that I have seen in all the real charmers I have known: she had a romantic personality; she had rich emotions; and a warm heart – indeed, one of the winning things about her was her affection for other people;[33]

Steele has noted critically 'the recurrent narrative of Gonne's life as a violent, irrational, facile and beautiful distraction', discerning a tendency on the part of biographers to 'romanticize Gonne's considerable political contributions and capitalize on a flourishing Yeats industry'. Those political contributuons have recently been noted.[34]

Born into a wealthy family in England, Gonne was brought to Ireland as a child when her father became brigade major of cavalry during the Fenian alarm. She spent much of her youth elsewhere. According to Yeats, she told him that when she returned to Ireland for a while before the age of twenty, she 'longed to have control over her own life'. Finding a volume on magic among her father's books, she 'asked the Devil to give her control of her own life and offered in return her soul.

At that moment the clock struck twelve, and she felt of a sudden that the prayer had been heard and answered. Within a fortnight her father died suddenly, and she was stricken with remorse.'[35] She came into a substantial inheritance after her father died.

Moving in wealthy circles abroad, in 1887 in France Gonne met Lucien Millevoye, an older man and a journalist who became an anti-Republican member of the French parliament. He was married, but perhaps then separated, and they began a relationship. In 1890 their son was born, only to die within a year. According to Yeats, Gonne said that at this point she had 'thought of breaking' with Millevoye 'and had engaged herself for a week to someone else', whom she did not identify. Yeats added pathetically 'I thought, I may have had that poor betrothal for my reward.' But she was reconciled with Millevoye and in 1893 (as Yeats says she told him) the couple had sex in the mausoleum where their son's remains were buried. Maud hoped for his reincarnation.[36] The child born to her in August 1894 was actually a girl, named Iseult, who was to be brought up in France. On visits to Ireland, Gonne did not acknowledge that she was an unmarried mother. At that time 'such an admission would have socially and politically destroyed her', it is said.[37]

Millevoye was a conservative conspirator. In 1899 Rowland Strong described him as 'a malicious lunatic whose great object is to "produce" himself'. Strong added, 'I have known him as a Boulangist [an assertive nationalist follower of Georges Boulanger] who was most anxious to be on good terms with the Jews, then as an anti-Semite.'[38] Strong, a critic and writer, was Paris correspondent for *The New York Times* and the London *Observer*. He moved in a small circle that included the disgraced Oscar Wilde, Alfred Douglas and Commandant Ferdinand Walsin-Esterhazy. The latter had engaged in the very spying for which the Jewish Dreyfus was both wrongfully convicted and jailed on Devil's Island, and Strong was hostile to Dreyfus.[39] Maud Gonne herself in her autobiography, even as late as 1938, seemed reluctant to acknowledge the innocence of Dreyfus.[40]

By 1899 Gonne's affair with Millevoye appears to have ended, although the couple had a lingering acquaintanceship.[41] Gonne later wrote that she got to know Griffith well that year. He had returned from South Africa in late 1898.

When in France, Gonne organised and spoke at events to highlight the cause of the Irish nation, and from May 1897 edited *L'Irlande Libre* (Free Ireland) in which she came to publish pieces by James Connolly, Griffith and Yeats. Its masthead proclaimed '*Organe de la colonie Irlandaise à Paris*'. A special issue of April 1900, for which Griffith wrote, had a cartoon on the cover showing Queen Victoria in a shamrock dress in a famine graveyard. It included Gonne's article on 'The Famine Queen' that Griffith also published in English in the *United Irishman* on 7 April, leading to police seizures of his paper. She helped to support Griffith's *United Irishman*, raising donations for it on her visits to America. In that regard she persuaded W.B. Yeats to write a supportive letter.[42] She also inspired much of Yeats' popular early love poetry. In 1900, a correspondent in Dublin's *Express* took a sideswipe at Yeats as 'poet laureate to the court of Miss Maud Gonne'.[43]

The police thought Gonne 'dangerous' and speculated about the source of the money that they believed she was providing to Griffith, James Connolly and others, suspecting that it came from the National Party of France, through Millevoye or even from some section of the Russian government. Informers and spies reported on her movements with Yeats and Griffith. She paid at least one printing bill for the *United Irishman* and claimed later to have wanted Griffith to accept £2.10.00 a week as its editor, 'but Griffith who was entirely unselfish and disinterested about money, refused'. He would take only half that amount, which was what (according to Gonne) he had to pay his mother for board. It was the case that he lived at home. Gonne continued 'I was never able to shake his proud resolve of living on a bare subsistence till the paper paid. It never did pay owing to its frequent seizures and difficulty of production under British coercion acts.'[44]

At the turn of the century Griffith was 'the driving force behind the Irish pro-Boer movement', most notably through the Irish Transvaal Committee that embraced 'all that is dangerous in Dublin', according to a police report.[45] Gonne worked closely with him to stir up opposition to Britain's presence in southern Africa.[46] It was a heady campaign that drew large crowds. The police also recorded her as often seeing the socialist James Connolly, believing that she funded his *Irish Worker* paper and that Connolly was 'a most willing agent in carrying out the behests of Maud Gonne'.[47] In late 1899, as will be seen, Griffith, Connolly and Gonne, in consultation with John O'Leary, planned a large protest meeting and confronted the police.

Griffith, partly reliant on her funding, gave Gonne much coverage in the *United Irishman*. Together they objected that the British Army had altered a rule requiring its men to sleep in barracks, and the pair started a campaign to shame Irish girls walking out with soldiers on Dublin's main street. This resulted in physical confrontations: 'fighting soldiers became quite a popular evening entertainment with young men – in which Arthur Griffith and Mary Quinn's brother used to take part, though Griffith I think hated it', wrote Gonne. Apart from exploiting Catholic concerns about morality, they also raised the issue of consequential 'illegitimate babies in the Workhouses'. William Rooney recoiled from 'the young and strong women of our country almost hanging on the necks of British soldiers'.[48] James Joyce's Leopold Bloom later refers to the campaign, in *Ulysses*:

> Redcoats. Too showy. That must be why the women go after them. Uniform. Easier to enlist and drill. Maud Gonne's letter about taking them off O'Connell street at night: disgrace to our Irish capital. Griffith's paper is on the same tack now: an army rotten with venereal disease: overseas or halfseasover empire. Half-baked they look: hypnotised like. Eyes front. Mark time. Table: able. Bed: ed. The King's own.

Gonne introduced Griffith to Paris, where wandering through the city at night he thought the new Eiffel Tower 'hideous'. He visited the Great Exhibition a number of times, writing 'we stood opposite the gloomy English building in the Paris exhibition and watched the cosmopolitan crowd'.[49] He was there with an Irish delegation for which Gonne helped to orchestrate a series of fine receptions. He and she were shadowed by English detectives.[50] He was back in Paris for a rendezvous with John MacBride, just returned from South Africa where Griffith had met him and where MacBride had subsequently fought in the Boer War. Griffith was staying in the 'little Paris flat' that Gonne maintained there. He ended up one night sharing a bed in it with MacBride, who ostensibly had not intended to sleep over until they and Gonne continued talking into the early hours.[51] Swathes of the *United Irishman* were devoted subsequently to accounts of a campaigning visit to the United States by Gonne and MacBride, including an unapologetically self-referential performance by Maud Gonne in Kansas on the theme of 'Who am I?'[52] A long unsigned poem praising Gonne appeared in the *United Irishman* on 1 June 1901.

The police informed the under-secretary for Ireland that John O'Leary and F.H. O'Donnell suspected Gonne of dishonesty. However, Griffith reacted angrily when Ramsey Colles, editor of the Irish *Figaro* referred to her as 'This lady – if a liar can be considered a lady'. Taking an object that he had brought back from Africa, he assaulted Colles: 'Mr Colles has a vigorous style with his pen, Mr Griffith has a ditto with his cow whip. So to jail [for two weeks] Mr Griffith went', wrote the *Evening Herald*. Gonne's Inghinidhe na hÉireann women's organisation, in its first public action, presented him with an inscribed blackthorn stick in thanks, and Millevoye's *La Patrie* praised him in Paris. Gonne then successfully sued the *Figaro* for libel, effectively closing it down.[53] Griffith also protested against Synge's *Shadow of the Glen*, and Mathews perceives in these two actions by Griffith a manifestation of 'his patriarchal propensity'.[54]

Griffith was appalled when Gonne decided to marry John MacBride. Their marriage was to be brief and almost certainly more disastrous than even Griffith foresaw. She chose to convert to Catholicism when she agreed to wed, despite having (as she later wrote) previously informed Lady Gregory that herself and W.B. Yeats 'were neither of the marrying sort, having other things which interested us more'.[55] Indeed, in her self-dramatising autobiography, she later claimed that a priest once cursed her ancestors, who had acquired land belonging to the Church, 'to the effect that no daughter of the Gonnes should ever find happiness in marriage'.[56] According to Gonne, Griffith wrote to her on hearing of her engagement:

Queen, forgive me. John MacBride, after Willie Rooney, is the best friend I ever had; you are the only woman friend I have. I only think of both your happiness. For your own sake and for the sake of Ireland to whom you both belong, don't get married. I know you both, you so unconventional – a law to yourself; John so full of conventions. You will not be happy for long. Forgive me, but think while there is still time.[57]

'The only woman friend'? No sign of Mollie Sheehan then, if Gonne is right. Gonne let MacBride read the heartfelt letter, and they laughed it off. Next morning in Paris, on 21 February 1903, they married.[58] In January 1904 their child Seán was born, destined one day to lead the IRA and later to win the Nobel Peace Prize and to work with the United Nations. She told John O'Leary that she thought that she was marrying Ireland when she married MacBride.[59] By 1905 she was complaining to Yeats that MacBride was 'insanely jealous', resenting money given to Griffith and suspecting her male friends of being lovers.[60] A heavy drinker, MacBride is said to have made sexual advances on her daughter Iseult, slept with Maud Gonne's half-sister and beaten Gonne herself.[61] Joyce in Trieste wrote to his brother, 'I have read in the *Figaro* of the divorce of the Irish Joan of Arc from her husband ... Poor little U.I. [*United Irishman*]: indignant little chap.'[62] Chrissie Doyle thought that Griffith took MacBride's side in the split, and Dan McCarthy who worked with him on the *United Irishman* said that he even went to Paris to try and settle the couple's differences, which proved irreconcilable. Gonne's life thereafter was centred on Paris.[63] In his poem 'Easter 1916', Yeats immortalised MacBride – after the latter's execution by the British – as a 'drunken, vainglorious lout'.

By some accounts Maud Gonne had a very limited interest in sexual intercourse, which seems incongruous given her dalliance with Millevoye. Joyce writes in *Ulysses*: 'Maud Gonne, beautiful woman, *La Patrie* [edited by Millevoye], M. Millevoye, Félix Faure, know how he died? Licentious men.' Faure, president of the French Republic, died in 1899 while having sex in the Élysée with a much younger woman. Yeats wrote later that Gonne told him that she often stayed away from Millevoye for, even if very much in love, 'sexual love began to repel her'. Yeats claimed that Millevoye had at one point urged her to become the mistress of another man to help Millevoye's political projects, and she refused: 'she thought that sexual love was only justified by children'.[64] Yeats and herself engaged in mystical experimentation together and had some kind of 'astral' relationship, one that clearly frustrated him and that ostensibly much later but only briefly passed into the physical realm. The journalist and reviewer H.W. Nevison wrote that he heard in 1903 that Gonne 'hates marriage & all sex' but he may have based this on what a hearsay source herself heard from Yeats.[65] The *Daily Mirror* sneered that her marriage was a surprise, because 'her friends believed she had vowed herself to celibacy'.[66] Nevinson adds that Yeats told him that Gonne 'ought not to have married but remained a romantic figure as a queen',[67] which regal status Griffith had conferred on her by his mode of address, as seen above. Much later she incorporated the word 'queen' in the title of her autobiography, to represent herself as 'servant of the queen' who is Ireland and whom she personified both in her political performances and in her brief stage role as 'Kathleen Ni Houlihan' in 1902.

Later, in a very long and quite spiteful passage, Sean O'Casey mocked Griffith for his infatuation with Maud Gonne and suggested that he was jealous of Yeats.[68] But when Gonne withdrew from activities in Ireland, Griffith also lost someone who, in the words of his acquaintance Padraic Colum 'kept him close to notable people', people whom someone of his social background and interests might not normally encounter.[69]

Was it of Griffith and Yeats that Mary Colum was thinking when she wrote about Maud Gonne, in the plural 'Men fell in love with her and stayed in love with her, and though they married afterwards, as most of them did, it was noticeable that they married rather plain and charmless women. It was as if, having once known all beauty and all charm, they did not care ever after for any of its lesser manifestations'?[70]

Mollie Again

After Peter Sheehan died in 1899, his widow and children (all born in Cook Street) moved across the Liffey to 3 Belvedere Place, adjacent to Mountjoy Square on Dublin's north side. His widow died the following year, leaving an estate now worth just £371.[71] The census of 1901 shows 'Mary' (Mollie/Maud) living there with her younger sister Anne and two older brothers. The eldest, who completed the census form, is alone shown as having an occupation, in the same rag trade as that of his father. Two of Maud's brothers joined the Franciscans on Merchant's Quay in Dublin, with Fr Leo (1871–1940) later serving as a chaplain to the British Army in Palestine during the First World War. He became the vicar-provincial of the Irish Franciscan order.[72]

After the family moved to Belvedere Place, their former home was soon listed in Thom's *Street Directory* as a tenement, with the derelict nature of Cook Street very evident from a photograph taken there about 1913. The census of 1901 indicates that only numbers 1–3 and 84–5 were inhabited then, with some coffin-makers still left in numbers 1 and 2, and with number 83 a store. The latter had been owned or rented by Sheehan. In 1904 the parish priest of St Audeon's complained that 'the houses in Cook Street were in such bad condition that one could scarcely walk up the stairs of any one of them with safety. One often found that a whole family were confined to one room.'[73]

Their wealthier neighbours in Belvedere Place included John Redmond and Timothy Sullivan, both members of parliament. Their near neighbour was David Sheehy BL, whose home was renowned for musical evenings that he hosted, and some of which James Joyce attended. However, the Sheehans appear to have remained at 3 Belvedere Place for only about seven years.[74]

In the course of an article in the *United Irishman* in 1900, under one of Griffith's usual pen names, its author wrote:

> It is natural for the young to lose the unattainable. When I was a child she had grey hair, a sweetshop and a husband. When I told her I loved her she gave me a packet of jujubes. I wept as I ate them on the doorstep for I felt I had not been taken seriously. Many, many years later, I again fell in love with the unattainable, but that's another matter.[75]

One assumes that the last sentence refers to his feelings for Mollie Sheehan, and not to his involvement with Maud Gonne. In any event, at some point thereafter he and Mollie began 'walking out' together again. He had a long friendship with Lily Williams and her sisters but 'did no lines whatever with girls, except with Miss Sheehan', thought Dan

McCarthy who helped him sometimes to produce the *United Irishman*.[76] Mollie took part in social events of the Celtic Literary Society and also joined Inghinidhe na hÉireann, and was present at the foundation meeting of Sinn Féin itself.[77]

Marriage

In December 1904 Griffith's father died in the home that the parents shared with their son, leaving Griffith to care for his widowed mother and sister in Summerhill. This was, noted Colum, 'his mother who, since the rest of her family were not successful, was then, and for the rest of her life, looked after by him, their livelihood being from the small returns he had from the *United Irishman*'.[78]

In November 1910, when he married Mollie, he was still living in Summerhill with his mother – while his bride had been residing at 4 Vernon Parade, Clontarf. The marriage, conducted by her brother Fr Leo, was witnessed officially by one James Connolly and by Maud's sister Anne.[79] The Connolly who witnessed Griffith's marriage worked as a civil servant at the Four Courts. He was 'elder brother of Joseph Connolly, afterwards Minister in Mr de Valera's Government'.[80]

The census for 1911 gives the newly married couple living at 136 St Joseph's Crescent, Botanic Road, Glasnevin, in what were rented rooms. He completed the census form in Irish as Art Ó Griobhtha and Máire bean Uí Griobhtha (giving her age as thirty-three when it was thirty-seven). He listed himself as 'editor', and as speaking Irish and English, but she as speaking English only and as having no occupation. The adoption of a Gaelic form of one's name was common among advanced nationalists at that time.

It was a mark of the considerable esteem in which Griffith was held that some 250 of 'your fellow-workers in the Sinn Féin movement, and of sympathisers outside that movement' now clubbed together to buy a house in Clontarf for Griffith and his wife. Among the subscribers were two future presidents of Ireland (Douglas Hyde and Seán T. O'Kelly), as well as Constance Markievicz, Chrissie Doyle (C. Máire Ní Dubhghaill), George Gavan Duffy, Eoin MacNeill, Fred Ryan, Áine Ceannt, George Russell ('Æ'), Richard Irvine Best, Cathal Brugha, Alice Stopford Green,

Roger Casement and the present author's grandfather Kevin J. Kenny.[81] Also subscribing was the Jewish gynaecologist Bethel Solomons, whose father – as the Austro-Hungarian honorary consul to Ireland – was to be mentioned by Joyce in *Ulysses*.

The couple soon had a son Naomhán (Nevin), born on 7 September 1911, and a daughter Ita, born on the last day of 1912.[82] He was at home minding the children when rebellion erupted in 1916. Mollie had gone to Cork to say goodbye to her sister who was sailing for America. In the course of her statement to the Bureau of Military History in 1949, a statement that is disappointingly short especially in respect to personal details, Griffith's widow recalled 'he took the children out to go to some relatives and got only to the end of the road as he was informed of the fighting. He then went home and asked a neighbour to take the children so that he might go to see what was happening'.

A few days later, having made a will,[83] Griffith was arrested. He feared that he might be executed, because the British so closely associated the Rising with his Sinn Féin. So he spoke with a priest, instructing the latter 'If the worst happens go to Maud and tell her I died thinking of her.'[84] He was interned without trial in England, first in Wandsworth and then at Reading. When Muriel Murphy, Terence MacSwiney's future wife, visited Wandsworth, Griffith was not allowed to meet her.[85] The Anglo-Irish writer Robert Lynd, who had known the lash of Griffith's tongue, was allowed to give him a copy of *War and Peace* through the railings.[86] Mollie was allowed in and wrote to Anna, sister of 'The O'Rahilly' that 'he looked fairly well & in good spirits ... and is confident of success', but 'I am very lonely, more so since my London visit.'[87] Oscar Wilde had also been imprisoned in Reading, and so Griffith asked Mollie to get him a copy of Wilde's *The Ballad of Reading Gaol*. She sent him a small edition that was thereupon signed by fellow prisoners and survives in the National Library of Ireland.[88] On their wedding anniversary he wrote from his cell in Reading 'My love ... we shall spend it happily hereafter. Tell Nevin to kiss you for me.' He asked if the children liked a certain picture that he had sent them, drawn by a fellow prisoner.[89] Griffith got to spend too little time with his children between then and his death, being in jail for much of the period when he was not hiding from the British or tied up on Dáil business in Dublin and London. Photographs show him gripping his children's hands as he walks up the path to their home after his release from jail (Plate 12). Their home was subjected to frequent official raids, including by the notorious 'Black-and-Tans', and his children heard terrifying threats made against him.[90]

Irish political prisoners were released from Reading on 23 December 1916, and Griffith returned home. With him for Christmas came Seumas Robinson from Tipperary, who never forgot the couple's kindness.[91] While the years that followed were fraught with tension, there were amusing moments for Mollie. Women visiting from America sometimes pursued her husband as 'admiring pilgrims'. Some wished to shake his hand, or, 'very frequently, to collect his autograph'. At least one cornered him for a kiss. Mollie overheard two girls talking: 'Look at what that one done. She kissed Arthur Griffith.' Thereupon the other replied 'Good Lord, I'd as lief kiss a granite wall.'[92] It is said that when Griffith was released from Mountjoy Prison in 1921, 'one of the women dealers at Nelson's Pillar, as he was passing by, recognized him, and rushing towards him, threw her arms around him and kissed him on both cheeks'.[93]

In London Together

During the treaty negotiations, we find Mollie sending him a touching note about family matters.[94] She went over near the end. 'First thing I noticed in London was his hair turning white,' she wrote a few days later, 'I feel so worried'.[95] She did not care to discuss politics with her husband, and told the Bureau of Military History:

> We had a lot of political publications but burnt them and all papers that might incriminate anybody from time to time for fear of raids. I never took part in any public functions or meetings, except once in Cootehill in the 1918 election where I went to stop people talking. Once when Mrs Sheehy-Skeffington wrote an article in *The Irish World* saying that my husband always kept me at home and gave me a bad time, for the only time in my life I wanted to write an answer to it, but he said it was better not as that would only give her statement more publicity which was probably what she wanted.[96]

Hanna Sheehy-Skeffington was fiercely against the treaty and wrote bitter columns for the *Irish World* in New York. She depicted the wives and sisters of pro-treaty politicians as puppets, claiming that they 'merely represent their husbands' and brothers' views' and that 'Treatyists desired to fire from behind their women'.[97] This and similar claims have recently been said to undermine the very real ideological positions that many pro-treaty women took, at great personal risk.[98]

In Joyce's *Ulysses*, Molly Bloom recalls that her husband Leopold Bloom 'was going about with some of them Sinner Fein lately or whatever they call themselves / talking his usual trash and nonsense / he says that little man he showed me without the neck is very intelligent / the coming man Griffith is he / well he doesn't look it thats all I can say … [forward-slashes added]'. Arthur Griffith's own Mollie was dissatisfied with her husband's political involvement: 'he's always been a Fool – giving his all – others having the benefit'.[99] She appears to have wanted her 'Dan' to draw back from politics, and he may have promised her that he would do so. Padraic Colum, to whom Griffith's widow spoke for his biography of her husband, quoted her saying that Arthur Griffith told her on the night the treaty was signed in London 'You will have your wish … In August I will be out of politics.'[100]

Griffith's prediction proved tragically accurate. When he died the following August she was understandably angry on behalf of her family, and became quite embittered not just against the anti-treaty side.[101] She proved reluctant to co-operate with some of those who wished to write about her late husband. Her friend Chrissie Doyle told Ó Lúing that Maud was 'very nice, but sometimes queer', while another interviewee told him that 'she is like that (indicating the table)', being 'very difficult' to approach.[102] She appeared to feel that her husband was a sacrifice on the altar of Ireland, and feared that people might come to think of him not as she believed and knew him to be.

Griffith, Race and Africa

In the first issue of his *United Irishman*, on 4 March 1899, Arthur Griffith strongly condemned imperialism. He wrote of a brutal engagement in Sudan, during which, in September 1898 near the town of Omdurman, a large British force led by the Irish-born General Horatio Herbert Kitchener slaughtered over 30,000 desert tribesmen (compared with the loss of just twenty-eight members of the British Army). The engagement lasted only a few hours, not least because the British had deadly new weapons such as the maxim-gun. On the British side was Winston Churchill,[1] who in 1921 as a government minister would negotiate a treaty with Griffith.

At Omdurman, Kitchener violated the corpse and tomb of an Islamic military and religious leader, Muhammad Ahmad, who was known as the Mahdi. In 1884–5 the Mahdi had successfully led his men against the British at Khartoum in the Sudan, showing little mercy and decapitating the body of Britain's General Charles Gordon. Nevertheless, in the first edition of a book that he wrote on the reconquest of the Sudan by Kitchener, *The River War*, Churchill criticised the British conduct of that campaign. Afterwards, having been elected to parliament and ostensibly for self-serving purposes, he moderated his account in a later edition of his book.

During 1897 and 1898, when Churchill served in Egypt, Griffith was working in mining and journalism in South Africa. He returned to Dublin as editor of the new *United Irishman* weekly. In it, on 4 March 1899, he criticised nationalist editors who were less 'advanced' or radical than himself and who were (he claimed) 'completely forgetful of the fact that a month or two since they were proudly claiming the general

[Kitchener of Omdurman] to be an Irishman'. Griffith also queried the meaning of the word 'civilization':

> we submit that the civilisation is narrow and selfish which opens a market for the sweat-produce of home centres; the civilisation which, with the gloating wild-eyed vengeance of the tiger, degrades, defiles, and outrages the tomb of a man who died unconquered; the civilisation which only sees in the dusky millions an increased percentage for home investments, or soft places and snug salaries for younger sons and poor relations … No! Ireland and the Empire are incompatible. One cannot be an African 'civiliser' and an Irish Nationalist; one cannot trample on the rights of other people and consistently demand his own.[2]

Griffith, who liked ballads and knew well their power to influence people, composed verses about Omdurman and published them in the second issue of his *United Irishman*. He passed over uncomfortable facts such as the presence of many Irishmen as well as 'Englishmen' in the British Army and the earlier decapitation of the corpse of General Gordon by the Mahdi. Yet this ballad, the 'Song of the Khalifa', is among his better efforts at composition. As a counterpoint to Rudyard Kipling's imperial versifying, it is notable if bloody. Written in the voice of Abdallah ibn Muhammed, the Mahdi's successor, it includes these lines:

> Vengeance, O Children of Allah! veng'ance on England's base
>   horde
> Who flung to the winds of the desert, the bones of our Prophet
>   and Lord –
> Who tore from the House of his Sleeping the corpse of our
>   Chieftain and Khan
> And carried his head o'er the waters to be spat at in far Frankistan.
>
> These dogs, with their canting of Issa [Jesus], the Prophet of Mercy
>   and Truth,
> Mow'd down with their cannon our women, nor mercy they
>   show'd them nor ruth,

And our brothers defenceless and wounded who lay when the
    battle was done
They stabb'd and they shot and they mangl'd and massacr'd
    everyone.

Veng'ance, O Children of Allah! revenge on each Infidel's head.
Revenge on the slayers of women, on the ghouls who dishonour
    the dead.
Strike for the land of your fathers – for the faith that is thine!
And be mercy unknown to your bosoms, for foes are Apes,
    Panthers and Swine![3]

However Griffith, like other advanced nationalists, saw himself in a
line of 'apostolic succession'[4] that descended from the 1798 Rebellion
through Young Ireland radicals who had grown tired of Daniel
O'Connell's parliamentary pacifism. This had implications for his views
on black Africans.

Griffith on Slavery

When Barack Obama came to Ireland in May 2011, many Irish people
learnt for the first time of a particular link between black liberation and
the struggle for Irish freedom. President Obama told the Irish

When we strove to blot out the stain of slavery and advance the
rights of man, we found common cause with your struggles against
oppression. [In the mid-nineteenth century] Frederick Douglass,
an escaped slave and our great abolitionist, forged an unlikely
friendship right here in Dublin with your great liberator, Daniel
O'Connell. His time here, Frederick Douglass said, defined him
not as a color but as a man. And it strengthened the non-violent
campaign he would return home to wage.

Obama diplomatically avoided mentioning the more radical political
movement known as 'Young Ireland': Young Ireland firebrands such
as John Mitchel looked to Irish-America for financial and other help,

and some of the Irish in America were not abolitionists. Some owned slaves. Because of this, Young Ireland decided not to take a firm position on slavery.[5] Indeed, for the same reason, O'Connell himself had some reservations.[6] Bruce Nelson has addressed more broadly the relationship between Irish nationalists and racial questions. Griffith should be seen in that context.[7]

Aged thirty, Griffith declared 'all my life I have worshipped [John] Mitchel'. He described him as 'the proud, fiery-hearted electric-brained, giant-souled Irishman who stood up to the might of the whole British Empire'.[8] Griffith's *United Irishman* was named after Mitchel's paper of the same title. Griffith republished in it and elsewhere many articles that Mitchel had written. So when Griffith was invited in 1913 to write a preface to a new edition of Mitchel's *Jail Journal*, he was not about to let the side down.

Mitchel had been transported by the British, but escaped and went to the United States where he voiced approval of slavery and supported the Confederate states. Such was the strength of the Confederate south in 1862 that William Gladstone, the United Kingdom's chancellor of the exchequer whose own father had kept slaves, described it as 'a nation' and was thought by some to have signaled that his government might recognise the Confederacy.[9] Mitchel, like his British acquaintance Thomas Carlyle, argued that black people were racially inferior and 'were better off as plantation slaves than living in barbarism in Africa, and that they had more secure and comfortable lives than had the exploited factory hands of Manchester or the starving cottiers of Mayo'.[10]

To some extent Griffith's preface to the new edition of Mitchel's book is a piece of devil's advocacy for his hero, pointing out that some saints and other admired historical figures tolerated slavery or kept slaves. In other ways Griffith's preface is a restatement of the Young Ireland policy that had avoided splitting Irish-American opinion by dodging a controversial question of no immediate relevance to the Irish nationalist cause. There was, after all, no slavery dispute in Ireland, and only a tiny number of non-white inhabitants on the whole island. Some Irish people wanted to keep it that way, violently, if a piece in the *United Irishman* of 26 August 1899 is any indication of public sentiment. The unidentified author seems to incite lynching: 'A correspondent of the *Daily Express* has hit on a plan for making Ireland happy and prosperous. He proposes introducing "black labour" ... We recommend the people of whatever district the "black labour" is first introduced into, to seek the advice and assistance of that excellent old Irish-American, Judge Lynch.' Pejorative terms such as 'nigger' and 'coon' were common then. A Gaelic League concert of dance music, for example, included 'De Gorn Coon' and 'Merry Little Niggahs', while a middle-class gathering in Dublin's Iveagh Gardens heard an English militia band play 'The Darkies' Cake Walk'.[11] When Lady Gregory of the Abbey Theatre went to Washington in 1911, she informed her friend W.B. Yeats that there were few people there 'except members of government and niggers'.[12]

Griffith defended Mitchel on the somewhat ingenious grounds that if citizens or subjects of other European states differed among themselves on questions such as slavery then Irish nationalists should not be obliged to take a common position on the question before Ireland itself was even a free nation. He wanted neither Ireland nor Irish-America distracted and divided by theories such as 'black equals white, that kingship is immoral, or that society has a duty to reform its enemies':

> It is the fate of four great Irishmen – Sean [Shane] O'Neill, Jonathan Swift, John Mitchel and Charles Parnell to have an inky tribe of small Irishmen in every generation explaining and apologizing for them. Mitchel has been explained as one who merely hated England, and apologized for as a good man unbalanced by the horrors he witnessed. Even his views on negro-slavery have been deprecatingly excused, as if excuse were needed for an Irish Nationalist declining to hold the negro his peer in right ... he laughed at theories of human perfectability and equality ... He was a sane Nietsche in his view of man ... The right of an Irish Nationalist to hold and champion any view he pleases, extraneous to Irish Nationalism, is absolute.[13]

Irish people had reason to understand the horrors of slavish oppression. Thus, in their 'Call to Arms', the Transvaal Irish Volunteers Association of Jo'burg had recalled that 'In the reign of Queen Anne, the Irish people were reduced to a condition closely resembling the bondage which black slaves endured in the Southern States of America.'[14]

The 1913 edition of Mitchel's *Jail Journal* was published and promoted by the leading publishing house of M.H. Gill, with *The Freeman's Journal* (no friend of Griffith) generously describing his preface as 'able'. The *Evening Herald* too reported 'a thoughtful, able, and vigorous preface by Mr Arthur Griffith, most competent of present-day writers'.[15] Mitchel's views, and Griffith's defense of Mitchel's right to hold them, caused no public outcry then.

Griffith's own *United Irishman* addressed the inhumane treatment of black people in Africa. However, it did so primarily to discredit the British. It is not clear if its editor saw black people as *intrinsically* inferior to whites, or only *extrinsically* so due to social, economic and other circumstances that could change. Those alternatives were debated through the nineteenth century, with a writer in London in 1838 putting the issue succinctly:

> It is an important question whether negroes are constitutionally, and therefore irremediably, inferior to whites in the powers of the mind. Much of the future welfare of the human race depends on the answer … Their actual inferiority of mind is too evident to be disputed; but it may be accounted for by circumstances amidst which negroes have lived, both in their own countries and abroad; while, if one single instance can be adduced of a man of jet-black complexion who has exhibited a genius which would be considered eminent in civilized European society, we have at least a proof that there is no incompatibility between negro organanizations and high-intellectual power.[16]

This 'negro question'– or 'nigger question' as it was more rudely framed by the British writer Thomas Carlyle – was debated by Carlyle and John Stuart Mill and others in England during the nineteenth century.[17] Carlyle had an ambiguous if intriguing relationship with the Young Ireland movement,[18] and his opinions on black people presumably did little to persuade Young Ireland to oppose slavery in America. Griffith himself appears to incline towards the view that black people were not intrinsically inferior, that any inferiority came from decadence and other circumstances. Having arrived by ship at Delagoa Bay in Portuguese Mozambique, a port of call on the voyage to and from South Africa, Griffith (using his pen name Cuguan) wrote:

> The negro, say the wise ones, is a child. The negro, say I, is an old, old, man. Once on a time when your father and mine, my white brother, were lusty barbarians, the Ethiop was a mighty man, a warrior, a sailor, a poet, an artist, a cunning artificer, and a philosopher. But he grew luxurious and degenerate, and the shepherds and fishers and thieves of Egypt drove him into the wilderness and razed his empire, even as the barbarians of thousands of years later drove out the last Imperial Roman to the marshes and hills.

He added 'The negro never changes. What he was when Hanno saw him, he was when I saw him,' but 'the negro' is actually 'degenerate, played out – as I fear me, when I look around and note the almond-eyed ones girding up their loins, that the Caucasian is becoming'.[19] The article elicited a rebuke to the *United Irishman* from one Edward Dalton, but not because of its references to black people. Dalton was offended by Griffith writing as he had about local Catholics at Delagoa Bay who displayed 'red-white-and-blue saints dressed in tinsel paper'.[20]

Irish people distinguished themselves from black people not least because of Anglo-Saxon caricatures that represented both the Irish and black people quite similarly as ape-like.[21] But Griffith was prepared to condemn cruelty in South Africa. He identified 'the filthiest and most savage beings dwelling on a savage continent' as 'the Rand capitalists'.[22] Elsewhere he wrote of how

> ... the Englishman treated the Kaffir [native peoples]. He taught him the Bible; he taught him that he was a man and a brother, and he treated him like a dog.

> The white men assumed a domineering attitude; rape and murder were frequent. But not until the English forcibly prevented Lo Ben

from collecting his annual tribute from the subject Mashona tribe did war break out. The war did not last long; the brave, but ill-armed Matabili, were no match for the maxim guns of Jameson. They were slaughtered and their country taken from them.[23]

Griffith reported that native people 'friendly' to Britain, those whom he described as 'the Matabili equivalent of our [Irish, pro-British] "Loyalists"' were 'blown to atoms by the English with their maxim guns when they had no further need of them'. He alleged 'since the conclusion of the war the natives have lived under a reign of terror which has degraded them below the level of the meanest animal that crawls the earth'. He claimed that an Irish trooper in the British Army was so appalled by the atrocities that in a fight with some Matabilis he let himself fall 'unresistingly beneath the assegais of the savages'. At present, Griffith continued, 'native men and women are bought and sold as "goods" by the English ... the white traveler through the Mashona country finds the timid natives fleeing everywhere before him, or, if unable to avoid him, prostrating themselves on the earth and moaning out to him appeals for mercy. This is no exaggeration. It is the literal truth.'[24]

However, having explained all this, Griffith then appropriated the Africans' suffering to score a point for Irish nationalists: 'After seven centuries experience the Irish people seem to be still unaware that their lords and masters are white barbarians.'[25] He later claimed in disgust 'I have known an English missionary to let the Kaffirs under his charge starve to death in order that he might pocket £1,000.'[26] Many white people, including Griffith and Michael Davitt, used the word 'Kaffir' as a matter of course then for native peoples.

In prose and verse Griffith cheered on the Boers against the British. He made what he described as 'a rude translation' of the Transvaal national anthem.[27] In Griffith's *United Irishman* 'The Foreign Secretary' made a statement that is particularly revealing of Irish opinion – in this case of self-interest masquerading as concern. The author, almost certainly the notoriously anti-Semitic F.H. O'Donnell, shook his head at justifications that the British offered for fighting the Boers. At the same time, he seemingly accepted the suppression of indigenous people by Boers:

But to pretend that the notorious nigger-drivers and nigger-slayers of the English mining rings are fighting to save the African natives from unequal treatment is a climax of cant to which only a religious hypocrite could hope to attain. Have not the Rhodes gang openly declared that when they get the Transvaal, they will imprison the Kaffir labourers in barracoons as at Kimberley, and make them slave twelve hours a day, as at Kimberley, *instead of the eight hours, which form the maximum permissible by Transvaal law*? [Italics thus].[28]

British ministers denied such claims and alleged in turn that the Boers were cruel. On 19 October 1899 the secretary of state for the colonies, Joseph Chamberlain, said in the House of Commons:

the treatment of the natives of the Transvaal [by the Boers] has been disgraceful; it has been brutal; it has been unworthy of a civilized Power ... The Great Trek took place mainly and chiefly because, in the words of the Boers themselves, and you can prove it from their own language, they wanted to 'wallop their own niggers.'

When immediately challenged on this by John Dillon (MP for Mayo East), Chamberlain reiterated that, in his opinion 'the main reason for the trek of the Boers from British rule was their disinclination to be interfered with in their treatment of the native races.'[29]

Many Irish nationalists supported the Dutch Boers, and when the *United Irishman* asserted that there were just two 'independent states, two guarantees of the rights of human freedom in this subcontinent ... the last rampart of an untrammeled future for Africa' it was in fact referring to the Dutch Boers' Transvaal and Orange Free State.[30] Among Irish advanced nationalists there appears to have been a sneaking regard for Napoleon as a more efficient conqueror than the British,[31] and for the French empire as a bulwark against a possible British monopoly in Africa.[32]

Those who opposed the British in South Africa included the socialist James Connolly, who was to die in the Rising of 1916. He supported a motion at a meeting of the Irish Republican Socialist Party proposed by a speaker who condemned 'every bloated Jewish capitalist and English adventurer'.[33] Yet in 1914 Irish trades unionists warmly welcomed a labour leader deported from South Africa who told them that white workers 'could not acquiesce in the standard of the white man being leveled down to that of the savage black race (applause)'. Thomas Johnson, president of the Irish Trade Union Congress and Labour Party, chaired this meeting. Connolly and the radical trade unionist James Larkin sat listening. As it ended, the whole gathering sang the socialist 'Red Flag' and the nationalist 'A Nation Once Again'.[34]

The following year Griffith seized on a report in William Randolph Hearst's New York *American* to score another point against England. In 1915 the *American* referred to accusations against African soldiers in the British and French armies in Europe. Griffith's *Nationality* described these soldiers as 'savages, and, in the case of some, cannibals', and their introduction into the war as 'the worst act ever committed by white men against the white race' and as 'a betrayal of the white race'.[35]

The *United Irishman* framed Ireland's relationship with the black peoples of Africa within an overall imperial context. China and India were similarly referenced. Newspapers such as *Le Monde* or the London *Times* have long reported foreign affairs in a way that gives precedence to stories of direct relevance to their domestic readers, which is how much news is prioritised everywhere. Irish nationalist readers were similarly served. Laffan bluntly summarises the self-serving critique of British colonialism in Griffith's papers:

> His exceptional interest in foreign affairs was dominated by anglophobia. He approved of the dowager empress of China because she was hostile towards Britain; he switched his support from France to Germany after the Entente Cordiale; and he defended Leopold II's record in the Congo against '[the old game of] calumny and mud-throwing [of which England is such a past mistress]' (*Nationality*, 16 Oct. 1915). Griffith sympathised instinctively with every anti-British interest and individual, however unworthy they might be.[36]

In fairness, Griffith praised Leopold for his use of colonial wealth to improve Belgium and not for his treatment of the Congolese. Griffith recognised colonial competition generally when referring in the same article to British indignation at Belgium: 'to be cheated out of your lawful and favourite occupation of exploiting the natives in the interests of Christianity and civilization by a little country one fourth the size of Ireland was unthinkable'.

Reading Griffith's *Sinn Féin* paper in Rome in 1906, James Joyce noted that Griffith had alluded to the British Army as the only mercenary army in Europe. Joyce exclaimed, no doubt with a twinkle in his eye: 'I suppose he prefers the conscription system because it is French. Irish intellectuals are very tiresome.'[37]

Connolly, Yeats, Synge and Larkin

Had he settled in South Africa, Griffith would not have become involved with James Connolly and W.B. Yeats, attended Synge's *Playboy of the Western World* at the Abbey Theatre or crossed swords with Jim Larkin.

In South Africa in 1897 and 1898, he worked briefly as a journalist, editing a small paper, and finding employment in the mining industry. With John MacBride he encouraged Irish immigrants there to assert their distinctive national identity, and together with MacBride and others, celebrated the centenary of the United Irishmen rebellion of 1798.[1] Some Irish were soon to fight alongside the Dutch Boers in their war against the British, while other Irish fought there in the British Army. In autumn 1898, before that war began, Griffith returned to Dublin, to a warm welcome from his friends in the Celtic Literary Society.[2] A group of nationalists, backed by the Irish Republican Brotherhood, had invited him to become editor of the new but poorly resourced *United Irishman*. It was the first of a number of influential small papers partly funded or supported by the IRB that he would edit and sustain during the next two decades.

'Looking for trouble': James Connolly

Griffith was honorary secretary of the Irish Transvaal Committee. On 1 October 1899 it held its inaugural public rally in Beresford Place, Dublin, between Liberty Hall and the Custom House. The meeting attracted a large crowd and was addressed by John O'Leary, who was on the organising committee along with Maud Gonne, Griffith, Yeats and others.[3] The strong reaction of nationalist Ireland to events in South Africa took authorities by surprise.[4]

Griffith continued to compose pro-Boer ballads or doggerel.[5] He also became centrally involved with Maud Gonne and the socialist James Connolly in a celebrated pro-Boer escapade in 1899 – when the British government's colonial secretary, Joseph Chamberlain MP, came to Dublin to be conferred with an honorary degree by Trinity College. Chamberlain had impeded Home Rule for Ireland and now, in the words of the *Dictionary of National Biography*, 'remained ready to do what he could by rough means as well as fair to strengthen the imperial power' in South Africa. The Irish Transvaal Committee organised a public protest for Sunday 17 December, again with John O'Leary due to be present. The authorities proclaimed this meeting and strong contingents of police barred all approaches. The day was bitterly cold but a large crowd gathered on Sackville Street. Connolly's *Workers' Republic* paper subsequently published a log of developments:

December 17. – All the tactical positions in and about and streets debouching on Beresford Place occupied by masses of police. Military confined to barracks and in readiness to turn out. Thousands of people thronging to the place of meeting. Dublin wild with excitement.

Home Rulers Funk. Leave the people to face the police as they had advised them to, but take their own miserable carcasses to the seclusion of a back room.

Miss Maud Gonne, Mr Griffith of the *United Irishman*, Mr [George] Lyons of the Oliver Bond '98 Club, comrades Stewart and Connolly of the Irish Socialist Republican Party step into the breach and drive down to Beresford Place to hold the meeting.

Baton charges by police. Hired driver of brake [two-horse wagon] seized by police, reins assumed by Connolly who had been moved to the chair by Griffith, procession organised through the principal streets, two meetings held, charges by mounted police, unsuccessful, but desperate efforts of the mounted police to keep their seats, triumphal conclusion of the procession, arrest of Connolly.[6]

The group had led the police on a merry chase, shouting out support for the Boers and unfurling the flag of the South African Republic. *The Irish Times* reported that a body of mounted constables was sent after it, and 'A brisk struggle for the Transvaal flag took place, ending in its capture by the police.' Some foreign media also noted the confrontation.

Le Petit Journal, 31 December 1899. Connolly and Griffith in action.

Lyons wrote that Griffith that day 'engaged in hand to hand struggle' with a police officer.[7] The next day it was reported 'A respectable-looking man named James Connolly', of 28 Fingal Street, was charged with having been disorderly and with 'acting as driver of a licensed hackney carriage, he not being a licensed driver'. But 'Griffiths [sic]', when called to give evidence, 'could not say for certain' whether he had thrown leaflets from the brake as they drove along. Connolly was fined £2 or a month in jail.[8] On the same morning that the court sat, Chamberlain slipped into Trinity College by its Provost's private entrance to avoid crowds gathered outside before his conferring. In a reaction to nationalists, some Trinity students, waving Union Jacks, broke into the garden of the lord mayor's Mansion House, assaulted his servants and tore up the city flag. They also removed floral tributes from the foundation of a planned statue of Wolfe Tone nearby.[9]

However, things were not going well for the government in London, with three British defeats in South Africa within one week in December 1899. Maud Gonne ensured that the anti-Boer escapade in Dublin was celebrated in Paris by the issuing of a special supplement of *Le Petit Journal*. Joyce was to memorialise the clash in *Ulysses* by having Bloom muse

> That horse policeman the day Joe Chamberlain was given his degree in Trinity he got a run for his money. My word he did! His horse's hoofs clattering after us down Abbey street. Lucky I had the presence of mind to dive into Manning's or I was souped. He did come a wallop, by George. Must have cracked his skull on the cobblestones. I oughtn't to have got myself swept along with those medicals. And the Trinity jibs in their mortar-boards. Looking for trouble.

It was at this point that Griffith and Connolly are said to have argued about the revolutionary merits and dangers of broader confrontation between workers and the military, with Griffith convinced that the time was not right for it. Lyons wrote that Connolly cried 'The people must become case-hardened to conflict', but Griffith retorted 'People don't become case-hardened to being dead.'[10] Lyons thought that Connolly thereafter kept his distance from the nationalists.[11] However, while

Connolly disagreed with Sinn Féin's economic policy, he and Griffith remained friendly to the end.[12] Connolly was one of just eight candidates whom Griffith publicly backed in the local elections of 1903,[13] and as late as 1915, Griffith is found reporting in his *Scissors and Paste* paper the seizure of *The Worker* (successor to the suppressed *Irish Worker*), then being edited by Connolly.[14] Griffith's friend and solicitor Michael Noyk said 'Although Griffith distrusted Larkin immensely, he had a very high regard for James Connolly, although they were ideologically opposed.'[15]

In 1900, the year after his escapade with Connolly, Griffith joined with Dr Mark Ryan of the IRB and others to support John MacBride for a parliamentary seat in South Mayo. The outcome disappointed him. Mayo-born MacBride had helped him to find work in South Africa and by 1900 was leading a pro-Boer Irish brigade against the British. The Mayo seat had been occupied by Michael Davitt, who objected to the Boer War and resigned from the House of Commons. The contest gave nationalists a clear chance to make a point, and electors were treated to the sight of Griffith and Rooney singing a special ballad that Griffith composed in support of their candidate.[16] However, John O'Donnell, who was supported by William O'Brien MP and other Irish parliamentarians, heavily defeated MacBride. Davitt's failure to support the latter was just one of the reasons why Griffith disliked him.

Yeats and Griffith

William Butler Yeats espoused republicanism before 1900, being influenced by his friendships with the veteran Fenian John O'Leary and the exciting Maud Gonne. He joined the Irish Republican Brotherhood (IRB) and was on the Irish Transvaal Committee with Griffith, Rooney and Maud Gonne.[17] He was, he said then, at one 'in wishing victory for the just cause of the Boers. I am not English and owe England no loyalty.'[18] He is mentioned in police files alongside Maud Gonne, and in 1898 it was reported: 'W.B. Yeats of London answers the description of the man who left Dublin for London' with the IRB's Fred Allan. Yeats and Griffith campaigned together to stop an eccentric British group excavating the historic Hill of Tara, and he attended with Griffith, Rooney and Gonne, prizegiving for the children of members of the

Celtic Literary Society. He publicly scorned the visit to Ireland of Queen Victoria.[19] He also wrote a letter of protest to a weekly Liberal paper on 'The Freedom of the Press in Ireland' following Dublin Castle's seizure of issues of the *United Irishman*.[20] Padraic Colum, who sometimes worked with Griffith, wrote:

> callers to the office [of the *United Irishman*] might encounter a figure that seemed out of place there: a young man seated on a pile of newspapers, his back to the wall. The visitor would be drawn to observe his dark clothes, dark, flowing tie, the lock of blue-black hair falling over his forehead, the dark oval-shaped face with the strangely placed eyes, glasses over them. He was William Butler Yeats whose lately published volume *The Wind Among the Reeds* [1899] was deemed esoteric even by the coteries.[21]

From the outset Griffith's *United Irishman* took Yeats seriously and boosted him, although a piece on the front page of its second issue by William Rooney reflected some of the tensions within the literary movement that later became acute. Referring to the foundation of the Irish Literary Theatre by Yeats and others in 1899, Rooney described 'Mr. Yeats' project' as 'an attempt to produce a really high-class Anglo-Irish drama.' But, he warned 'such plays as he meditates can never be popular. They are too far above the people's heads, and while they shall not want for an audience, they will not appeal to the taste of the multitude, for whom melodrama is for a long time yet the best field of work.' He thought 'If the Irish drama is to be, as all such undertakings should be, educational, it must make due allowance for the deficiencies which still exist in our tastes.'[22]

The Countess Cathleen

One of the defining moments of the Gaelic Revival, inspiring to advanced nationalists, was the Irish Literary Theatre's production of Yeats' play *The Countess Cathleen* in May 1899. The story of the aristocratic countess, prepared even to sell her own soul for her people, preoccupied Yeats in his struggle to become a playwright. According to Yeats, he wrote it before he met Maud Gonne.[23] Yet it somewhat echoed an account that he later recalled the wealthy Gonne once giving him of her own youth – when she purportedly made a pact with the devil to surrender her soul for the realisation of her ambitions.[24] He was to rewrite the play a number of times before 1912, making changes that reflected the state of his obsessive relationship with Gonne.[25] Dedicating all editions to her, he was 'determined that this play should shape the conceptual formation of a new national movement'.[26]

The title of Gonne's memoirs, *A Servant of the Queen*, itself refers to the personification of Ireland as aristocracy, which is evident from her somewhat boastful foreword:

> I was returning from Mayo triumphant. I had stopped a famine and saved many lives by making the people share my own belief that courage and will are inconquerable ... Tired but glowing I looked out of the window of the train at the dark bog land where now only the tiny lakes gleamed in the fading light. Then I saw a tall, beautiful woman with dark hair blown on the wind and I knew it was Cathleen ni Houlihan ... I heard a voice say: 'You are one of the little stones on which the feet of the Queen have rested on her way to Freedom.'[27]

Such personifications constituted a rival symbol (or rival 'maternity')[28] to that of Queen Victoria, who had been on the throne since before the great Irish famine of the 1840s. Victoria's visit to Dublin in 1900 was the occasion of one of a number of seizures of Griffith's *United Irishman* by the police, not least because he had published in it the translation of Gonne's 'Famine Queen' article from *La Patrie*.[29] Two weeks later Griffith's paper carried a piece by Yeats asking 'What can these Royal Processions mean to those who walk in the procession of heroic and enduring hearts that has followed Kathleen Ny Hoolihan [sic] through the ages?'[30] Griffith also criticised T.W. Rolleston's new *Treasury of Irish Poetry* for various omissions of Irish patriotic work, writing 'I paid down certain coins bearing the image and superscription of the lady [Victoria] for whom he jilted Kathaleen [sic] Ni Houlihan.'[31]

The former MP and controversialist Frank H. O'Donnell took potshots at *The Countess Cathleen*, both in *The Freeman's Journal* and by pamphlet. According to the IRB organiser Dr Mark Ryan, both O'Donnell and Yeats had been 'prominent figures in the [1798] centenary movement in London'.[32] But Yeats came to regard O'Donnell as his 'enemy'.[33] O'Donnell scoffed at the 'demented' countess 'who is rewarded for her blasphemous apostasy by Mr W.B. Yeats, dramatist and theologian, by being straightaway transmigrated to the Heaven of Heavens, where, as a special inducement to all good little Irish girls to go and do likewise', she is well received.[34] Although O'Donnell also wrote for the *United Irishman* at that time, Griffith disagreed with him about the play. Yeats wrote that on the opening night, Griffith, 'at that time an enthusiastic anti-cleric', claimed to have brought 'a lot of men from the Quays and told them to applaud everything the Church would not like'.[35]

Some nationalist objectors drew attention to the foreign inspiration of the play and objected vehemently that, while purporting to 'show the sublimity of self-sacrifice', Yeats represented 'the Irish peasant as a crooning barbarian, crazed with morbid superstition' and thus provided grist to the mill of Ireland's enemies.[36] Griffith disagreed. Cardinal Logue thought that lines such as 'The Light of Lights looks always on the motive, not the deed' implied a heretical claim by Yeats that it was acceptable to barter one's soul for material objectives. However, Yeats was resolute and satisfied.[37]

At that first performance, in Dublin's Antient Concert Rooms, Yeats and Maud Gonne sat side by side watching May Whitty play the countess. Protesters included students of the Royal University, 'the majority of them friends of James Joyce', although he had refused to sign their letter.[38] Joyce himself attended the opening and later set to music some of its lines. He also drew on the play in *A Portrait of the Artist as a Young Man* and *Ulysses*. A number of daily newspapers praised the production, but Yeats was sensitive to any criticism of his 'spiritual drama' and wrote to the *Morning Leader* to complain about 'the blind bigots of journalism who have made no protest against the musical burlesques full of immoral suggestion which have of late possessed the Dublin theatres' but who called his play 'a blasphemy and a slander'.[39] Griffith had not ignored such musicals, and the *United Irishman* was peppered with criticism of them.

'The Greatest Living Poet'

Days after the opening of *The Countess Cathleen* in 1899, George Moore in London told a meeting of certain promoters of the Irish Literary Theatre 'England's delight in a rhymer [Rudyard Kipling] who expressed the lust of an African millionaire and the artistic taste of a drunken soldier returning from Hampstead, and England's neglect of the author of *The Countess Cathleen* could only have happened at the same moment.'[40] Griffith shared Moore's disdain of Rudyard Kipling, and the *United Irishman* frequently flung jibes at that English writer whose verses inflamed popular sentiment and jingoism.

In January 1901, Griffith parodied Irish MPs as the 'Irish Nationalist Imperialist Party', conjuring up a banquet at which one speaker 'believed that the great danger confronting the twentieth century was W.B. Yeats (loud cheers).'[41] However, Yeats was not entirely pleased at this time, for Griffith had also lambasted T.W. Rolleston's *Treasury of Irish Poetry* for omitting both Oscar Wilde and Alice Milligan among others, and for including John Todhunter but with the latter's 'fierce, brave Irish "Aghadoe"' carefully omitted', and for cutting Michael Doheny's 'Cuisle Geal Mo Croidhe'. The Offaly-born Rolleston was highly regarded in cultural circles and was a friend of John O'Leary and Yeats. Letters from O'Leary appeared in the *United Irishman* criticising the paper's tone and the review itself as unfair.[42] Yeats made one of his visits to the editorial office in Fownes Street where Dan McCarthy sometimes helped to produce the paper. There was a wobbly chair against the wall and McCarthy later recalled that the protesting Yeats 'sat on the chair while expostulating. I heard a commotion myself, and on looking in – I occupied the outer office – Yeats was floundering on the floor, the seat having collapsed under him, to Griffith's intense amusement.'[43]

The following month the *United Irishman* quoted with approval Yeats' views on the 'Gaelic speaking Irish and their attitudes', while in April Griffith extravagantly praised him in a review of Yeats' *Poems*, just published in London by T. Fisher Unwin: 'Mr Yeats is the greatest living poet and the greatest of Irish poets. He has interpreted the Celt to the world and the Celt to himself, and the Celt is exceedingly fortunate in having a great artist for his interpreter.' Griffith mischievously recommended that 'who so may be too poor to buy it should borrow or steal a copy.'[44] In the same paper 'FJF '(Frank Fay) enthused about Yeats' earlier play *The Land of Heart's Desire*, and Yeats wrote to thank him.[45] Fay and his brother William were leaders of a dramatic group, and their efforts with others resulted in a round of Irish stage productions preceding the foundation of the Abbey Theatre in 1904.

Just weeks after Griffith's friend and collaborator William Rooney died in 1901, Yeats brought a man to George Moore to propose a Gaelic dramatic touring company, acknowledging 'It was in part a scheme of poor Rooney's.'[46] Yeats also wrote to Douglas Hyde, praising Griffith's work on Cuchulain.[47] On 31 August 1901 Griffith provided two and a half columns to Yeats to expound on 'Ireland and the Arts'. Two months later, not only was W.B. Yeats himself boosted but his father and brother, both painters, as well as his two sisters in 'this very gifted family' were also praised.[48] Griffith subsequently laid a restraining paternal hand on Yeats' shoulders when the latter sought to respond in the *United Irishman* to a reviewer in *The Freeman's Journal* who accused Yeats of wishing to substitute the Irish mythical hero Cuchulain for Christ. Griffith declined to publish his response, telling him, 'Anything we write must show kindly dignity not vexation – They are only untaught children,' and 'the attack on reviewers leaves an impression of fretfulness.'[49]

Kathleen Ni Houlihan

Yeats had not finished with Mother Ireland. On 2 April 1902, Maud Gonne appeared in the lead of his new one-act play *Kathleen Ni Houlihan*, which he dedicated to Griffith's late friend and comrade William Rooney (and the title of which he would later alter to *Cathleen Ni Houlihan*). This play, which was set near Killala, Co. Mayo, in 1798, is said to have 'represented the high zenith of Yeatsian revolutionary fervour, and Maud was the embodiment of an Ireland that demanded the blood of her sons'.[50] She was also a crowd-puller, or 'draw', as Yeats pointed out to Lady Gregory.[51] On the bill that night, in the hall of St Teresa's Total Abstinence Association, his play followed the première of Æ's three-act *Deirdre*. W.G. Fay's Irish National Dramatic Company produced them both.

Advertisement for the first performance of Yeats' *Kathleen Ni Houlihan*, 1902 (National Library of Ireland [EPH C 821]).

Gonne's Inghinidhe na hÉireann, to which Griffith's sister belonged and the banner of which hung in the hall, made the dresses and provided Irish actors. This was a significant development, not least because the presence of an excessive number of English players on the Irish stage then had some results that were 'little short of ludicrous.'[52]

The closing lines of *Kathleen Ni Houlihan* were emotionally powerful. They included a promise to Ireland's loyal sons. Thus Kathleen ('some call me the Poor Old Woman') proclaims to Peter Gillane and his family 'It is a hard service they take that help me' but

> They shall be remembered for ever,
> They shall be alive for ever,
> They shall be speaking for ever,
> The people shall hear them for ever.

Kathleen exits. When Patrick enters a few moments later, Peter lays a hand on his arm and asks 'Did you see an old woman going down the path?' Patrick replies 'I did not, but I saw a young girl, and she had the walk of a queen.' The curtain falls. Yeats in old age, in his poem 'The Man and the Echo', was to ask 'Did that play of mine send out / Certain men the English shot?'

Seamus O'Sullivan attended on the opening night, and he long remembered its impact: 'I was with Arthur Griffith, and I can still see his face as he stood up at the fall of the curtain to join in the singing of what was then our national anthem.'[53] This anthem was 'A Nation Once Again', with its rousing chorus by Thomas Davis that foresaw a day when 'Ireland, long a province' would regain its freedom.

While Yeats had the idea for the play, it is now believed that Lady Gregory wrote most of it.[54] He also consulted George Moore, who advised that Kathleen 'not sit down by the fire and croon but walk up and down in front of the stage'.[55] Remarkably, in 1914, Griffith wrote that Yeats 'added the present ending of that very beautiful little allegory at the suggestion of the present writer to emphasise its propaganda'.[56] Yeats sometimes read his manuscripts aloud to acquaintances, and is said to have done so on this occasion to Griffith. As the play stood originally, so Griffith told Robert Brennan after 1916, the ending was bald and Yeats knew that he needed a last line but could not get it. So Griffith gave him the question and answer above, referring to the old woman and a young girl, except for the word 'path' with which Yeats replaced Griffith's suggested 'road'. Griffith told Brennan that Yeats said the lines several times over before he made the change. Brennan was interned with Griffith, but by the time that he recalled this conversation in 1950 he had served as Irish ambassador in Washington (appointed by de Valera) and subsequently as director of broadcasting at Radio Éireann. Brennan admitted that several poet friends of his doubted the story but wrote 'I knew Griffith very well. He was the most unassuming and modest of men and he would never have dreamed of making a claim of such a nature if it was unfounded.'[57] Not every biographer of Yeats has addressed Griffith's accounts.

In his thesis that the rebellion of 1916 was liturgy as well as theatre, the Jesuit Séamus Murphy has written 'The prophecy of the [1916] Rising was the staging of Yeats' 1902 play.[58] Indeed, as it happened, *Kathleen Ni Houlihan* was scheduled for a revival at the Abbey Theatre on Easter Monday 1916. The player Sean Connolly (Plate 7) was then allocated the role of Peter Gillane. However, he joined the rebellion that week and died. In notes on the Abbey Theatre programme in 1916, Yeats explained his inspiration:

> One night I had a dream, almost as distinct as a vision, of a cottage where there was well-being, and firelight, and talk of a marriage, and into the midst of that cottage there came an old woman, in a long cloak. She was Ireland herself, that Kathleen Ni Houlihan for whom so many songs have been sung, and about whom so many stories have been told and for whose sake so many have gone to their death. I thought if I could write this out as a little play I could make others see my dream as I had seen it.

In 1997, in old age, Conor Cruise O'Brien reportedly told a columnist that he had once asked Noel Browne, a left-wing minister in an Irish government who famously clashed with the Catholic hierarchy, if he had to choose between Kathleen Ni Houlihan and Mother Mary Church, which would he choose? Browne is said to have replied 'Mother Church, every time', and O'Brien agreed because 'Mother Church can be exacting, but unlike Kathleen Ni Houlihan at her most exacting, she does not demand the blood sacrifice.'[59]

At the time that *Kathleen Ni Houlihan* was first performed in 1902, the *United Irishman* carried an interview with Yeats about it: 'My subject is Ireland and its struggle for independence … It is the perpetual struggle of the cause of Ireland,' he said. A week later, again in Griffith's paper, he enthused that 'nothing but a victory on the battlefield could so uplift and enlarge the imagination of Ireland, could so strengthen the National spirit … as the creation of a [National] Theatre where beautiful emotion and profound thought … might have their three hours' traffic'.[60] At the same time, in the London press, he acknowledged the influence of the *United Irishman* in the large towns of Ireland. He added that, in comparison to D.P. Moran's *Leader*, Griffith's paper 'has more ideas, and is more literary in tone, and yet this paper, which represents the national aspirations of a large section, was three times suppressed by the Government'.[61]

In November 1902, Griffith even published a play in five acts by Yeats, *Where There Is Nothing*, as a special supplement with the *United Irishman*. The following year, Yeats used Griffith's paper as his platform for three articles responding to an attack on the Irish National Theatre by the *Irish Independent*.[62] Later, in an essay on Synge, Yeats was to speak scornfully of 'a school of patriotism that held sway over my youth'.[63] But as the new century began that school surely helped him to graduate with honours.

Yeats was well aware of Griffith's belief that art should serve national objectives, at least until Ireland won its independence, and he raised with George Russell ('Æ') and Lady Gregory the 'amusing' idea of a debate with Griffith 'in public on our two policies – his that literature should be subordinate to nationalism, and mine that it must have its own ideal?' He thought that Griffith 'would be a little embarrassed'.[64] Maud Gonne summed up the contemporary tensions as 'Art for Art's Sake or Art for Propaganda'.[65]

Synge and *The Playboy*

In late 1904, Yeats had what he described as his 'first serious quarrel with Arthur Griffith'. This was when the *United Irishman* hinted that Hugh Lane acted partly out of self-interest in offering a collection of his paintings to Ireland. The following week Griffith published a generous retraction of his slur.[66] During 1905, Yeats and Griffith engaged in a public academic tussle in the *United Irishman* over the authenticity of Synge's *In the Shadow of the Glen* when this was performed at the

Abbey Theatre. Griffith liked Synge's *Riders to the Sea* but took an intense dislike to some of Synge's other work and now claimed that *In the Shadow of the Glen* was unoriginal and un-Irish, that it was based on an old Greek story of an unfaithful wife rather than a true Irish tale. Yeats and Griffith traded intellectual blows over it.[67] This was a foretaste of broader disagreements as tensions between art and politics opened up fissures in the 'Gaelic Revival'. Frayne notes that the attack in the *United Irishman* on Synge's *In the Shadow of the Glen* prompted Yeats' summary description of Griffith in *Dramatis Personae* as the 'slanderer of Lane and Synge, founder of the Sinn Fein movement, first President of the Irish Free State, and at that time an enthusiastic anti-cleric'.[68]

Both Griffith and Yeats wanted plays that showed Irish life as it was, but ultimately disagreed about what that meant or should mean. When Griffith impugned Synge's artistic integrity, Yeats wrote to the patron John Quinn about 'my squabble with Arthur Griffith' and said 'I could not avoid it, as the story [allegation] that Synge had taken a plot from Petronius and pretended that it was Irish was calculated to do a deal of mischief'.[69]

Tensions over the role of a national theatre notoriously erupted in January 1907 with the production of Synge's *The Playboy of the Western World*. Griffith, whose motives in support of the staging of *The Countess Cathleen* had been described by Yeats as avowedly anticlerical,[70] now found himself on the same side as conservative Catholics. He described the play as representing 'the peasant women of Mayo contending in their lusts for the possession of a man who has appealed to their depraved instincts by murdering, as they believe, his father'. It was, he said 'as vile and inhuman a story told in the foulest language we have ever listened to from a public platform ... told in language much of which is too coarse to be printed in any public journal'.[71] Reading the play today, in a world well-used to very explicit media and entertainment, it is hard to fathom why people were so shocked by *The Playboy*, just as it is baffling to consider the long list of seemingly innocuous books and films that were banned in Ireland decades after Griffith's death. Griffith denied that opposition to the play was 'organised' as the Abbey Theatre claimed, and he published, for no fee, the Abbey's advertisement inviting support against 'he who strikes at freedom of judgment' as well as a lengthy letter in defence of *The Playboy*. He wrote that the author of the play 'is entitled to have independent opinion in his favour published', and also commended the actors for their pluck in contending with protests in the theatre. He criticised what he regarded as the rough seizure of a man who hissed the play by policemen whom the Abbey's management had called in, and pointed to the provocative singing of 'God Save the King' by a section of the audience. When Synge died young two years later Griffith wrote sympathetically of him, forecasting that his *Riders to the Sea* would keep his name alive and – while not resiling from his views on *The Playboy* which he stated were written when Synge was ill – describing Synge as 'a potentially great dramatist'.[72] Maye has clearly demonstrated that Griffith was by no means exceptional in his response to *The Playboy*.[73]

Some years later, Yeats wrote a brilliant defence of Synge's representation of a life that 'is the most primitive left in Europe', in which Yeats referred not to Griffith by name but to a corrosive 'patriotic journalism' – and thus used that 'big word' that Joyce had avoided uttering in his criticism of Rooney's poetry.[74] There was to be no meeting of minds. For Griffith was spinning a new kind of democratic, bourgeois patriotism, and this play about patricide was in its own way an assault on 'the father of Sinn Féin'. It might be seen as the throwing over of order by reversion to wild stereotypes in line with the Yeatsian trope of a race of romantic peasantry. That seemed to critics not very far removed from recurrent stage-Irishry.

Griffith willingly published an article that scorned the painting of wisps of straw as a form of fig-leaf to conceal natural nudity in art.[75] But to Griffith, Synge's manner of depicting his people was at times not merely crude – or a 'foul echo from degenerate Greece' in the case of *Shadow of the Glen* – but was unrepresentative of Irish women and another form of what the *United Irishman* had called 'brogue and balderdash'.[76] Irish emigrants had long objected to patronising and insulting representations of Irish people on the stage in Britain and the United States. The *United Irishman* berated a particularly odious example of such stage-Irishry that it reported from the St Louis World's Fair of 1904.[77]

The power of Mother Ireland was far from exhausted, as is clear from the appearance in 1907 of a remarkable painting by Beatrice Elvery that is said to have inspired at least one youth to 'die for Ireland'.[78] Elvery (later Lady Glenavy) represented Éire in a suffocating, dark-green cloak over a long, shapeless white gown, with peasant figures no higher than her knees huddled like poor, banished children of Eve under its folds; a supercharged, highlighted, naked Christ-like child reaches out from the canvas towards the observer. Éire sits upright, supported by the shaft of a grey Celtic cross. The English Maud Gonne purchased this painting from the Anglo-Irish artist and donated it to Patrick Pearse, the son of an English sculptor, for his St Enda's School.

Pearse and his brother were both to be executed for their parts in the 1916 Rising. Not long before his death, he wrote a poem entitled 'The Mother' in which he articulated the voice of a doleful woman proclaiming bravely or even masochistically that she did not grudge 'them' her 'two strong sons' whom she had seen 'go out to break their strength and die'. She predicts, like Yeats' *Kathleen Ni Houlihan* had of such martyrs, that 'They shall be spoken of among their people / The generations shall remember them / And call them blessed'. Pearse's poem, partly prophetic and wholly theatrical, abides in the Irish collective memory of the 1916 dead and echoes an earlier translation by Pearse of a renowned ancient Irish invocation of the motherland ('Mise Éire/I am Ireland') that Ernest Jones later included in his analysis as a 'typical' example of references to Ireland as a woman.[79]

Some critics of *The Playboy* did not like seeing Irish sin represented on the stage, particularly in the form of women less pitiable and immaculate than Mother Ireland. But that was not the only reason for unease about Synge's work. For within the world of real politics and ideology, *The Playboy* might also be taken to support the view that the Irish were not fit enough to assume self-governance. Synge and Yeats dropping in on remote Irish peasants did not result in cutting modern European dramas that challenged the class of Yeats and Gregory or confronted the demeaning and destructive effects of British imperialism, but it might reinforce stereotypes. The appropriation of the label 'national' for a private Abbey Theatre controlled by Gregory and Yeats raised a fair question about that theatre's function.[80]

A Dubliner such as Griffith quite possibly also found the airy Anglo-Irish Yeats hard to take. The Dubliner James Joyce was certainly sceptical of Yeats and his coterie. Class and church, politics or aesthetics, were complicating factors in the dispute. Not all who objected to *The Playboy* were necessarily offended because of its reference to a petticoat, said to have sparked uproar in the theatre. This was included in the phrase 'If all the girls in Mayo were standing before us in their shifts', upon which Joyce commented drily 'Wonderful vision'. Joyce at this time declared sympathy for the advanced nationalists, thinking malignly that 'the Irish Theatre will beat Y[eats] and L[ady] G[regory] and Miss H[orniman], which will please me greatly, as Yeats cannot well hawk his theatre over to London'.[81]

After all that, when Michael MacWhite returned to Ireland later that year and called in to see Griffith at the *United Irishman,* 'in the office that morning was John B. Yeats', the poet's father.[82]

Hysterics and Eunuchs

Yeats and Lady Gregory themselves were self-censorious when it came to publishing material that affected their own objectives or sensitivities, with Yeats' powerful poem about those who rebelled at Easter 1916 (whom Gregory called the 'rabble') not being published in full for years after it was written, in order to avoid offending influential people they were trying to persuade to help secure the Hugh Lane collection of pictures for Ireland. And a poem by Yeats about Lady Gregory's dead son was suppressed because it did not project the image she wanted. Art for art's sake was clearly not the whole story. Nor was censorship the preserve of narrow Irish Catholic nationalists, for Britain's lord chamberlain ensured that George Bernard Shaw's *The Shewing-Up of Blanco Posnet* was kept off the stage in London then, and Anglo-Irish authorities in Ireland moved to have it suppressed in Dublin.[83]

Moreover, the Abbey Theatre of Yeats and Gregory happily staged some plays that were baldly propagandist in intent, including one by Casimir Dunin Markievicz in 1910 and one by Patrick Pearse in 1913.[84] The former was *The Memory of the Dead*, which shared its name with that of the popular ballad beloved by Griffith. Casimir Dunin Markievicz was a Polish count and the husband of the Anglo-Irish Constance Gore-Booth, who played the title role in the play (Plate 7). She was widely known as 'Countess Markievicz', an aristocratic title resonant of the heroic '*Countess Cathleen*'. On occasion, she also played the part of Joan of Arc, and was referred to as 'Ireland's Joan of Arc' when she went to New York – a sobriquet previously enjoyed by Maud Gonne. Constance had joined Sinn Féin in 1908. *The Freeman's Journal* described *The Memory of the Dead*, which dealt with the French landing in Co. Mayo in 1798, as 'romantic'.[85]

While intellectuals might yearn to maximise what freedom there was in Ireland for artists to develop as they did in other European countries, and for Irish people generally to transcend national or nationalist preoccupations, the fact remained that centuries of harsh colonialism and the suppression of the wishes of the majority of the population in Ireland ultimately determined the nature of the economy as well as Irish cultural and social superstructures. Griffith recognised this fact by his insistence that independence was a fundamental precondition of development, as perhaps Yeats himself implicitly did when he responded to the rebellion and executions by writing to Lady Gregory on 11 May 1916 that 'all the work of years has been overturned, all the bringing together of classes, all the freeing of Irish literature & criticism from politics'.[86] The artist cannot escape history.

Yeats and Griffith diverged. They became disaffected acquaintances who for years were not on speaking terms. In January 1916 Griffith resorted to one of those very pointed verbal assualts to which he sometimes gave vent, attacking Yeats as both an imperialist and imperious, and questioning his knowledge and scholarship.[87] But later, as president of the new Dáil, Griffith nominated Yeats to represent Ireland at a convention in Paris concerning the Irish 'race', and Yeats admitted that he would be tempted to accept a possible offer to become minister for fine arts in Griffith's government.[88] A friend of Griffith thought that 'Griffith loved Yeats; it was just a quarrel', and Griffith, when interned in Gloucester Prison in 1918, is said to have organised a celebration of Yeats' birthday with recitations of the latter's poetry.[89] To use a word such as 'malevolent' to describe Griffith's later attitude to Yeats, as Foster does, is to fix it too solidly.[90] In any event was Yeats' own attitude any less 'malevolent', not least when at the height of his fame he described Griffith posthumously as 'hysterical'?

Yeats could not resist some gentle mockery when Griffith, in 1921, got more from the treaty negotiations with Lloyd George than Yeats thought he would get. Yeats then wrote: 'I expect to see Griffith, now that he is the universal target, grow almost mellow, and become the fanatic of broadmindedness and accuracy of statement. Hitherto he has fired at the cocanuts [sic] but now that he has become a cocoa nut himself, he may become milky.'[91] Amusing as this is, it also reflects Yeats' attitude as someone who did not doubt his own intellectual superiority. The writer Seumas MacManus was puzzled later when Yeats, in his autobiographical writings, did not make anything of his earlier connections with Griffith:

> I wrote to tell him my surprise. He answered that he didn't know him well. This again surprised me and I told Y[eats] that I walked into the shabby two-by-four office in which poor G[riffith] immersed himself (in dirty Fownes St) and saw him (Y[eats]) sitting on [the] floor, back resting against the wall, nursing his knees, conversing with A[rthur] in this most emphatically intimate manner. Y[eats] did not reply.[92]

In the 1930s, Yeats included Griffith awkwardly in a poem that celebrated 'The Municipal Gallery Revisited' ('where my friends' portraits hang'). It begins:

> Around me the images of thirty years:
> An ambush; pilgrims at the water-side;
> Casement upon trial, half hidden by the bars,
> Guarded; Griffith staring in hysterical pride;[93]

The use of the adjective 'hysterical' here is unexplained, yet has had a long afterlife in respect to Griffith. In the portrait by Sir John Lavery to which Yeats referred, which was painted during the treaty negotiations in London in 1921 when the Laverys were friendly with Griffith and Collins, there is no obvious or self-evident representation of 'hysterical pride' (Plate 13). Nor is there any reason to think that John Lavery saw Griffith that way. Indeed the posture and expression of the sitter appear quite subdued. The epithet is a projection by Yeats, presumably based on his ostensibly gendered theory that Ireland had for generations pursued fixed ideas until 'at last a generation is like an hysterical woman who will make unmeasured accusations and believe impossible things, because of some logical deduction from a solitary thought which has turned a portion of her mind to stone.'[94] If it is the case as Harris avers that Yeats somehow followed an enlightened path by articulating a conception of gender that subverted a 'nationalism that requires its adherents to "believe impossible things"',[95] Griffith spent much of his life grounding his nationalist objective within the realms of possibility. His 'thing' of an independent Irish state turned out to be not at all 'impossible'. As early as 1903, in Griffith's *United Irishman*, the socialist Fred Ryan took issue with Yeats for depicting nationalist fervour in a way that Ryan saw as attempting to define advanced nationalists clinically and thus reduce patriotism to pathology.[96]

Yeats subsequently recalled both his visit to the Dublin gallery and the poem that he wrote about it. However, he passed over his sideswipe at Griffith when he then explained simply that the poem dealt with his 'many friends', including 'statesmen' in 'Ireland in the glory of her passions'.[97] Foster thinks that the 'friends' invoked in the poem 'certainly' did not include Griffith,[98] but that certainty may be misplaced given that Griffith had once been the poet's booster, as demonstrated above.

Yeats himself was not immune from great pride, as evidenced by lines of that same poem which articulate the outlook of a cultural elite that ostensibly scorned the middle class upon whom it relied for its income:

John Synge, I and Augusta Gregory, thought
All that we did, all that we said or sang
Must come from contact with the soil, from that
Contact everything Antaeus-like grew strong.
We three alone in modern times had brought
Everything down to that sole test again,
Dream of the noble and the beggar-man.

It is not clear to what 'contact with the soil' Yeats referred, unless it was his meeting farmers occasionally. His romantic idea of the noble and the beggar-man or peasant was some distance from Sinn Féin's concept of Ireland when that party won a resounding victory on a substantially expanded democratic franchise in 1918. Yeats' vision may have more in common with the backward-glancing Jacobite versifiers echoed in Mangan's poem 'Kathleen-Ni-Houlahan'. Griffith's 'hysterical' stare or 'steadfast will' was focused less on the landed gentry than on people beggared by Ireland's economic and political plight and disrupted by wholesale emigration.

Griffith's efforts to create a national debate by giving Yeats and other intellectuals a platform in the *United Irishman* does not seem to have earned the artisan's son a right to be considered cultured, for in 1909 Yeats told Lady Gregory that in using the phrase 'culture is the sanctity of the intellect' when writing of those who hated *The Playboy*, he was 'thinking of men like Arthur Griffith and how they can renounce external things without it but not envy, revenge, jealousy and so on.' He continued 'I compare Griffith and his like to the Eunuchs in Rickett's picture watching Don Juan riding through Hell.'[99] The comparison of playwrights such as Synge and (ostensibly) Yeats himself to Don Juan is worthy of its own psychosexual analysis. For one thing the analogy was inaccurate, with Rickett pointing out to Yeats that in this painting those who watch Don Juan are not in fact eunuchs but old women.[100] For another, among those who did not much like Synge's *Playboy* was that old woman and business partner of Yeats at the Abbey Theatre, Lady Gregory herself. Yet despite her misgivings, and with the residual hauteur of the Anglo-Irish elite that had long governed Ireland, she dismissed the *Playboy* row as 'the old battle, between those who use a toothbrush and those who don't'. The present author cannot say whether or not Griffith used a toothbrush, but in his case the culture war was between those whose motivations were primarily political and those whose motivations were ultimately not.

The 1913 Lock-Out

James Connolly neatly summed up a difference between the economic perspective of socialists and of his friend Arthur Griffith's Sinn Féin movement when, in 1909, he addressed a certain proposal in *The Peasant* that they might combine politically: 'With its economic teaching, as expounded by my friend Mr Arthur Griffith in his adoption of the doctrine of Friedrich List, Socialists have no sympathy, as it appeals only to those who measure a nation's prosperity by the volume of wealth produced in a country, instead of the distribution of that wealth among its inhabitants.'[101] Griffith thought that one first had to have the wealth before deciding how to distribute it, and that political independence as well as a degree of economic protectionism were needed to achieve that. He did not believe that socialism appealed to a majority of Irish voters, and it has never been proven otherwise in a national election. To Griffith, Larkin's brand of socialist agitation in particular was yet another factional distraction from the agenda of political independence, and he suspected that the philosophy of internationalism would benefit English workers more than Irish workers due to market factors within the United Kingdom.[102] Indeed, Larkin did then and later divide even the trade union movement.

Larkin's paper, the *Irish Worker*, competed to some extent with Griffith's *Sinn Féin*, and the two editors had sharp tongues. The son of Ulster emigrants, Larkin had first come to Ireland in 1907, when in his thirties. He proved himself a formidable trade union organiser and fighter. When Dublin employers combined to lock out striking workers, it led to clashes that are commemorated today on Dublin's O'Connell Street by a statue of this 'man of seething energy', as Lenin called Larkin. However, the workers did not win in 1913. Larkin left Dublin in 1914 and only returned when the Irish Free State had been founded and the civil war was over. He is said to have resented Connolly's status as a national martyr after 1916.[103]

Seamus O'Farrell, who helped to produce the *Irish Worker* at that time, later claimed 'Arthur Griffith's attitude towards Larkin and trade unionism caused the majority of the Dublin workers, especially the members of his union, to look on Sinn Féin and, to some extent, on the Volunteers, as being opposed to their interests. This, in my opinion, was the reason for the formation of the Citizen Army.' O'Farrell wrote that some replies to attacks on Larkin in *Sinn Féin* went unpublished by its editor.[104] Yet Griffith had been for many years a firm and 'honoured' member of the printers' union before becoming an editor and was not antagonistic to labour. He set out his views in a key article on 'Sinn Féin and the Labour Question'.[105]

Although at times hostile to James Larkin, in 1913, Griffith had what Noyk and Yeates and others have indicated was a warm regard for Larkin's principal lieutenant James Connolly and he praised the latter for suggesting a conciliation board to resolve industrial disputes.[106] Would Connolly, his acquaintance of earlier years,[107] have advertised the *Irish Worker* in Griffith's *Éire-Ireland* during the year following the great 1913 lockout had he believed that his old acquaintance was anti-worker? In 1922, H.E. Kenny claimed that Pearse and Connolly had told him 'several times' that they considered Griffith to be 'the truest of friends', although Pearse criticised his management of Sinn Féin.[108]

Griffith was accused of pandering to big money, of wanting to swap British rule for the domination of Irish capitalists. J.J. O'Kelly, who had enjoyed Griffith's company in earlier years, later complained that 'it was very easy for any man of substance to get Griffith's ear. By people of substance, I mean men like Martin Fitzgerald, the wine merchant. He was a great racing man, and he thought it an event of some importance to bring Arthur to meet the American, Boss Croker.' The Cork-born Croker, infamous Democratic Party boss of Tammany Hall in New York and freeman of Dublin City, kept racing horses in Ireland. O'Kelly continued 'Cathal Brugha would have no use for such men, nor would I. At once, I would feel in some way culpable. They all had Griffith.'[109]

Richard Davis has weighed up the pros and cons of such criticism, some of it not based on substantial evidence.[110] Where Griffith saw a significant role for Irish and foreign capital in building up an independent Ireland, his policy was in line with that of many independent nations and similar to that of governments of the future Irish state. It was never suggested, even by his enemies, that he lined his own pockets. While Boss Croker is thought to have provided monetary support and perhaps arms to republicans in the years leading up to independence, Griffith's widow said that when Griffith was jailed in 1916, Croker drove up to their house in Clontarf and opened a cheque book on her table, offering to write it for any amount. 'We do not have to take anything' was her reply, reportedly.[111] It is the case that, among the honorary pallbearers at Croker's funeral in Ireland in April 1922, were Griffith and Gogarty and a future lord mayor of Dublin, the popular Alfie Byrne.[112]

Griffith died before there was time for his likely attitude towards labour in an independent Irish state to become clear, but Cathal O'Shannon and others had already found him approachable. There is no reason to believe that he would ever have been a socialist, nor is there reason to think that his disdain for Larkin and for English unions meant that he would have been any further to the right than the principal Irish political parties have been since 1922.

Journalist, Editor and Crusader

Arthur Griffith was the only editor willing to publish in full James Joyce's letter of 1911 referring to Joyce's difficulties in getting *Dubliners* into print. He did so in his *Sinn Féin* paper, notwithstanding Joyce's dismissive review of William Rooney's poems when Griffith published them.[1] A decade earlier, both Griffith and Frank Fay in the *United Irishman* had recommended that people read Joyce's 'The Day of the Rabblement' essay, which Joyce himself published in pamphlet form following the refusal of the literary magazine *St Stephen's* to include it as an essay. Griffith and Fay disagreed with some of what Joyce wrote in that essay but Griffith enquired 'why we should grow Censors at all in this country':

> Turnips would be more useful. I hope this little pamphlet will have a large sale, if only to convince blooming Censors and budding Censors that this is the twentieth century, and that it is a holy and wholesome thing for men and women to use the minds God gave them and speak out the things they think.[2]

Griffith and D.P. Moran were the leading Irish journalists of the early twentieth century. Griffith was more 'advanced' in his advocacy of political independence. His papers were sued and suppressed, but he resurrected them under different titles. He edited, and wrote much of

- *The United Irishman*, 1899–1906
- *Sinn Féin*, 1906–14
- *Éire-Ireland*, 1914

- *Scissors and Paste*, 1914–15
- *Nationality*, 1915–19

James Connolly advertised the *Irish Worker* in his pages. Joyce admired Griffith, if not always agreeing with him, and was influenced by his papers. Archbishop William Walsh of Dublin 'read them most carefully and often discussed them.'[3] Griffith's attitude towards women in public affairs has been praised. Yet his reputation has been tarnished by some of what he penned or published. For, although he supported the establishment of a Zionist homeland, his paper's views on Jews and black people were sometimes prejudiced. However, while 'it is right', as Kelly says, 'to be appalled' by occasional anti-Semitism in Griffith's earlier papers,[4] it is not appropriate to overlook either a change in his outlook on Jews or the contemporary context in which others such as Michael Davitt and James Larkin also evinced anti-Semitic attitudes.

Described as 'a born journalist' by one who worked with him on *Sinn Féin* before joining the editorial staff of the *Irish Independent*,[5] Griffith became an office-boy with the Underwoods when he left school at the age of fourteen. They owned a small printing firm in Dublin. Jane Underwood, well regarded by other printers, lent young Griffith books and discussed ideas with him.[6] He subsequently served his apprenticeship as a compositor at the *Nation*, where his roles included that of copyholder. A copyholder was a proofreader's assistant who read copy aloud to the proofreader. He worked there with Adolphus Shields, one of Dublin's master compositors and a 'red-hot socialist and an anarchist.'[7] By 1891, Griffith had become a copyreader at the *Daily Independent*. Due to the development of new technologies and transport systems, as well as better education, the circulation and number of newspapers was growing rapidly. Griffith was to create an influential niche for his own advanced nationalist titles in the midst of what has recently been described as 'an explosion in the number of newspapers published in Ireland.'[8]

His training suited not only apprentice printers but also those who aspired to be journalists, as he did. The author of a professional textbook noted then 'In the first ten years the young journalist masters reporting, copy-reading, and the rest of the routine work.'[9] Griffith was soon in print himself. Thus in 1892, under the joint byline of Griffith and his close friend William Rooney, a series of eight long articles entitled 'Notable graves' appeared in Dublin's *Herald*. Why did that series include Lord Clare, architect of the despised Act of Union, and Charles Lucas, notwithstanding 'his intolerance of his Catholic countrymen ... [in] an age of bigotry'? It seems that it was because Griffith thought that Clare had an independent spirit, and the 'incorruptible' Lucas 'almost single-handed ... carried on the fight which Molyneux had begun and Swift continued'.[10] That fight was for a representative assembly, independent of Westminster, albeit under a single monarch.

Griffith was not yet a full-time journalist, and in the 1890s worked as a proofreader on Dublin's *Evening Telegraph*. He was employed too as a compositor at Thom's, where the Dublin *Gazette* and the police *Hue and Cry* were printed, and where they knew him as 'the son of old Arthur Griffith, the pressman'. He is said to have been a relatively slow but methodical compositor; a fact that reduced his potential earnings when compositors were paid on a piece-work basis.[11] On 17 February 1894 he was admitted as a member of the Dublin typographical craft union, his sponsors being Patrick Seary and Christopher Timmins, who were prominent in Dublin trade union and nationalist circles.

Early in 1897 Griffith emigrated to South Africa.[12] There he was invited to edit the *Courant*, a very small weekly paper in the sleepy town of Middelburg. It was not a success, wrote Griffith, 'as the Britishers withdrew their support, and the Dutchmen didn't bother about reading a journal printed in English'.[13] Although editor for only a few months, he learnt useful skills, and saw that readers had a mixture of news, analysis and lighter items. His personal 'fondness for versifying' was evident in the *Courant*, as later in the *United Irishman*.[14]

Griffith returned to Dublin in need of a job.[15] He was invited to edit a new advanced nationalist paper, the *United Irishman*. Alice Milligan and Anna Johnston facilitated its launch on 4 March 1899. They had been publishing in Belfast the *Shan Van Vocht*, that title being an anglicisation of Gaelic words meaning 'poor old woman', a personification of Ireland. It was also the name of a song from the time of the United Irishmen rebellion of 1798. The women now closed their paper and gave their list of subscribers to Griffith and Rooney, who had written pieces for

Shan Van Vocht.[16] Griffith's new paper took its name from the defunct *United Irishman*, started in 1848 by the rebel John Mitchel. It is said that the Irish Republican Brotherhood in the late 1890s also considered renaming itself 'The United Irishmen'.[17]

It is no easy task running a newspaper. The circulation of the Parnellite *United Ireland* paper had reportedly dropped from 5,000 to 2,000 by June 1898, when it became bankrupt.[18] Griffith himself would sometimes set the type at the printers to save money.[19]

The socialist Fred Ryan wanted Griffith's new *United Irishman* to be hard-hitting and discomforting, as he bluntly told its editor in an early issue:

It is not so much England that has kept Ireland in chains as Irish ignorance, Irish folly, and Irish dissension. You are in the habit of using very plain speech about some of your contemporaries. And I admire it. Let me then speak plainly. The Irish people in many respects are more ignorant, more superstitious, and more vain than the majority of peoples in Western Europe. They have become so accustomed to flattery from their Press, that they have come to really think that Providence has a special eye on this island, and that they are somehow holier than the rest of common humanity.

The first issue of Griffith's *United Irishman*.

Now all this vanity and conceit – which is debited, of course, to England – has to be destroyed. And it requires direct speech.[20]

The editorial office of the *United Irishman* was first at 9 Upper Ormond Quay, but moved to 17 Fownes Street in July 1900. James Stephens recalled that, when a required piece was not forthcoming, Griffith 'would write the missing articles himself and write them much better than anybody else could … He would turn out, with equal ease, an article on [the earl of Tyrone] Red Hugh O'Neill, an appreciation of [the poet] Raftery, a biographical notice, a comic ballad, or a parody on any person whom Fate, at the moment, had doomed to this treatment.'[21] In the robust spirit of frankness and debate that marked the small Dublin societies that he joined, Griffith boasted of his new paper 'We have at all times opened our columns to our critics. The want of a free, tolerant, and intelligent public opinion in Ireland is directly traceable to the Irish politicians and their press.'[22] It is impossible to know how far he was open to criticism, but he certainly published some feedback that was robust.

Maud Gonne raised funds in America for his paper and personally supported it financially.[23] She sometimes wrote articles for it too. In 1900, when Victoria visited Dublin during the Boer War, police seized all copies of the *United Irishman* containing Gonne's description of her majesty as the 'Famine Queen'. W.B. Yeats protested publicly about police seizures of that and other editions of the paper.[24] Gonne wrote of Griffith 'living on a bare subsistence'.[25] When Griffith accompanied Maud Gonne to France the following year, it was reported that English agents were 'shadowing an Irish journalist in Paris'. In 1903, when the pair opposed a visit to Dublin by Edward VII, Griffith ran a story alleging a Unionist conspiracy to sideline the nationalist lord mayor of Dublin. Recognising the limitations of Griffith's anonymous sources, W.B. Yeats told Maud Gonne that because Griffith had not stated where he got his information 'it won't carry much weight'.[26]

In November 1910, in the first issue of the radical republican *Irish Freedom*, a contributor ('Lucan') vividly remembered 'how the advent of *the United Irishman* came to me with the heaviness and bewilderingness of wine, with the sense of comradeship, with hope and confidence, with the dawn of a new interest in life'. Steele has praised the *United*

Irishman for giving a platform to women writers.[27] O'Sullivan described Griffith then as 'the most powerful figure in national affairs'. Sales of newspapers were not audited as they are today but Inspector Thomas Lynham of the Dublin Metropolitan Police thought that the *United Irishman* had 'a large circulation throughout the county and city'.[28] Horgan wrote that the *United Irishman* 'quickly became the mouthpiece of a new political movement. Griffith's sincere and powerful articles soon attracted attention.' Horgan remembered calling on Griffith at Fownes Street:

> To find him I had to climb the narrow stairs of an old house in a street running down to the Liffey. There in a dusty back office surrounded by piles of MSS [manuscripts], files, and the other odds and ends of a small newspaper office, he sat at a little table, a small, stocky man, his short-sighted eyes peering from behind thick glasses, his mouth hidden under a heavy moustache.[29]

That house was shared by various commercial tenants. Numbers 16 and 17 together were listed in Thom's *Street Directory* as 'Colonial Chambers' (now demolished), although Griffith did not include this name in the address of his paper! Here he had one room divided into two by a thin partition of board. Among the paper's subscribers was Canon Hannay ('George A. Birmingham') who wrote that Arthur Griffith 'worked away silently in his cubby-hole of an office at the production of his weekly paper. The circulation of the paper increased steadily. It came to be recognised that Arthur Griffith was a man who would not be frightened out of saying what he thought true or seduced into saying anything else by the prospect of some advantage.'[30]

H.E. Kenny claims to have been present when Griffith rebuffed an American newspaper owner who pressed the editor of the *United Irishman* to take a job in the United States as a 'paragraph writer' for £1,000 per year.[31] Other people who worked with him, including Yeats, also spoke of his being offered employment that would have paid him well had he accepted it.[32]

By any standards, the *United Irishman* was a lively and wide-ranging publication, particularly in the early years of the twentieth century, when

Joyce was having it sent to him in Italy and when a writer in the New York *Sun* on 25 June 1904 described it as 'the most vigorous paper, and far and away the best, if the youngest, paper in Ireland'.

Griffith's most influential polemic was 'The Resurrection of Hungary'. It first appeared in 1904 as a long series in the *United Irishman*, and later that year as a pamphlet. It is said that 5,000 copies were sold within twenty-four hours, 'a record in the Irish publishing trade'.[33] Among its readers was James Joyce. The polemic expressed Griffith's own brand of nationalism. It held up the dual monarchy of Austria and Hungary as a model for Ireland, and articulated economic arguments in support of Griffith's ideal. F.S Lyons, a leading historian, later wrote:

> That the *United Irishman* made the impact it did was largely due to the editor himself … Griffith was an inspired journalist who combined style and temper in a way no one else could match. He recalled both the savagery of Swift and the ruggedness of John Mitchel, but to these he added his own intensity and his own intimate knowledge of the political and economic environment about him.[34]

Brennan penned a vivid description of Griffith at work, wrestling with the angel of his editorials, his mood changing daily relative to deadlines: 'During all his adult years, except the last few, he slaved for four days of the week at his paper which, for a long time, he not merely wrote, but set up as well.'[35] Griffith's style may now seem dated but was then regarded as refreshing. Seán T. O'Kelly, who worked with Griffith and other nationalists as their newspaper manager, and later became president of Ireland, recalled the impact of the paper:

> Griffith was a forceful writer, and had a style that was then new in Irish journalistic work. The old-fashioned verbose tirades that were always associated with Parliamentarianism soon went out of fashion. The subscribers to the *United Irishman* were taught to be prudent, careful and precise in their statements. Every fact should be checked … something more than wild words were necessary to attain the objects that Sinn Féin and Irish-Ireland and the Gaelic League had.[36]

When refinancing the *United Irishman* in 1903, Griffith vaunted it as 'the pioneer of the Irish industrial movement and the supporter of the Irish language revival movement'.[37] Looking back in 1923, George Lyons described the paper as 'teeming with articles on the Irish language, history and topography. A vigorous campaign on behalf of Irish industries was kept up, and trenchant denunciations of emigration and enlistment in the British armed forces.' In 1937, Stephen Brown thought that Griffith in its pages had 'preached an aggressive anti-British policy', but de Roiste thought it 'literary rather than propagandist'. Colum was 'surprised at the absence of attack' in the early issues. Politics, news, history, economics, literature, mythology, science, ballads and art were discussed in its pages. Contributors included J.B. and W.B. Yeats, George Moore, Edward Martyn, Æ, 'John Eglinton' (William Magee), J.M. Synge and Kuno Meyer. Stephens wrote that 'All the poets of Ireland were then solid for Mr Griffith.'[38] Callinan notes that 'the magnificent ambition of Griffith's *United Irishman*' was epitomised by the publication of a series of 'Old Irish Bardic Tales', accessible but with scholarly exegeses, by Richard Irvine Best. These included a rendering of 'The Destruction of Da Dearga's Hostel', a tale from which derives a rich subtext of James Joyce's 'The Dead'.[39] Joyce 'said that the *United Irishman* was the only paper in Dublin worth reading, and in fact, he used to read it every week'. Scholars have demonstrated its cultural and political influence on Joyce's oeuvre, with Callinan, for example, complaining that the import of Joyce's interest in the *United Irishman* 'has been overlooked as the consequence of a lack of curiosity as to Joyce's intellectual relation to Irish nationalism in 1902–4', on the mistaken assumption that the sometime socialist Joyce was then indifferent to Irish politics.[40]

As any editor may, Griffith risked provoking deadly defamation suits. His 'pugnacious style of journalism' led to a legal action that is believed to have hastened his demise at the *Middelburg Courant*.[41] Another legal action killed off the *United Irishman*. On 12 August 1905, Griffith wrote and published an article referring to Michael Donor, a parish priest in Limerick who had objected to the Gaelic League holding its local 'Feis' on a Sunday. Donor claimed that Griffith had impugned his reputation and initiated what Lyons described as 'a splenetic libel action'. He was awarded damages of £50 and costs of £200, but the *United Irishman* was said to be worth only £150 and went into liquidation. To Donor's chagrin, Griffith successfully sought a preferential payment of £50 due on his notional salary as editor of £208 annually. Donor's counsel described Griffith as 'the Pooh-Bah of the establishment – director, manager, editor and libeller'. Judge Johnson reportedly thought Griffith 'too saucy in his attitude'.[42]

Indeed, no sooner had the struggling *United Irishman* gone than Griffith 'cheerfully rebaptized it under the still more appropriate name of *Sinn Féin*'. It was appropriate because Griffith had recently been instrumental in founding the political movement of that name. Joyce drew directly on Griffith's *Sinn Féin* when he wrote articles for an Italian newspaper between 1907 and 1912.[43] He also advertised his Volta cinema in *Sinn Féin*. This was Dublin's first custom-built cinema, opened by Joyce in 1909 but sold the following July.[44]

Griffith's friend George Lyons wrote 'In business affairs Griffith had a weakness for depending upon those immediately surrounding him, rather than making a systematic selection on the basis of efficiency from a list of his far flung supporters. It is something of an Irish failing'.[45] But perhaps for Griffith it was a case of 'needs must'. Griffith boasted in his *United Irishman* that the paper was not incorporated, thus allowing its editors and writers the freedom to 'write what they think – not what any board of directors or political bosses may find it profitable to think'.[46] In the case of *Sinn Féin*, paradoxically, it was the creation of a board of sympathetic directors that enabled him to hold the IRB and other republican hardliners at bay and to keep his paper afloat in adverse circumstances.[47]

Griffith 'inaugurated a period of muck-raking protest journalism which had certain affinities with the American radical periodicals of his day'.[48] The editor of *Sinn Féin* thought it was a cut above other papers.[49] The *Cork Examiner*, for example, was 'notorious for the lack of principle and backbone'. The failure of the daily press to cover more Irish stories was lamented.[50] Joyce read *Sinn Féin* as he had the *United Irishman*, sending back from Rome to his brother on one occasion a cutting from of a piece by Griffith signed with his most common pen name 'Shanganagh'.[51] This was the pen name explicitly associated with

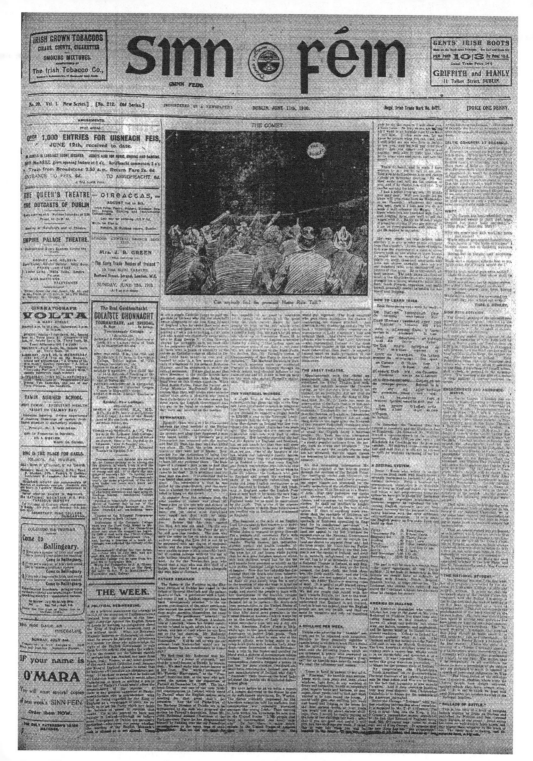

Sinn Féin, 11 June 1910. The 'Home Rule Comet' cartoon seen here inspired James Joyce to write an article in Italian for *Il Piccolo della Sera* (22 Dec. 1910). Note also (left column) the advertisement for Dublin's Volta cinema ('cinematograph'), of which Joyce was then the manager.

Griffith in *Ulysses*: 'Is that by Griffith? says John Wyse. —No, says the citizen. It's not signed Shanganagh. It's only initialled: P.'

Pen Names

One hundred years ago it was less common than it is today to find the names of journalists attached to what they wrote. Various pen names were used in Griffith's papers. Besides 'Shanganagh', Griffith himself used 'J. P. Ruhart' even before he went to South Africa. His work also appeared above Cuguan, Ier, Rathcoole, Mise, Nationalist, Old Fogey, Mafosta and (Joseph) Smith, as well perhaps as Viking and Lasairfhíona.[52] Glandon gives Griffith too as Calma, Lugh, Cloakey, Rover, JAP and Hop and Go One, but this is unreliable. While the style of Calma may resemble that of Griffith, at least some of the content seems incompatible with Griffith's known biography. JAP was almost certainly Joseph A. Power (later editor of *An t-Óglách* and an *Evening Telegraph* journalist), while W.J. Stanton Pyper seems to have identified himself to Yeats as 'Lugh'.[53] William Rooney used Fear na Muintire, Hi Fiachra, Criadhaire, Shel Martin, Sliabh Ruadh, Gleann an Smoil, Knocksedan, Killester, Feltrim, Ballinascorney and Baltrasna – and also wrote the 'All Ireland' column until his death.[54] His girlfriend Maire Killeen wrote under 'Maire'. Fred Ryan was 'Irial', while the actor Frank Fay was 'FJF' and W.K. Magee was 'John Eglinton'.[55] F.H. O'Donnell was for some months 'The Foreign Secretary', and also 'Red Hand'. Joyce identified Gogarty as 'Mettus Curtius'.[56] 'Michael Orkney' was possibly Thomas Keohler. Chrissie Doyle lay claim to the 'Man of the Week' column, while Anna Johnston was 'Ethna Carberry', Alice Milligan was 'Irish Olkyrn' and Sidney Gifford-Czira was 'John Brennan'.[57]

Daily *Sinn Féin*

Griffith briefly published *Sinn Féin* as a daily, from August 1909 until January 1910, although he knew the financial risk involved.[58] Twenty-five years later Senator Thomas Farren of Labour remembered seeing him when the first issue of that daily was being prepared 'and he was not only editor of the paper, but he was porter and everything else; I saw him with his coat off wheeling in trucks of paper before they went to the machine room. His heart and soul was in whatever he was doing.'[59] However, keeping the daily afloat was not easy and P.S. O'Hegarty, an IRB man and writer, accused him of sensationalism in trying to do so, of 'scandal-making' and 'encouragement of mania in … controversy' and regretted that the organisation itself had no control over the newspaper of the same name. O'Hegarty at the time also criticised Griffith's *Sinn Féin* paper for being 'chiefly a manifestation to the Unionists of how they may be Unionists and good patriots at the same time. Our business is to show Unionists and Home Rulers that until they have become Nationalists they cannot be good patriots.' Despite all that, O'Hegarty still considered it 'the best daily paper in Ireland'.[60]

'The Daily National Industrial Journal', as *Sinn Féin* styled itself, incurred such debts that Griffith had to mortgage his printing plant to save even a reduced weekly edition. He earned extra money from time to time by writing for Dublin's *Evening Telegraph*, including in 1913 seventeen substantial and illustrated features on Irish language revivalists.[61] In the years preceding the First World War he was behind an attempt to launch an Irish news agency too, and published an annual Sinn Féin *Irish Year Book*.[62] Griffith also wrote some articles for the new women's nationalist paper, *Bean na h-Éireann* (subtitled 'The Woman of Ireland').[63]

Articles in the *United Irishman* on the Dreyfus affair in France included a number in late 1899 and early 1900 by 'The Foreign Secretary', who was then the former MP and notorious anti-Semite F.H. O'Donnell. Extracts from *La Patrie*, an organ controlled by the anti-Semitic Lucien Millevoye, also featured prominently among European newspapers quoted in Griffith's paper. Maud Gonne, Millevoye's friend and lover, is herself described identically by the *Dictionary of Irish Biography* and the Oxford *Dictionary of National Biography* as a 'vehement anti-Dreyfusard'.[64] The bulk of anti-Semitic statements that Griffith published, including with reference to Dreyfus, appeared in the second half of 1899 during the Boer War. However, on 23 April 1904, passages in the *United Irishman* referred to attacks on Jews in Limerick and mentioned a priest there 'who warned the people against being caught in their usurious toils'. The writer thought that accusations of a persecution were not justified by 'a few charges of trivial assaults preferred by Jews' and defined nine-tenths of the Jewish people as 'usurers and parasites of industry. In this category we do not include the Zionist minority of the Jews.'

Griffith published in the *United Irishman* some criticism of pieces in it relating to Jews and, in an apparent paradox, expressed strong support for a Jewish state in Palestine.[65] Laffan explains 'Although he supported Zionism, he attacked Jewish "cosmopolitans" such as the "Jew-Jingo brigands" of Johannesburg.'[66] This perhaps 'corresponds to the historical split in perception of the Jews as at once a noble, ancient people, but unacceptable as individuals in modern society.'[67]

James Joyce, creator of the Hungarian-Irish rambling part-Jewish Leopold Bloom, endorsed Griffith's journalism as a whole. He told his brother

> In my opinion Griffith's speech at the meeting in the National Council justifies the existence of his paper [*Sinn Féin*]. He, probably, has to lease out his columns to scribblers … what I object to most of all in his paper is that it is educating the people of Ireland on the old pap of racial hatred whereas anyone can see that if the Irish question exists, it exists for the Irish proletariat chiefly.[68]

This mention of 'racial hatred' is sometimes assumed only to refer to anti-Semitism but, from its context, it clearly encompasses comments on the English in a recent article by Joyce's old acquaintance Oliver St John Gogarty ('Buck Mulligan' of *Ulysses*). This was one of three articles in *Sinn Féin* between August and December 1906, under the general title 'Ugly England.'[69] Nevertheless, Joyce, when writing to his brother in November, defended Griffith: 'You complain of Griffith's using Gogarty & Co. How do you expect him to fill his paper: he can't write it all himself. The part he does write, at least has some intelligence and directness about it.'[70]

In August 1912 Joyce consulted Griffith about his continuing difficulties with Irish publishers in respect to *Dubliners*: 'I went then to Griffith who received me very kindly and remembered my letter [of 1911], he told his brother. In Italy Joyce had been receiving copies of Griffith's papers, and later had issues of them in Ireland searched for a review of *Dubliners* when it was eventually published.[71] He was to have a character in *Ulysses* claim that Leopold Bloom 'gave the ideas for Sinn Fein [i.e. the paper *Sinn Féin*?] to Griffith to put in his paper'. Was this the origin of reported rumours that Griffith had 'a Jewish adviser-ghostwriter'?[72]

It was for Griffith's opinions on national issues, not for publishing Joyce's letter, that the government suppressed *Sinn Féin*. Griffith soon afterwards brought out *Éire-Ireland*, which survived for just a few weeks in 1914, on Mondays and Saturdays from 26 October until 4 December. It was anti-Redmond, being opposed to Irish involvement in the European war that had begun in July that year. He included in its launch issue an article on the Irish Volunteers by Patrick Pearse, who had once criticised Griffith strongly in one of Pearse's own small papers. Griffith now announced that 'Today we issue the first number of "Ireland" in order to report the proceedings of the Irish Volunteer Convention, which the prostitute daily Press of Ireland will, in so far as it does not suppress, attempt to misrepresent and distort'. Griffith used *Éire-Ireland* to attack some other publications as supine, particularly *The Freeman's Journal*, while promoting others. Thus, in the year following the great 1913 lockout, he carried notices for 'The *Irish Worker* – champion of the Rights of Labour', published at Liberty Hall.[73] But on 4 December 1914, Griffith distributed a letter to readers of *Éire-Ireland*. Printed separately, it was signed by himself and by that paper's manager, the future president of Ireland, Seán T. O'Kelly. He explained that their printer ('Mr Mahon') felt unable to continue producing the journal because the *Irish Worker* had just become the latest nationalist publication to be forceably suppressed and to have its printing machinery seized. Griffith claimed that, to the best of his knowledge, he had 'complied with British military orders' in respect to what journalists were free to write about during the war.[74]

Just eight days after Griffith ceased publishing *Éire-Ireland*, he was back in business with a new title, *Scissors and Paste*. Its first issue appeared on 12 December 1914, and the last of its twenty-two issues on 27 February 1915. Four pages long, it was published on Wednesdays and Saturdays. The first number contained a short editorial headed 'Ourselves', this word being a translation of 'Sinn Féin'. In it he stated that

It is high treason for an Irishman to argue with the sword the right of his small nationality [sic] to equal political freedom with Belgium, or Serbia, or Hungary. It is destruction to the property of his printer now when he argues with the pen. Hence while England is fighting the battle of Small Nationalities **Ireland** [the use here of bold typeface presumably a reference to the title of Griffith's preceding publication] is reduced to **Scissors and Paste**. Up to the present the sale and use of these instruments have not been prohibited by the British Government in Ireland.

One finds also in the first issue an article and advertisement relating to Sinn Féin's Aonach na Nollag, the annual Irish goods fair which that year took place at the Abbey Theatre. The editorial and report were among very few original items in *Scissors and Paste*. This paper almost wholly consisted of extracts from other titles at home and abroad, along with some quotations from Irish patriotic writers of earlier generations and occasional snatches and verses from old songs or poems intended to make a contemporary point. I have analysed the content and significance of *Scissors and Paste* at some length elsewhere.[75]

On 2 January 1915, *Scissors and Paste* reported that the *Irish Worker* had reappeared, having been printed by the press of the Socialist Labour Party in Glasgow. It noted that James Connolly was editing it in place of James Larkin who had gone to America. On 10 February it reported that the new *Worker* had been seized when the vessel carrying it arrived in Dublin.

In the final issue of *Scissors and Paste* before its suppression, Griffith reported that the assault on Turkish forces at the Dardanelles had begun. He included some pointed material relating to it. There was also a striking piece from the London *Daily Express* which itself cited a German report in the *Deutsche Zeitung* that the number of recruits to the British Army had dwindled away to nothing and that emigration to America was 'proceeding on a scale never before seen'. The twenty-third issue of *Scissors and Paste*, due on 3 March 1915, never appeared. On that morning national newspapers reported that police and military police had entered the editorial offices of Griffith's publication in Middle Abbey Street and taken possession of various papers, and that *Scissors and Paste* had been suppressed under the Defence of the Realm Act. Police also visited the offices of its printer, Patrick Mahon of Yarnhall Street, and ensured that the machinery was dismantled in such a manner as to prevent its further use.[76] About this time Griffith is said to have also written more than twenty articles for *The Spark*, a very small Dublin paper.[77]

Despite Griffith encouraging people to begin 'thinking for yourselves about books and their writers',[78] some have claimed that Griffith himself might have approved of censorship in the Irish Free State in respect to works of literature that he considered indecent. Robert Brennan, for example, thought him in some respects 'the narrowest of puritans' and recounted a conversation with him about a novel by Compton Mackenzie that Griffith described as 'filth'. He recalled that Griffith said the book 'has everything that appeals to the lower English taste: adultery, a suggestion of sodomy, and tears for the poor prostitute'.[79] However, while Griffith no doubt shared many contemporary mainstream attitudes on such matters, the Irish Free State in due course had a very high level of censorship for which the dead Griffith cannot be held responsible and which was widely supported in the Dáil and elsewhere.

Never long silenced, Griffith was in print again in June 1915, with the launch of *Nationality* which was backed by the IRB. Seán Mac Diarmada managed it with Griffith, at its office in D'Olier St.[80] They employed a Belfast Protestant firm as its printer, hoping thereby to reduce the chance of being suppressed again. *Nationality* proved so popular that it required two reprints in its first four days and is said to have achieved a circulation larger than any Irish publication save the daily *Independent*. Chief Secretary Augustine Birrell is reported to have described Griffith as 'an extraordinarily clever journalist', and the *Catholic Bulletin* thought him 'brilliant'.[81]

After the Easter Rising of 1916, publication of *Nationality* was suspended until a new series began in February 1917. It ran until 1919. Griffith was imprisoned twice during its lifetime. It was edited by others in his absence, and sued by one Malcolm Lyon – on behalf of the government he believed.[82] Ever the editor, Griffith even started manuscript journals when jailed, these being *The Outpost* in Reading (named by Terence MacSwiney) and *The Gloucester Diamond* in

Gloucester.[83] Griffith also helped in the writing and production of *Young Ireland: Éire Óg*, which first appeared on 5 May 1917.[84]

In 1919 O'Hegarty said of Griffith 'As leader-writer he is unequalled, and as a writer of obituary notices he is unsurpassable.' But, it had to be admitted, 'He always splits his infinitives'![85] Griffith's journalism deserves closer scrutiny than it has received to date, and critical studies of its content in respect to discrete areas such as literature, religion and social affairs would be fruitful.

11

1902–16: Sinn Féin and the Rising

The night before Griffith, Connolly and Gonne mounted their protest at Joseph Chamberlain's visit to Dublin in 1899, they met the Fenian veteran John O'Leary. As he sipped a Jameson 'white whiskey' at a late hour, O'Leary asked 'Can you defend the people you are tempting to danger?' One of those present later wrote: 'O'Leary abhorred "flash-in-the pan" exploits, and he could only discern in our proposal a piece of elaborate bravado by which we would get the defenceless citizens battoned in the streets.'[1] Despite this, Griffith took part in the protest.[2] Yet he too considered the unintended repercussions of confrontation and did not take them lightly, in 1916 or later. In 1919, for example, he reportedly criticised the Soloheadbeg ambush that came to be seen as the opening shot in the guerilla War of Independence, because it was not sanctioned democratically by the Dáil and might lead to a split. He worried too about the impact of killing British officers on 21 November 1920, an event that led hours later on 'Bloody Sunday' to British forces murdering civilians at Croke Park. His concerns sprang from his usual wish to avoid divisions, but also perhaps partly from his memory of the death of a brave IRB man in activities with which a much younger Griffith was ostensibly connected.[3]

Griffith was not against an insurrection in principle. Those responsible for one in 1916 took him partly into their confidence when he was invited to a significant meeting attended by members of the supreme council of the Irish Republican Brotherhood in September 1914. The organisers of the meeting wanted Griffith to keep writing about events and this, along with his poor eyesight, was reason enough for him not to fire a shot during the later insurrection. He was promised that he would be kept informed of developments.

The Foundation of Sinn Féin

In August 1900 Griffith advocated a 'federation' of nationalist groups.[4] He and Rooney and others then founded Cumann na nGaedheal ('Confederation of the Gaels' – not to be confused with the later political party of that name). It was intended to increase resistance to anglicisation. Gonne recalled Griffith and Yeats drawing up its programme at her house.[5] At its 1902 convention – during which Maud Gonne appeared in the title role of a production of Yeats' *Kathleen Ni Houlihan* – Griffith made a speech during which he first advocated that Irish MPs withdraw permanently from parliament in Westminster in order to convene a separate assembly in Ireland.[6]

The police regarded Griffith and Maud Gonne, along with 'Miss Quinn' (Mary Quinn, actor and secretary of Inghinidhe na hÉireann), as 'evidently the prime movers' in opposition to the visit of King Edward VII to Ireland during 1903.[7] The trio campaigned to stop local councils agreeing to addresses of welcome, with 'a daring attempt by a well organised mob headed by Arthur Griffith to take possession of the platform' at a meeting in the Rotunda chaired by the lord mayor of Dublin. Griffith wanted the mayor to declare his intentions in the matter. Chairs constituted the principle weapon used in the fracas, with some injuries.[8]

Griffith also founded a 'National Council' to bring together 'advanced nationalist' groups and to oppose enlistment in the British army. This council held its first annual congress on 28 November 1905, when it endorsed his Sinn Féin policy.[9] As the National Council merged with Cumann na nGaedheal and the Dungannon Clubs, he played a central role in creating the composite movement known as Sinn Féin. In March 1906, Griffith declared 'The policy for which the National Council stands is summarized in its title – "SINN FÉIN."'[10] He reportedly insisted to an American journalist in June 1922 'Sinn Féin was not my exclusive creation', that it was 'conceived by two of us – and the other man was William Rooney', who died in 1901.[11] Although the new movement contested and won seats in local elections in Dublin in 1904 and 1905, it decided that it would not yet directly challenge existing political parties by contesting the general election of 1906.

THE RESURRECTION

OF HUNGARY:

A PARALLEL FOR IRELAND.

It is impossible to think of the affairs of Ireland without being forcibly struck with the parallel of Hungary.—SYDNEY SMITH.

DUBLIN:
JAMES DUFFY & CO.,
M. H. GILL & SON,
SEALY, BRYERS & WALKER.

PRICE ONE PENNY.

1904

Arthur Griffith's *The Resurrection of Hungary,* title page.

Griffith gave Máire Butler the credit for persuading him to settle on the name 'Sinn Féin' (Irish for 'we ourselves').[12] Butler, an activist and writer, and her sister Belinda (later Mère/Mother Columba) were regular contributors to Griffith's papers. They also happened to be first cousins of the prominent unionist Edward Carson. However, the 'brand concept' of Sinn Féin had been in the air for years. For Sinn Féin emerged from the womb of a cultural renaissance or 'Celtic revival'. It was nourished with nutrients that were part poetic and part political, being the offspring of a union between Irish cultural or language revivalists and political activists inspired by the rebels of 1798, and by Thomas Davis' Young Ireland movement of the 1840s. Davis himself wrote a poem called 'Self-Reliance', and the Young Irelander John O'Hagan composed one entitled 'Ourselves Alone'.

On 14 June 1892, *The Freeman's Journal* reported that Tim Healy had invoked for voters 'the good old watchword of Ireland – shin fain – ourselves alone'. At the first meeting of the Celtic Literary Society in 1893, Griffith's friend William Rooney lectured on Samuel Ferguson, quoting that poet's 'Lament for Thomas Davis' which looks forward to 'Erin a nation yet; self-respecting, self-relying, self-advancing'.[13] When Griffith was in South Africa in 1898, a short poem in Irish by Douglas Hyde of the Gaelic League appeared in *Shan Van Vocht*, that Belfast paper to which both Griffith and Rooney occasionally contributed before their *United Irishman* superseded it. Hyde's poem was a clarion call to self-reliance, ending with the cry '*Sinn Féin amháin!*' The verses, published under Hyde's pen name 'An Chraoibhín Aoibhinn', were accompanied by this translation:

> Waiting for help from France, waiting for help from Spain; the
>   people who waited long ago for that, they got shame only.
> Waiting for help again, help from America, the lot who are now
>   waiting for it, my disgust for ever on them.
> It is time for every fool to have knowledge that there is no watch-
>   cry worth any heed but one, *Ourselves Alone!*[14]

The use of the word 'fool' identified a distinction between the aspirations of patriots such as Thomas Davis, who emphasised self-reliance, and the traditional Jacobite laments for Mother Ireland that yearned for salvation from abroad: 'We wait the Young Deliverer of Kathleen-Ni-Houlihan'.

. J.J. O'Kelly was to recall clearly that 'Sinn Féin, Sinn Féin' was 'very much used' in the Gaelic League and at meetings of the Celtic Literary Society.[15] One contrarian in the *United Irishman* in 1900 was not yet convinced that Irish youth was up to it, writing paradoxically 'Self-help alone deserves exterior aid and Irish manhood is in such a rudimentary stage that it knows scarce how to help itself.'[16] In 1902 nationalists in Co. Meath launched a short-lived review entitled *Sinn Féin*, which trumpeted the words 'sinn féin, sinn féin, amháin' that the paper reported having seen on a banner in Dublin at the Gaelic League's 'Imtheachta an Oireachtais' cultural gathering.[17]

When the *United Irishman* closed in 1906, following a libel action by a priest, Griffith named its immediate weekly successor *Sinn Féin*. Through this he promoted Sinn Féin policies such as those urging the withdrawal of Irish MPs from Westminster and the appointment of Irish consuls abroad, the latter policy being endorsed by the first Dáil in 1919 when adopting its 'democratic programme'.

Aodh de Blacam in 1921 neatly described Sinn Féin as 'the impulse of the new generation':

> Initially, Sinn Féin was not a party: it was the amorphous propaganda of the Gaelicised young men and women. The principles of this journalistically-united *Intelligentsia* might be well summed up in Bishop Berkeley's famous query: '*Whether it would not be more pertinent to mend our state than to complain of it; and how far this may be in our power?*' [Italics in original][18]

The Green Hungarian Band

The great majority of voters, when the franchise was more restricted than it would be for the election of 1918, chose Irish MPs who sought only limited Irish self-government, or 'Home Rule', within the United Kingdom. Griffith was more ambitious. He recalled that Ireland had appeared to prosper in the decades prior to the Act of Union of 1800 when it and Britain each had a separate parliament under the same king and when that Irish parliament became assertive. The model of king, lords and a house of commons with greater powers than those envisaged under 'Home Rule' appealed to this Dubliner, who saw around him the continuing effects of an industrial and administrative decline and urban decay that had followed the abolition of the Irish parliament. Sovereignty in substance, rather than the form of a republic over a monarchy, was his priority. After all, had not Parnell been styled 'the uncrowned king of Ireland', not the president-in-waiting? Thus it was that Griffith's *Resurrection of Hungary* in 1904 earned him a reputation to this day of being a monarchist. For he proposed in it a relationship between Britain and Ireland based loosely on that between Austria and Hungary, two countries that shared one crown. His economic ideas in the pamphlet derived from those of the German economist Frederick List (1789–1846). He also admired the Hungarian statesman Ferenc Deák. His argument was strategic, using the Austro-Hungarian example like he did the example of Grattan's and Flood's pre-Union Irish parliament in order to galvanise political support as best he could in the circumstances of his time. He 'mythologised or simplified both for distinctly presentist purposes', as Kelly recently observed.[19]

A pragmatist, Griffith looked for ways to achieve his objective that stood a chance of success, and he thought that his particular idea of a dual monarchy might appeal to a broad cross-section of people. His model in the *Resurrection of Hungary* harked backed to the Irish parliament before the Act of Union, when that exclusively Protestant institution asserted independence from England, but now Catholics as well as Protestants would be allowed to participate. Griffith, the man who spearheaded resistance to royal visits to Ireland, had not suddenly become an enthusiastic royalist. He saw his proposal as a means to an end, and it excited great interest when published weekly in his *United Irishman* during the first six months of 1904 – and then as a best-selling booklet. As it happened, in citing with approval the efforts of the Hungarian Ferenc Deák, Griffith also endorsed a reformer who came to be fiercely attacked for his willingness to compromise.

Earlier, in his *United Irishman*, Griffith had complained 'The misrepresentation of Irish history for party purposes has been persistent and injurious to the nation.'[20] He himself has been accused of the same sin in respect to the *Resurrection of Hungary*. Canon Hannay described it as 'not so much history as tendentious romance, founded on a very prejudicial manipulation of the facts. But it was written in plain vigorous prose, like the prose of John Mitchel, the Young Irelander whom Griffith in many ways resembled.'[21] While historians and parliamentarians have been unconvinced by Griffith's references to the Austro-Hungarian system,[22] his version of it served his political purposes. It was necessary for Irish nationalists such as Griffith to construct alternative scenarios to counter British myths and ideology so as to win support for a policy of parliamentary abstention from Westminster. In that regard, Griffith's *Resurrection of Hungary* has been described as one of the seminal documents of modern Irish history.[23]

Given the title of Griffith's popular pamphlet and the fact that certain immigrant musicians who were well known in the United Kingdom at the time had earlier formed themselves into 'The Blue Hungarian Band', his journalistic competitor and political critic D.P. Moran ridiculed him and his followers as 'the Green Hungarian Band'.[24]

Sinn Féin Struggles

While Griffith himself admired the Hungarian statesman Ferenc Deák, James Joyce saw in Griffith something of the Italian syndicalist and socialist Arturo Labriola. Inclined towards socialism at the time, Joyce favoured the Sinn Féin policy in principle. His biographer Richard Ellmann writes that he 'had absorbed enough Marxist thought to argue that capitalism was a necessary transition to socialism'.[25] In late 1906 Joyce wrote from Rome to his brother:

You ask me what I should substitute for parliamentary agitation in Ireland. I think the Sinn Féin policy would be more effective. Of course I see that its success would be to substitute Irish for English capital but no one, I suppose, denies that capitalism is a stage of progress. The Irish proletariat has yet to be created. A feudal peasantry exists, scraping the soil but this would with a national revival or with a definite preponderance of England surely disappear. I quite agree with you that Griffith is afraid of the priests – and he has every reason to be so. But, possibly, they are also a little afraid of him too. After all, he is holding out some secular liberty to the people and the Church doesn't approve of that ... either Sinn Féin or Imperialism will conquer the present Ireland. If the Irish programme did not insist on the Irish language I suppose I could call myself a nationalist. As it is, I am content to recognise myself an exile ...[26]

In 1908 Sinn Féin contested and lost to the Irish Parliamentary Party a signal by-election in North Leitrim. For a decade more, the movement was to remain electorally marginal. In fact the first Sinn Féin party candidate was not elected to parliament until 1917. While Sinn Féin was in the doldrums politically Griffith appeared to become more conservative and at times illiberal, perhaps with a view to attracting more voters nationally. He now declined to publish further articles by the socialist Fred Ryan.[27] In 1911 he came late to the idea that a truly independent Ireland must be exclusively Irish-speaking.[28]

The struggle for self-reliance and sovereignty took different forms. An experimental Sinn Féin Co-operative Bank opened in 1908. This came to be housed in the party's new headquarters:

I recall that summer evening of lightning and volleying thunder in 1910 in which the Sinn Fein headquarters at no. 6 Harcourt Street were opened ... Alderman Tom Kelly telling how he had nailed the Tricolour to a flagstaff on the roof ... The O'Rahilly speaking in his proud Quixotic manner ... P.J. Ryan singing 'Pomeroy' ... and the man whom we craved to see, our hero, Griffith himself – who in modest, low, but confident tones reviewed a year's work. The least impressive figure? No. But the most self-effacing.[29]

James Joyce was inspired to present the Sinn Féin argument to Italian newspaper readers between 1907 and 1912, not least because he was irritated by representations of Ireland and the Irish in the British press. He told the Italians 'The new Fenians have regrouped in a party called "ourselves alone"', and he added that they had established a direct ferry link between Ireland and France and were trying to develop the industry of Ireland that had long suffered under British rule: 'From many points of view, this latest form of Fenianism is the most formidable.' At one point he appears to have been preparing these Italian pieces for publication in English in a book but nothing came of it.[30]

However, the rise of the Sinn Féin organisation between its foundation and its electoral triumph in 1918 was neither constant nor certain. The Gaelic League organiser Seumas Mac a Muilleora (Millar) of Laois gave a taste of public opinion in rural Ireland when he stated 'all wrongs were to be righted in the English Parliament by the members of the Parliamentary Party ... Here and there in the county there were a few who hearkened to Griffith, but they were classed as cranks and soreheads.'[31] Sinn Féin may have wanted a form of political independence more robust than Home Rule, but voters remained unconvinced. Cognisant of political realities, Griffith toyed with the idea of a parliamentary alliance and Sinn Féin decided not even to contest the general elections in 1910. At that time the passage of a Home Rule Act in London once more seemed politically possible. Griffith was caught between the rock of a conservative electorate and the hard place of criticism by those who felt that Sinn Féin was too moderate. Bulmer Hobson, never Griffith's greatest admirer, summed up the frustrated critical perspective when he wrote later that Griffith's views were often narrow and reactionary: 'he was dogmatic to a very unusual degree. He did not easily tolerate any opinion which differed from his own and this made it very difficult to work with him. In the Sinn Féin organisation his attitude caused many of the most active members to withdraw and work in other organisations.'[32] Yet Denis McCullough of the IRB Supreme council, who had sworn Hobson into the IRB, disagreed with his colleague, pointing out 'The opinion of Griffith expressed by Hobson is purely a personal one which I share in no way, though Griffith treated me coldly, largely because of his differences with Hobson, with whom I was always closely associated, particularly in the formation of the Dungannon Clubs, of which I was Secretary ...'[33]

When in 1910 Hobson and others founded the *Irish Freedom* paper it made Griffith's task of keeping his *Sinn Féin* afloat no easier, although in its first issue in November 1910 the new paper put a positive spin on developments by trumpeting that there were now 'two separatist journals to place our faith before the people'. Pat McCartan, another of the firebrands of that time, later entered a note of caution about exaggerating the impact of extremists on the national movement:

> McCullough & Hobson take themselves too seriously. They remind me of the Connolly children's attempt to make it appear Labour & James Connolly were responsible for the revolution of 1916 … Of course the three of us contributed something but nothing compared to Arthur Griffith by his paper and John Devoy in the *Gaelic American*. To my mind were it not for these men there would be no 1916. They prepared the minds of the young men who were the driving force before and afterwards. The readers of Griffith were also Gaelic Leaguers and GAA men who carried the hurleys where there was a parade.[34]

Sinn Féin was 'practically moribund' between 1910 and 1913.[35] Griffith, past his fortieth birthday and with a lifetime of effort and not much by way of personal or political reward to show for it, may have been thinking partly of his own destiny when he ended his preface to the 1913 edition of Mitchel's *Jail Journal* as follows: 'John Mitchel met the crisis of 1848 with a policy. Practical Posterity, from its easy chair, has pronounced the policy extravagant and impossible: even, in unctuous moments, reprehensible. Let the Censor stand in the Censured's place and declare what its wisdom would have counseled a people whose life was assailed … This was a man.'

Howth Gun-Running, 1914

Protestant unionists in the northern counties of Ireland formed the Ulster Volunteers in 1912, landing guns there with a view to fighting any attempt to force them to accept Home Rule for an island dominated by Catholic nationalists. Some Irish nationalists then founded the Irish Volunteers (Óglaigh na hÉireann) in 1913. Griffith joined them. On 26 July 1914 they took delivery of a consignment of guns at Howth in Co. Dublin (Plate 8). Griffith was present, demonstrating that he was not against the use of force where he thought it merited and wise. An eye-witness later recalled 'Arthur Griffith marching up from the yacht with his Mauser rifle on his shoulder ... It was interesting to see a man who had been more or less a pacifist march the whole way with his rifle on his shoulder.' Griffith wrote a substantial account of the episode, including a description of confrontations and scuffles between nervous soldiers from the King's Own Scottish Borderers and the marchers.[36] Later that day, people jeered and threw stones at some of the Scottish Borderers as they marched alongside the Liffey, at Bachelor's Walk. The soldiers opened fire, killing four civilians and wounding dozens. One of Griffith's colleagues later said 'I saw him at the funeral of the Bachelor's Walk victims carrying his Howth rifle.'[37] An old friend present when the Volunteers were drilling at Croydon Park in Dublin saw him there too 'with hat cocked on one side like a Boer commando, and rifle in hand ... His gaze, as always, is removed from the scene: the greatest intellect in Ireland is meditating the nation's interests, till at the word '"shun [attention]!" from Captain Thomas Markham, the heels click, and A.G. stands as taut and alert as the youngest soldier of them all'.[38] J.J. O'Kelly, a member of his Volunteer company, said that Griffith attended drill regularly.[39] Griffith wrote at the time 'If I were asked what impressed me most in the day [at Howth], I would answer: The profound truth of the saying that every Irishman is born a soldier ... We have got the guns, but better still, we have got back some of our respect and confidence in ourselves.'[40]

A staunch Irish Parliamentary Party activist of that time wrote of the decline of Sinn Féin in the years following its foundation, claiming that Griffith 'was essentially a city man and had little knowledge of rural Ireland': 'His policy had consequently not much support outside Dublin ... Its subsequent revival in another form is perhaps therefore all the more remarkable and proved the stubborn pertinacity of the man.'[41]

The IRB and Griffith

Griffith struggled to maintain Sinn Féin. Due to the outbreak of war in 1914 there would be no further general election until 1918. He played cat-and-mouse with the government as he kept his successive papers going. In 1921, De Blacam was to identify an intellectual factor intrinsic to Sinn Féin's survival, writing that the principal merit of its policy 'was that no political reverses could leave it, like a defeated political party, at a dead end; its constructive program gave its adherents something to work at through good fortune and ill, popularity or disdain'.[42] However, events were also about to shape its destiny.

A standard view of Griffith's relationship with the secretive Irish Republican Brotherhood (IRB) is that he joined it before 1900 but kept it at arm's length, and that he left it later while still being prepared to accept its financial assistance to run his papers so long as he could maintain their editorial independence. The very secrecy of the brotherhood makes it impossible to be sure what exactly was its relationship with him.[43] The fact that he was invited to a very important meeting called by some members of the IRB Supreme Council in 1914 suggests that he was seen as not far removed from them. With war declared, this meeting of a small number of people was called to consider how England's difficulty might be Ireland's opportunity. They met on 9 September 1914 in the Gaelic League's premises at 25 Rutland (now Parnell) Square, in a room that the future president of Ireland, Seán T. O'Kelly, used for his political work. O'Kelly, a founding member of the Irish Volunteers. had a month earlier supervised the landing of arms in Co. Wicklow. Present at the meeting were O'Kelly himself, Patrick Pearse, Tom Clarke, Seán Mac Diarmada, Joseph Plunkett, Thomas MacDonagh, John MacBride, Arthur Griffith, the labour activists William O'Brien and James Connolly, and possibly Éamonn Ceannt and Seán Tobin. Most of these men were to sign the 1916 proclamation and to be executed as leaders of the Rising, but O'Kelly survived and later gave an account of the long meeting to the Bureau of Military History. He said that Tom Clarke and Seán Mac Diarmada had convened it 'to try to organise the progressive – or as others might call them, the extreme Nationalist – element to work together to promote certain activities they had in mind towards achieving independence while the war continued':

> Everyone in turn gave his views, and as I remember, all agreed that a joint effort by all the progressive Nationalist organisations that favoured independence should be made before the end of the war to do everything possible to secure independence. All present fully accepted this policy. All the I.R.B. people present were most anxious to hear what Arthur Griffith would say, and Griffith expressed full

agreement with the policy of getting all the progressive Nationalist forces to work together to win complete independence before the end of the war.[44]

In the *Irish Press* on 8 July 1961 O'Kelly added 'In a private chat Clarke and MacDermott had with Griffith before we left the room at the end of the meeting, Griffith asked that he should be kept informed of all important decisions before any serious action would be taken. MacDermott, with Clarke assenting, promised Griffith he would keep him informed.' Elsewhere, O'Kelly recalled that, during the chat, Clarke told Griffith that the IRB would make funds available for a new paper. This was to be *Nationality*, the fifth title that Griffith edited. O'Kelly noted that Griffith agreed, subject to his being briefed about all important decisions between then and any future rising: 'Clarke and MacDermott promised to keep Griffith fully informed. I was then invited to become manager of the new paper.' Griffith was not in fact kept fully informed of plans for the Rising in 1916 and 'was quite sore and vexed about being kept in the dark' about the final decision to proceed.[45]

William O'Brien noted that one outcome of the meeting in September 1914 that both he and Griffith attended was the formation of a short-lived but 'useful' Irish Neutrality League of which Connolly was president and Griffith and O'Brien members of the committee.[46] Seán T. O'Kelly, who was a key figure in the IRB and who would be a vital witness after so many of those at that meeting were executed, was long accustomed to meeting Griffith for a midday meal. He wrote soon after the meeting

I think I had lunch most days of the week with Seán MacDermott and Arthur Griffith. We would lunch in the restaurant of Mrs Wyse Power in Henry Street and sometimes in the Red Bank Restaurant, D'Olier Street, which was just across the street from MacDermott's office then situated at 12 D'Olier Street. Every day we would have problems of one kind or another relating to the Volunteers or the newspapers to discuss.[47]

It was agreed also at the meeting attended by Griffith and IRB leaders in 1914 that arms would be accepted from Germany provided that this connection itself did not constitute a threat to Irish independence. Preparations were set back when arms from Germany failed to reach the Volunteers, this being the latest in a long line of disappointed hopes for salvation from overseas. In 1916 Roger Casement was arrested on Good Friday in Kerry in connection with that attempt. The next day O'Kelly found Griffith in a barber's shop in Dublin. It was clear by now that trouble was brewing:

> Griffith made a bitter complaint to me that he had been promised at the time that the agreement was come to in September, 1914, as to working together, by Clarke and MacDermott that he would be kept fully informed of what they were doing and what steps they were taking to carry out the agreement that had been arrived at. He said that there were many things happening these times – things of importance – not one of which he had been consulted about or informed of. He said that he felt very hurt that Clarke and MacDermott had not taken him, according to their promise, into their confidence.[48]

Griffith was not opposed to defensive action, should the British try to disarm the Volunteers or to force Irishmen into the army by means of conscription. However, he was by no means the only one concerned about the complications of offensive action. Attempts by Eoin MacNeill, leader of the Volunteers, and others to stop a rebellion proceeding at that point were only partly successful. Some more militant Volunteers and members of James Connolly's Irish Citizen Army went ahead anyway. Fighting broke out in Dublin.

The Easter Rising, 1916

That Easter weekend Griffith's wife was away in Cork, and he at home in Clontarf with their two children when rebels seized key buildings. It was Monday 24 April 1916. She later wrote:

> He did not take any part in the Rising as he was against all that and Seán McDermott had promised him that a Rising would never be started without his – Arthur's – knowledge … Before Seán

MacDermott was executed he sent a message to Arthur by someone who was in the prison, asking him to forgive him for not having kept his promise to inform him about the Rising, but he and others thought it would be better not – so that Arthur might live on after themselves to keep the National Movement alive. My husband was a member of the I.R.B. and of the Volunteers and had been present at the Howth gun-running with his Unit.[49]

Michael Noyk, Griffith's friend and solicitor, was present at a dinner party given by Liam O'Brien (Ó Briain) when the latter was appointed a professor in Galway in 1917. Noyk recalled Griffith being called on to address the dinner party:

During the course of his speech Griffith stated that the reason he was not out in 1916 was that he was asked to remain out by the leaders on the grounds that he was more useful outside by carrying on propaganda through his papers and otherwise. I referred to Liam O'Brien for confirmation of my recollection and he stated in a letter to me as follows:

'To the best of my recollection what you say is true and you would be safe in giving it to the Bureau [of Military History]. He said the same to me afterwards and I have published it. He said he had sent in a message to the G.P.O. telling them what he thought of them, for leaving him in the dark, (contrary to promise), but that he would join in. He said he got a message back from them saying they wanted his pen and brain to survive the fight for their memory – and not to join in. The only confirmation I ever got of that was from Gearóid O'Sullivan (Adjutant General to the I.R.A. Pre-Truce). He (Gearóid) said he remembered Seán MacDermott saying: "We have got a very nice letter from Griffith". You see they didn't mind his "blowing them up"; they knew they deserved it, in a way, but they did appreciate his saying he would join in.'[50]

Bulmer Hobson wrote that Griffith made it clear at Easter 1916 that he regarded the insurrection as a potential calamity, just as Eoin MacNeill did. Hobson admitted 'At that moment there were very few people in Ireland who would not have agreed with him.'[51] Nevertheless, during that week of revolt Griffith cycled by a circuitous route to a meeting with MacNeill and, according to an account by Liam O'Brien published in 1924 and not then contradicted, O'Neill and Griffith agreed that Griffith should issue a call to the country to rise and relieve Dublin. Griffith was to attach their two names to the call, and circulate it if he could. But the plan was overtaken by the collapse of the rebellion that week.[52]

Liam O'Brien himself gave a compelling statement to the Bureau of Military History in which he indicated that he spoke to Griffith a number of times about the Easter Rising and his account of what Griffith said confirms the versions of Griffith's wife and Griffith's solicitor above. He adds the detail that some of Griffith's neighbours were immediately afraid to have anything to do with him: 'It is well-known that the "rebels" were universally called the "Sinn Féiners" from the very beginning of the Rising and wasn't he the Sinn Féiner par excellence?'[53] In fact it was from within the IRB and the Volunteers, rather than from within Sinn Féin, that the actual impetus for the rebellion of 1916 came. Yet the British and others immediately attributed it to Sinn Féin, thus reflecting Griffith's status as a leading advocate of the nationalist cause, and perhaps intending to discredit the revolt in the eyes of more moderate nationalists. The Irish Times copper-fastened the link when, in 1917, it published its Sinn Féin Rebellion Handbook: Easter 1916. Some of the Volunteers who did not like Griffith or Sinn Féin were displeased.

The arrest and speedy execution of rebel leaders, including a wounded James Connolly who was strapped to a chair, was politically inept on the part of the British. Here now was a blood sacrifice, rather than simply a bloody revolt, and in 1916 Yeats wrote, wide-eyed, 'A terrible beauty is born'. An acquaintance of Pearse and MacDonagh remarked in 1917 'What a nightmare is the reality of life, thrusting itself into the country of a golden dream.'[54] Reflecting on 'The Man and The Echo', a poem in which Yeats later expressed self-doubts about the impact of his earlier words, Seamus Heaney wrote 'there is no perfect fit between the project of civilization represented by thought and the facts of violence and death.'[55] The United Kingdom government used violence to stop German expansion, while rebels in Ireland used it to resist British rule.

By 4 May 1916 British forces had arrested Griffith. He reportedly said later that when he learnt of the execution of his acquaintances and friends who had led the Rising, 'Something of the primitive man awoke in me. I clenched my fists with rage and longed for vengeance. I had not believed they would be stupid enough to do it. Had I foreseen that, perhaps my views on the whole matter might be different.'[56] Notwithstanding the danger to himself, he never disassociated himself from the rebels once they took up arms.

It was possible that the British would shoot Griffith but, in the end, he and many more arrested nationalists were interned in England until 23 December that same year. There survives a small notebook containing verses which prisoners composed while in Reading Gaol along with Griffith.[57] The entries of Terence MacSwiney and Ernest Blythe could scarcely be more different. MacSwiney, who was to die on hunger strike in another British prison in 1920, concluded

The poet is born from birth
Just at a touch he'll forget the earth
And wrap himself in a robe of dreams.

Blythe, a future minister for finance, was not inclined towards romance:

To Reading Gaol I have been sent
And must endure the punishment
That every bloke is writing rhyme
And I must praise it every time.

The two entries are divided only by a quotation from John Mitchel: 'No country can be conquered whose sons love her better than their lives.' MacSwiney seems to have adopted the quotation as something of a personal motto because he used it when signing his autograph before his release from Reading Gaol. The socialist Cathal O'Shannon signed out with a less reverential 'Home to the flappers [flighty young women]!'[58]

In November 1916 in Reading Gaol Griffith heard the explosion of bombs dropped from German Zeppelins onto London. His mind turned to the current British threat to introduce conscription in Ireland and he wrote to his artist friend Lily Williams that 'England can never enforce conscription if Ireland fights, and Ireland must fight conscription with tongues, pens, sticks, stones, pitchforks, guns and all the resources of civilization.'[59] This was a declaration that again demonstrated that he was not opposed to the use of physical force when he thought that it was justified. It was also the identification of an issue that was to be crucial in delivering to the Sinn Féin movement its stunning victory in the general election of 1918.

When Francis Hackett put the finishing touches to his study of Irish nationalism, for publication later in 1918, it was still not evident that the movement that Griffith had founded was about to sweep away the Irish Parliamentary Party. Hackett lamented 'In the House of Commons Parnell had what Griffith lacked – a contact with the enemy. Where Parnell could injure, Griffith could only fulminate … He preferred to flash lightening from his heights.'[60]

James Joyce in exile was to be implicated in Sinn Féin's remarkable resurgence, for by 1920 one of the various rumours circulating about him was that he was its emissary abroad, even its 'spy'.[61]

Irish and Jewish

When Arthur Griffith declared in 1915 in his *Nationality* paper, 'We do not know of one Nationalist Irishman ... who holds the creed that an Irish Jew should be ineligible for any office he was competent to fill in an Irish government,' the then president of Sinn Féin sent a signal.[1] The previous year, as seen above, he had attended a private meeting organised by the IRB, at which all or nearly all of the future signatories of the proclamation of the Irish Republic were also present and which agreed to use the opportunity of the First World War to take action to oust British forces from Ireland. In December 1915 he made it clear then that Jews would be welcome in an independent state. Griffith's inclusive statement may be seen in a context in which even five years later the Jewish Edwin Samuel Montagu MP, the United Kingdom's secretary of state for India, would be condemned as 'unEnglish' by a fellow member of the House of Commons. That accusation, by the Irish Unionist leader Edward Carson MP, was greeted by cheers from the backbenches and has been seen as standard anti-Semitic innuendo.[2]

The issue of his paper in which Griffith affirmed a place for Jews in a future Irish government.

That there were certain positive statements about Jews in Griffith's papers is seldom if ever mentioned when other statements, especially those by F.H. O'Donnell and Oliver St John Gogarty, are cited against him. He is often contrasted unfavourably with Michael Davitt, although Davitt himself explicitly defended forms of anti-Semitism. Jim Larkin, as well as some other socialists, also evinced anti-Semitic sentiments. Anti-Semitism was rife in the Catholic Church. The national newspapers carried Jewish 'jokes' and advertisements boasted that no Jews were involved in particular businesses.

Griffith's early prejudices were on parade not least because he was responsible for producing so many pages in print. However, the great bulk of any anti-Semitic commentary in his *United Irishman* appeared in late 1899 during the Boer War. At that time many English leftists or liberals also lamented the perceived influence of Jewish capitalists and newspaper owners. Apart from that period, anti-Semitic references are rare and progressively absent from his pages. Laffan, in the *Dictionary of Irish Biography*, has described Griffith's offensive attitudes as the 'habits or prejudices of his youth' and added 'with occasional lapses, he outgrew them'.[3]

'Reptiles Breathe Not'

The foremost Irish nationalist leader Daniel O'Connell MP became known widely in Ireland as 'The Liberator' because of his successful campaign for Catholic emancipation from legislative discrimination. During September 1829 he also expressed support for Jews who were campaigning for civil liberties within the United Kingdom of Great Britain and Ireland. He told the English Jewish leader Isaac Goldsmid 'Ireland has claims on your ancient race as it is the only Christian community that I know of unsullied by any one act of persecution of the Jews ...'[4] Despite that fact, in 1835, O'Connell clashed publicly with Benjamin Disraeli, politician and Jewish convert to Anglicanism, whom he believed to have acted treacherously. Assuring his audience in Conciliation Hall that he knew very many fine Jews, O'Connell noted ambivalently that there were also 'miscreants' among Jews and suggested that Disraeli was descended from the impenitent thief who died alongside Jesus. Disraeli then wrote to O'Connell: 'I admire your scurrilous allusions to my origins. It is quite clear that the "hereditary bondsman" has already forgotten the clank of his fetter. I know the tactics of your church; it clamours for toleration, and it labours for supremacy. I see that you are quite prepared to persecute.'[5] Nor was the path of Irish public life always smooth for a Jew, even one married to a Christian. When in 1881 Albert Altman as chairman of a meeting disagreed with a fellow member of the Irish Home Manufacture Association, the latter reportedly withdrew complaining about 'a lot of Jewish curs and pups (Great confusion and cries of "Shame")'. Nevertheless, the meeting later passed a vote of thanks to Altman.[6] In 1888 *The Times* of London reported that Jews were being persecuted by nationalists in Cork, although the mayor of Cork, John O'Brien, denied this.[7] However, consecrating a new synagogue in Dublin in 1892, Chief Rabbi Hermann Adler of the United Kingdom (of which all Ireland was then part) expressly recalled O'Connell's words of 1829 (above) and told Jewish immigrants from recent 'tyrannous persecutions' in eastern Europe who were present:

> You have come here from a country like unto Egypt of old to a land which offers you hospitable shelter. It is said that Ireland is the only country in the world which cannot be charged with persecuting the Jews. 'Alas, poor Erin [Ireland]!' an eloquent writer says, 'thou art thyself an eternal badge of sufferance, the blood of my people rests not on thy head. Is it not true that reptiles breathe not in thy Emerald Isle?'[8]

The 'eloquent writer' whom Adler quoted was Hertz Ben Pinchas, one of two winners of an essay competition of which Adler's father had been one of three judges.[9]

Thomas Moore, hailed as the 'Irish national poet', penned verses addressing the 'sad one of Sion' following his 'perusal of a treatise by Mr Hamilton, professing to prove that the Irish were originally Jews'.[10] But an Irish-American paper in Boston mocked any such ahistorical theory that implied O'Connell and Disraeli might 'turn out to be members of the one race'.[11]

In 1893 Michael Davitt wrote to Con Crowley, a nationalist and labour activist in Co. Cork, to say that an old and staunch supporter of the Irish cause 'who belongs to the Hebrew race' had brought to Davitt's attention a speech delivered by Crowley recently in which Crowley was reported as having said 'The Jews ought to be kept out of Ireland.' Davitt continued:

> there is a section of working men in London and other places who are allowing themselves to be deluded by the Tory protectionists into the belief that low wages and trade depression in the East End of London and in some other densely crowded labour centres are traceable for cause to the influx of 'foreign workmen, mainly Jews'. No intelligent artisan … can allow himself to be gulled by the Jew-baiting tactics of the 'fair traders' and protectionists.[12]

Crowley claimed that there had been a misunderstanding and that a jest he made at the meeting was misreported. Yet Fr Thomas Finlay, the prominent Jesuit intellectual, regretted that Crowley 'gave up his case so readily'. Finlay penned three long articles arguing for the exclusion of an 'obnoxious' large Jewish influx to Ireland, fearing (as he indicated) that Jewish moneylenders had designs on Irish farms and warning of the possible rise of an anti-Semitic party as existed in Germany in response to any such conspiracy.[13] Finlay's influence on Catholic thought in Ireland was significant, and the calmly considered tone of these three closely argued articles made their rationalisation of prejudice all the more insidious. In purporting to distinguish for the purposes of exclusion between good Jews and bad Jews, as it were, he engaged in a kind of discursive strategy that was not unique to Ireland and that has been closely analysed in recent years by Bryan Cheyette in particular.[14]

Immigration

From late in the nineteenth century, an influx of Jewish immigrants from eastern Europe to Britain and Ireland ensured that romantic notions of commonality were tempered by actual social strains. The immigrants in Ireland joined a very small but established Jewish community that had tended to support the status quo of a united kingdom of Britain and Ireland rather than Irish nationalism. The growth of Ireland's Jewish population was in marked contrast to a steady and continuing decline in the number of native people in Ireland from the Great Famine of the 1840s onwards. Census returns indicate a rise in the number of Jews on the whole island of Ireland from 285 in 1871 to 5,148 in 1911. During the same period, the population of what is now the Republic of Ireland declined by 913,500. Some Jewish newcomers found ways to make their living that caused resentment, especially in respect to moneylending, deferred payment or hire-purchase sales by pedlars, the importation or production of cheap wares in competition with Irish businesses and certain trades. Strains were reflected in the press, and in a 'bifurcation' of Jews in Ireland, as abroad, into an historical, almost mythological people of exodus, and a modern European body.[15]

The *Cork Examiner* of 16 March 1888 reported that the local trades' council fought to prevent two Jewish employers hiring 'German Jews at half the current wages of the city'. One council member accused Jews of crucifying gypsies and another referred to Jews as 'swindlers'. During the 1890s and later, some people wishing to borrow money placed small advertisements in leading Irish newspapers that specified that 'no Jew' would be lending it. A clothing retailer who offered hire-purchase terms made it clear that he was 'no Jew man'.[16]

Close connections between the Irish Catholic Church and Catholics in France also ran the risk of infecting Irish discourses with anti-Semitic perspectives that were rampant there.[17] In an essay James Joyce wrote in 1899 about an Irish exhibition of a painting of Pilate presenting Jesus to a hostile crowd, 'Ecce Homo', by the Hungarian painter Mihály Munkácsy, the young Joyce referred stereotypically to Jews' 'small beady eyes' and 'the bitter unwisdom of their race'.[18] Prejudice of various kinds was widespread. Thus, job notices commonly specified that a cook, gardener, farm hand or shop assistant must be Protestant. And while the *Belfast Telegraph* might run a series of articles celebrating the 'singularly clean' record of Ireland in respect to Jews ('We left them whatever molars they were possessed of ... We never burned them ... We never massacred them'), not all Protestant Unionist councillors in that city were inclined to treat even a prominent Jewish colleague as they would one of their own.[19] Advertisements in Dublin newspapers and signs in shops sometimes boasted that no Jews were involved in a business.[20] James Duffy & Co., a well-known firm of Catholic publishers, anxiously let it be known in *The Freeman's Journal* of 11 November 1911 that, contrary to rumour, 'no Jew has any financial interest direct or indirect, in the firm, or is in any way connected with it'. *The Irish Times* published a few Jewish 'jokes' as fillers, such as an incitement to violence on 6 July 1901, headed 'Why the Jew Ran'. A certain 'Hebrew pedlar' enters a tenement house and knocks on a door. He is told to enter:

> 'Oh, it's you, is it?' exclaimed the occupant of the room, a broad-shouldered labourer. 'Eh, did anybody see you coming in?' 'No, no', replied the pedlar. 'Then, none will see you go out. Johnnie, fetch me the razor.' But the Jew did not wait to see matters out.

The reality for a Jew actually prevented by someone wielding a razor from collecting a debt or instalment due was no joke. He was, as a Dubliner later recalled, cheated out of his money.[21] On 29 October 1910 another *Irish Times* filler was the stereotypical 'Jew's Nature', on the predictable theme of penny-pinching.

D.P. Moran, influential editor of *The Leader* and champion of 'Irish-Ireland' self-sufficiency, advised his readers how they might avoid the ascendancy of Jews in the financial affairs of Ireland – 'a frequent theme in some nationalist and Labourite newspapers' according to Glandon in her study of the nationalist press then. Yet Moran claimed 'We have no sympathy with any agitation against the Jews as Jews.' Like Fr Finlay, he feared their supposed designs on Irish farms. Moran's opinions on Jews were perhaps no more hostile than his frequent denunciations of Protestants in Ireland, the latter being 'sourfaces' who were sectarian 'bigots' as he saw it, but this fact did not vitiate his anti-Semitism.[22]

F.H. O'Donnell

Griffith edited and produced advanced nationalist newspapers for almost twenty years, the first being his *United Irishman*. At the outset its pages contained no derogatory references to Jews. The Boer War changed that, partly by way of Griffith's relationship with Maud Gonne. Her sometime lover in France, Lucien Millevoye, was a prominent anti-Semitic member of the French parliament. He was very hostile to Alfred Dreyfus, a Jew whose trial for treason was highly controversial both within and beyond France.[23] Griffith's paper was amongst Irish nationalist titles that came to express views concerning the Dreyfus affair that were unkind to Jews in general, although his very first observation on the affair was quite open-minded.[24] Moreover, the paper was also supported by the Fenian organiser Mark Ryan 'upon whom the *United Irishman* became financially dependent'.[25] An associate of Ryan in London, Frank Hugh O'Donnell, began to write for it four months after its first appearance. When he wrote as 'The Foreign Secretary' that column included some virulent anti-Semitism. O'Donnell and Griffith soon fell out, ostensibly in part because the latter as editor decided that 'decency and honour' constrained him to reject an article in which O'Donnell had compared the conciliatory nationalist leader and newspaper owner William O'Brien to Judas, who betrayed Jesus. O'Brien's wife, as it happened, was the daughter of a Russian Jewish banker. The 'Foreign Secretary' byline appeared for the last time on 31 March 1900, but even before then the incidence of anti-Semitism in the paper had declined steeply and it was rare thereafter.[26] O'Donnell subsequently pursued his anti-Semitic arguments in England, a fact that has gone quite unnoticed until recently.[27] When anti-Semitic sentiment in the *United Irishman* of the period is said to be 'summarised' by the statement 'we know that all Jews are pretty sure to be traitors, if they get a chance', it might be pointed out that it was not Griffith himself but a German officer who reportedly made the remark, as quoted by the 'Foreign Secretary'.[28]

Michael Davitt

British cultural elites and liberals during the nineteenth century welcomed the assimilation of Jews on both intellectual and material grounds, albeit ambivalently. Thus, where there was an Irish sense of affinity with persecuted Jews, Matthew Arnold for example claimed an affinity between the English and Jews. This was based, seemingly, 'in some special sort' on 'the genius and history' of both.[29] Leftist radicals in England such as J.A. Hobson, on the other hand and on grounds that can seem quite similar to those articulated by Griffith, opposed what they saw as the malign international power of Jewish capitalists acting in concert.[30] Griffith believed that Britain supported Dreyfus largely in order to embarrass France, and Britain fought against the Boers whom he backed in the war of 1899–1902. He resented the propagandist content of the British press, which he and other advanced nationalists and socialists believed was dominated conspiratorially by Jewish proprietors with self-serving agendas related to universalising commercialism.

Critics have roundly and understandably condemned the articles, anti-Semitic in tone or content, that Griffith published during the earlier part of his editorial career but most particularly in late 1899.[31] Yet he was informed about and supported Zionism in its own right (and not, as some did, simply as a mechanism to rid Europe of Jews). He became a close personal friend of more than one prominent Jewish member of the nationalist movement. The Irish Jewish historian Louis Hyman considered Griffith's earlier anti-Semitism to have 'stemmed from inherent xenophobia rather than from principle', and it should be seen within the context of his life's work, as Maye sees it.[32] He is sometimes compared unfavourably to Michael Davitt, who publicly spoke up to defend Jews in Ireland, as seen above. Davitt was not only the leader of a great Irish land reform movement but also a working journalist. He wrote about the treatment of Jews in the Russian empire for William Randolph Hearst's *New York American* and for Ireland's *Freeman's Journal*. Some of his writings on the pogrom in Kishinev (today Chişinău, capital of Moldova), published in the United States as a book in 1903, are said to have made him 'a folk hero among Jews'.[33] Yet, remarkably, in his preface to that book, Davitt delivered an apologia for anti-Semitism when it stands, as he put it, 'in fair political combat, in opposition to the foes of nationality, or against the engineers of a sordid war in South Africa, or as the assailant of the economic evils of unscrupulous capitalism anywhere'. In such cases, he added 'I am resolutely in line with its spirit and programme.' He also condemned the role of forty 'Anglicized German Jews' in respect to the Boer conflict and quoted approvingly in that context an English newspaper report about

'Jew boys' who were 'sharpers and swindlers' and who 'had the press in their hands'.[34] Like some other Irish journalists, such as Griffith, he was unsympathetic to Alfred Dreyfus, but his views were amplified by receiving international attention. While reporting social disturbances in Russia he also expressed anti-Semitic sentiments. I have written elsewhere of his contradictions, and of the rivalry between Davitt and Griffith and their support for Zionism.[35]

The Limerick Boycott

Griffith, too, would later publish reports critical of pogroms in eastern Europe, but not in 1904. On 23 April of that year, his *United Irishman* carried a vituperative article during a boycott of Jews in Limerick, and this frequently quoted article has done his reputation damage. A Catholic priest was whipping up hostility in that city.[36] Absent a by-line (as so many newspaper articles then were), it is the piece that is most often cited against Griffith, not least because the editor himself may well have written and not just published it. In it the writer describes nine out of ten Jews as 'usurers and parasites of industry'. He graciously exempted from these categories 'the Zionist minority of the Jews'. Thus, he tolerated Jews who were nationalists, just as he had contempt for Irish Catholics or Protestants who were not. He cited in support of his argument a Protestant member of the bench:

> Attack a Jew – other than a Zionist Jew – and all Jewry comes to his assistance ... Thus, when three years ago, the Recorder of Dublin, Sir Frederick Falkiner, denounced in strong terms the extortion which the Jews of Dublin practiced on the poor, Jewry combined and was powerful enough to rig the whole daily Press against him, and to influence official quarters to force the Recorder to withdraw.

It is evident from this quotation that some newspapers regarded expressions of hostility towards Jews as unacceptable. The Irish *Evening Telegraph* and *Evening Herald* had recently discontinued an advertisement for a company of tailors that included the words 'No connection with Jews'.[37]

In contrast to Griffith's efforts to justify the Limerick boycott, the leader of the Irish Parliamentary Party, John Redmond, wrote that he had 'no sympathy ... with the attacks upon the Hebrew Community in Limerick and elsewhere'.[38] Some of Griffith's associates were uneasy about his views and he printed in his own *United Irishman* harsh criticism of what he had published there – criticism by his socialist friend Fred Ryan ('Fraidrine' in Joyce's *Ulysses*). Ryan described certain statements in the *United Irishman* as 'anti-Semitic ravings', and in a journal that Ryan co-edited also castigated D.P. Moran and Catholics who supported 'anti-Jewish' boycotts.[39] Griffith insisted that his attitude towards the Limerick boycott was posited only on the unacceptable behaviour of particular Jewish moneylenders, not on hostility to Jews as such. He protested that 'if Jews – as Jews – were boycotted, it would be outrageously unjust', and wrote 'we do not object to the Jew seeking an honest livelihood in Ireland'. He saw no reason for 'silence in the face of injustice or attack' and claimed 'the Jew in Limerick has not been boycotted as a Jew, but because he is a usurer. And we deny that we offend against ethics by most heartily advocating the boycott of usurers, whether they be Jew, Pagan or Christian.'[40]

Griffith gave credit to a Jew, when that Jew's policies were aligned with some of his own, as Albert Altman discovered. Altman was brought to Ireland as a child in 1854. As a successful businessman he stood for election to Dublin Corporation in 1903. He and the socialist James Connolly – the latter already endorsed by the East London Jewish Branch of the Socialist Federation – were two of only eight candidates whom Griffith recommended to voters.[41]

Gogarty and Joyce

As mentioned earler, Griffith's sharp tongue led to a successful defamation action by a Catholic priest that in 1906 put his *United Irishman* out of business. It was succeeded by his *Sinn Féin*, which included a viciously anti-Semitic article penned by James Joyce's old acquaintance Oliver St John Gogarty ('Buck Mulligan' in *Ulysses*). In a short series entitled 'Ugly England', Gogarty, a medical doctor, claimed that pure English blood had been contaminated by that of Jews. He foreshadowed the

Holocaust by trumpeting 'the struggle is approaching … Germany is healthy and must expand' while 'Israel is rotten within and … must die … Already her grave is open'. Joyce checked his anger at Griffith for publishing 'the old pap of racial hatred', for he understood that Griffith was under financial pressure and believed that what the editor was trying to achieve nationally 'justifies the existence of his paper'.[42] He distinguished between Griffith as editor and those who wrote for him, thus setting a precedent that is not always followed by others. To state, for example, that Griffith 'wrote' certain pieces identifying 'the Three Evil Influences' of the nineteenth century as the pirate, the freemason and the Jew is a mere guess. F.H. O'Donnell almost certainly penned that nasty anti-Semitic assertion.[43] A series 'Ireland at Auction' did not run for six months as a kind of anti-Semitic campaign, as has been suggested, but was in fact a much shorter serialisation of what was an older political satire by Martin Mahony; and the only Jew to whom it refers was Daniel O'Connell's sometime foe Disraeli, who as a politician personified Britain's damaging laissez-faire attitude towards Ireland.[44]

In 1908 the first issue of the Sinn Féin *Yearbook* included an advertisement for a firm of tailors that boasted 'no Jews employed' there. This was exceptional for the *Yearbook*, and similar notices are found in contemporary publications that included the Gaelic League's *Claidheamh Soluis*.[45]

Joyce reminds us that it was not just Catholics or nationalists who were anti-Semitic. In *Ulysses* 'Mr Deasy', a Tory and an Orangeman, reveals a deep and abiding anti-Semitism. And it was not Irish nationalists who secured the passing of the United Kingdom Aliens Act 1905 and further laws that restricted immigration to Britain before 1922. Indeed, the fact that Ireland had a small number of Jewish inhabitants, especially until the twentieth century, meant that anti-Semitic incidents were unlikely to occur widely.[46] Joyce recognised this, lampooning in *Ulysses* O'Connell's famous declaration that Ireland had the honour of being the only country which never persecuted the Jews. 'Do you know why?' asks Deasy. 'Because she never let them in … She never let them in, he cried again through his laughter as he stamped on gaitered feet over the gravel of the path. That's why. On his wise shoulders through the checkerwork of leaves the sun flung spangles, dancing coins.'

The Pedlar

William Bulfin, a prominent Sinn Féin supporter whom Griffith once thought might become its president one day, wrote a long and widely read account of a cycling tour in Ireland which included a brief description of one Jewish trader whom he encountered. It echoes the English novelist Anthony Trollope's prejudicial descriptions of Jews, such as that of Joseph Emilius in *The Eustace Diamonds,* as 'nasty, greasy, lying, squinting' and 'oily'. Bulfin's account appeared under the pseudonym 'Che Buono' as a serial in *Sinn Féin* in 1906, and subsequently as a best-selling and often reprinted book published in Ireland and the United States. Almost a decade earlier in the Irish-Argentinian paper that he edited, Bulfin had written 'The Jews with their Masonic literature and journalism prostituted France.' Anti-Semitism appears to bubble to the surface just once in the course of his long account of cycling in Ireland – when he refers sarcastically to Ireland's 'grateful Sheenies' (then a slang term used internationally for Jews and found in *Ulysses*). Bulfin is describing in stereotypical detail a Jewish pedlar ('outland merchant') seen on a warm day in the Irish countryside 'mopping the perspiration from his forehead with a big red handkerchief'.[47]

The appearance of Jews was no doubt fascinating, if threatening, to the overwhelmingly Catholic and Protestant native population of Ireland that had seen few immigrants. Their sweat rendered the grasping outsiders 'oily' or greasy rather than simply industrious. In 1939, the playwright and former member of the IRB, Sean O'Casey, recalled from his youth half a century earlier the cruel persecution of a Jewish itinerant glazier by Dublin boys. The boys tricked him into replacing a window for no payment and then drove him away throwing stones, one of which drew blood. The glazier's 'deep black eyes stared out from a white fat face … The sweat was trickling down his cheeks, and glistening patches showed where it had soaked through his clothes and the inner parts of his thighs'.[48] Other stories of the ridiculing and cheating of Jewish pedlars and moneylenders in Ireland, and of the 'teasing' of Jews by Dublin's 'mischief-loving corner-boy', have also been recorded.[49]

McSheeneys and the *Lepracaun*

The *Lepracaun* was a worldly and satirical Irish magazine, and Joyce had copies of it sent to him in Italy. It sometimes let fly at Jews with swingeing cartoons and text. Thus in 1906 it represented a Jewish moneylender as a spider trapping people in its web, and identified the 'principal characteristic' of this spider as the 'chosen boko [nose]' able to smell cash at great distances. The author referred to Jewish names being 'almost completely Hibernianised into McSheeney, of Ballystibem or O'Barron, of Mosestown', and wrote that this 'animal is daily increasing in numbers and energy with such rapidity that if the indigenous inhabitants of this country have the slightest regard for their future they will place in the forefront of their educational programme neither Irish not English, but that which converts everything into gold ... the melodious, ear-splitting, euphonious, blood-curdling Yiddish'.[50]

More common in Dublin than the slang term 'sheeney' has been 'Jewman', which a writer in the *Jewish Chronicle* of 1906 recalled frequently seeing on newspaper placards and hearing dropped informally but often 'from the lips of highly placed personages and officials' in Ireland. The lecturer, essayist and critic Abraham 'Con' Leventhal, knew from his experience as a child that the term Jewman might well be a contemptuous jibe, although he thought that it 'was not, in the first instance, pejorative' and was descriptive like 'Frenchman' or 'Englishman'. A popular Irish ballad 'The Waxies' Dargle' refers to 'the Jewman moneylender'. Some tenement dwellers recalled Jewish lenders more fondly than they did native loan-sharks.[51]

On 13 May 1907, the *Lepracaun*'s theme was preferential treatment for Jews. A cartoon shows the sea parting and drowning Irish manufacturers while persons with stereotypical Jewish features enter an industrial promised land in Ireland. Jews were suspected of raising finance and getting ahead in Ireland in ways that many Catholics and nationalists could not. Irish banking and other support services were still dominated by the Protestant unionist minority while established, wealthier Jews were generally unionist and not averse to joining Protestants in the Masonic Order, forbidden to Catholics.[52]

The Lepracaun, 1906, worldly but anti-Semitic.

The urbane *Lepracaun* was packed with advertisements placed by respectable companies willing to promote themselves alongside such content. Its anti-Semitic jibes did not deter even Hoseas Weiner, an immigrant Jewish furniture dealer, from advertising in its pages. The fictional Leopold Bloom's tailor, George Mesias, was based on a real Jew of that name who lodged with Weiner.[53] Another Dublin Jew responded to hostile depictions of Jewish moneylenders by writing a novel in which undesirable practices by moneylenders were castigated. A remarkable feature of his book was the drawing on its cover, which as Jewish stereotypes go, was a piece of work of which any anti-Semite might be proud. It depicted a Shylock-like figure, head and shoulders set off by flung spangles in the form of big dancing coins. 'In some shops in this enlightened capital of Ireland, its author wrote in 1908, 'we see cards bearing the words: "No connection with Jews."'[54]

Griffith's Evolution

Griffith's opinions of Jews evolved. This was perhaps due partly to his association with individual Jews who supported Irish nationalism and, in particular, due to his close friendship with Michael Noyk. Noyk, a future life councillor and honorary solicitor of the Dublin Hebrew Congregation, drank with him often in The Bailey pub. Noyk, son of a Litvak immigrant, first met Griffith about 1910, the year in which the Jewish Bethel Solomons, who was to deliver Griffith's daughter, subscribed to a fund to buy Griffith a house. Noyk considered Griffith a 'very close friend', and they frequently went walking together: 'I spent many evenings in his home where I got a very intimate knowledge of his character.' Noyk visited him in Reading Gaol in 1916 and long acted as his solicitor. Their children played together and Griffith's daughter was a flower girl at Noyk's wedding.[55] Griffith was also friendly with other Jews including Abraham Briscoe, Jacob Elyan and Eddie Lipman.[56]

On 16 October 1909, Griffith's *Sinn Féin* paper acknowledged the role of the Jewish enlightenment in spreading medical knowledge throughout the world. And while the ugly pieces by O'Donnell and Gogarty that Griffith published are frequently noted with justifiable disapproval, critics of Griffith seldom appear to notice a very different kind of article in *Sinn Féin* in 1912, written by 'A de B'. This was probably Aodh de Blacam, then living in London and later a speechwriter for the popular left-wing Irish government minister Noel Browne TD. He is said to have 'regularly made pejorative remarks associating Jewish people with exploitation, mass culture, and other undesirable features of modernity',[57] but in *Sinn Féin* wrote 'The Jews have given us the finest nationalist literature in the world: they have also set the finest nationalist example.' Referring to the recently published *Zionist Work in Palestine* (edited by Israel Cohen) and declaring 'Israel represents the triumph of Sinn Féin', the author added 'One lays down the book with a new respect for that much maligned race.' He recalled the words of Chief Rabbi Adler who had expressed his pleasure at visiting Ireland, 'the only land in which his race has not been persecuted'. Ten years later, in a mainstream Irish newspaper, this same author attacked G.K. Chesterton and Hilaire Belloc for attacking the Jews.[58]

During the First World War Griffith also published reports highlighting the plight of persecuted Jews in Russia, now an ally of England. His socialist friend James Connolly did likewise in the *Irish Worker* and elsewhere. Griffith cited Israel Zangwill as an authority on the matter.[59] This was at a time of growing anti-Semitism in Britain, when immigrant Jews from Europe came under suspicion. In 1915 too, Griffith as editor of the new *Nationality*, published on its front page as firm a rebuttal of anti-Semitism as may be found in any Irish paper of the period.[60] It was quoted above in the opening paragraph. He wrote it in the context of criticism of the appointment of Matthew Nathan as the United Kingdom's under-secretary for Ireland. On 23 March 1918, furthermore, Griffith's *Nationality* praised as 'impartial' an official report by 'an Anglo-Jew, titled Sir Maurice Levy' on manufacturing services in Ireland. The government had delayed publishing Levy's report.

Griffith's *Nationality* was said to have achieved a circulation second only to the daily *Irish Independent*, being ostensibly far greater than that of his papers in which some anti-Semitic sentiments were printed years before, and so this declaration of equal opportunity is relatively significant, even if not often acknowledged.[61] It was consistent with another declaration in the very first issue of his *United Irishman*, in 1899: 'One cannot trample on the rights of other people and consistently demand his own.'

James Larkin and Jews

James Larkin's *Irish Worker* first appeared in 1911 and its reputed circulation of up to 21,000 exceeded that of Griffith's earlier papers.

Emmet Larkin puts its success down to James Larkin's 'appointment of himself as the keeper of the public conscience'.[62] A statue on O'Connell Street, Dublin's main thoroughfare, today prominently commemorates Larkin as a labour leader. Yet, as I have demonstrated elsewhere, Larkin and some other labour activists were not above taking sideswipes at Jewish immigrants.[63] The *Cork Trade and Labour Journal* of 1908, for example, had 'a peculiar antisemitic twist', and in Larkin's own paper one reads the startling headline 'Worse than the Jewman'.[64]

The nature of a cartoon in Larkin's *Irish Worker* of 26 August 1911 corresponds quite closely to some of what Griffith and Bulfin had published about Jews and to one particular cartoon in *Sinn Féin* on 11 December 1909 that shows 'Moses O'Toole' outside his shop. Larkin's illustration likewise was an objection by the editor to 'foreigners masquering under Irish names'. Larkin deployed stereotypical physical characterists as well as mock-immigrant pronunciation and the

GENTLEMEN OF THE JEWRY

[We have no objection to any man, Jew or Gentile, on account of his Nationality or Creed. What we do object to is the practice, which is becoming all too common, of Foreigners masquerading under Irish Names.—Ed.]

James Larkin's *Irish Worker*, 26 August 1911, reflects annoyance at Jewish immigrant traders who allegedly pretended to be Irish.

common derogatory nickname 'ikey'. The ridiculing of immigrants' broken English had long been a feature of anti-Semitic communications in Britain, as noted in Ireland by Maria Edgeworth as early as 1817 in her novel *Harrington*, in her perceptive observation on the expression of prejudice towards Jews for which she herself had been reproached.[65]

Larkin also gratuitously published twenty lines of a poem referring to Jewish avarice or economising. He did so not once but twice, and on the first occasion quite oddly in a smaller-than-usual number of the *Irish Worker* that was produced as a special edition during one particular lockout of workers in 1911. The poem, replete with mock-Jewish pronunciation, was written by Peter Pindar in the eighteenth century and has a Jewish mother asking for her son's theatre ticket to be refunded when he accidentally falls to his death from a theatre balcony. It is not evident why Larkin bizarrely printed these verses even once, never mind twice.[66]

Jews after Independence

Bethel Solomons' republican sister, the painter Estella, married James Starkey, who was to publish in his *Dublin Magazine* work by Samuel Beckett. Known as Seumas O'Sullivan, Starkey greatly admired Griffith and wrote an essay honouring him after he died.[67] That he did so, given his connection with Estella and her brother Bethel, who contributed to the fund for Griffith's house, suggests that Griffith was neither exceptionally nor ultimately anti-Semitic.

Griffith died suddenly in 1922 and was long gone by the time some Irish people, such as members of the Blueshirts, openly sympathised with fascism.[68] It was not Griffith but his nemesis Éamon de Valera – himself once accused by the republican John Devoy of being a 'half-breed Jew'[69] – who, as leader of Fianna Fáil and prime minister, permitted Charles Bewley, a Nazi sympathiser, to be the Irish ambassador in Berlin and who signed a book of condolences upon Hitler's death. De Valera's acquaintanceship with Robert Briscoe, Ireland's first Jewish member of Dáil Éireann and a member of his Fianna Fáil parliamentary party (and an admirer of Griffith),[70] appears to have made little or no difference to the official policy of rebuffing Jewish immigration to the

Irish state at that time. Although Griffith foresaw a place for Jews in an Irish government, de Valera failed to appoint Briscoe to a ministry. Nor did prejudice against Jewish, Muslim or other immigrants end with the declaration of an Irish republic in 1949.

Dublin Jewish Students' Union

One academic has referred to 'the casual anti-Semitism endemic to Irish political life'. She sees a failure to consider fully the extent of that prejudice.[71] Griffith struggled to come to terms with it. Yet, notably, when the Dublin Jewish Students' Union reportedly learnt with 'dismay' of his death in 1922, its members were reported to have sent a message to his widow expressing 'its sincere and respectful sympathy'.[72]

Bryan Cheyette, in an essay on T.S. Eliot, writes 'I have always thought that it is a mistake to overdetermine or moralize individual writers as particularly unforgivable anti-Semites or racists as this lets the rest of the culture off the hook'.[73] Cheyette, a leading Jewish studies scholar, articulates an attitude that is also useful when considering Griffith's attitude to Jews, not least because that attitude matured. Had it not done so it seems quite unlikely that Jewish students in Dublin would have expressed as they did 'sincere and respectful sympathy' to his widow upon Arthur Griffith's death.

1917–20: Griffith and de Valera

Implicit in the Irish state's current 'Decade of Centenaries' programme is the idea that there was a continuum from 1912 to 1922 that carried Ireland toward its destiny. It 'aims to commemorate each step that Ireland took between 1912 and 1922', thus mirroring in words a cartoon image of stepping stones published after significant Sinn Féin by-election victories in 1917.[1] It is a narrative of national liberation that moves seamlessly to a satisfying climax. Such too is the spirit of the last line of a verse of a patriotic ballad written in about the year 1940 and subsequently sung frequently for its nationalist fervor, even by members of the Irish army on parade: 'We're on the one road, swinging along, singin' a soldier's song!'[2]

However, from 1912 the Irish experienced a decade of exclusions that was far from being the 'one road'. Orange was pitted against Green, 'Northmen' against 'Southmen', workers against employers, Anglo-Irish against Catholic Irish, World War veterans against veterans of the Rising, nationalist against nationalist, Free Staters against Irregulars. The 'steps' taken led to neither a progressive nor a pluralist nor a united Ireland. The decision by Griffith to yield the presidency of Sinn Féin in 1917 reflected some of those strains.

Before 1917 Griffith was already widely known as the voice of Sinn Féin, his dream of a dual monarchy based loosely on a 'Hungarian' model more radical than Home Rule. Until 1916 few people had heard of de Valera (1882–1975), who had not joined Sinn Féin. De Valera avoided execution for his part in the rebellion of 1916 and went on to become the towering political figure in Ireland in the mid-twentieth century. Many people admired and even loved him.

To see Griffith and de Valera as they were in 1917, one must put aside our image of them now. For this was Ireland before Sinn Féin surged in the polls in 1918, before Dáil Éireann ever met, before the War of Independence. Forget too the civil war, Griffith's tragic death, Collins gunned down, de Valera's foundation of Fianna Fáil, the so-called 'Emergency' (World War II), de Valera's roles as taoiseach and later president of the republic declared in 1949.

The Threat of Conscription

It was not by magic that Éamon de Valera became president of Sinn Féin in 1917. It was to some extent by manipulation and the threat of violence. After the 1916 Rising, Griffith was eclipsed by those who eschewed Sinn Féin's aim of a dual monarchy or dominion status in favour of more militant objectives. The latter now saw the party as a useful vehicle for driving forward their struggle for an all-island republic, particularly as Griffith's less militant Sinn Féin had in the public's eye accrued the credit for their revolt.[3]

Griffith's self-effacement worked against his elevation politically. He had long yearned to find a leader equal to Parnell in terms of uniting the nation in a great movement. He somehow convinced himself that William Rooney or William Bulfin might be that man, before their deaths.[4] Now Griffith decided that de Valera could be the next great leader.

By-election victories in early 1917 in North Roscommon and South Longford heartened Griffith and gave Sinn Féin its first members of parliament. De Valera had at first opposed the party's participation in those by-elections,[5] but afterwards changed his mind about the benefits of such contests. De Valera then became Sinn Féin's successful candidate in the by-election in East Clare in July 1917. Co. Clare had the third-highest number of paid-up Sinn Féin members of any county in Ireland, and Laffan describes it as 'one of the constituencies which was most likely to elect a Sinn Féiner'.[6] De Valera, campaigning in his Volunteer uniform, cultivated the active support of the local Catholic bishop and priests and won by a landslide. He had evinced, perhaps for the first time, or one of the first times, what John Bowman describes as 'his genius for the bespoke formula'.[7] For he managed to find words of sufficient ambiguity to assuage all factions and convince them that he had their interests at heart, while not firmly committing himself to any particular course of action. Lloyd George reportedly referred to him that year as 'a man of great ability'.[8] Griffith too spoke well of de Valera, believing that the latter had 'the capacity of a statesman'.[9] He would continue to speak well of him after yielding the presidency of Sinn Féin, and even after de Valera rejected the Treaty. According to the *Dáil Debates* of 9 January 1922, Griffith declared: 'I want to say now that there is scarcely a man I have ever met in my life that I have more love and respect for than President de Valera. I am thoroughly sorry to see him placed in such a position. We want him with us.'

But one must put all that happened after 1917 out of mind in order to understand clearly what determined Griffith's surrender of the presidency of Sinn Féin to a man ten years his junior and far less experienced and less informed in many ways than Griffith was. Three years earlier, it would not have occurred to the senior IRB men who then met Griffith to invite de Valera to that meeting, even if they knew of him. He came late even to the Gaelic League and had not joined Sinn Féin. He mistakenly thought that the IRB's strategy of controlling the Gaelic League's national executive was orchestrated by Sinn Féin and directed against him personally, and 'vowed that he would never have anything to do with it [Sinn Féin]'. He appears to have kept to that vow until elected its president.[10] He was undoubtedly an enthusiastic organiser within the Irish Volunteers and led his company out of it after the Redmondite split, but then he failed to retain most of the company's members and was a relatively minor figure in the preparations for 1916. It was only after his escape from execution that he performed what one writer has described as 'personal acrobatics' and 'the teacher turned soldier became a politician'.[11] And who was the person whom Longford and O'Neill, in their sympathetic biography of de Valera, credit with persuading de Valera to devote all his time 'to the national cause'? It was Arthur Griffith.[12]

Did de Valera rise simply because he survived the executions of 1916, being just one of three commandants to do so? He assumed a leadership role among Irish political prisoners when interned with them in Britain. Ironically, in view of later events, de Valera had earned a reputation as something of 'a unifying moderate', first in 1913 when he successfully proposed a compromise between factions in the Gaelic League, and then after the Rising when he ensured that Eoin MacNeill, the leader who at the last minute tried to stop it, was paid the respect due to a leader both while interned and later on the hustings in Clare.[13]

De Valera's election as president of Sinn Féin was followed by a reversal of its recent fortunes, by three by-elections in which Sinn Féin candidates lost.[14] Only when the UK government, in 1918, added the blunder of proposing compulsory military conscription in Ireland to their inflammatory executions of 1916, and after the Catholic Church actively criticised the government for doing so, did many voters swing decisively behind Sinn Féin. Yet a striking phrase is found in David Dwane's somewhat simpering account of de Valera's early life published in 1922. He wrote that his subject 'was not known to the general public until Easter Week. Perhaps his first public appearance in Ireland as a leader was in June 1917, when, after the general amnesty, he marched home at the head of the prisoners ... From that moment ... de Valera became, as if by magic, the accepted leader of the Irish nation.'[15]

So what kind of '*magic*' was involved in de Valera's replacing the 'father of Sinn Féin' as Sinn Féin president on 26 October 1917? To answer that question it is necessary to consider the context. In January 1917 Griffith had tried to bring together the various factions or 'sections of national opinion' when it appeared that opinion was very divided as to the proper policy to be adopted for the future: 'Only the younger Irish Volunteers favoured physical force, but the others could not agree on a constitutional policy', thought a contemporary.[16] Now, at a crucial moment in 1917, Griffith might have split his beloved Sinn Féin had he been unwilling to step aside to allow de Valera, newly elected as an abstentionist MP, to become its president. The pragmatic Griffith assessed realities and decided to avoid a divisive contest with de Valera for the presidency of Sinn Féin because it was made clear to him that he would not win it.

In 1917 Griffith was not only older than de Valera. He was also much more experienced in political and cultural organisation, had travelled to France, Africa and elsewhere as an adult (while a young de Valera hastened back to Ireland from Liverpool after a day or two in England and had not yet visited America). Griffith in his columns had also stood up to the Catholic Church. De Valera was beholden to the church for his education and job as a teacher, and mingled at Blackrock College with future cardinals.[17] As a child on a poor farm in rural Munster, de Valera had yearned to be reunited with his mother in America, where she later married Charles Wheelwright, a non-Catholic Englishman with whom she was to have two children reared as Catholics, one of whom became a priest in the same year of 1916 in which de Valera hazarded his life in the rebellion. Ryle-Dwyer writes 'it was something else for a former widow not to reclaim a legitimate child after she had remarried, especially after she had started a second family'.[18] When de Valera won his scholarship to Blackrock, it was as if Mother Church adopted him, and he stayed living in a room at the college even after finishing school.

The sociable image of Griffith, having a glass of stout among acquaintances at The Bailey pub, contrasts with that of the ostensibly austere de Valera. The US state department was later told that de Valera 'dresses habitually in black, so appears to be in perpetual mourning for a nation in bondage' and that the papal nuncio in Ireland believed de Valera 'never smoked, never took a drop of alcoholic drink except in public when as a matter of courtesy he forced himself to gulp down a few swallows of wine'.[19] Interned in England, Griffith organised activities for his comrades and even played handball with them, while de Valera inspired awe among his fellow prisoners by an aloofness reflected in his playing handball on his own.[20] Biographers refer to a boyhood hobby that the latter shared with a neighbouring lad of digging for water, or what in 1922 one admiring writer described as 'de Valera's incessant search for deep springs'.[21]

It was surely out of deep springs that they drew up the second article of the new Sinn Féin constitution adopted in 1917: 'Sinn Féin aims at securing the international recognition of Ireland as an independent Irish Republic. Having achieved that status the Irish people may by referendum freely choose their own form of government.' This clearly did not preclude a lesser constitutional arrangement along the way, but it could be read, if one pleased, as distancing the party from Griffith's willingness to approve some form of dual monarchy that might be more palatable to unionists than an outright republic.

It has been suggested that Griffith decided to yield to de Valera when they met for tea in a café on Grafton Street one week before the Sinn Féin convention of 1917. Indeed, newspapers reported from the convention that 'the [outgoing] chairman [Griffith] said he told Mr de Valera a week ago that he would propose him instead of himself.'[22] But a cup of tea on Grafton Street alone did not swing it for 'Dev'. For it appears that on the evening before the vote for president was scheduled to occur, the Irish Volunteers held a secret meeting at which its members who were about to attend the convention were instructed to vote for certain candidates for the executive.[23] Griffith was not naïve and no doubt understood clearly that the IRB and the Volunteers had now stacked the cards against him; it would have gone against his political instincts to force a split on the issue. Dan McCarthy, an IRB man, thought that Griffith would have won any contest, but on the evening before the vote, Griffith told him that he was not going to contest the presidency.[24] Only one other potential candidate was mooted – George Noble Plunkett, whose son Joseph had been executed in 1916 and whose Liberty League was to be subsumed into Sinn Féin at that party's forthcoming convention. Plunkett also withdrew.

The militant Cathal Brugha reportedly said that Griffith had been obliged to accept the new objective of a republic rather than a dual monarchy, or he would have had to 'walk the plank' (as Brugha put it).[25] By this Brugha signified that Griffith had been obliged to accept de Valera as president. Griffith in 1917 appears to have believed most Irish people shared Cardinal Michael Logue's perspective, that the objective of an Irish republic was 'ill-considered and Utopian' and 'a dream which no man in his sober senses can hope to see realised'.[26] The republic of which people then spoke was envisaged as inclusive of all thirty-two counties on the island of Ireland.

In 1952 Seán T. O'Kelly, when president of Ireland, recalled what happened behind the scenes in 1917:

At the branch meetings held before the big re-organisation meeting of Sinn Féin which was held that year in the Mansion House in

October 1917, the decision seems to have been taken ['was arrived at' crossed out] that Griffith would not be acceptable to the 'military' men as the leader for the re-organised movement. I was present at some of these meetings, and amongst those who took part in some of these discussions were Cathal Brugha, Michael Collins, Seán McGarry, Pearse Beaslaoi, John O'Mahony, [and] Joseph Murray ... there was a lot of discussions going on everywhere as to the new leadership, and it eventually emerged that the 'military men' – as we might describe them – those who had actually taken part in the Rising of 1916, favoured the election of Éamon de Valera; but a number of Griffith's friends, and he had a number of friends and admirers even amongst the men who had been active in the fight, disliked deposing Griffith because of the excellent work he had done over a period of nearly twenty years and the heroic sacrifices that he had made in the interests of the movement ... We also decided that when Griffith arrived, he should be told what our considered view was. He was told by Walter Cole, and he himself entered into the discussion in the most objective kind of way. After a discussion of half an hour or so on the matter of the presidency of the new organisation, he said that he would give serious consideration to our advice, and that next day when the question of the presidency arose, he would announce his decision. At the meeting itself the next day, when the point was reached where the election of the new president was to take place, Griffith stood up and, if my recollection serves me correctly, himself proposed Éamon de Valera for the presidency.[27]

O'Kelly's memory served him more or less well, although at the meeting on 25 October 1917 Griffith *announced* as much as 'proposed' de Valera as president. The *Evening Herald* of that day described the latter's unanimous election as 'a mild sensation'. According to *The Freeman's Journal* next morning,

Mr. Griffith, chairman, made a short address entirely without oratorical ashes, without a single gesture, and in almost a conversational manner. It was a speech which a chairman might have delivered at a shareholders' meeting. It is quite different from the old style when the heroes of the occasion almost brought out a rash on themselves with excess of rhetoric. Mr. Griffith sits at the table like a director at a board meeting.

The newspaper observed that Griffith had 'gracefully' given way. That was as generous as its partisan writer got, for he went on to claim that 'It was pretty clear from the temper of the [Sinn Féin] convention that it wanted a president who had given earnest of his courage and readiness to make sacrifices, and that a purely pacifist presidency would not have been to its taste.' Next day, the party's joint treasurer, Laurence Ginnell MP, referred to Griffith's 'noble conduct' in withdrawing and described him as 'a man who during the dark days when Ireland was in the lurch devoted his life to the creation of a true party and the educating of Ireland in the true principles of Sinn Féin (applause).'[28] Rising after Ginnell, de Valera did not hesitate to describe his own ascendancy as 'a monument to the brave dead'.[29]

The handover to de Valera at the convention was unostentatious, and on Griffith's part generous. He dealt with it in two paragraphs in the course of his 'almost conversational' or subdued address:

I told Mr. de Valera that for the presidency I would propose him instead of myself. I have been six years president of Sinn Féin. Mr. de Valera is twelve years younger than I am. During the last eight or nine months I have endeavoured to combine the business of president and the editing of *Nationality*, and doing a considerable amount of going about the country. Well, I now withdraw my name in favour of Mr. de Valera. (Cries of 'No'). He is a man whose sincerity and courage and determination you all know. But I know more about him than that from recent experience. I know that he is a man of cool judgement, in whose judgement I have absolute confidence, and I believe that in him as president of this movement you will have a statesman as well as a soldier. I therefore withdraw my name, and as Count Plunkett has also withdrawn, Mr. de Valera is unanimously elected president. (Prolonged cheers).[30]

In a telling reference to Eoin MacNeill, whose attempt to call off the Rising in 1916 largely frustrated it outside Dublin, and whose nomination to the executive was opposed by a small number of delegates led by Constance Markievicz, Griffith made an observation that may have been seen as a defensive riposte to those who resented his own lack of militancy in 1916. He said of MacNeill 'when the onus was put on him, and he was faced with the responsibility, as it seemed to him, of offering up the young men of Ireland as a holocaust, he did his best to save the young men of Ireland. (Cheers).'[31]

If Griffith's speech was generous to de Valera, de Valera appears to have been ungenerous to him. When de Valera spoke the next day as Sinn Féin's new president, he was not reported to have paid any personal tribute to Griffith such as Griffith had paid to him, but merely presumed to convey thanks 'in the name of the convention and in the name of the people of Ireland' to the two candidates who had retired in order to strengthen 'the new position which we occupy'. He proceeded somewhat bizarrely to assure delegates that 'I am a Catholic', by way of a guarantee that whatever he advocated was morally compatible with the Catholic Church's theology.[32] Within days delegates to a convention of the Irish Volunteers, who had all been delegates to the Sinn Féin convention, also chose de Valera as the president of that organisation. While Griffith had (as even an unsympathetic newspaper reported) 'gracefully' yielded, and continued later to speak well of de Valera, the latter during the treaty debates in the Dáil twice used a graceless and humiliating word to describe what had happened in 1917. He said that Griffith 'surrendered at the convention his chairmanship of the Sinn Féin organisation, surrendered it to me'. De Valera added that Cathal Brugha had likewise 'surrendered' to him the top position in the Irish Volunteers.[33] It seems that when Brugha (reportedly) said that Griffith faced having 'to walk the plank' at the Sinn Féin convention of 1917, he knew whereof he spoke.

With de Valera becoming president of the party in 1917, Griffith was elected its vice-president.[34] Voters were not just angry about the executions of 1916 and not simply dreaming of independence. They were also exercised by the immediate threat of conscription. During the First World War, in January 1916, conscription was imposed in

Britain. Provision for its introduction in Ireland during 1918 threatened more than two hundred thousand eligible men who had not already volunteered to serve, and was stiffly opposed by farmers and bishops amongst others.[35] Notably, in April 1918, de Valera made a key presentation of 'Ireland's Case Against Conscription', which was also published as a pamphlet.

In May 1918 the British alleged Sinn Féin's involvement in a 'German plot', and arrested and interned de Valera and Griffith along with more than seventy other members of the party. In Gloucester Prison Griffith obtained a postcard of Gloucester town and sent it to his son (Plate 9). In June, while still interned, Griffith was for the first time nominated for election as an MP, in a by-election in Co. Cavan in which the possibility of conscription loomed large. He won the seat. There were said to be 'mean and vile stories circulated' about him by the Ancient Order of Hibernians, who backed the Irish Party.[36]

With some of the prisoners dying of influenza and other medical conditions, Griffith's wife wrote anxiously to the home secretary a number of times, asking on one occasion 'Are you married? Have you a daughter? Put them in my place and you in my husband's cell and how would you feel?'[37]

On 21 January 1919 Dáil Éireann first sat, and on the same day the first shots were fired in what became known as 'the War of Independence'. Griffith was still interned in England. Released in March 1919 he continued to play a central role in political affairs. He was appointed acting president of Dáil Éireann in June 1919 after de Valera went to America for eighteen months to seek support.[38] The volunteer Mortimer O'Connell, who had been 'out' in Jameson's Distillery at Easter 1916 and who 'knew fairly well and admired immensely' Griffith, would later recall

He was a man of charm and great moral courage and not by any means the pacifist ... he was alleged to be. In the height of the Black and Tan terror in 1919–21, as acting head of the Government of Ireland, he gave unstinted approval to all the measures taken to meet the British onslaught. He knew the British mind so well that, rather than remain as we were, he was prepared to meet them at their own game, to fight hard for the maximum, to get the best bargain he could …[39]

George Lyons wrote that Griffith abhorred militarism but 'readily consented to military action when such became necessary or feasible'. Referring to the fact that the presidency of Sinn Féin was not continually held by Griffith, Lyons said of him: 'He was always Hamlet though the king's part was played at different times by Martyn, Sweetman and de Valera' (each being a president of Sinn Féin).[40]

It is tempting to expand the analogy with Hamlet, a Shakespearian character around whom violence exploded but who was slow to perpetrate it. A signal moment in Griffith's youth had been the destruction of Parnell by those who formerly backed him and who then sought to supplant him, even as Hamlet's uncle supplanted Hamlet's murdered father in Hamlet's mother's bed. Although self-avowedly not a Parnellite, Griffith took Parnell's betrayal almost personally. Haunted by the damaging divisions it caused, Griffith wrestled with the wrong and for some years was torn between the poles of violent reaction and despair. In Shakespeare's play, Hamlet is for a while paralysed by inertia in the face of his uncle's poisoning of Hamlet's own father, an inertia where one might expect and even excuse revengeful violence.

Ernest Jones sought to explain Hamlet's response by reference to the Oedipus complex.[41] Hamlet feared for his mother while resenting her union with his uncle, a union that Hamlet felt branded her 'harlot', just as union with Britain had compromised Mother Ireland. With the Irish earls having fled abroad in 1607, and with the Jacobite kings in London dethroned by 1690, Irish Catholics were tempted to compromise with their oppressors for the sake of survival. There were dubious land transactions in the seventeenth century intended to circumvent extensive Anglo-Protestant expropriation (deals that disadvantaged other native Catholics); compromising conversions of convenience to Anglicanism in the eighteenth century; unspeakable strategies of survival during the Great Famine; and Catholic careerism abroad within a colonial service that was oppressing the Irish at home in Griffith's lifetime. Griffith railed against the cloying myth of political purity in his newspapers, even as he lashed the English interloper and was haunted like Hamlet by the past. James Joyce, who had a complex relationship with his own father, was also interested in Hamlet. He devoted a scene in *Ulysses* to the significance of the relationship between Shakespeare as writer and Hamlet as character.[42] But he also has one of his own creations in *Ulysses* warn that 'Shakespeare is the happy hunting-ground of all minds that have lost their balance'!

Griffith's status as a leader is reflected in the fact that, between May 1918 and July 1921, the British imprisoned him for a total of seventeen months. When free and acting as president of Dáil Éireann, Griffith occasionally received transatlantic advice from de Valera. On Christmas Day 1919, for example, came 'greetings to persecuted people of Ireland'. De Valera advised 'Endure yet a little while', and sent 'our affectionate regards to every Irish citizen'. In January 1920, in the run up to Irish urban elections, de Valera telegraphed Griffith personally from Washington DC to remind his substitute as president, already under many pressures and harassed by raids on his home and family during the continuing War of Independence, that he had a new responsibility in the chief's absence: 'Lloyd George cannot find his Ulster boundaries. Elections must show that they are not there to be found. Every lover of Ireland to the polls then. Victory – Ireland's fate – is dependant on you. The world is watching and the world will note.' A copy of this message survives in a Colonial Office file, evidence of the police's interception and disruption of Griffith's mail. There too one finds the London publisher Thomas Fisher Unwin complaining, in March 1920, that his private letter to Griffith, suggesting a new history of Dublin Castle, was among correspondence opened and detained by the authorities. However, Griffith had more on his mind than writing history, not least the wrecking of Sinn Féin's offices by government forces (Plate 10).[43]

De Valera caused controversy in America by making a remark about Cuba, which was a zone of particular US sensitivity. Griffith defended him – 'as usual' according to de Valera's most recent biographer.[44] He remained supportive of his chief's long mission to stir up support and raise funds in the United States.[45]

We should pause before attributing the level of agency to de Valera personally that David Fitzpatrick allowed him in respect to his 'astonishing success' after 1916 in 'cajoling' the men of blood to subsume their energies within an open political movement. Objective circumstances largely explain the tactics adopted then, for the 'military' men were aware of Britain's strength once the First World War ended and knew that they could not take and secure the whole island. Fitzpatrick's admiration for what he termed, in this context, 'feats of legerdemain' by Dev is a curious echo of Dwane's wonderworker reference to 'magic' in the latter's narrative of the rise of de Valera. The *Oxford English Dictionary* defines 'legerdemain' as 'skillful use of one's hands when performing conjuring tricks; sleight of hand'. Perhaps Dev's true gift was actually one of articulation rather than agency, with his resort to 'bespoke formula' (to use John Bowman's term) being a useful means of papering over cracks in the republican movement until he chose to do otherwise in 1922.[46] Was it intended to be indicative of a difference between Griffith and de Valera that, at the former's graveside in 1922, William T. Cosgrave said Griffith 'abhorred those magicians of political metaphysics who say one thing and mean another'?[47]

Archbishop William Walsh's secretary thought that 'if Arthur Griffith had been in USA for a few months in the 1919–21 period, the history of the treaty would have been quite different. He was never there.'[48] And had de Valera gone to London as leader of the treaty delegation in October 1921, de Valera would have had to take ownership of those talks in a way that he never did.

14

A Fateful Weekend

The pressure was intense. In June 1921, while the War of Independence continued, King George V travelled to Belfast and opened a parliament for that part of the old Irish province of Ulster that he called 'the Six Counties'. There would now be two Irelands constitutionally. The British insisted that 'the six counties' (Northern Ireland) must not be coerced, and Irish republicans were in no position militarily to force them into an all-island state. Economic sanctions against northern traders, 'The Belfast Boycott', had done nothing to persuade unionists to throw in their lot with nationalists on the island.

On 30 June 1921 Griffith was released from Mountjoy Prison, no doubt to his childrens' relief (Plate 12). When a truce came into effect in July he accompanied Éamon de Valera to London, where de Valera, as president of the Dáil, met Prime Minister Lloyd George to discuss setting up substantive peace negotiations. Getting to London from Dublin by boat and rail took, as usual, about eleven hours. It was quicker than going by boat and road, with flying between Ireland and Britain not yet established as a usual means of civilian transport. Later that same day, Horace Plunkett, the co-operative movement pioneer and campaigner for Irish dominion Home Rule, also crossed. Disembarking at Holyhead, he drove his Morris Oxford to London, a distance of some 416 km (260 miles). He noted that he had 'averaged 24 m.p.h. [miles per hour] while running. Left 8 AM arrived … 9.30 P.M. dead tired'.[1] On previous trips to Britain de Valera and Griffith had gone as captured rebels transported to English jails. Now large crowds cheered them. There was a heat wave and they stayed on deck throughout the three-hour crossing.[2] British authorities provided a special rail carriage for their onward journey from Holyhead. A reporter in London thought that de Valera 'looked somewhat tired after his long journey', and Griffith 'was also feeling the strain'. Griffith was said to be 'regarded by the English Press as one of the sharpest intellects in the Sinn Féin movement'.[3] When De Valera then met Lloyd George a number of times they agreed to open treaty negotiations. On 22 July 1921 the lean de Valera and stocky Griffith were warmly welcomed back to Dublin by a large crowd – an Irish Don Quixote and Sancho Panza, observed one French woman (Plate 11).[4]

Protracted correspondence between the Irish and British ensued. Nearly three months passed before substantive peace negotiations began in October 1921.[5] De Valera himself did not return to London for those talks. He stayed in Dublin, for reasons never clearly articulated that have long generated controversy. Over the years he was to seek to explain his refusal by way of 'many versions and many reasons'.[6]

The Irish seem to have been unconcerned about the physical circumstances in which they were set to meet some of the shrewdest politicians in Europe. They did not seek a neutral venue, nor even one in Britain that lay away from the metropolis and nearer Dublin. De Valera freely sent his team into Downing Street. To put this in context, nearly half a century later, US and Vietnamese enemies, having agreed to peace talks, held them in Paris and wrangled over the very shape of a negotiating table.

October 1921

With de Valera staying in Dublin, he appointed Griffith to lead the delegation of negotiators to London in October 1921. It consisted of Griffith, Michael Collins and Robert Barton, who were all ministers in the Dáil cabinet, as well as Éamonn Duggan (chief liaison officer for the IRA) and George Gavan Duffy (Irish envoy at Rome). Gavan Duffy, a London-Irish solicitor, had acted for Roger Casement at the latter's trial for high treason in 1916 and would now face across the negotiating table Lord Birkenhad, who as attorney-general had successfully prosecuted Casement. The party going to London also included Erskine Childers as its secretary, and John Chartres as second secretary. The Anglo-Irish Childers was a former civil servant and soldier who came to support Irish nationalism and whom de Valera trusted highly.[7] In addition to Prime Minister Lloyd George, the principal negotiators for the British were his Liberal Party colleague Winston Churchill (colonial secretary), the Conservative Party's Lord Birkenhead (F.E. Smith, lord chancellor) and Austin Chamberlain (lord privy seal and leader of the commons). Some other UK ministers attended particular sessions. Thomas Jones was secretary to the British delegation, with Lional Curtis second secretary. Childers and Curtis had both attended Haileybury College, a private school near Hertford, and both fought in and wrote about the Boer War.[8]

When the peace negotiators left Ireland for England on Saturday 8 October 1921, enthusiastic crowds once more gathered at the pier to cheer off their team, which included women typists and personal secretaries.

Griffith with his treaty negotiations staff, Ellie Lyons, her sister Alice Lyons and Kathleen McKenna, aboard the mailboat *Curraghmore*, October 1921 (National Library of Ireland [NPA MKN 32]).

British authorities again provided a special saloon on the express train from north Wales down to London. One newspaper reported that on their arrival at Euston Station after their long trip, 'none of them betrayed the weariness which usually marks those who make the journey from Dublin to London'.[9] Yet even on that optimistic day in October there was a sign of tensions to come. One newspaper reported:

> Mr Arthur Griffith, who is at all times emotionless as the sphinx, appeared to be unmoved by the reception accorded him. When questioned by a Press Association representative he maintained his taciturnity, and would not breathe a single word as to the hope or fear of the party for the success of the conference … Nor would Mr Griffith say whether the delegates are endowed with plenipotentiary powers. It was learned, however, on good authority that any decision or agreement between the [UK] Government and the Sinn Féin delegates, will have to be placed before Dáil Éireann.[10]

So were the five Irish peace negotiators actually 'plenipotentiaries', as officially described? The Latin roots of that word indicate 'full power' to make decisions. Or had certain 'instructions' and promises ultimately bound them to refer back to the Irish cabinet every last detail of any final draft treaty before signing it and submitting it to Dáil Éireann for approval?[11] This distinction later became a matter bitterly debated in Ireland. Was it an omen that on that same Saturday when the Irish treaty negotiators crossed to England, a passenger steamer, *The Rowan*, left Glasgow for Dublin but never reached its destination? While sailing through fog banks on the Irish Sea it was struck successively by two other vessels and sank. About twenty passengers died.[12]

The treaty negotiations dragged on through October and November. There were seven plenary sessions in October, followed by twenty-four sub-conferences between 24 October and 6 December, as well as many other committee sessions and less formal contacts. Griffith bore the brunt of the work attending these, with Collins in mid-November describing him as 'a good man. Only, I fear, much the worse for the strain of a life spent in toil and trouble. I reminded him of how, when I was young, I thought of him *as* Ireland.'[13] The fact that not all five Irish delegates attended every session gradually fostered distrust among them. The Irish found themselves struggling in imperial surroundings as they tried to outsmart ministers whose social class and educational privileges were all too evident. And, always, delegates looked over their shoulders to Ireland, where Éamon de Valera, together with a couple of more hardline nationalist cabinet ministers, stood ready to disown them – and where unionists in northern Ireland loyal to the United Kingdom had armed themselves to resist inclusion in any independent Irish state. The Irish took some comfort from their religion, with both Collins and Griffith carrying rosary beads in their pockets. The militant Collins regularly attended Mass in the Brompton Oratory, lighting a small candle for his friend Kitty Kiernan back in Ireland.[14]

The Irish were housed in fine rented accommodation where, today near Harrods, Russian oligarchs and rich Arabs have residences. Rolls Royce cars were provided to transport them to Downing Street and back (Plate 14). Yet a graphic indication of the tension surrounding the peace negotiations was that the Irish provisional government arranged to have a small aircraft, capable of carrying five passengers to Dublin, standing by at a London airfield to evacuate Griffith and the four other delegates quickly in the event of negotations collapsing acrimoniously.[15] During October, Griffith bought conjuring tricks for his son in Dublin. By late November he could only promise to look for more 'if I can get time one day'.[16] Collins wrote to an Irish businessman in London that 'From Dublin I don't know whether we're being instructed or confused. The latter I would say'.[17] Collins worried that Griffith was 'in poor health and further burdens will do no more than grossly exaggerate his condition'.[18]

December 1921

Matters came to a head on Thursday 1 December 1921. During that afternoon the Irish 'received an outline of the [UK] Government's latest proposals' and Robert Barton left immediately for Dublin. The other negotiators remained in London where there was an air of crisis and 'feverish Ministerial consultations that were noted until a late hour in

Downing Street'.[19] That evening Prime Minister Lloyd George presented them with full details of the revised proposals, if not an ultimatum. The Irish Free State was to remain linked to the British Crown in a manner that was symbolically contentious. To make the terms more palatable the British promised to establish a boundary commission that 'could be directed to adjust the line [of the new frontier on the island] both by inclusion and exclusion so as to make the boundary conform as closely as possible to the wishes of the population'.[20] Griffith and Collins hoped that any such adjustments would make a separated northern Ireland unsustainable. Griffith informed the British cabinet secretary Thomas Jones 'It is not our proposal ... we would prefer a plebiscite, but in essentials a Boundary Commission is very much the same. It would have to be not for Tyrone and Fermanagh only but for [all of] the Six Counties.' Jones noted his reply to Griffith ('I said that was enough for me') and added in a note to himself that 'a boundary commission was the idea of Edward Carson, the unionist leader, who thought that unionists would gain if unionist communities in Ulster outside the six counties were transferred to the northern side of the new border'.[21] In fact, adjustments to the new frontier would never be made and the Irish border has remained problematic to this day, as seen during the 'Brexit' controversy.

The evening negotiations on Thursday 1 December 1921 were described at the time as 'most exacting'.[22] *The Irish Times* reported that 'Between 6.30 and midnight the tension was at its highest, and it constitutes the most strenuous period of any during the negotiations.'[23] Proposals were carefully considered clause by clause, with various amendments made: 'The examination of the proposals was a sharp battle of wits between Mr Griffith and Mr Lloyd George', remarked one newspaper correspondent.[24] Finally, an agreed draft document emerged about 1.30 a.m.

Having been awake well into the early hours of the morning of Friday 2 December, embroiled in tough talks and always under implicit if not explicit threat of imminent military hostilities from the British, Irish negotiators felt obliged to rush back to Ireland later that same Friday in order to consult their colleagues in Dublin next day, before then immediately returning to London for a meeting on Sunday. This all required a journey of twenty-two hours travel, eleven in each direction, as well as a difficult cabinet meeting in Dublin that would include not only de Valera but also their two intractable cabinet colleagues, Austin Stack and Cathal Brugha. Now, on short winter days, the Irish Sea could be rough. A boat on which some of the delegates sailed was about to be be involved in another fatal collision.

'Awful Day'

Arthur Griffith and Éamonn Duggan caught that Friday morning's train from Euston Station to Holyhead. After Griffith ate breakfast, he returned to his seat in another carriage but left behind on the luggage rack in the dining-car his old attaché case. In that unlocked case was the negotiated text of the proposed treaty. His forgetfulness was perhaps a symptom of the pressure he was under. Fortunately for him, a senior civil servant and not one of the many journalists also on board recognised the attaché case and ensured that a relieved Griffith recovered it before reaching Holyhead.[25] Meanwhile, Collins was having yet another meeting at Downing Street. There, at about 7.00 p.m. on the Friday, he liberated a sheet of its headed notepaper and scribbled on it a love letter to Kitty Kiernan while the secretaries agreed final details of a promised report. He had told Kiernan on 30 November that his maxim was 'It's better to wear out than to rust out', but at this point confided 'I have had a most awful day – conferring all the time and I am preparing to clear off now for Euston station' to catch the night mail to Holyhead.[26]

The tone of a comment that de Valera made to Joe McGarrity later that month suggests that the former was irked to be involved at this point. He wrote: 'I was suddenly summoned to Dublin to meet Griffith and the plenipotentiaries who had returned'.[27] A driver conveyed him back from the west of Ireland where de Valera had been touring groups of rebel volunteer soldiers (the IRA) to boost their morale, and warning them of the dangers of consuming too much alcohol. He also advised them that the IRA might have to resume the War of Independence if peace negotiations failed. Many of those whom he addressed were recruits who had never fired a shot in anger.

Griffith disembarked in Ireland on the evening of Friday 2 December, and then stayed up to meet de Valera after 11.00 p.m. that night. By then Michael Collins, George Gavan Duffy and Erskine Childers had also left London, intending to make it back to Ireland on the overnight boat with just a few hours to spare before the cabinet meeting on Saturday morning. Theirs was already a tight schedule, but it became even tighter when their boat hit and sank a schooner. Their vessel, a new *Cambria*, was on its maiden voyage, carrying with Collins and Duggan 272 other passengers and many bags of mail. It left Holyhead at 3.12 a.m. and was at full speed just off the coast of north Wales when at 3.28 a.m. it rammed and cut in two the *James Tyrel* from Arklow ('as if it were a piece of cheese' according to one account).[28] Three of the schooner's crew died. Michael Collins reportedly helped to lower the *Cambria*'s lifeboats and offered the delegates' rooms on board to those who were rescued. He is said to have refused a lifebelt, reportedly remarking with a smile 'I have been in tighter corners than this, and got out of them.'[29] The *Cambria* cruised about the area for over an hour before returning to Holyhead around 6.00 a.m. Its passengers were subsequently transferred to the *Hibernia*, which left for Ireland at 7.50 a.m. and arrived in Ireland at 10.31 a.m.[30] Among others on board the *Cambria* that night was John Ford, later director of the quintessential Irish-American film *The Quiet Man* (1952) and the son of an Irish emigrant whose home district he was now to find badly damaged by British forces.[31] The boat's very late arrival meant that Collins and Gavan Duffy had to go straight from it to the cabinet meeting due to start at 11.00 a.m. at Dublin's Mansion House. They arrived in time, but with little chance to consult their fellow peace negotiators before the fraught session began. Horace Plunkett called on Erskine Childers and his wife later that day, noting 'He, who arrived this morning and goes back [to London] tonight looked very tired.'[32]

According to the publicity department of Dáil Éireann, the Irish cabinet met in Dublin on Saturday 3 December from 11.00 a.m. until 7.00 p.m., with a break for lunch. Members of the delegation to London who were not members of the Dáil cabinet were permitted to attend part of the meeting.[33] Minister for Defence Cathal Brugha, a hardliner who had chosen not to be in London, demanded to know more about the splitting of the delegation for various meetings with the British in London that meant Griffith and Collins did most of the key work, claiming that 'the British Government selected its men'. Griffith reassured the cabinet that Dáil Éireann would have the final say. He invited de Valera himself to go to London, which de Valera still would not do.[34] 'Confused and inconclusive discussion in Irish cabinet,' recorded the prompt and well-informed British cabinet secretary in his diary.[35] It is said that British intelligence had an informant whom Griffith and others on the Irish team trusted to the point of being 'quite frank as to their views and their future negotiating tactics'. The identity of that informant, whether deliberately disloyal to the Irish delegation or simply reckless, is unknown.[36]

Secret Diplomacy

Within twelve hours of that difficult meeting ending in Dublin on Saturday, Griffith was already back in London with de Valera's latest suggestions. By now it was Sunday morning. The fact that he, Collins and Duggan travelled by one boat while Barton, Gavan Duffy and Chilters boarded another vessel may have reflected divisions in the cabinet.[37] De Valera himself returned to the west of Ireland and resumed his tour of IRA volunteers, a decision that McCullagh in his recent biography finds 'inexplicable' because it put the president of Dáil Éireann even further out of contact with developments at Downing Street.[38] At 5.00 p.m. on that Sunday 4 December Griffith, Barton and Gavan Duffy found themselves again in Downing Street, facing Prime Minister Lloyd George and other senior British ministers in a very tense session. Reporters commented on the absence of Michael Collins, 'although he was believed to be in London'.[39] Collins explained his absence as being 'for the reason that I had in my own estimation argued fully all points', but the British cabinet secretary thought that he was bluntly 'fed up' with the muddle.[40] Indeed, on that day, Collins wrote from London to Kitty Kiernan: 'I dislike this place intensely on a Sunday; everything so quiet, and still, and so drearily dull. The outlook now is not inviting – through smoky, grimy windows, to a drab Square. Very, very unpleasant indeed – different from our own places, but then there's a job to be done, and for the moment here is the place. And *that's that*.'[41]

At the meeting that Collins missed that Sunday, Griffith read out de Valera's latest proposals from Dublin – only to find Lloyd George retorting that these were 'a complete going back upon the discussions of the last week'. At the nub of British concerns was the Irish reluctance to be associated formally with 'the British Empire'. De Valera wanted a looser kind of external association with the British Commonwealth, under its figurehead of the Crown. Griffith at the outset in October had neatly expressed an underlying distinction between Ireland and places such as Australia or Canada. He said 'We do not feel ourselves to be a colony but a nation.'[42] He now reported to de Valera,

> They [the British] asked what was the difficulty about going in like Canada in the Empire? Gavan Duffy said that we should be as closely associated with them as the Dominions [such as Canada] in the large matters, and more so in the matter of defence but our difficulty is coming within the Empire. They jumped up at this and conversation came to a close, we undertaking to send them copies of our proposals tomorrow and they undertaking to send in a formal rejection tomorrow. They would, they said, inform Craig [leader of the Ulster unionists] tomorrow that the negotiations were broken down. We then parted.[43]

Newspaper reports next morning suggested that expectations of an agreement were low. A correspondent for *The Freeman's Journal* reported 'Journalists who have been accustomed to visit Downing Street almost daily for years past informed me that they never remember seeing so much depression within the portals of No. 10 as prevailed last night.'[44] Griffith was so worried that, very late after the formal session ended on the Sunday, he arranged a private meeting with the British cabinet secretary, Thomas Jones. The latter wrote in his diary at 1.30 a.m. on Monday morning after they parted, 'I saw Arthur Griffith at midnight for an hour alone. He was labouring under a deep sense of the crisis and spoke throughout with the greatest earnestness and unusual emotion. One was bound to feel that to break with him would be infinitely tragic.'[45] Griffith is said to have described the meeting to Jones as 'our first attempt at secret diplomacy'.[46] He tried to impress upon Jones the need for further concessions if a civil war among nationalists was to be avoided. Jones agreed to a request from Griffith that Lloyd George would meet Michael Collins a few hours later to 'have a heart-to-heart with him', and 'so Arthur Griffith went over at 1.00 [a.m.] to hunt out Collins to fix this up'.[47]

What was Griffith feeling as he 'went over' to Collins at Chelsea in the early hours? He was beginning his ninth week of talks in London, having within the previous ten days made not one but two tiring journeys to Dublin and back.[48] He was wrangling with Lloyd George, a man nicknamed 'the Welsh wizard', all the time on solid English 'home turf' that was well within the social and political comfort zones of the British. Although the Irish had high-class lodgings at 22 Hans Place and 15 Cadogan Gardens, they cannot have found their extended stay abroad anything but difficult. Collins in England and Kitty Kiernan in Ireland daily exchanged love letters that reflected the pressures under which he laboured. Collins told her 'It's so lonely and so sad being far away.'[49] She visited him, and Griffith's 'Mollie' came in December.[50] De Valera's absence made matters worse. If the prospects of even limited statehood slipped away, nationalists might face outright war with the British army and armed Ulster unionists. Someone painted the word 'MURDERERS' in letters a foot wide on the footpath outside the house in Hans Place.[51]

Collins accepted the invitation to go alone to see Lloyd George, at 9.30 a.m.[52] By the time that they met, the prime minister had already been up and working for over four hours: 'His patience and alertness have been extraordinary, even for him,' wrote Jones then.[53] When Griffith and Barton returned to Downing Street on the afternoon of that same Monday 5 December, Collins joined them.

As on the previous day and on the previous Thursday, the formal session of the talks on Monday 5 December began in the afternoon and ran into the evening. This may have been a negotiating ploy on the part of the British to exploit fatigue. Starting about 3 o'clock in the afternoon, the talks continued until about 7.15 p.m. and resumed later from around 11.15 p.m. Under intense personal pressure from Lloyd George, Griffith eventually announced that he would accept the document as it then stood. This seemingly took his colleagues by surprise. However, by 2.15 a.m., in the early hours of Tuesday 6 December 1921, all of the Irish had followed his lead, finalising and signing articles of agreement for a treaty.[54] What ultimately decided Collins in favour of signing appears to have been the British promise to establish a boundary commission to adjust the new Irish border in accordance with the wishes of local populations. The day before signing, Collins had predicted that the work of the boundary commission would mean 'We would save [the northern counties of] Tyrone and Fermanagh, parts of Derry, Armagh and Down.' He noted that Lloyd George had remarked that it was Collins himself who pointed out on a previous occasion 'that the North [of Ireland] would be forced economically to come in.'[55] However, this did not mean that Lloyd George himself thought so.

The decision by Griffith to commit himself unilaterally to signing, and by the team to agree to a boundary commission without clearer terms of reference, were perhaps tactical errors due partly to exhaustion.[56] Or perhaps they simply felt that there was no realistic alternative at that point. A statement that when the Irish returned to Hans Place Griffith spent what was left of the night pacing the hall with his head in his hands was later described by his private secretary as 'a grave untruth.'[57] Whatever the facts on that occasion, the psychological implications of logistical pressures on negotiators, and in particular the impact of the physical arrangements made for or by them, cannot be overlooked by historians as a factor quite possibly contributing significantly to the outcome of negotiations.

15

1921: 'He Signed the Treaty'

The long-running 'Brexit' debacle in Britain is a reminder of just how fraught and subjective intense political debates involving international treaties and national identities can become. Perceptions of reality shift unpredictably, even when those arguing their causes are well intentioned. Both principle and prejudice are at play, both the rational and irrational.

Caesar, crossing the River Rubicon in 49 BC to banish his opponents from Rome, declared 'the dice is cast' [*iacta alea est*]. In December 1921, Griffith crossed his Rubicon when he declared he would sign the treaty proposal in Downing Street. He was not sure that even Michael Collins would follow his lead, never mind any other member of his team (Barton, Duggan and Gavan Duffy). But they all did. Griffith sealed what he believed was the best deal possible for Ireland in difficult circumstances. He was under no illusion about the British. His widow later told Michael Hayes how her husband described to her Lloyd George entering a room 'like a benevolent old gentleman with white hair and a smooth face showing no line on it':

Mrs A.G. He must have an easy conscience.
AG: He has no conscience.[1]

British ministers were worried about their own political futures, but also anxious about the international implications of committing their army to fighting again in Ireland. The Irish were worried about the lives of their countrymen in the event of no deal. Collins and Griffith regarded the treaty as a step in the direction of an all-Ireland state, or even of a republic. Nevertheless, later on the day that he signed the articles of agreement Collins wrote dramatically:

> When you have sweated, toiled, had mad dreams, hopeless nightmares, you find yourself in London's streets, cold and dank in the night air. Think – what have I got for Ireland? Something which she has wanted these past seven hundred years. Will anyone be satisfied at the bargain? Will anyone? I tell you this; early this morning I signed my death warrant. I thought at the time how odd, how ridiculous – a bullet may just as well have done the job five years ago.[2]

There had been years of pleading, a sacrificial rebellion, a guerilla war for independence. There were months of painful negotiations. Now the plenipotentiaries returned to Dublin with an agreement for Dáil Éireann to approve or to reject, for it was only a resolution of the elected members of Dáil Éireann and not the negotiators' signatures on the proposed treaty that could make it a reality. The Dáil approved it. Voters too endorsed it, not by means of a referendum as some wanted but by electing a majority of pro-treaty candidates in the subsequent general election. No later Irish government ever proposed revoking that treaty.

The fact that the exact final version of the articles of agreement for a treaty had not been referred back to the cabinet in Dublin for approval, before being signed in London on 6 December 1921, infuriated de Valera. Yet, later on that very evening he calmly donned academic robes in his capacity as the new honorary chancellor of the National University of Ireland and chaired an event marking the centenary of Dante's death.[3] The inferno of civil war was still not inevitable.

De Valera may always have planned to reject any 'final' offer by the British, in order to send delegates back for one last push that they might then blame on their intransigent chief in Dublin. Now he insisted that the team had broken a promise or obligation to refer the very final draft back to him for approval before signing. Griffith said that they were not bound to do so, that the Dáil and not de Valera had made them plenipotentiaries. Whoever was right, the Dáil made its decision and the short civil war that followed poisoned Irish politics.

A Point of 'Honour'?

Some thought the canny Lloyd George had outsmarted Griffith as early as November 1921. The British cabinet secretary had then worked on Griffith and Collins to see if the Irish would settle for a new state with dominion status within the empire, similar to Canada, along with a commission to determine the precise boundaries of those parts of Ulster where its inhabitants wished to remain within the United Kingdom. On the evening of 13 November 1921 Griffith wrote to de Valera explaining that he had just then met the prime minister who discussed with him the British government's position in respect to the Ulster unionists at that point:

> Lloyd George and his colleagues are sending a further reply to the Ulstermen ... offering to create an All-Ireland Parliament, Ulster to have the right to vote itself out within 12 months, but if it does a Boundary Commission to be set up to delimit the area, and the part that remains after the Commission has acted to be subject to equal financial burdens with England.

> Lloyd George intimated this would be their last word to Ulster. If they refused, as he believed they would, he would fight, summon Parliament, appeal to it against Ulster, dissolve, or pass an Act establishing the All-Ireland Parliament.

> I told him it was his proposal, not ours. He agreed, but he said that when they were fighting next Thursday with the Die-hards and 'Ulster' in front, they were lost if we cut the ground away behind them by repudiating the proposal.

> I said we would not do that, if he meant that he thought we would come out in public decrying it. It was his own proposal. If the Ulstermen accepted it, we would have to discuss it with him in the privacy of the Conference [treaty talks]. I could not guarantee its acceptance, as, of course, my colleagues knew nothing of it yet. But I would guarantee that while he was fighting the 'Ulster' crowd we would not help them by repudiating him. This satisfied him.[4]

What Lloyd George wanted was that Irish nationalists would not 'break' on Northern Ireland, that they would hope instead that a boundary commission must certainly favour increasing the territory of the Irish Free State and thus perhaps render Northern Ireland unviable or less viable. As seen above, Collins seems to have convinced himself that it would do so. But if that was the Irish understanding of the ultimate outcome, it was not necessarily shared by the British and might possibly have been tied down more clearly. Moreover, Griffith did not mention in the letter to de Valera, and seemingly did not mention to his colleagues, that he had assented to a memorandum being prepared based on the proposal that he alone had discussed with the cabinet secretary. That official memorandum was to seem colder and more definitive in respect to the status of Northern Ireland than Griffith's letter to de Valera, and its later revelation and use by Lloyd George came as an unpleasant suprise at a sensitive moment in the final talks, on 5 December 1921. Another Irish negotiator present with Griffith and Collins that December afternoon recorded what happened:

> Lloyd George got excited. He shook his papers in the air, declared that we were trying deliberately to bring about a break on Ulster because our people in Ireland had refused to come within the Empire and that Arthur Griffith was letting him down where he had promised not to do so. He produced a paper from an envelope, stated that he had shewn it to Arthur Griffith ... and that Arthur Griffith had agreed to its contents. Lloyd George referred to this document as a letter and thereby mystified me and appeared to mystify Michael Collins. I could not recollect the existence of any letter on this subject other than the one Arthur Griffith wrote to Lloyd George on November 2nd after consultation with the other members of the Delegation. The paper was then passed across the table. It proved to be a memorandum, not a letter, and read partly as follows:
>
> If Ulster did not see her way to accept immediately the principle of a Parliament of All-Ireland ... she would continue to be represented in the British Parliament and she would continue subject to British

taxation except in so far as already modified by the Act of 1920. In this case, however, it would be necessary to revise the boundary of Northern Ireland. This might be done by a Boundary Commission which would be directed to adjust the line both by inclusion and exclusion so as to make the Boundary conform as closely as possible to the wishes of the population.

Arthur Griffith declared his adhesion to his undertaking but argued that it was not unreasonable for us to require that [the Unionist leader] Craig should reply before we refused or accepted the proposals now before us. Lloyd George declared that to make receipt of such a reply conditional before accepting or refusing was letting him down on his proposals because the only alternative to Craig's acceptance of the unity of Ireland was the Boundary Commission and that his Government would carry the Boundary Commission proposal into effect with strict fidelity.[5]

This was the moment to which the priest and professor of history F.X. Martin referred in 1965 when he asked the biographer Séan Ó Lúing if Griffith was not 'either vain or rigid so as to be caught by Lloyd George on the point of "honour" in the Treaty negotiations – any typical Irishman would have dismissed Lloyd George's objection'. Whatever one thinks of a Catholic priest suggesting – even in the role of an intellectual 'devil's advocate' – that a 'typical Irishman' might not be so 'vain or rigid' as to keep his word of honour, it may be noted that Griffith's immediate response to Lloyd George was in fact ambiguous rather than fixed. He declared his adhesion to the understanding, such as that was and not necessarily as others thought it to be, but at the same time argued that it was reasonable that his colleagues only accept or refuse the proposals before them when they had heard further from Craig on behalf of the unionists. Moreover, it was still necessary for Dáil Éireann to agree to the treaty. In any event, Griffith by this stage almost certainly thought that the memorandum reflected the only way forward in practice, whatever about honour or principle.

However, he had wrong-footed his fellow delegates by not obtaining and sharing a copy of the memorandum with them when he conveyed its substance to de Valera, albeit perhaps reluctant to do so in case the idea somehow leaked out. But that omission was perhaps not as crucial as some have suggested. Pakenham, in his influential early account of the treaty negotiations, made much of the November memo and felt that 'Griffith's promise excluded any further possibility of a break coming on the Ulster question.' Yet Pakenham himself conceded at the same time that Griffith by agreeing to the memo had made 'no definite promise' to assent to the terms mentioned before Craig had consented or had even replied on the unionist side.[6] The influence of Pakenham's work is evident in the fact that F.X. Martin not only uses but places in inverted commas the word 'honour' that Pakenham earlier deployed in print in order to bolster the theory that Griffith was somehow 'caught' by Lloyd George.

Bones of Contention

Griffith had long wanted a degree of independence for Ireland stronger than that envisaged by 'Home Rule', and most of Ireland now had it, thanks to him and to the others who negotiated the creation of an Irish state in London. There would not yet be a republic, but it had been clear from the outset that the Irish could not achieve in negotiations what they had failed to win by fighting. De Valera knew that, even if some were not willing to accept the reality.

Before briefly posing a few of the 'what if' questions that are still so maddening and ultimately unanswerable, questions that can inflame even the most austere and intellectual observer and drive one to 'take sides' (as if such questions had simple 'sides'), it is worth identifying three of the short treaty's most significant articles of agreement in particular.

Article 1: Ireland shall have the same constitutional status in the Community of Nations known as the British Empire as the Dominion of Canada, the Commonwealth of Australia, the Dominion of New Zealand, and the Union of South Africa with a Parliament having powers to make laws for the peace, order and good government of Ireland and an Executive responsible to that Parliament, and shall be styled and known as the Irish Free State.[7]

While this article met the British pre-condition that Ireland remain within the empire, the freedom and status envisaged by it for Ireland had been inconceivable twenty years earlier. Griffith's clarion call for elected Irish MPs to withdraw from Westminster was now consolidated by the recognition of an Irish parliament that ranked alongside those of Australia and Canada. De Valera hoped for something symbolically more unique, a relationship that might be more external to the empire than such dominion status.

> Article 4: The oath to be taken by Members of the Parliament of the Irish Free State shall be in the following form:- I [NAME] do solemnly swear true faith and allegiance to the Constitution of the Irish Free State as by law established and that I will be faithful to H.M. King George V, his heirs and successors by law, in virtue of the common citizenship of Ireland with Great Britain and her adherence to and membership of the group of nations forming the British Commonwealth of Nations.

De Valera detested this oath. It stuck in the throats of many on both sides of the subsequent treaty divide, notwithstanding that the editor of the British cabinet secretary's diary has described it as 'a mishmash of legal verbiage, making the oath almost meaningless'.[8] In addition to political distaste at swearing to be 'faithful' to the British monarch, which for nationalist Ireland had connotations very different from those for the colonial settlers of Australia or Canada, there was also a religious implication. The British monarch was head of the Church of England, the church of the old enemy and occupier, and aspects of the British monarchy and government remained sectarian. How significant was this religious factor for de Valera in particular? The priests of Blackrock College had been his surrogate parents and he had stayed living there even after he left school. He reportedly told the electors of Clare that 'all his life he had been associated with priests, and the priests knew him and were behind him'.[9]

Difficult or not as it may be to grasp now, this article was one of the key sticking points that led to civil war. De Valera and his followers later took the oath and entered government as the Fianna Fáil party.[10]

Meanwhile there was that Boundary Commission on which Collins and Griffith, both dead by the end of 1922, pinned their hopes when it was promised in the treaty:

> Article 12: … a Commission consisting of three persons, one to be appointed by the Government of the Irish Free State, one to be appointed by the Government of Northern Ireland, and one who shall be Chairman to be appointed by the British Government shall determine in accordance with the wishes of the inhabitants, so far as may be compatible with economic and geographic conditions, the boundaries between Northern Ireland and the rest of Ireland, and for the purposes of the Government of Ireland Act, 1920, and of this instrument, the boundary of Northern Ireland shall be such as may be determined by such Commission.

Griffith and Collins regarded this as a vital component of the treaty, ostensibly deluding themselves into believing that it must result in large portions of 'the Six Counties' being transferred to the Irish Free State once the provision was given 'effect with strict fidelity' as Lloyd George reportedly promised just hours before they signed in London.[11] However, the treaty did not define aspects of such a commission enough and it proved inadequate. It was not only unionists who had problems with the concept. The fact that people in some areas of the province of Ulster, lying within the Irish Free State, might wish to be transferred into Northern Ireland subsequently alarmed Dublin and exacerbated sensitivities. In the end the Boundary Commission did not serve as a stepping-stone to a united, independent Ireland. Had the cabinet of the new state itself been united from the outset, more might have been achieved.

What If?

An old adage has it that there is no use crying over spilt milk. But it is still difficult to resist taking sides on the treaty even today and, once a side is taken, difficult to resist stacking up details in support of an argument. The use of history for political or cultural purposes did not start or end with the Irish civil war.

Was de Valera right or wrong when he convinced himself that his cabinet as a whole must have the last word before the proposed treaty was signed and brought to the Dáil? Was Griffith acting arrogantly, or being a statesman within his terms of reference from the Dáil as a whole, when he decided to sign the document without further referral back to cabinet colleagues who had passed up their chance to be part of the Irish team in London?

What if the Irish had walked out of the talks on 6 December 1921 and insisted on returning to consult with de Valera yet again? Would the British have conceded more? Might not their doing so have brought down the United Kingdom government and undone whatever had been negotiated? Might the possibility of such an outcome have made the British even more likely to call the Irish bluff and order military re-engagement in Ireland? Now, with the war in Europe ended, Irish fighters would face not merely policemen and ragged auxiliaries but large contingents of well-trained and heavily armed forces with nothing to distract the British from a ruthless suppression of insurgency and the liquidation of its leaders? Might the negotiating team have failed even to reach home?

Or perhaps London would have waited patiently for the Irish to see sense, from a British perspective. Maybe de Valera would have found one of his formulas of words, mastering ambiguity to own the agreement as his while making it seem more than it actually was. We shall never know. A letter written by de Valera to Joseph McGarrity in Philadelphia before the end of 1921 neatly frames the frustrating questions of what might have been. He was justifying his decision not to go to London even in early December 1921:

The British would think I had gone because I was anxious to prevent a breakdown. They would accordingly not make any further advance to me, but might stiffen instead ... I probably would have gone over, nevertheless, had not Griffith [having] been shown that if he accepted the Crown he would split the country, given an *express undertaking* [words stressed on the original] that he would not sign a document accepting allegiance but would bring it back and

> refer the matter to Dáil Éireann. This made us all satisfied; we were
> certain that Dáil Éireann would reject it.[12]

The negotiators did in fact 'refer the matter to Dáil Éireann'. For approval
of the treaty was ultimately contingent on Dáil Éireann accepting it,
regardless of whether or not the 'plenipotentiaries' signed it first. Was not
de Valera proven wrong by history when the Dáil did not in fact 'reject
it' despite concessions on the Crown? Griffith never tired of indicating
that the final decision was a democratic one, saying for example in Dáil
Éireann on 10 January 1922 'If the Irish people turn down the Free State
for the Republic, I will follow in the ranks'.

Meanwhile Ulster's unionists were looking on. It might not have
mattered much to them if the Irish Free State styled itself a republic, but
if their six counties came under imminent threat of outright military
activity by the IRA or by the new state then Ireland might have been
plunged into a civil war even more damaging and certainly more bloody
and harmful to civilians than what soon followed. Sectarian violence
against Catholics in Northern Ireland at the time did not bode well for
the future.

If we cannot answer the 'what if' questions definitively, we may
consider them as dispassionately as possible. George Santayana's warning
is something of a cliché but still worth heeding. In his *Life of Reason*,
published in 1905 when Sinn Féin was emerging as a movement, he
wrote 'Those who cannot remember the past are condemned to repeat
it'. By studying what happened in 1921, its roots and causes, we may
avoid future errors.

President of Ireland

Having signed the treaty, Griffith returned to Dublin. There, the next
morning, he scribbled a note and asked his private secretary to issue
it: 'I have signed a treaty of peace between Ireland and Great Britain. I
believe that treaty will lay foundations of peace and friendship between
the two Nations. What I have signed I shall stand by in the belief that
the end of the conflict of centuries is at hand'.[13]

In 1917 Griffith absented himself from competition when he yielded to de Valera the position of president of Sinn Féin, rather than risk a split, and this resulted in de Valera becoming president of Dáil Éireann after Sinn Féin's stunning election victory in 1918. However, de Valera's own role in respect to Griffith may be defined as a series of absences. Absent from Sinn Féin before 1917; absent in the United States for eighteen months, during which time Griffith was appointed his substitute as president; absent from the treaty negotiations in London in late 1921; absent from Dáil Éireann in 1922 once it voted to support the treaty. Was de Valera's unsettling personal experience of absent parents in any way a factor in this peculiar political relationship with 'the father of Sinn Féin'?

In 1922 Griffith became president of Dáil Éireann, pending the formal creation of the Irish Free State. In de Valera's mind the office to which Griffith now succeeded had made de Valera both president of the Dáil and president of the notional republic proclaimed by the rebels of 1916. During his absence in America he had been been publicly addressed in some quarters as 'President of Ireland'. This led to a somewhat farcical exchange in the Dáil on 10 January 1922:

MR. GRIFFITH: President de Valera yesterday threw this body into confusion by resigning and leaving no government in existence. Public order and security have to be maintained. If I am elected I will occupy whatever position President de Valera occupied.

MR. DE VALERA: Hear, hear.

MR. GRIFFITH: Now, that is right. In that position he was not the President of the Republic, but the President of Dáil Éireann, according to the constitution ('No! no!').

MR. DE VALERA: It is President of Dáil Éireann, which is written down as the Government of the Republic of Ireland. So I was President of the Republic of Ireland.

MR. GRIFFITH: I do not mind a single rap about words. I say whatever position – if you like to put it that way – that the President resigned from yesterday, I will, if I am elected, occupy the same position until the Irish people have an opportunity of deciding for themselves.

MR. DE VALERA: That is a fair answer.[14]

Unsurprisingly, such distinctions defeated the editor of *The New York Times*. When the paper devoted the whole front page of its 'Mid-Week Pictorial' supplement to a photograph of Griffith in January 1922, it described him in a large caption simply as 'Head of the Irish Free State' (Plate 1).

Getting There

Years after the treaty debates, Griffith's private secretary recalled that he liked to travel in the open air. She wrote 'It must be pointed out that the usual method of transport of this humble man, even after he became president of the Provisional government, was "Shank's Mare" [i.e. walking] or, when absolutely necessary, a hackney car.' She was remarking on the fact that in March 1922 Griffith was obliged to explain that his hire of a motor car at the expense of the provisional government in December 1921 was not personal but had been needed to take him late at night to a cabinet meeting.[15] If methods of transport reveal personality it may be instructive that those used by the leading players to get to the Dáil treaty debate on 15 December 1921 were a matter for comments in the media. Next day, for example, the *Cork Examiner* reported that 'Mr de Valera drove up in a somewhat old-fashioned car, Mr Michael Collins lolled back in a Rolls-Royce, Mr Arthur Griffith balanced himself on the side of a jaunting car [see p.3 above], while Mr Cathal Brugha laboriously pedalled along on a bicycle.'

1922: Destruction and Death

Griffith was visited during the prolonged treaty negotiations by 'a sculptor named Jacob Epstein, who brought in his arms his baby rolled up in swaddling-clothes which resembled an Egyptian mummy'.[1]

As if he had not enough on his mind, Griffith was being asked to play host at his temporary home in London to a number of renowned intellectuals, including George Bernard Shaw. Another was James Joyce's friend Ezra Pound. Pound arrived to promote his economic theories, for besides being a poet he had political interests. Of his meeting in London he later said: 'One of the most illuminating hours of my life was that spent in conversation with Griffith,' whom he called 'the inventor of Sinn Féin'.[2] At one point, wrote Pound, Griffith replied 'All you say is true. But I can't move 'em with a cold thing like economics.' According to a biographer of the poet this remark would 'stay with Pound for the rest of his life, as a constant reminder that intelligence by itself did not bring about change, that it counted for very little without the will to change'.[3] More than once Pound recalled the remark in his work, most notably in the Cantos where he somewhat rudely describes Griffith as 'stubby':

And the stubby little man was up-stairs.
And there was the slick guy in the other corner reading The Tatler,
Not upside down, but never turning the pages,
And then I went up to the bed-room, and he said,
The stubby fellow: Perfectly true,
'But it's a question of feeling,

'Can't move 'em with a cold thing, like economics.'
And so we came down stairs and went out …[4]

Pound observed 'Not one man in a thousand can be aroused to an interest in economics until he definitely suffers from the effects of an evil system.'[5] He may have pressed Griffith on Sinn Féin's abstentionist policy, for he indicated that Griffith explained to him 'I am pledged not to come here [London] to Parliament.'[6]

If the visit by the anti-Semitic Pound was odd, that by the controversial Jewish sculptor Jacob Epstein seems stranger. The man who earlier designed the tomb for Oscar Wilde's grave in Paris presented himself with his babe-in-arms to the 'father of Sinn Féin'. Griffith had at least once in his United Irishman defended Wilde's literary reputation, and the Polish-American sculptor may have heard about this. The nude, angel-like figure that he created for Wilde's grave in Paris, influenced by the style of winged Egyptian and other sphinxes, is today regarded as an Irish and French national treasure but attracted controversy when first unveiled. Prominent testicles accentuated its phallic thrust.[7] Now its creator stood in front of a man described in the press as being 'emotionless as the sphinx'.[8] Earlier, Epstein had created a bust of Lady Augusta Gregory, and is said to have struggled generally with the question of nationality and its value.[9] Among his patrons was the Irish-American collector John Quinn.[10] In 1947, Epstein would make a bust of the English national hero Winston Churchill, a cast of which bust Donald Trump returned to its former place in the Oval Office when he became US president. But if Epstein had it in mind to create a sculpture of Griffith – who in 1921 sat across a negotiating table from Winston Churchill – nothing came of the idea. Irish newspapers do not appear to have reported Epstein's visit, which was later remembered but not explained by Griffith's private secretary in London. The latter's comparison of the swaddled baby to an Egyptian mummy is striking. This 'baby' was probably Epstein's two-year-old daughter Peggy Jane, of whom Epstein about this time sculpted a number of figures and who grew up to be an art student alongside Lucien Freud, later her sister's husband. Given Griffith's place of internment in 1916, did he and Epstein discuss the lines inscribed on Wilde's tomb, from Wilde's 'Ballad of Reading Gaol'?

And alien tears will fill for him
   Pity's long-broken urn,
For his mourners will be outcast men,
   And outcasts always mourn.

If Griffith himself was no longer a political outcast, the role in which he now found himself had its discomforts. His detractors alleged that he and Collins were flattered and influenced by their reception in London. He usually lived very simply and was notoriously shy. He had a keen sense of who the outcasts were in his world. Perhaps by attending performances of the revived *Beggar's Opera* when in England, he not only soothed his nerves musically but also reminded himself of the everyday lives of poor people in the face of more abstract political arguments.

Turning White

Griffith's earlier deputising for de Valera, absent in America, and his periods of incarceration in England and Ireland since Easter 1916, as well as his anxiety about the impact of raids on his family and other personal dangers, took their toll on a man who was now almost fifty years old. He received several death threats.[11] The kind of stress to which he was subjected is evident from the fact that, during his time interned in Gloucester Prison, the acting editor of his paper *Nationality* collapsed and died following a raid on its premises by British soldiers.[12] Griffith himself had been unwell before being released from Mountjoy Prison earlier in 1921.[13]

In December 1921, Mollie Griffith crossed the Irish Sea to join her 'Dan' at Hans Place (Plate 15). She wrote to a friend soon afterwards: 'First thing I noticed in London was his hair turning white.' He is said to have told her 'You will have your wish. In August I will be out of politics.'[14] The day after the treaty was signed and the couple returned to Ireland she told a friend 'A pressman pounded the knocker at 1 a.m. I thought for a while it was the B[lack] & T[ans] again.' She added that her husband had not had a sleep since before the weekend, so 'how must he feel now'? She thought 'He's always been a fool giving his all, others having the benefit. But we must pray for peace, as never again will the same terms be offered.'[15]

Standing by the Treaty

Speaking in the treaty debates in the Dáil, on 19 December 1921, Griffith said among other things:

> Nearly three months ago Dáil Éireann appointed plenipotentiaries to go to London to treat with the British Government and to make a bargain with them. We have made a bargain. We have brought it back. We were to go there to reconcile our aspirations with the association of the community of nations known as the British Empire. That task which was given to us was as hard as was ever placed on the shoulders of men. We faced that task; we knew that whatever happened we would have our critics, and we made up our minds to do whatever was right and disregard whatever criticism might occur. We could have shirked the responsibility. We did not seek to act as the plenipotentiaries; other men were asked and other men refused. We went. The responsibility is on our shoulders; we took the responsibility in London and we take the responsibility in Dublin. I signed that Treaty not as the ideal thing, but fully believing, as I believe now, it is a treaty honourable to Ireland, and safeguards the vital interests of Ireland.

> And now by that Treaty I am going to stand, and every man with a scrap of honour who signed it is going to stand. It is for the Irish people – who are our masters (hear, hear), not our servants as some think – it is for the Irish people to say whether it is good enough. I hold that it is, and I hold that the Irish people – that 95 per cent of them believe it to be good enough. We are here, not as the dictators of the Irish people, but as the representatives of the Irish people, and if we misrepresent the Irish people, then the moral authority of Dáil Éireann, the strength behind it, and the fact that Dáil Éireann spoke the voice of the Irish people, is gone, and gone forever ... Does all this quibble of words – because it is merely a quibble of

words – mean that Ireland is asked to throw away this Treaty and go back to war? So far as my power or voice extends, not one young Irishman's life shall be lost on that quibble.

In the end, most members of Dáil Éireann accepted the treaty as the best agreement possible in the circumstances. De Valera and a minority did not, and they walked out. Neither Collins nor Griffith wanted a civil war, but both agreed that military action was necessary when anti-treaty forces occupied the Four Courts in Dublin. Griffith and Collins believed that they were enforcing the will of the people, as expressed both by the Dáil itself and by most voters in a general election during 1922 that returned a majority of pro-treaty candidates. The Labour Party had wanted a plebiscite or referendum on the treaty, rather than letting it become the dominant issue in that election. Others objected that the franchise on which that election was based was outdated and inadequate, and that updating it to include more women and young people would make a difference to the outcome. But Griffith dismissed de Valera's demand for a new register, writing to him 'You are also prepared, judging from your speeches, to put forward subsequent claims with the object of consuming time, in order that the electorate may be muzzled, while the Treaty is being destroyed.'[16]

Soon, matters were exacerbated by explicit threats by de Valera and others to wade through Irish blood in order to achieve a full republic.[17] Griffith defied danger and went to Sligo in early April 1922 (Plate 16), carrying in his pocket 'a last message' in case he died there. It would be opened after his death in August and it read: 'Let the people stand firm for the Free State. It is their national need and economic salvation. Love to the Irish people, to all my colleagues and friends.'[18] In January 1921 he was already taking steps to have Ireland join the League of Nations.[19] Later in April there were acrimonious exchanges between ministers at a meeting convened in the Mansion House to attempt reconciliation. Cathal Brugha accused Griffith and Collins of being agents of the British government, while Griffith told de Valera, regarding the latter's attitude to negotiations, 'a penny postcard would have been sufficient to inform the British Government without going to the trouble of sending us over.' The cartoonist 'Shemus' caught the mood of the times (Plate 17).[20]

The Wind of Hope

'The atmosphere of the year 1922 is not easy to recapture in the year 1951', wrote George Gavan Duffy decades after he had helped to negotiate the treaty.[21] Griffith disliked a proposed electoral pact between both treaty sides, thinking that it was unrealistic and would negate democracy by effectively rigging the distribution of Dáil seats without providing voters with a clear choice. He very reluctantly went along with the idea, as a colleague later recalled:

> When Griffith was asked whether he approved or disapproved, he seemed to me to be under tremendous emotional stress. He worked nervously with his neck-tie in silence. He took off his glasses and wiped them, and I noticed that his hand was shaking so that he could hardly hold them. He put on the glasses, fiddled with his tie again; again he took off his glasses and wiped them, the whole thing occupying, it seemed to me, three or four minutes while dead silence reigned round the table. We all realised that if Griffith said no, a split, the consequences of which could hardly be foreseen, would be almost upon us. On the other hand, I think the majority of us almost wished that he would say no, in the hope that Collins would be forced to reconsider his support of the Pact. Ultimately, however, Griffith said: 'I agree' and made no further comment.[22]

In the event, this proposal failed to stop civil war erupting in late June 1922. That war was a terrible economic and psychological blow to the emerging state. Griffith and Collins felt that they had to defend the new state or yield to military dictatorship. They feared that the British would not tolerate instability and might return to crush what had taken so much to achieve. Republican intransigence prompted one *Punch* cartoonist to suggest that de Valera was stuck in the year of rebellion 1798, but few were laughing.

Among the 'Irregulars' who fought against the emerging new state in the civil war were people who believed that it might be possible to drive the British off the whole island by force and to suppress Irish unionists – or at least believed it best to die trying. They were brave or foolhardy

A DIAGNOSIS.

Dr. M. Collins. "A SOMEWHAT OBSCURE COMPLAINT. SAY '99.'"

Mr. De Valera. "I AM SORRY, SIR, BUT I CAN NEVER PROCEED ANY FURTHER THAN '98."

Punch, 16 August 1922.

soldiers, but Griffith was primarily a politician and an intellectual. To make the distinction in his case that he made in the case of John Mitchel, one may say that Griffith, a nationalist, cared not twopence for republicanism in the abstract. So he was willing to do what was necessary to secure the state's future.[23]

A Broken Heart

Griffith cut a sad figure in his last days. It would be claimed that 'Arthur Griffith died of a broken heart. Shortly after the start of the Civil War workmen were delayed in getting into his office as he was seated at his desk with his hands to his face. On arranging his desk for removal, one of the workmen discovered the blotting pad was quite wet with his tears.'[24] He 'endured tortures of anxiety' and slept on a bed where he and his ministers worked in premises on Upper Merrion Street.[25] Ernest Blythe was with him there at a cabinet meeting, some days after the Four Courts was recaptured from the anti-treaty side. Men taken prisoner were causing uproar in Mountjoy Prison and a note from Griffith's old friend Maud Gonne arrived during the meeting. She wanted Griffith to go outside and talk to her. Griffith refused to go.[26]

Griffith's doctor was another of his old friends. This was Oliver St John Gogarty, with whom he used to swim when younger at Sandycove and whom Joyce immortalised in *Ulysses* as 'stately, plump Buck Mulligan'. Gogarty wrote vividly of the last days:

Arthur Griffith lay on a small mattress in a room off the Ministry for Justice high up in the Government Buildings, as the place intended for a College of Science in the days of the British Administration was now called … If you wished to see him as a medical attendant, you had to put your face into a large letter-box-like grille and hold it against the revolver of the sentry on duty, before the door was opened. When you were admitted into the Hall you found yourself in a small chamber, walled by bullet-proof sheets of steel … Through dirty marble halls and up dirty staircases of a building never designed for dwellings, at last you reached … the small closet where Arthur Griffith lay. At a glance you recognised a man who was very ill. He had a solicitor administering to him. The hour was nine o'clock in the morning. My mind was made up at once. Out of this he must be taken.[27]

On Sunday 31 July 1922 Griffith had an attack of tonsilitis to add to his woes. It passed soon and no operation was deemed necessary, but he was prevailed upon to rest for a few days in a nearby nursing home on

Lower Leeson Street, run by the Sisters of Charity.[28] On some of those days he may have walked around to his office. At the time, the anti-treaty Harry Boland was brought to St Vincent's Hospital, close to the nursing home, where he died of his gunshot wounds on 1 August 1922.

Gogarty arranged for an influential Irish-American, James Duval Phelan, former mayor of San Francisco and US senator for California until 1921, to meet the 'very ill' Griffith at the nursing home. Phelan, who had spent an anxious night in Dublin on his arrival, with the city's roofs resounding to sniper fire, found Griffith 'a nervous wreck' when they met: 'He was obsessed with the idea that, in the cruel vendetta disgraceful and abhorrent to him, he was the next in turn to be sacrificed. He, the originator of the Sinn Féin movement, whose intellectual prowess was the pride of his countrymen, there miserably dying in an hospital.'[29] Griffith's guards reportedly claimed that on the night before he died they heard the banshee wail.[30] On the following morning his sister Frances visited him, and he convinced her that he was fine.[31] But later on 12 August 1922 Gogarty was summoned and arrived quickly to find Griffith lying on his back at the top of the stairs: 'His left arm was outstretched and bloody. A long incision of four inches gaped where his pulse was.' There had been a vain effort to counteract a cerebral haemorrhage. Perhaps into Gogarty's mind came an image of the two of them swimming together years earlier, far out in Dublin Bay. 'Take up that corpse at once,' ordered Gogarty, admitting later that he let something of the bitterness of his spirit escape into that harsh word. He regretted doing so, and a moment later added 'Take the President's body into the bedroom.' The last rites were administered. Gogarty later denied that Griffith was actually poisoned:

the poison that slew Griffith was envy and jealousy and calumny, which can be deadlier than prussic acid, and, what is more mortal to a martyr, ingratitude. He had not the armour with which I, for one, was invested, be it irony or motley. His sincerity was a bow and his belief an arrow which, if deflected, slew his faith ... from the idea of a Dual Monarchy for Ireland, he never advanced or retreated. Therefore it is absurd to write of his parley with English Ministers, Churchill, George, Birkenhead and that ilk, as an 'ordeal' [Pakenham's *Peace by*

Ordeal had recently been published when Gogarty wrote]. It has been presented lately to the Irish public as if it were a campaign in which Griffith fought a rearguard action. A battle wherein Griffith was on the retreat. What is the truth? When I think of what Griffith set out to acquire and the character of the man, which was indeflectible, his achievement of the 'Treaty' is a conquest which excelled all that he set himself to accomplish twenty years before. His 'concessions' were conquests. His camp followers may have expected more loot, but the General's plan of campaign cannot be decided by the avarice of the hangers-on or the *vivandières*. A Dual Monarchy was Griffith's ambition, His triumph went beyond it.[32]

Griffith's widow had a simple diagnosis: 'It was overwork that killed Dan,' she told Michael Hayes.[33] Her late husband's remains were laid out for the public to inspect at Dublin City Hall where a great statue of Daniel O'Connell, whose restraint he once scorned but then in ways emulated, and which was especially draped in black for the occasion, loomed over her 'poor Dan'.

Lloyd George was represented at Griffith's funeral by Thomas Jones, who after the church service in Marlborough Street stood on O'Connell Bridge and watched the procession going to Glasnevin Cemetery. Jones wrote to his wife: 'Sackville St. [now O'Connell St.], in a long stretch is still a heap of ruins, and houses standing are dotted with bullet marks.' The grim intensity of the time is seen clearly etched in the faces of mourners, including Michael Collins, Richard Mulcahy and other Free State troops at Glasnevin.[34]

Yet, in a remarkable comment on how little some people were being inconvenienced by the civil war, Jones also informed his wife that he went afterwards to have lunch at 2.30 in Jammet's, Dublin's leading 'French' restaurant, before going out to the annual 'Horse Show' at the RDS in Ballsbridge: 'There was Society and a gathering of many beautiful Irish women and magnificent horses. We saw the jumping for an hour or more. Met Martin Fitzgerald, owner of the *Freeman*.' That evening, Jones attended a dinner for the Royal Irish Constabulary in Dublin Castle, which was due to be handed over to the nascent Irish Free State on the next day.[35]

VOL. XIV. NO. 21. **MID-WEEK PICTORIAL** PRICE TEN CENTS
JANUARY 19, 1922 (CANADA 15 CENTS)

AN ILLUSTRATED WEEKLY PUBLISHED BY The New York Times COMPANY

ARTHUR GRIFFITH
Head of the Irish Free State.

1. *New York Times* supplement, January 1922.

2. Maud Gonne (MacBride).
(NLI, NPA POLF85)

3. John MacBride and his mother.
(NLI, NPA POLF 107)

4. Mollie (Maud) Sheehan, Griffith's wife.
(NLI, 49,530/24/1)

5. William Rooney, Griffith's 'best friend'.
(NLI, NPA POL175)

6. Sandycove, Co. Dublin, before 1904, with Martello Tower: here Griffith swam and James Joyce set the opening of *Ulysses*. (NLI, L_CAB_02917)

7. *The Memory of the Dead*, Abbey Theatre, 1910. Constance Markievicz holds the player Sean Connolly, in a play by her husband. (NLI, NPA POLF 204)

8. Howth Harbour, gun-running, 1914. Griffith got a rifle there. (NLI, NPA ASG3)

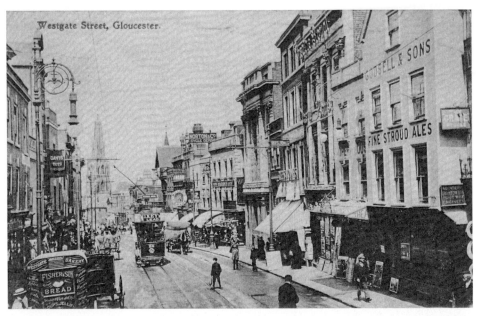

9. Griffith sent his son this postcard from Gloucester Prison, 1919. (NLI, 49,530/5/6/)

10. Sinn Féin HQ, damaged by a British raid in 1920. (NLI, KE 207)

11. Griffith in July 1921: 'Sancho Panza next to Don Quixote – his friend de Valera', wrote French journalist Simone Téry that summer. (NLI, NPA CIVF1)

12. Griffith at home from Mountjoy Prison, 1921, with his children. (NLI, HOGW 83)

13. Griffith, by Sir John Lavery, 1921. A claim by W.B. Yeats that Griffith stares 'in hysterical pride' in this portrait is contested. (Dublin City Gallery/The Hugh Lane)

14. Griffith and Collins (behind) exit Downing Street, October 1921. (NLI, NPA MKN33)

15. Griffith and his wife at 22 Hans Place, December 1921.

16. Griffith and Collins in Sligo in the Spring of 1922. (NLI, INDH400A)

17. *Freeman's Journal* cartoon by 'Shemus', 10 May 1922. Éamon de Valera (in his robes as chancellor of the National University of Ireland) and Erskine Childers confront Griffith and Collins against a background of growing concern that political strains are hitting Irish business. Civil War will erupt in June. (NLI, PD 4309 TX126)

Griffith's remains laid out for the public at Dublin City Hall under a statue of
O'Connell draped in black (National Library of Ireland [NPA POL F91]).

Griffith laboured for years to achieve what he scarcely lived to see.
After he died, a sealed envelope he had given to James Montgomery to
mind was opened at government buildings. It read:

> In case of anything happening to me, all I possess to go to my wife.
> Let a sum of £50, however, be provided for my sister. I hope she will
> be looked after.

> Let the people stand firm for the Free State. It is their national need
> and economic salvation.

> Love to the Irish people, to all my colleagues and friends.[36]

Michael Collins, Richard Mulcahy (right) and their men, at Griffith's funeral (National Library of Ireland. [49, 835/15/14]).

A few days after Griffith's death both *Young Ireland* and *Scéala Chatha* published verses that Yeats had written and published in the week that Parnell died, entitled 'Mourn – And Then Onward'. Some readers, including Minister for Defence Richard Mulcahy, thought then that these were composed to mark Griffith's death. Some lines were reproduced on a memorial poster for Griffith. But in 1965, when Mulcahy publicly described the poem as a tribute to Griffith, he was quickly put right by Austin Clarke. Conor Cruise O'Brien believed that Yeats had cunningly seized the moment of Parnell's death to get his poem published prominently in *United Ireland*, a Parnellite paper in which his work sometime appeared – just as he later benefitted by using the platform that Griffith provided him in the *United Irishman*. Eoin O'Mahony suggested that the belief that Yeats wrote these verses in honor of Griffith was a reason that the new government appointed him to the senate, and he suspected Gogarty of complicity in a 'deception'.[37] Whatever about the literary merit of the poem, Yeats preferred to forget it as he advanced his career in the twentieth century. It is easy to see why the sixteen lines, ending with the nationalist trope of an Irish Moses leading his people out of bondage, were seen as a tribute to Griffith:

Ye on the broad high mountains of old Eri [Ireland],
Mourn all the night and day,
The man is gone who guided ye, unweary,
Through the long, bitter way.

Ye by the waves that close in our sad nation,
Be full of sudden fears,
The man is gone who from his lonely station
Has moulded the hard years.

Mourn ye on grass-green plains of Eri fated,
For closed in darkness now,
Is he who laboured on, derided, hated,
And made the tyrant bow.

Mourn – and then onward, there is no returning
He guides ye from the tomb;
His memory now is a tall pillar, burning
Before us in the gloom!

Griffith was eleven days dead when the *Cork Examiner* published a sharp commentary on the state of Ireland. Michael Collins was also dead, shot just a few hours before the piece appeared. The writer was Hugh Martin, a correspondent of the English *Daily News*, founded by Charles Dickens. His life had been threatened following publication of his reports on the behaviour of British forces during the guerilla War of Independence. He was aghast at the civil war:

Remember, the great thing that Sinn Fein did for Ireland was to give it self-confidence and self-esteem. Ireland's besetting sin – as all the world knows, and nobody better than the Irish – is strong talk and weak action, boastfulness and inefficiency, a passion for glory and a dislike of getting up early to win it. In short, Synge's *Playboy* has held the field as a symbol, and Shaw had to cease breathing Irish air in order to be himself.

Sinn Fein, through Arthur Griffith, ingeniously assisted by the absurdities of Dublin Castle, struck the heaviest blow in history at that conception of the Irish character. For a time it seemed as though if the impact was not causing a transformation, it must be revealing the real Ireland that lay below the surface. Certainly the people thought so. They had been accustomed to hold a low enough estimate of their national character in private, while expressing the highest possible estimate in public. Now at last they found it possible to believe in themselves. They believed in their past, their present, their future. 'The wind of hope' blew through the land. De Valera's adventure has changed all that. Its inefficiency, rather than its stupidity, has been a revelation.[38]

Griffith's widow thought that she was the only person who saw his death coming,

Every day for four months I had to see him going out, and he as calm near death as in life. Poor boy; he was tormented and tortured to the grave by men who in the old days used to call themselves his friends, and I'm happy for him that he has escaped them all. His poor exhausted face will haunt me for as long as I live. We have had so little happiness, the two of us ...[39]

The British signatories of the treaty later made a gift to Ireland of a drawing of Arthur Griffith on his deathbed, one of three such sketches by the artist Paul Henry. Their suggestion that a surviving treaty signatory on the Irish side be associated with the purchase was rebuffed.[40]

Senator Yeats and Griffith

In 1923 W.B. Yeats was awarded the Nobel Prize in Literature. He was also appointed a senator of the new state for which Griffith had so long struggled. When the government introduced legislation to make provision for Griffith's surviving family, Yeats paid him a tribute, while at the same time not quite acknowledging just how much Griffith and Yeats had once agreed politically or how much Griffith's *United Irishman* initially boosted the career of the poet:

> I was on many points deeply opposed to Mr. Arthur Griffith during his lifetime on matters connected with the Arts, but time has justified him on the great issue that most concerns us all. He was a man with the most enduring courage and the most steadfast will. I have good reason for knowing how enduring his courage was. I first met him a great many years ago, when he and his friend Rooney were editing a little paper which they set up with their own hand as well as writing it. They also paid for the weekly expenditure on that paper. I know how hard a struggle it was for him to edit and print that paper, and I remember in those days, on hearing how hard that struggle was, I offered to get some of his articles placed in, I think, *The Speaker*, which was an English Liberal paper. I remember his reply that he had taken a vow to himself never to write for any paper outside Ireland. That was for him a vow of poverty, and he kept it. For many years, at least two or three years, before the end, it must have seemed to him that he was carrying on an almost hopeless struggle and when the final crisis came he showed himself a man of particular value to this country, if it were only in this, that when the final test came he gave his faith, not to an abstract theory, but to a conception of this historical nation – and we are all theory mad. On that point he kept himself thoroughly sane, and we owe, therefore, to his memory great honour – honour that will always be paid by this country.[41]

As far as it went it was a gracious tribute, particularly from a sometime adversary who had known the lash of Griffith's sharp tongue. Only a handful of senators felt the need to speak at all.

Arthur Griffith and Joyce's *Ulysses*

As Griffith struggled to finalise a treaty, James Joyce declared 'now the writing of *Ulysses* is ended'. He remarked that the date of its conclusion, 30 October 1921, was the birthday of his acquaintance Ezra Pound, who, as seen above, visited Griffith in London about this time. After further adjustments, *Ulysses* was published in February 1922, on Joyce's fortieth birthday.[1]

Richard Ellmann, Joyce's best-known biographer, believed that the references in *Ulysses* to Griffith, particularly those in the final section, are 'more than coincidence' given Griffith's elevation as president of the Dáil in January 1922:

> Joyce wished to salute Griffith's at last successful efforts. Bloom is described as having once picked up Parnell's hat and handed it back to him, a homely gesture more attractive than rhetorical ones. Joyce offers Griffith, through the unwitting agency of Molly, a backhanded tribute, homely too. It was Griffith's programme, and not Parnell's, which had eventually won through. Ireland was achieving independence just as *Ulysses* was achieving publication. The political emancipation of Ireland had been accomplished by his old ally Griffith, and the emancipation of its conscience – Joyce's own lifetime work – was also approaching culmination.

Ellmann adds 'in Joyce's own fashion' the author was hailing the new state 'and the political leader to whom he felt most closely allied'.[2] Joyce himself described *Ulysses* as 'the work of a sceptic' but added 'I don't want it to appear the work of a cynic. I don't want to hurt or offend those of my countrymen who are devoting their lives to a cause they feel to be necessary and just.'[3] One of those whom he possibly had in mind was George Clancy, a member of the Celtic Literary Society who once taught Joyce some Irish and who, as mayor of Limerick in 1921, was murdered by men believed to have been 'Black and Tans'. Another was Griffith.

It seems likely that on one of the occasions on which he met Joyce, Griffith told him of going to Broadstone Station to see off Parnell in sad circumstances years earlier. Joyce may also have kept a cutting of the piece in the *United Irishman* of 1901 referring to 'blooming censors' when advising the public to read an essay by Joyce that had been rejected elsewhere. Joyce's principal character in *Ulysses*, the part-Jew Leopold Bloom, had, like Griffith, an Austro-Hungarian connection. Did Joyce know from meeting Griffith that the latter called his wife 'Mollie'? She had lived for some years in Belvedere Place and may even have attended one of those musical evenings hosted there by her neighbours, Joyce's friends the Sheehys, at which Joyce was present.[4]

Given the well-known way that Joyce's mind worked playfully, by a 'mere hint of resemblance', by 'shadowy similarity' and 'salient indications' as one student of that author puts it,[5] it is worth teasing out such random associations a little further and suggesting parallels between Arthur Griffith and Leopold Bloom. For, besides the Austro-Hungarian connection and each man's wife being known to him endearingly as 'Mollie' or 'Molly', there is Bloom's address in north Dublin at 7 Eccles Street and Griffith's in nearby Summerhill; Griffith's night spent in Glasnevin Cemetery and the funeral there in *Ulysses*; both Griffith and Bloom's immersion in newspaper work; Griffith's proclivity for long walks through Dublin with convivial breaks in pubs along the way and Bloom's wandering about the city on 16 June 1904; the two men's friendship with Oliver St John Gogarty ('Buck Mulligan') and their visits to the Forty Foot and its nearby Martello Tower in Sandycove (Plate 6) where Joyce set the opening scene of *Ulysses*; Mollie Griffith's disinterest in politics and the other Molly's sceptical musings about her husband and about Sinn Féin in the famous soliloquy that ends *Ulysses*; Bloom's imperfect Jewishness and Griffith's anti-Semitic failings. Did Joyce even think of Griffith himself as a kind of Odysseus (or 'Ulysses' in the Latin form), journeying with a shifting and unreliable crew on a long voyage filled with perils towards a homeland from which fate had expelled the Irish, namely self-government? Joyce's friend Padraic Colum, whose children's version of the adventures of Homer's *Odysseus* was published in New York in 1918, and who – on a ship from America to Ireland – learnt of Griffith's death, certainly saw Griffith thus. By 1923 he had written a poem on the theme in memory of Griffith that included these lines:

> And could we pray, touching the island-homeland,
> Other than this: 'Odysseus, you who laboured
> So long upon the barren outer sea;
> Odysseus, Odysseus, you who made
> The plan that drove the wasters from the house,
> And bent the bow that none could bend but you:
> Be with us still:
> Your memory be the watcher in our house,
> Your memory be the flame upon our hills.'[6]

The interplay between Griffith and Joyce, reflected in Joyce's seeking the older man's advice and in his body of writing, goes deeper than Joyce's abiding interest in Irish politics and daily life and is richer than specific mentions of Griffith in *Ulysses,* or than the echoes of Griffith's friend Rooney in both 'The Dead' and *Ulysses* as discussed above. Far from turning his back on Ireland, Joyce in self-exile liked to read about his country, order books about it, quiz visitors from his homeland and even listen to Irish radio at night. The very content and structure of Joyce's texts have been demonstrated to be informed by some of Griffith's work. For example, among various distinguished writers whom Griffith encouraged and published in his *United Irishman* was Richard Irvine Best, an employee of the National Library of Ireland who later became its director. In her remarkable account of the extent of the *United Irishman*'s influence on Joyce as 'a significant and documentable source', Tymoczko has identified Best's translation of *The Irish Mythological Cycle* by Henri d'Arbois de Jubainville that appeared in weekly installments in the *United Irishman* between 9 November 1901 and 19 July 1902 – as well as other work by Best in Griffith's paper. Best was one of those who contributed to the fund to buy a house for Griffith and Mollie Sheehan when they married in 1910.[7] Even more subtle but intriguing is Ungar's exposition of how the search for kinship between Stephen and Bloom in *Ulysses* is rooted in a 'finely modulated' representation of Austro-Hungarian history that qualifies Griffith's analogy in *The Resurrection of Hungary*, while at the same time Joyce made errors of detail that are demonstrated to originate in that work which Griffith published in the year 1904 in which *Ulysses* is set.[8]

It is not known if Griffith and Joyce chatted from time to time under the portico of the National Library of Ireland, where readers habitually mingled and smoked. It is quite possible that they did so in the late 1890s and early 1900s, unless constant visitors such as Griffith, without a college education, always stood at a mute distance from those such as Joyce who attended university. The library precincts were quite intimate, and regular visitors could scarcely avoid acknowledging one another. In the ninth episode of *Ulysses*, set at the National Library, four of the five participants to whom Stephen (Joyce's alter ego) expounds his theory about Shakespeare's *Hamlet*, had some of their work published by Griffith in his papers. These were Best, George Russell ('Æ'), William Magee ('John Eglinton') and Oliver St John Gogarty ('Buck Mulligan'). The fifth person present was the chief librarian, Lyster, renowned for being helpful to readers. During the episode Fred Ryan is identified as being a contributor to *Dana*, but he also wrote in the *United Irishman*.

Joyce's interest in the relationship between Shakespeare and the characters in *Hamlet*, including the question of whether or not Shakespeare saw himself as Hamlet, is too complicated to pursue at length here. Its theme of a father–son relationship is relevant to how Joyce thought of Griffith and understood his own creative role in relationship to the political role of 'the father of Sinn Féin'. During that scene in the National Library, 'A father, Stephen said, battling against hopelessness, is a necessary evil'. He argued that when Shakespeare (or whoever it might be) wrote Hamlet 'he was not the father of his own son merely but, being no more a son, he was and felt himself the father of all his race'. As the bard of England thus served as 'father of all his race', Joyce had hoped to fulfil a key creative and inspirational role for Ireland. The coincidence between Griffith's reputation as 'father of Sinn Féin' (where these two Irish words mean 'we ourselves'), or even as 'father of us all', and Joyce's identification of a nation's chronicler as 'father of all his race' takes one to a point in the recurrent possibilities of Joycean speculation that is as intriguing as it may be delusional. Did Joyce see himself and Griffith as a Scylla and Charybdis between whom Irish people would navigate their future?

Tymocsko observes that the national literary revival, of which Griffith and these men in the National Library were part, 'was haunted by the desire for a national epic'.[9] Indeed, during the National Library episode in *Ulysses*, Best remarks: 'Our national epic has yet to be written.' If Griffith supplied one sort of epic through the collected pages of the *United Irishman* or in the analogy of *The Resurrection of Hungary*, Joyce's contribution was *Ulysses*, a myth that subverted orthodoxy for a new state growing into the postmodern twentieth century. If few other politicians might find a place in that everyday epic, Joyce could scarcely not have acknowledged Griffith, the emerging state's founding father or father figure.

The New State and Joyce

In March 1922 Dáil Éireann's minister for publicity, Desmond FitzGerald, who had been in London in 1921 to support the treaty negotiators and who would soon become the first foreign minister of the Irish Free State, called on Joyce in Paris and asked if he intended to return to Ireland: 'I told him not for the present. One redeemed city [Trieste] (and inhabitants thereof) will last me for a few years more. He has proposed a resolution to his Irish cabinet to send my name to Stockholm as candidate for the Nobel prize.' Joyce was sceptical enough to add 'He will probably lose his portfolio without obtaining the prize for me.'[10] In fact, in 1923, the Nobel Prize in Literature went to Yeats.

However, while Joyce was to complain that Thom's Irish *Who's Who at Home and Abroad* in 1923 'contains 2,500 names but not mine',[11] he could not now complain that Griffith's emerging state had ignored him. Joyce was amused when his sister-in-law later gave him a metal copy of the Irish Free State's flag. The words of the ancient prayer known as 'St Patrick's Breastplate' were inscribed on it. Writing that the donor was 'a devotee of S[aint] Patrick and keeps his statue on her mantelpiece', he referred indirectly to a well-known Irish decision by a Gaelic king (said to be 'the first [decision] we know of in the law of copyright')[12] who declared in respect to a manuscript owned by St Finnian of Moville that 'as with every cow her calf, so with every book its son'. Joyce wrote: 'She gave me a pocket breast-plate in the new Irish colours [green, white and orange] with part of the famous prayer on it cut in the form of a shield. At the top is a cross and at the end are the words: all rights reserved. This must be the first case of copyright in the history of humanity.'[13]

However, when Griffith collapsed and died, Joyce was in no humour for jokes. His own health was in crisis. His eyesight had deteriorated badly and, in August 1922, a journey to London was 'disastrous'. There were '1,000 drops of stuff in my eye, profuse nightly perspirations and pain', making him fatigued and irritable.[14] His published letters during the period are quite sparse and include no references to Griffith.

The Virtue of Fortitude

Both Griffith and Joyce, as we have seen, were conscious of the memory of the dead and its influence on the living. But even if Griffith's widow was aware that her late husband's name featured in *Ulysses* a number of times she would scarcely have considered that a fitting enough tribute for him. Nor was she impressed by the efforts of the new government of the Irish Free State to remember him. A temporary monument to Griffith and Collins was erected on the lawn of Leinster House, where the new state's parliament sat in Dublin. Years later that monument would be replaced by a smaller but more elegant one. Albert Power also sculpted some memorial busts of Griffith.[15] Griffith soon had a barracks and a new avenue in Glasnevin named after him, but his 'desolate' widow boycotted ceremonies and remained unhappy about what she regarded as the new state's half-hearted efforts to honour her late husband. That sad story has been well told.[16] Even thirty-four years after Griffith's death, de Valera thought it worthwhile to take steps to establish that Griffith had not originated either the name of Sinn Féin or the policy of abstention from Westminster. In 1956 he wrote to New York seeking a copy of an old editorial in the *Irish World* that he believed had advocated the Sinn Féin policy of abstention from the British House of Commons 'many years before Arthur Griffith proposed it. What has fixed this in my mind was the fact that the editorial was dated the 14th of October 1882, the day of my birth.'[17] Unlike Griffith himself, contemporaries who survived to old age were free to shape his reputation.

Freeman's Journal, 24 August 1922: 'Shemus' on 'Ireland's Via Dolorosa' (National Library of Ireland [PD 4309 TX145]).

Griffith's widow decided to mark her husband's grave with a broken column. Such a column indicates life cut short – but formerly too was a renaissance signifier of fortitude, one of the four cardinal virtues. A broken column had been used for other Irish memorials. One that was erected in Co. Wexford when the Fenian Charlie Farrell of Enniscorthy died in 1913, was subsequently taken to mean 'when Ireland was free, his monument would be finished'.[18] Floral arrangements in that shape adorned the funeral cortege of Michael Collins.

That Griffith was by no means the only Irish leader whose life had been cut short was a point made graphically by a striking illustration published after the death of Michael Collins.[19] It shows a female personification of Ireland weeping at the foot of a broken column on which is inscribed his name. Behind are other columns of a ruined temple bearing the names of Arthur Griffith, Charles Stewart Parnell, Thomas Davis, Robert Emmet, Wolfe Tone and Owen Roe O'Neill.

The sides that fought the civil war later evolved into separate political parties. Sometimes Griffith's memory suited the purposes of one and sometimes the other. Sometimes neither. In a life of complexities, he had published and done many things, and some of what he said or did might now embarrass those who ruled the state that he ushered into existence on a winter's afternoon in London – 'men who through all our sacrifices are put in the good paid positions', as his widow wrote to Ernest Blythe. She thought that her late husband 'was much too good & followed the Lord in poverty, charity, humility etc. Awaiting a reply'.[20]

Griffith could only dream of the time when Irish citizens would enjoy robust democracy and relative control of our economy, even if such self-reliance in practice has allowed the state to risk bankruptcy during the boom of the 'Celtic Tiger' years. He erected signposts and coaxed, cajoled or pushed people into following their directions. Gradually an independent Irish state grew into what it is today. If you seek his monument, look around.

2022: Commemorating Griffith

Griffith knew poverty, cared for his widowed mother and sister and loved his wife Mollie and their two children. By the start of the twentieth century he was editing a small but influential paper and making enemies. When Joyce went abroad – famously 'to forge in the smithy of my soul the uncreated conscience of my race' – Griffith stayed at home to build a cultural and political movement and to help forge in the smithy of the polling booth an Irish state. He came to disagree with W.B. Yeats, whose career he first boosted but whom he later criticised. The papers that he edited were for twenty years a wealth of debate and information, and today they merit overdue digitisation and analysis.

Groups to which Griffith belonged as a young man encouraged the robust exchange of views. And so, for example, members who wrote essays for the Leinster Debating Club's manuscript journal read them aloud at meetings where they argued about them, before the editor circulated their essays in manuscript form with quite strong criticism. This was thought to be in the spirit of the Young Ireland movement so admired by Griffith and his friends. It also became the editorial spirit of the *United Irishman* under Griffith, who published in his paper a range of opinions and of reaction to them on cultural, political and other matters, and who attracted to its pages some very bright minds. Anyone who reads the *United Irishman* as if Griffith approved or held every opinion expressed in it, will be misled. In a piece that its editor wrote about books he set out his philosophy:

If your friends dispute with you consider, not their assertions, which don't matter a straw, but their arguments, and hold, modify, or change your opinions, when you have calmly considered them. Do not be afraid of changing your opinion when you are convinced your opinion is a wrong one. The wise man, say the Spaniards, changes his opinion often, the fool never does. But never *desert* your opinion.[1]

Griffith's second influential paper, *Sinn Féin*, was coloured by its affiliation to the political movement of the same name that he founded, but it was not simply a party organ. James Joyce, according to his brother, regarded Griffith's *United Irishman* as 'the only paper in Dublin worth reading'.[2] He also sought out copies of *Sinn Féin*.

Griffith's criticisms of *The Playboy of the Western World* did not make him an uncritical Catholic conservative. Indeed, Yeats described him as 'anti-clerical'. Griffith criticised priests and bishops who impeded the struggle for independence and social justice, or who unduly inhibited personal relationships. He asserted a proper distinction between the public and private lives of figures such as Charles Stewart Parnell and Oscar Wilde. He was a Zionist who struggled to overcome within himself contemporary anti-Semitic prejudice. His anxieties about the challenges of immigration are all too familiar today.

At great cost to himself, including personal poverty, a late marriage and deteriorating health leading to an early death, Griffith kept his successive newspapers afloat. In 1914 he was one of the few people who were parties to a decision that foreshadowed the rebellion of 1916, from which event its leaders excluded him, apparently for strategic reasons. They recognised the role that he played in building up and keeping alive a new concept of independence, as did British authorities and the unionist press when they mistakenly attributed to his Sinn Féin party authorship of the rebellion itself.

He was sometimes intolerant, his persona being more petit bourgeois than bacchanalian or 'Big House'. While he did much to develop Irish culture, his response to Synge betrayed his obsession with political objectives over other priorities. His critics have at times been unsparing. Horgan accused him of having 'no interest in, and little sympathy with, labour demands or problems of social reform'.[3] Lentin and McVeigh condemn what they call his 'proto-Fascist' ideas, writing 'Griffith was indeed "a repugnant figure", the enemy of other races, the working classes, and no friend to the Rights of Man ... The possibility that had Griffith become the head of state for any length of time, he might have put his anti-Semitic politics into effect is, of course, even more chilling.'[4] It is the case that a small proportion of what Griffith wrote or published in his papers spanning two decades was 'repugnant', particularly by today's standards, but his ideology was neither fascist nor undemocratic. There is much in Griffith's journalism to undermine the extravagant claim that he was 'the enemy' of the working-class and 'no friend to the Rights of Man'. He cared a great deal about matters that deeply affected the lives of working people. He was no socialist but many articles in his papers are concerned compassionately with justice, slums and economic growth. He backed the socialist James Connolly in local elections.

Even sympathetic biographers of Griffith have felt it necessary to point out apologetically that he rubbed people up the wrong way, although that particular characteristic is not so rare among successful politicians or statesmen that it requires special emphasis in Griffith's case. Others less sympathetic to him use Griffith's faults or perceived faults as a foil against which some of his contemporaries are set more favourably.

A shy man, Griffith yielded the presidency of Sinn Féin to de Valera only to find himself burdened with the responsibility of running the provisional government after Sinn Féin swept to power in 1918 and de Valera subsequently went to America for eighteen months. In 1921 de Valera again put him in the firing line by appointing him head of the plenipotentiaries sent to negotiate the terms of an Anglo-Irish Treaty. That treaty, whatever its flaws or the possible errors made by those who negotiated and signed it, is the basis of opportunities and status that we enjoy today, unimaginable to most Irish people at the start of the twentieth century, but not to Griffith.

Having yielded the presidency to de Valera, Griffith then let Collins chair the body that was to become, after Collins was killed, the cabinet of the new Irish Free State. Griffith even proclaimed that a government of women might be best for Ireland. His widow said that he had intended to quit politics in 1922. That he exited as he did, by collapsing and dying, was an Irish tragedy.

Griffith was first and last a political activist, one with a vision of Irish independence related to his keen grasp of economic and other harsh realities. Determined to avoid factional distractions, he clashed with those who had different priorities. Griffith was more pragmatic than idealististic. It has been suggested that he was 'a man with a mission, not a politician'.[5] But he was actually both. His chief political objective, the withdrawal of Irish MPs from Westminster in order to re-establish an independent Irish legislature, was achieved in his lifetime, and by his death most of Ireland had some degree of that economic and political independence for which he long laboured. He once declared that a republic was the best form of government, and Maume astutely observes 'Griffith was more republican than is generally realised'. However, he was not prepared to insist on imposing republican status on the whole island regardless of the cost of attempting to do so.[6]

'The Greatest Intellectual Force'

As I was completing my research for this book, bound on a bus for the National Library once more, I fell into conversation with its driver while we waited in traffic to reach my stop. He asked what I was reading, and I mentioned Arthur Griffith. 'Ah, Griffith! He's one of my heroes', replied the driver to my surprise. He added 'Have you ever read any Lloyd George? Now, there's someone – he said that negotiating with de Valera was like trying to pick up mercury with a fork.' If de Valera had not withdrawn from the Dáil, the treaty that he sent Griffith to negotiate and the state founded upon it might have led sooner to better things.

I grew up in a family where my father supported Fine Gael and my mother inclined to de Valera, but I have no loyalty to any of the parties that claim descent from Griffith's Sinn Féin. As it happens, Griffith entrusted one of my grandfathers with the commercial management of later editions of his pioneering annual Sinn Féin *Yearbook*. Those yearbooks and other initiatives, including Sinn Féin's experiment in banking and the voluntary Industrial Development Association, serve as useful reminders that advanced nationalism was about more than bare politics. Not until Seán Lemass and T.K. Whitaker launched their first programme for economic expansion in 1958 was there again such an imaginative and optimistic effort to envisage Ireland's material and social future as that developed by Arthur Griffith, except perhaps that of his friend James Connolly from a socialist perspective.

Some who disagreed with Griffith about the treaty were still prepared to praise him after he died. One was Seán T. O'Kelly, who had long been at the heart of advanced nationalist agitation and who, in 1922, wrote from Kilmainham Jail where he was a guest of the Free Staters. O'Kelly predicted 'Future generations of Irish men and women shall draw inspiration [from a man] whose political philosophy so eloquently taught, and whose long years of toil and sacrifice brought the present generation of Irishmen from their knees to their feet, and rekindled in their hearts the almost extinct flame of liberty.'[7] For the most part, Griffith was respectfully and even warmly remembered by witnesses of the period who later made statements to the Bureau of Military History.

If Griffith was an 'enigma' to his contemporaries, as Stephens suggested in 1922,[8] it is possible to see him clearer in hindsight. For he straddled two eras in ways that others did not. By the dawn of the twentieth century, more than half of his life was already over and he had not yet even founded Sinn Féin. He was deeply rooted in the pre-industrial history of Ireland and in the Victorian hardships of Dublin. It was presumably for this reason that when Michael Lennon was researching a possible biography of Griffith that was never actually published, he adopted as its working title 'Arthur Griffith: A Nineteenth-Century Man'.[9] Yet Griffith also understood the dynamics of industrialisation, becoming an informed advocate of modern economic development and a consistent promoter of parliamentary independence as a driver of statehood and opportunity. He ultimately eschewed the old heroics, of which both Collins and de Valera were in their own ways the latest standard-bearers, and committed himself to the pragmatic politics that a greatly enlarged franchise was to favour after 1918. Stephens asked 'How would he have borne himself or grown in the exercise of power?' had he lived longer, and we can only guess the answer to that question, even as we wonder might he have retired from politics altogether – as his widow said he had indicated to her he would do in 1922. However, to Stephens' other question 'What were his capacities?' we can respond confidently that they were precisely these: a steady hand on the tiller of advanced nationalism at a vital moment; an assured pen as editor of successive newspapers that fanned the flame of Irish freedom; and the courage to sign an agreement for a treaty when others had declined even to participate in the necessary negotiations. He was modest rather than anonymous, declining opportunities to work at home or abroad for more money in order to concentrate on his Sinn Féin vocation; and while his character was sometimes contradictory or faulty he was no great riddle or unknowable secret. With Griffith you got what you saw, like it or not.

Yet, after independence, Griffith's reputation would come to be selectively appropriated by Fine Gael in a way that is too seldom interrogated. Unsurprisingly, he was largely ignored by the Fianna Fáil party founded by Éamon de Valera. His failure even notionally to embrace socialism meant that the Left in turn did not embrace him. And he was not militant enough for the party that continued to call itself Sinn Féin. A few biographers have attempted to do him justice. McGee's recent critique of how some Irish historians have represented Griffith was sharp but merits consideration by those who intend to address his legacy and who should avoid cherry-picking the extensive writings of 'the father of us all' to make points that may be unfair to Griffith's memory.[10]

In the economic arena, Griffith's advocacy of protectionism has been seen as problematic, even though he came to combine it with a vision of the kind of inward investment that has greatly benefitted the Irish economy since the 1950s. In any event, protectionism was by no means an unusual doctrine for nations far more robust that Ireland was in the early twentieth century. Indeed, Britain had long used selective protectionist and free trade ruses to disadvantage Irish manufacturers. In August 2016, the present Taoiseach Leo Varadkar, who was then the minister for social protection, paid Griffith a tribute that was a riposte to those who, in the economic as in the cultural field, seem intent on defining 'the father of Sinn Féin' as 'narrow'. He said of Griffith 'it was with economic ideas he was most preoccupied. He realised Independence without economic sustainability was not acceptable. He wanted Ireland to be a modern democratic state and his approach was always pragmatic, concerned with issues such as industrialisation, mining, afforestation, excessive taxation and the protection of Irish goods.'

Varadkar also recalled that Erskine Childers had described Griffith 'magnanimously it has to be said, as "the greatest intellectual force stimulating the national revival of 1916–19".[11] The latter was not just magnanimous, coming as the compliment did from 'the other side' of the treaty split, but was an acknowledgement that Griffith's policies were based on a rational assessment of the problems facing Ireland.

For his vision in articulating a practical form of Irish independence, for his identifying and analysing so cogently in his papers many of the ills that then beset his country and prescribing remedies, for his reluctance to use physical force except defensively and for his dedication and personal sacrifices in working tirelessly to persuade his people that each of us has a responsibility to stand on our own two feet as citizens – *sinn féin, sinn féin amháin* – the Irish state today owes Griffith a great debt.

ACKNOWLEDGEMENTS

The writing of this new assessment has been made possible not least because certain studies of Arthur Griffith already exist. I owe their authors a debt, specifically Colum, Davis, Laffan, Maye, McGee, Jordan, Younger and Ó Lúing. The latter also bequeathed a rich collection of research notes and letters to the National Library of Ireland.

When I discovered by chance that one of my grandfathers both knew Griffith and undertook some work for him, my interest in the founder of Sinn Féin was whetted. Later, Felix Larkin invited me to explore Griffith's extensive and influential journalism for a collection of essays on periodicals in the twentieth century that he and Mark O'Brien edited. I am grateful for that opportunity, and for his directing me to two cartoons by 'Shemus' that are reproduced here.

The present book has grown from my research into the representation or misrepresentation of Griffith since his tragic death in 1922, aged just fifty-one. Along the way I have written articles relating to him for *Éire-Ireland* in the United States, for the journal of the International Commission for the History of Representative and Parliamentary Institutions, for *Media History* and for the *Journal of Modern Jewish Studies*. Further details of these are included in the bibliography, with the last three published by Taylor & Francis Ltd and each being copyrighted. The editor of *History Ireland* also kindly allowed me space to develop some of my ideas.

Letters and other documents belonging to Griffith were destroyed during the War of Independence and civil war. His widow appears to have burned others. The bulk of what remains is in the National Library. My thanks are due to its archivists, librarians and donors, and to those of Dublin City University, UCD Archives, the National Archives, King's Inns, the Bureau of Military History, Trinity College Dublin, Dublin

City Library and Archive, Dublin City Gallery/The Hugh Lane, the Irish Jewish Museum and the public library on Eglinton Road, Bray, Co. Wicklow. We are particularly grateful to the National Library of Ireland for its generous assistance with the choice of illustrations for the volume, and to Dublin City Gallery/The Hugh Lane for permission to reproduce John Lavery's portrait of Arthur Griffith. Ms Máire Ní Mhurchú of Bray kindly translated some passages in Irish by Patrick Pearse, while the estate of Padraic Colum gave me permission to reproduce lines from his poem 'Odysseus: In Memory of Arthur Griffith'.

My thanks to Conor Graham, Fiona Dunne and others at Merrion Press for their enthusiastic response to the idea of this book and for seeing it through into print.

As ever, when finding the space necessary for research, reflection and writing, I greatly appreciate the support and suggestions of my wife Catherine Curran and the encouragement of our sons, Oisín, Conor and Sam.

Reading Room, National Library of Ireland, 1890s: 'a haunt loved by us' wrote a friend of Griffith. Note the hats worn indoors (National Library of Ireland [RR2]).

ENDNOTES

Chapter 1
Griffith and Mother Ireland

1   Stephens, *Arthur Griffith*, p. 26; House of Commons, 1 June 1916.
2   Gogarty, 'The Passing of Arthur Griffith', p. 54.
3   *Cork Examiner* and *Irish Independent*, 17 August 1925; *An t-Óglách: The Army Journal*, 3, no. 17 (22 Aug. 1925), p. 4.
4   Téry, *En Irlande*, p. 155, translation by this author.
5   Letter from Griffith's wife, location now unknown, reproduced in Ó Lúing, *Ó Gríofa*, facing p. 385.
6   Hutchinson, *Dynamics of Cultural Nationalism*, pp. 171, 181.
7   Tóibín, *Fathers*, passim.
8   Bureau of Military History, Witness Statement (hereafter BMH WS) 1,770, pt. 3, p. 383.
9   Dáil Éireann, 7 Jan. 1922.
10 Jeffares, *Yeats*, p. 265; *Irish Press*, 23 June 1965 (letter from Eoin Ó Mathghamhna).
11 UCD MacWhite Papers, P194/582, 4 Jan. 1949.
12 Joyce, *A Portrait of the Artist as a Young Man*.
13 Colum, *Life and the Dream*, p. 100.
14 White, *The Significance of Sinn Féin*, p. 57.
15 Jones, 'The Island of Ireland', pp. 402, 414.
16 Gallagher, 'Ireland, Mother Ireland', p. 12.
17 Bender, *Israelites in Erin*, pp. 54–5; Fanny Parnell, 'Michael Davitt'; [Boston] *Pilot*, 19 Dec. 1880.
18 Jones, 'The Island of Ireland', pp. 403–5.
19 Dáil Éireann, 7 Jan. 1922; McCullagh, *De Valera*, vol. 1, 5–19.

Chapter 2
The Name of the Father

1   BMH WS 205 (Maud Griffith), p. 1 (3 March 1949); Glandon, *Griffith and the Advanced-Nationalist Press*, pp. 65–6.

2   Kenny, "'God Help Us!'", pp. 90–1, with sketch reproduced on the cover; Takagami, 'Fenian Rising in Dublin', pp. 340–62.

3   Sheehan, *Arthur Griffith*, p. 4.

4   R.F. [Robert Flood?] 'Some Early Memories', *Irish Times*, 26 Aug. 1922.

5   Ferriter, *A Nation and Not a Rabble*, p. 25, citing an address to the Irish Society at Oxford University.

6   Colum, *Griffith*, p. 8; Colum, *Road Round Ireland*, p. 299.

7   National Library of Ireland (hereafter NLI) Celtic Literary Society Minutes, at 20 and 27 January 1899; NLI Ó Ceallaigh Papers, MS 27,700, Address to Cumann Tír Conaill, p. 3.

8   *United Irishman*, 23 Feb. 1901 (editorial).

9   Hannay ('Birmingham'), *Pleasant Places*, pp. 187–8.

10   BMH WS 391.

11   See, for example, 'The slum tenements', *Sinn Féin*, 18 Oct. 1913 (3.5 columns).

12   Daly, *Industrial Development*, p. 3.

13   IG Register of Pro-Catherdral N/R, p. 95, no. 124, ID DU-RC-MA-120491 gives Mary as the daughter of Peter and Marcella Whelan of 14 Langrish Place (off Summerhill) and Griffith's paternal grandmother as Anna.

14   NLI Ó Lúing Papers, MS 12,038, box 3, Francis Griffith interview notes, 17 Oct. 1945, p. 2.

15   IG Civil Register, Births, Dublin North, 5 Jan. 1874 for Francis H. (no. 450, ID 8509837), born at 61 Upper Dominick Street; NLI Lennon Papers, MSS 6957, 22,288.

16   IG Civil Register, Births, Dublin North, 16 Jan. 1865 for William Peter (no. 124, ID 7666922), born at 14 Langrishe Place (his mother's parents' home), off Summerhill; *Freeman's Journal*, 7 Jan. 1924; NLI Lennon Papers, MS 22, 288 (2), and MS 22,293, Orange File No.1, p. 3b and inside front cover, for letter from the secretary of the Irish Union of Hairdressers and Allied Workers to Lennon, 24 April 1952, and for John Mullett hairdresser, 5 May 1952.

17   IG Civil Register, Deaths, Dublin North, 16 Dec. 1900 for Marcella (aged 34, no. 401, ID 4450319) dying 16 Dec. 1900 at 42 Britain St; *United Irishman*, 16 Dec. 1900 (notice in Irish).

18   BMH WS 909 (Sidney Czira), appendix; *Irish Press*, 30 Dec. 1949.

19   NLI Ó Lúing Papers, MS 12,038, box 3, Maud Griffith to Seán Ó Lúing, 23 March 1949; Colum, *Griffith*, p. 8.

20   IG Registry of Deaths, Dublin North, ID 4732437, no. 470 ('Hemiplegia 14 yrs. Asthenia'); Ibid., ID 5750349, no. 426 for his mother's death aged 80, at 37 Summerhill, on 6 March 1920 (of 'senility').

21   NLI Ó Lúing Papers, MS 12,038, box 3, Patrick Carey interview notes, 31 March 1966, pp. 1–2.

22   McCarthy, *Priests and People in Ireland*, p. 282.

23   *United Irishman*, 16 June 1900.

24   Hackett, *Ireland,* pp. 191–4 ('The Human Refuse Heap'); *Report of the Departmental Committee into the Housing Conditions of the Working Class in the City of Dublin* (London, 1914).

25   NLI Ó Lúing Papers, MS 12,038, box 3, Chrissie Doyle to Seán Ó Lúing (1945), p. 3.

26   Ibid., box 4, Dan McCarthy interview notes (1946), p. 4; *Irish Press*, 18 August 1947; Colum, *Griffith*, p. 74.

27   Joyce, *Letters*, vol. 2, p. 167, Letter to Stanislaus Joyce, 25 Sept. 1906.

28   *United Irishman*, 19 May 1900 (as 'Cuguan').

29   Sinn Féin, *Ethics of Sinn Féin*, p. 7.

30   *United Irishman*, 19 May 1900, 9 and 16 June 1900.

31   *United Irishman*, 8 Dec. 1900. See also *United Irishman*, 29 Dec. 1900, p. 8 for a comment on William Sharp ('Fiona Macleod'), 'the private life of an author was not a matter of concern, an author being properly judged merely by his works'.

32   *United Irishman*, 19 Jan. 1901.

33   *United Irishman*, 30 March, 6, 13, 20 and 27 April, 4, 11 and 18 May 1901.

34   *Irish Independent*, 24 May 1927.

35   Colum, *Arthur Griffith*, pp. 26–7.

36   *United Irishman*, 15 July 1899.

37   *United Irishman*, 7 Oct. 1899.

38   *United Irishman*, 9 June 1900.

39   *United Irishman*, 16 June 1900 and editorial, 18 May 1901.

40   *United Irishman*, 25 May 1901.

41   *United Irishman*, 15 Sept., 6 and 13 Oct., 10, 17 and 24 Nov. and 8 Dec. 1900.

42   *United Irishman*, 12 and 26 January, and 2 and 16 February 1901; 'Kavanagh, Patrick Fidelis', in *DIB*, by Patrick Maume.

43   *United Irishman*, 16 March and 13 April 1901. See also 3 Feb. 1900 for 'JAP' disagreeing with Finlay.

44   *United Irishman*, 11 May 1901; *Irish Worker*, 1 July 1899.

45   Yeats, *Autobiographies*, p. 309.

46   *United Irishman*, 2 Nov. 1901.

47   UCD De Valera Papers, P150/1427, letters.

48   Hackett, *Ireland*, pp. 399–404.

49   *United Irishman*, 18 Aug. 1900 and 2 Feb. 1901.

50   *United Irishman*, 15 Sept. 1900.

51   Mulhall, *Dictionary of Statistics*, p. 190.

52   *United Irishman*, 21 Sept. 1901.

53   *Nationality*, 2 Oct. 1915; NLI Lennon Papers MS 22,288 (2), Morison to Michael Lennon, twice in 1952.

54   Hackett, *Ireland*, p. 331.

55   Kelly, *The Fenian Ideal*, p. 176.
56   Manganiello, *Joyce's Politics*, pp. 142–3.
57   BMH WS 1,765, pt. 1, p. 13.
58   Davis, *Griffith and Non-Violent Sinn Fein*, p. 69; Kenny, *Kevin J. Kenny*, p. 116; *Irish Press*, 9 Dec. 1933, including a photograph of the first Aonach committee.
59   *Nationality*, 22 Jan. and 5 Feb. 1916; Kenny, *Kevin J. Kenny*, pp. 22–3, pp. 46–58.
60   *Sinn Féin* 16 April 1910; Kenny, 'The Advertising Problem', *passim*; Kenny, 'Not So Quaint', pp. 12–22.
61   *Irish Independent*, 21 June 1910.
62   Davis, *Griffith and Non-Violent Sinn Féin*, p. 139.
63   Brown, *The Way of My World*, pp. 178–9; 'Brown, Ivor John Carnegie (1891–1974)', in Oxford *Dictionary of National Biography*, by Philip Howard.
64   *United Irishman*, 1 June 1901 (editorial).
65   Letter and message, *Capuchin Annual 1969*, pp. 330–5.
66   Lynch, 'The Irish Free State and the Republic of Ireland', pp. 333–4.

Chapter 3
1871–1901: Hard-Working Men

1   *United Irishman*, 26 May 1900 (as 'Cuguan').
2   R.F. [Robert Flood?], 'Some Early Memories', *Irish Times*, 26 Aug. 1922.
3   Griffith, 'Speech, 28 Nov. 1905'.
4   NLI Ó Lúing Papers, MS 12,038, box 3, Maud Griffith to Seán Ó Lúing, 6 April 1949; Ibid., Francis Griffith interview notes, 17 Oct. 1945, p. 3.
5   *Freeman's Journal*, 27 June 1885; Quinn, 'History and the Making of National Citizens', pp. 63–4; Foster, *Yeats: A Life*, vol. 1, pp. 39, 112.
6   'O'Leary, John' in *DIB*, by Patrick Maume.
7   NLI Leinster, *passim*.
8   'Evelyn Herbert' (John Doyle), at NLI Eblana, p. 20.
9   NLI Eblana, p. 189.
10   NLI Arthur Griffith Papers, Recollections of Arthur Griffith, by James Moran, 1951, MS 49,530/14, pp. 5–7; Colum, *Road Round Ireland*, p. 296; Lyons, *Recollections*, p. 49.
11   NLI Leinster, 4 Dec. 1891; NLI Arthur Griffith Papers, Recollections of Arthur Griffith, by James Moran, 1951, MS 49,530/14, pp. 5–7.
12   Brennan, *Allegiance*, p. 9.
13   NLI Leinster.
14   Joyce, *Irish Names of Places*, p. 73.

15   NLI Eblana, MS 3493.

16   NLI Eblana, p. 701 (second sequence of pagination, 5 May 1889); R.F., 'Some Early Memories', *Irish Times*, 26 August 1922, recalls Griffith writing for Eblana and is probably by Flood.

17   NLI Eblana, pp. 221–33 (6 April 1889).

18   Colum, *Griffith*, p. 22.

19   NLI Leinster, 21 Nov. 1890.

20   NLI Leinster, 14 Oct. 1892.

21   NLI Leinster, 22 Nov. 1889, 25 Sept. 1871, 28 Oct. 1892.

22   NLI Minutes 28 March 1890 and 4 March 1892.

23   NLI Minutes, 30 Jan. 1891.

24   NLI Eblana, p. 43 (22 Feb. 1889) and p. 210 (6 April 1889).

25   NLI Eblana, p. 44 (8 March 1889).

26   NLI Eblana, p. 55 (22 Feb. 1889).

27   NLI Leinster, 15 Jan. 1892.

28   NLI Leinster, 21 Dec. 1888, 14 Feb. and 14 March 1890, 15 Jan. 1892.

29   NLI Eblana, p. 31 (22 Feb. 1889), p. 31 (gives 'p. 81' also), by Edward Whelan.

30   NLI Eblana, 8 March 1889, pp. 123–9.

31   NLI Leinster, 28 Nov. 1890 and at 18 Sept. 1891; *United Ireland*, 6 Dec. 1890.

32   Colum, *Griffith*, p. 24; Colum, *Road Round Ireland*, p. 296.

33   NLI Leinster, 19 Dec. 1890.

34   *Cork Examiner*, 28 Sept. 1891.

35   *Sinn Féin*, 7 October 1911. Unsigned even with a pen name but evidently the editor's in style and tone.

36   Note added under NLI Leinster, 9 Oct. 1891.

37   NLI Leinster, 25 Nov. 1892.

38   Colum, *Griffith*, pp. 9–10.

39   Ibid., p. 19.

40   *United Irishman*, 15 Feb. 1902.

41   BMH WS 1,765, part 1, p. 90.

42   NLI Celtic Literary Society Minute Books, vol. 1, 26 and 31 Dec. 1896.

43   NLI Arthur Griffith Papers, Recollections of Arthur Griffith, by James Moran, 1951, MS 49,530/14, p. 9.

44   Whelan, 'Literature and Nationality'; NLI Celtic, 6 May 1897; *United Irishman*, 16 Jan. 1897 and 15 June 1901; Fallon, *MacBride*, p. 50; NLI Ó Lúing Papers, MS 12,038, box 3, Francis Griffith interview notes, 17 Oct. 1945, p. 3; NLI Lennon Papers, MS 22,289, Lennon to P.C. Vercueil, Middleburg, 7 Feb. 1950; UCD Archives, Hayes Papers P52/222 (10–11), interview with Maud Griffith, 29 Aug., 1950.

45   NLI Ó Lúing Papers, MS 12,038, box 3, Francis Griffith interview notes, no. 2 (29 Aug. 1945), p. 8; Ibid., Nevin Griffith interview notes (25 March 1953).

46 *Irish Daily Independent*, 31 Dec. 1896.

47 NLI Celtic, 7 Jan. 1897.

48 BMH WS 302 (Maire O'Brolchain citing old 'Mr Murphy').

49 NLI Celtic, 26 Nov. 1897 for an unidentified press cutting.

50 O'Sullivan, *Essays and Recollections*, pp. 112–17.

Chapter 4
An 'Un-Irish' Personality?

1   *Irish Freedom*, no. 1 (November 1910), by 'Lucan' (who wrote also for the *United Irishman*).

2   Talbot, *Michael Collins*, p. 48; Téry, *En Irlande*, pp. 156–8.

3   *Irish Weekly Independent,* 17 August 1946 (Butler sisters); UCD MacWhite Papers, P194/657; Lyons, *Recollections*, pp. 32–3; Béaslaí, 'Arthur Griffith', p. 17.

4   NLI Ó Lúing Papers, MS 12,038, box 3, Carey interview notes, 31 March 1966, p. 3.

5   Gonne, *Servant of the Queen*, p. 343.

6   NLI Lennon Papers, MS 22, 288 (i), J.H. Hutchinson to Michael Lennon, 20 May 1952.

7   McCullagh, *De Valera*, vol. 1, pp. 5–14.

8   NLI Kenny (H.E.) Papers, MS 15,082 (3).

9   Ó Lúing, 'Arthur Griffith and Sinn Féin', pp. 55–66.

10 NLI Ó Lúing Papers, box 1 [Anon.], Reader's Report.

11 BMH WS 205 (3 March 1949); UCD Hayes Papers, P52/222 (10–11).

12 NLI Ó Lúing Papers, MS 12,038, box 4, Dan McCarthy interview notes (1946), p. 8.

13 NLI Lennon Papers, MS 22,913, file 29.

14 Sadlier, 'The Fate of Fr Sheehy'.

15 Ó Lúing, *Ó Gríofa*, p. 211.

16 *Evening Herald,* 13 Feb. and 14 May 1889.

17 *United Irishman*, 18 Aug. 1900.

18 Dunleavy, *Hyde*, p. 209; De Brún, *Revivalism and Modern Irish Literature*, pp. 119–20.

19 UCD Hayes Papers, P53/217, Hayes to Milroy, 1 May 1943.

20 UCD Aiken Papers, P104/2592, p. 4, John Devoy to Jeremiah J. Lynch, Butte, Montana, 20 Jan. 1921.

21 Lloyd George, *Where Are We Going?*, p. 344

22 'Childers (Robert), Erskine', in *DIB*, by M.A. Hopkinson.

23 Hannay, *Pleasant Places*, pp. 187–8; Sinn Féin, 24 Dec. 1909, 'Spanish Gold'.

24   NLI Ó Lúing Papers, MS 12,038, box 3, Maud Griffith to Ó Lúing, 23 March 1949; BMH WS 1,698 (de Róiste), pt. 1, p. 29.

25   Nadel, *Joyce and the Jews*, p. 191.

26   *United Irishman*, 23 Feb. 1901 (five columns), 13 April 1901; Colum, *Road Round Ireland*, p. 303.

27   Davis, *Arthur Griffith and Non-Violent Sinn Féin*, p. 14.

28   NLI Ó Lúing Papers, MS 12,038, box 3, Chrissie Doyle to Seán Ó Lúing (1945), p. 9; ibid, Michael McWhite interview notes (July 1953); UCD MacWhite Papers, P194/663, pp. 10–13.

29   NLI Ó Lúing Papers, MS 12,038, box 3, Mr and Mrs Charles Fox (1945).

30   NLI Ó Ceallaigh Papers, MS 27,700, Address to Cumann Tír Conaill, pp. 30–4.

31   McKenna, 'In London with the Treaty Delegates', p. 324.

32   Gonne, *Servant of the Queen*, p. 307.

33   Lyons, *Griffith*, p. 61.

34   BMH WS 1765 pt. 1, p. 84.

35   Lyons, *Griffith*, p. 61.

36   Maume, *Long Gestation*, p. 51.

37   Colum, *Road Round Ireland*, p. 299, p. 301.

38   NLI Johnson Papers, MSS 17, 239; *Irish Times*, 17 March 1951.

39   O'Casey, *Drums Under the Window*, pp. 14–15.

40   BMH WS 1770 (Kevin O'Shiel), pp. 709–16, p. 714; NLI Ó Ceallaigh Papers, NLI MS 27,700, Address to Cumann Tír Conaill, p. 30; NLI Lennon Papers, MS 22,289, Klerk and Klerk, attorneys in the Transvaal to Michael Lennon, 9 Jan. 1951, stating that 'Cuguan' is 'not a Kaffir [native] word'; NLI Ó Lúing Papers, MS 12,038, box 4, Dan McCarthy interview notes, p. 3.

41   NLI Arthur Griffith Papers, Personal Recollections of Arthur Griffith, by James Moran, 1951, MS 49,530/14, p. 1.

42   R.F. [Robert Flood?], 'Some Early Memories'; Gibson, *The Strong Spirit*, pp. 58–63; Joyce, *Occasional Writing*, pp. 52–60, 297–301.

43   R.F. [Robert Flood?], 'Some Early Memories'.

44   O'Sullivan, *Essays and Recollections*, p. 106; NLI Ó Lúing Papers, MS 12,038, box 3, Chrissie Doyle to Seán Ó Lúing (1945), p. 8.

45   NLI Ó Lúing Papers, MS 12,038, box 3, Patrick Carey interview notes, 31 March 1966, p. 2.

46   Colum, *Road Round Ireland*, p. 301; *Sunday Independent*, 11 Sept. 1949; NLI Ó Ceallaigh Papers, Address to Cumann Tír Conaill, p. 2.

47   Béaslaí, 'Arthur Griffith'; Brennan, *Allegiance*, p. 229.

48   NLI, Arthur Griffith to Lily Williams, 1 April 1909 (MS 5,943/5); NLI Lennon Papers, letter from Griffith, 1 April 1910; *Sunday Independent*, 11 Sept. 1949; Brennan, *Allegiance*, p. 224; Briscoe, *For the Life of Me*, p. 50; McKenna, 'In London with the Treaty Delegates', p. 320.

49   BMH WS 1,765, pt. 1, p. 85.

50   BMH WS 1,170, pt. 5, pp. 709–16.

51   Ibid.; Brennan, *Allegiance*, p. 207; Gogarty, *Sackville Street*, p. 80.

52   Lyons, *Recollections of Griffith*, p. 61.

53   Colum, *Griffith*, p. 173.

54   BMH WS 707, p. 11.

55   NLI Arthur Griffith Papers, Recollections of Arthur Griffith, by James Moran, 1951, MS 49,530/14.

Chapter 5
Ballads, Songs and Snatches

1   O'Sullivan, *Essays and Recollections*, p. 105; Gaeul, *P. J. McCall*, p. 15, p. 162.

2   BMH WS 707 (Michael Noyk), p. 6; NLI Lennon Papers, MS 22,293.

3   NLI Irish Transvaal Committee Minute Book, 17 Oct. 1899.

4   McCracken, 'The Irish Literary Movement, Irish Doggerel and the Boer War', p. 101.

5   *United Irishman*, 17 Nov. 1900, p. 4, editorial.

6   *Freeman's Journal*, 27 June 1885; Duncathail, *Street Ballads, passim*.

7   Barry, *Songs of Ireland*, preface.

8   O'Donoghue, 'The Literature of '67'.

9   NLI Eblana, pp. 9–16 (8 Feb. 1889).

10   'Lilly, William', in Oxford *Dictionary of National Biography*, by Patrick Curry; Ó Buachalla, 'Lillibulero'.

11   See   http://www.bbc.co.uk/worldservice/us/001221_sigtunes.shtml   (at   2 August 2019).

12   Bagwell, *Ireland Under the Stuarts*, vol. 3, 164.

13   Ó Buachalla, 'Lillibulero', pp. 51–2.

14   Lyons, *Recollections*, p. 60; NLI Ó Lúing Papers, MS 12,038, box 3, Francis Griffith interview notes, no. 2, 29 Aug. 1945.

15   See, for example, 'Irish Life as Instanced in Irish Songs' and 'Songs and Humour' (*United Irishman*, 4 and 18 March 1899).

16   *United Irishman*, 29 June 1901.

17   Joyce, *Chamber Music*, no. 31.

18   McKenna, 'In London with the Treaty delegates', p. 324.

19   BMH WS 939 (Blythe), p. 67.

20   NLI Celtic, at 20 and 27 Jan. 1899; NLI Ó Lúing Papers, MS 12,038, box 3, Chrissie Doyle to Seán Ó Lúing (1945), p. 6.

21   Colum, *Griffith*, p. 190.

22   NLI Collins Papers MS 40.432/2, Letter from Mary Clare Collins-Powell, *Irish Times*, 27 April 2015; Béaslaí, 'Arthur Griffith'.

23   NLI Eblana, pp. 9–16 (8 Feb. 1889).

24   *United Irishman*, 8 and 15 June 1901 including interview with Duffaud.

25   *United Irishman*, 29 June 1901.

Chapter 6
His 'Best Friend' Rooney Dies

1   Yeats, *Collected Letters*, vol. 3, p. 72, Yeats to Gregory (21 May 1901).

2   Yeats, *Cathleen ni Hoolihan*, dedication; *Samhain*, October 1902.

3   Kenny (H.E.), 'William Rooney'.

4   Collins, *Path to Freedom*, p. 145.

5   Rooney, *Poems and Ballads*.

6   Sheehy-Skeffington, *British Militarism*; *Shan Van Vocht*, 12 March 1897. There is another song of the same name.

7   Rooney, *Poems and Ballads*, pp. xiii–xlvi.

8   Kenny, 'William Rooney'.

9   Kelly, '... and William Rooney spoke in Irish'.

10   *Irish Freedom*, no. 1 (November 1910), by Lucan (3 cols).

11   *United Ireland*, March 1897; Rooney, *Poems and Ballads*, pp. xxviii, 32–3.

12   Gonne, *Servant of the Queen*, p. 266.

13   NLI Ó Lúing Papers, MS 12,038, box 3, notes of interview with Maire O'Brolchain (Máire Bean Uí Brolcháin), pp. 11–13.

14   NLI Celtic, 24 and 28 Oct. 1898.

15   'Clancy, George' and 'Rooney, William', in *DIB*, by William Murphy; Ellmann, *James Joyce*, pp. 62–3.

16   *United Irishman*, 11 May 1901; Kenny, 'William Rooney'; Rooney, *Poems and Ballads*, p. xxxiv.

17   Kenny, 'William Rooney'; Rooney, *Poems and Ballads*, p. xviii.

18   Gonne, *Servant of the Queen*, pp. 98, 240; *United Irishman*, 16 March and 1 June 1901; Yeats, *Uncollected Prose*, vol. 2, pp. 470–2.

19   Levenson, *Maud Gonne*, pp. 142–3.

20   Gonne, *Servant of the Queen*, p. 288.

21   *United Irishman*, 27 Jan. 1900, under a heading 'Recruiting Songs'; Rooney, *Poems and Ballads*, pp. 146–8.

22   Thornton, *Allusions in* Ulysses, p. 242; Worthington, 'Folk songs in Joyce's *Ulysses*', p. 337.

23   Rooney, *Poems and Ballads*, p. xxiii.

24   *United Irishman*, 11 and 25 May 1901 for this and other tributes.

25   Rooney, *Poems and Ballads*, p. xvii for a long extract from the paper.

26   Gonne, *Servant of the Queen*, pp. 94, 266.

27 Rooney, *Poems and Ballads*, pp. xxx, xliii quoting unidentified pieces by Rooney.

28 Ibid., p. xxxi–xxxii.

29 For example, *United Irishman*, 11 March, 19 April, 14 and 28 October, 11 and 18 Nov. 1899 and 13 Jan. 1900.

30 *United Irishman*, 'All Ireland' column, 11 and 25 March 1899, 10 March 1900.

31 Kenny, 'William Rooney'.

32 Rooney, *Poems and Ballads*, p. xxxii.

33 *Daily Express*, 11 Dec. 1902.

34 Rooney, *Prose Writings*, p. vii; *United Irishman*, 9 Sept. 1899.

35 *Evening Herald*, 6 and 8 May 1901; *United Irishman*, 11 May 1901 and 25 May ('Celt') 1901; Kenny (H.E.), 'William Rooney' and Alice Milligan, 'By the Graveside', *United Irishman*, 15 June 1901.

36 *United Irishman*, 29 June 1901.

37 *United Irishman*, 11 May 1901.

38 IG Register of Deaths, Dublin North 1901, no. 314 (ID 4497840).

39 *United Irishman*, 11 May 1901.

40 Griffith, 'Preface', in Rooney, *Poems and Ballads*, pp. ix–xi.

41 Gonne, *Servant of the Queen*, p. 349.

42 *United Irishman*, 11 May 1901.

43 'Rooney' in *DIB*, by William Murphy; *United Irishman*, 11 May 1901, 12 and 19 Oct. 1901.

44 *United Irishman*, 6 April 1901.

45 Kelly, *Collected Letters*, p. 72 (Yeats to Lady Gregory, 21 May 1901); Wade, *Letters*, p. 351.

46 Gonne, *Servant of the Queen*, pp. 312–13.

47 Ibid., pp. 313–15.

48 Collins, *Path to Freedom*, pp. 148–50.

49 Joyce, *Occasional Writing*, pp. 50, 295–6.

50 Ibid., pp. 60–99, 301–10.

51 Marx, 'The Excitement in Ireland'.

52 Joyce, *Dubliners*, p. 233; *Sinn Féin*, 5 Jan. 1907.

53 *United Irishman*, 4 and 11 March, 27 May, 24 June, 23 Dec. 1899.

54 Yeats, *Where There is Nothing*; Ellmann, *James Joyce*, pp. 109–15.

55 Ellmann, *James Joyce*, pp. 83–7.

56 Rooney, *Poems and Ballads*, pp. 68–9, beneath Hyde's pen name 'An Craoibhín Aoibhinn'; *United Irishman*, 11 May 1901; *Evening Herald*, 11 May 1901, which again published it after his death under the headline 'A Beautiful Poem'.

57 *United Irishman*, 20 Dec. 1902; Ellmann, *James Joyce*, p. 116.

58 *Daily Express*, 26 March 1903; Joyce, *Occasional Writing*, pp. 74–6, 304.

59 Ellmann, *The Consciousness of Joyce*, p. 125.

60   Ellmann, *James Joyce*, pp. 246–8; Joyce, *Occasional Writing*, pp. ix–x.

61   *United Irishman*, 15 June 1901.

62   Callinan, 'James Joyce and the *United Irishman*', p. 91.

63   Shovlin, 'Who Was Father Conroy?', pp. 255–65.

64   Rooney, *Poems and Ballads*, pp. xxiv, 141–5.

65   Whelan, 'The Memories of "The Dead"', pp. 59–97.

66   Nagy, *Conversing with Angels and Ancients*, *passim*.

67   Hannay, *Pleasant Places*, p. 189; McCartney, 'The Political Use of History', p. 12.

68   Joyce, *Dubliners*, p. 274.

69   *United Irishman*, 27 May 1899, 15 June 1901.

70   *United Irishman*, 3 Feb. 1900, 14 and 28 July 1900; *Hansard*, HC Deb., 1 Feb. 1900, vol. 78, col. 264 and 6 Feb. 1900, vol. 78, cols 701–3; McCracken, *Forgotten Protest*, pp. 58, 82.

71   Joyce, *Occasional Writing*, pp. 41, 294; *Fortnightly Review* NS, 67 (London, 1 April 1900), 575–90.

72   *United Irishman*, 15 June 1901.

73   *United Irishman*, 31 March 1900.

74   *United Irishman*, 14 April 1900.

75   *United Irishman*, 9 June 1900.

76   *United Irishman*, 8 June 1901.

77   Yeats, *Essays*, p. 313.

78   Joyce, *Dubliners*, pp. 273–4.

79   Gonne, *Servant of the Queen*, p. 312.

80   Ellman, *James Joyce*, p. 252.

81   Kelly, '… and William Rooney spoke in Irish'.

82   Mathews, 'A Battle of Two Civilizations?', p. 29.

Chapter 7
Women as Comrade and Wife

1   Gonne, *Servant of the Queen*, pp. 94–5, 266, 306, 312–13.

2   Steele, *Women, Press and Politics*, pp. 73–4.

3   Ryan, 'Philosophies in Little'.

4   *United Irishman*, 10 Aug. 1910, by 'Sean-Ghall'.

5   'Inghinidhe na hÉireann', by 'Ier', *United Irishman*, 24 Aug. 1901.

6   *United Irishman*, 2 Nov. 1901.

7   *Sinn Féin*, 20 March 1909, 15 and 22 April 1911, 6 and 13 April 1912; Kate O'Callaghan, in Dáil Éireann, 2 March 1922; Maume, *Long Gestation*, pp. 122–3; Maye, *Griffith*, pp. 22–7.

8   See, for example, Martin, 'Review'.

9   Gonne, *Gonne-Yeats Letters*, pp. 165–6 (Gonne to Yeats, 1905).

10   IG Civil Records, Births, Dublin North, no. 85 of 1871 (ID 10826836) to Arthur and Mary née Whelan at 61 Upper Dominick Street; Ibid., Death of Arthur Griffith (senior, aged 66, 'hemiplegia'), Dublin North, no. 470 of 1904 (ID 4732437); Ibid., Death of Mary Griffith (widow aged 80, 'senility/cardiac failure'), Dublin North, no. 426 of 1920 (ID 5750349).

11   IG, Civil Records, Births, Dublin South, no. 271 of 1874 (ID 8596121).

12   Gonne, *Servant of the Queen*, p. 239.

13   Nicholson, *Annals of the Famine in Ireland*, pp. 44–6, 117, 233; *Freeman's Journal*, 20 April 1847, 28 Dec. 1853, 1 Feb. 1864, 12 Dec. 1891, 18 May 1889, 11 July 1899; Census 1901 shows coffin-makers living at numbers 2 and 3 Cook Street; NLI Ó Lúing Papers, MS 12,038, box 3, Chrissie Doyle to Seán Ó Lúing (1945), p. 7.

14   *Freeeman's Journal*, 28 Dec. 1853, 1 Feb. 1864.

15   Magee, *Paper Industry*, pp. 105–08.

16   *Freeman's Journal*, 11 July 1899; National Archives of Ireland, 'Calendar of Wills and Administrations 1858–1922', online database.

17   UCD Hayes Papers, P52/222 (10–11), Notes of an interview with Mrs A. Griffith, August 1950; Colum, *Griffith*, p. 30.

18   NLI Arthur Griffith Papers, MS 49,530/1/3, to 'Mollie', unsigned, undated.

19   Quoted at Colum, *Griffith*, p. 30, unreferenced. The author has not found this invitation among the Griffith Papers in the National Library.

20   NLI Arthur Griffith Papers, MS 49,530/1/1, to 'Molly', unsigned, dated 22 Dec. 1894.

21   NLI Arthur Griffith Papers, MS 49,530/1/2, to 'Molly', unsigned, also dated 22 Dec. 1894.

22   NLI Arthur Griffith Papers, MS 49,530/1/4, to 'Molly', unsigned, dated 26 Aug. 1895.

23   O'Shea, *Charles Stewart Parnell*, passim.

24   NLI Celtic, 26 Dec. 1896; NLI Ó Ceallaigh Papers, Address to Cumann Tír Conaill, pp. 3–4.

25   NLI Ó Lúing Papers, MS 12,038, box 3, Chrissie Doyle to Seán Ó Lúing (1945), p. 5.

26   BMH WS 205 (Maud Griffith), 3 March 1949, p. 1.

27   Gonne, *Servant of the Queen*, p. 94.

28   Ibid.

29   NAI CBS Précis, box 6, 23 Oct. 1900; BMH WS 317 (Gonne), p. 6.

30   Levenson, *Maud Gonne*, p. 1.

31   Gonne, *Servant of the Queen*, pp. x–xvii, 8; Steel, 'Biography as Promotional Discourse' and Pratt, 'Maud Gonne', passim.

32   Gonne, *Servant of the Queen*, p. 84, citing the *Review of Reviews*, 7 June 1892.

33 Colum, *Life and the Dream*, p. 130.

34 Steele, 'Biography as Promotional Discourse', p. 138; Ferguson, *Maud Gonne, passim*.

35 Yeats, *Memoirs*, pp. 132–3.

36 Ibid.; Ward, *Maud Gonne*, pp. 54–5.

37 'MacBride, (Edith) Maud Gonne', in *DIB*, by M. O'Callaghan and C. Nic Dháibhéid; Balliet, 'Lives – and Lies', pp. 17, 27–9.

38 *New York Times*, 5 March 1899, p. 7.

39 Maguire, 'Oscar Wilde and the Dreyfus Affair', pp. 5, 9–10, 22–3; Ellmann, *Oscar Wilde*, p. 530.

40 Gonne, *Servant of the Queen*, p. 292.

41 Balliet, 'Lives – and Lies', pp. 29–30, 40.

42 Gonne, *Servant of the Queen*, p. 235; *Gonne–Yeats Letters*, pp. 152–3.

43 *Express*, 9 April 1900, cited at Yeats, *Collected Letters*, vol. 2, p. 510.

44 NAI Colonial Office boxes, MFA 54/122; NAI CBS Précis, box 6, 10 Oct. and 9 Nov. 1898, 25 June 1900, 12 June 1901, etc.; Gonne, *Servant of the Queen*, pp. 238–9.

45 McCracken, *The Irish Pro-Boers, passim*; BMH WS 104 (Lyons), p. 3.

46 NAI CBS Précis, box 6, 21 Nov. 1900; *United Irishman*, 14 Oct. 1899, p. 6; McGeee, *Griffith*, pp. 32–52.

47 NAI CBS Précis, box 6, 10 Oct. and 9 Nov. 1898, 22 Aug. 1902.

48 *United Ireland* 13 Oct. 1900, by 'Shel Martin'; Gonne, *Servant of the Queen*, p. 267; NLI Ó Ceallaigh Papers, Draft of RTE Talk *c.*1960, no. 2, includes Oliver St John Gogarty on the rate of VD among British forces.

49 *United Irishman*, 27 April 1901, p. 4, editorial.

50 *United Irishman*, 21 and 28 July 1900, 19 Oct. 1901.

51 Gonne, *Servant of the Queen*, pp. 197–9, 202, 278, 307–09.

52 *United Irishman*, 27 April 1901.

53 Inghinidhe na h-Éireann, *First Annual Report, 1900–1901*, p. 2; NAI CBS Précis, box 6, 8 March 1898; *Irish Figaro*, 7 April 1900; *Evening Herald*, 9 and 10 April 1900; *Daily Nation*, 10 April 1910; *United Irishman*, 14, 21 and 28 April, 12 and 19 May 1900; Yeats, *Collected Letters*, vol. 2, p. 511; Gonne, *Servant of the Queen*, p. 201; Lyons, *Griffith*, pp. 10–11.

54 Mathews, 'Stirring Up Disloyalty', p. 115.

55 Gonne, *Servant of the Queen*, p. 321.

56 Ibid., p. 322.

57 Ibid., p. 349; *United Irishman* 25 Nov. and 23 Dec. 1899.

58 Gonne, *Servant of the Queen*, p. 349; Gonne, *Gonne–Yeats Letters*, pp. 185–6.

59 McCracken, *Irish Pro-Boers*, citing NLI John O'Leary Papers, MS 8001 (34), Gonne to O'Leary.

60   Gonne, *Gonne-Yeats Letters*, pp. 185–6.

61   Foster, *Yeats*, vol. 1, pp. 330–1.

62   Joyce, *Letters*, vol. 2, p. 185.

63   NLI Ó Lúing Papers, MS 12,038, box 3, Chrissie Doyle to Seán Ó Lúing (1945), p. 3; Ibid., box 4, Dan McCarthy interview notes (1946), p. 10.

64   Yeats, *Memoirs*, p. 133.

65   Schuchard, 'Attendant Lord', p. 104.

66   *Daily Mirror*, 27 Feb. 1903, cited at Balliet, 'Lives – and Lies', p. 37.

67   Schuchard, 'Attendant Lord', p. 104.

68   O'Casey, *Drums Under the Window*, pp. 14–15.

69   Colum, *Griffith*, p. 74.

70   Colum, *Life and the Dream*, p. 130.

71   IG Civil Records, Death of Mary Sheehan (aged 58, 'heart disease'), Dublin North, no. 124, ID 4442635 (1900); *Calendar of Wills and Administrations 1858-1922*, p. 477; Census 1901; *Freeman's Journal*, 25 Aug. and 28 Dec. 1900; *United Irishman*, 1 Sept. 1900.

72   NLI Ó Lúing Papers, MS 12,038, box 3, Interview with Patrick Carey (aged 91, 31 March 1966), p. 4; Fennessy, 'Irish Franciscan Chaplains', p. 459 with photo of Leo. Her brother Michael was Fr. Peter in religion.

73   *Irish Times*, 15 July 1904.

74   *Thom's Street Directory*, 1900–1908.

75   *United Irishman*, 26 May 1900, by 'Cuguan'.

76   NLI, Arthur Griffith to Lily Williams, MSS 5,943 (1-18); NLI Ó Lúing Papers, MS 12,038, box 4, Dan McCarthy interview notes, p. 4.

77   BMH WS 205 (Maud Griffith); BMH WS 909 (Sidney Czira), appendix, 'First Meeting Easter Sunday, 1900: list'; *United Irishman*, 2 March 1901.

78   Colum, *Griffith*, p. 74.

79   IG Civil Records, Marriages, Dublin North, no. 202 of 1910 (ID 2015190).

80   BMH WS 1,765 (Seán T. Ó Ceallaigh); Letter re Griffith from C. Kenny, *History Ireland*, November/December 2017.

81   NLI Arthur Griffith Papers, MS 49,530/7/1, Leabhar Tighe Uí Ghríobhtha 1910.

82   IG Registry of Births, Dublin, ID1109968 and ID1317850; NLI, Arthur Griffith to Lily Williams, MS 5,943/6 (9 Sept. 1911).

83   NMI HE:EWL.207, Griffith's will.

84   McKenna, 'In London', p. 324.

85   BMH WS 637 (Muriel Murphy), p. 7.

86   Cathal O'Shannon, *Irish Times*, 17 March 1951.

87   UCD Humphreys Papers, P106/184/1/1 (13 Sept. 1916).

88   Colum, *Griffith*, pp. 162–3; NLI Arthur Griffith Papers, MS LO12348.

89   NLI Arthur Griffith Papers, MS 49,530/4 (24 Nov. 1916).

90   Maye, *Griffith*, pp. 74–5; NLI Arthur Griffith Papers, MS 49,530/5.

91   BMH WS 1,721 (Robinson), p. 66.

92   Brennan, *Allegiance*, p. 241; O'Sullivan, *Essays and Recollections*, p. 115.

93   NLI Ó Lúing Papers, MS 12,038, box 3, Notes of interview with Maire O'Brolchain (Máire Bean Uí Brolcháin), June 1953.

94   NLI Arthur Griffith Papers, MS 49,530/8/1/v.

95   Ó Lúing, *Ó Gríofa*, plate at p. 385 for letter from Maud, location now unknown.

96   BMH WS 205 (Maud Griffith); NLI Lennon Papers, MS 22,289, Lennon to P.C. Vercueil, Middleburg, 7 Feb. 1950.

97   NLI Sheehy-Skeffington Papers, MS 33,617 (2); *Irish World*, 8 April and 13 May 1922.

98   McAuliffe, 'An Idea Has Gone Abroad', p. 179.

99   Ó Lúing, *Ó Gríofa*, plate at p. 385 for letter from Maud, location now unknown.

100   Colum, *Griffith*, p. 333.

101   Dolan, 'The Forgotten President'.

102   NLI Ó Lúing Papers, MS 12,038, box 3, Chrissie Doyle to Seán Ó Lúing (1945), p. 10; Ibid., Notes of interview with Padraig Ó Caoimh (March 1945).

Chapter 8
Griffith, Race and Africa

1   'Churchill, Sir Winston Leonard Spencer', in Oxford *Dictionary of National Biography*, by Paul Addison.

2   *United Irishman*, 4 March 1899.

3   *United Irishman*, 11 March 1899, by 'Cuguan'; Griffith, *Songs, Ballads and Recitations*, p. 25. For other references to the Sudan, including the use of dum-dum bullets see *United Irishman*, 11 and 25 March, 1, 8 and 22 April, 3, 10, 17 and 22 June 1899.

4   Maume, 'Young Ireland, Arthur Griffith and Republican Ideology', p. 171.

5   *The Nation*, 13 Jan. 1844, 9 Aug. and 1 Nov. 1845.

6   Dugger, 'Black Ireland's Race', p. 474.

7   Nelson, *Irish Race, passim*.

8   *United Irishman*, 20 July 1901, by 'Cuguan'.

9   *Observer*, 12 Oct. 1862.

10   'Mitchel, John', in *DIB*, by John Quinn.

11   *United Irishman*, 3 March 1900 and 2 Feb., 8 and 19 June 1901.

12   Tóibín, *Lady Gregory's Toothbrush*, p. 78.

13   Mitchel, *Jail Journal*, preface, pp. xiii–xiv.

14   *United Irishman*, 28 Oct. 1899.

15   *Evening Herald*, 23 Aug. 1913; *Freeman's Journal*, 26 Sept. 1913.

16   *The Penny Magazine* [London], monthly supplement, 28 February – 31 March 1838, pp. 121–2.

17   Spurr, *Rhetoric of Empire*, pp. 66–7.

18   Dugger, 'Black Ireland's Race', *passim*; Morrow, 'Thomas Carlyle'.

19   *United Irishman*, 9 Sept. 1899. Also see 27 Jan. 1900.

20   *United Irishman*, 16 Sept. 1899.

21   Curtis, *Apes and Angels: The Irishman in Victorian Caricature, passim*.

22   *United Irishman*, 27 May 1899, by 'Ier' (Griffith).

23   *United Irishman*, 11 Nov. 1899, by 'Ier'.

24   *United Irishman*, 9 Dec. 1899, by 'Ier'.

25   *United Irishman*, 9 Dec. 1899, by 'Ier'.

26   *United Irishman*, 20 Jan. 1900.

27   Griffith, *Ballads: Arthur Griffith*, p. 23 and *passim* for 'A Ballad of Bezuidenhout' and 'The Song of the British 'Ero' etc.

28   *United Irishman*, 27 Jan. 1900. See also O'Donnell's 'An Englishman's Cawnpore', *United Irishman*, 17 June 1898.

29   *Hansard*, House of Commons, 19 Oct. 1899, vol. 77, cols 254–371.

30   *United Irishman*, 21 July 1900, by 'Celt'.

31   *United Irishman*, 10 Feb. 1900.

32   *United Irishman*, 16 June 1900.

33   *United Irishman*, 26 Aug. 1899.

34   *Irish Worker*, 25 July 1914.

35   *Nationality*, 30 Oct. 1915.

36   'Griffith, Arthur', in *DIB*, by Michael Laffan.

37   Joyce, *Letters*, vol. 2, p. 189.

Chapter 9
Connolly, Yeats, Synge and Larkin

1   McCracken, *Forgotten Protest, passim*; McGee, *Griffith*, pp. 32–9.

2   NLI Celtic Literary Society minutes, NLI MS 19,934 (i), 24 and 28 Oct. 1898.

3   *Freeman's Journal*, 2 Oct. 1899; NLI Irish Transvaal Committee Minute Book.

4   McCracken, *Forgotten Protest*, p. 45.

5   McCracken, 'Irish doggerel and the Boer War', pp. 97–115.

6   *Workers' Republic*, 30 Dec. 1899; *United Irishman*, 23 Dec. 1899.

7   *Irish Times*, 18 Dec. 1899; Lyons, *Recollections*, pp. 12–26.

8   *Evening Herald*, 18 Dec. 1899.

9   *Cork Examiner* and *Irish Times*, 19 Dec. 1899.

10   Lyons, *Recollections*, p. 19.
11   Ibid., p. 14.
12   NLI Ó Ceallaigh Papers, Address; Connolly, 'Sinn Féin, Socialism and the Nation', *Irish Nation*, 23 Jan. 1909.
13   *United Irishman*, 17, 24 and 31 Jan. 1903.
14   Kenny, *'Scissors and Paste'*, p. 339.
15   BMH WS 707 (Noyk), p. 3.
16   Lyons, *Recollections*, pp. 39–40 for the lyrics of this 'disconcerted' duet.
17   'Yeats, William Butler' in *DIB*, by Terence Brown; Foster, *Yeats*, vol. 1, pp. 112–14; *United Irishman*, 27 Oct. 1900.
18   Yeats, *Collected Letters*, vol. 2, p. 477 (Yeats to Gonne, *c*.15 Dec. 1899).
19   NAI CBS Précis, box 6, August 1898; NAI CO 904, MFA 54/122, 18 Oct. 1900; *United Irishman*, 21 April 1900.
20   *The Speaker*, 7 July 1900; *United Ireland*, 28 July 1900.
21   Colum, *Griffith*, p. 46; *United Irishman*, 6 May 1899.
22   *United Irishman*, 11 March 1897. Rooney wrote all 'All Ireland' columns until his death.
23   Yeats gave the date of their first meeting as 1889, and is followed by the authors of *DIB* entries for both, but Gonne claimed it was earlier (Foster, *Yeats*, vol. 1, p. 57).
24   Yeats, *Memoirs*, pp. 132–3.
25   Yeats, *Countess Cathleen*, *passim* for that rewriting.
26   Ibid., p. xxxvii.
27   Gonne, *Servant of the Queen*, Preface (entitled 'I Saw the Queen').
28   Bobotis, 'Rival Maternities', pp. 63–83.
29   *United Irishman*, 7 and 14 April 1900.
30   *United Irishman*, 21 April 1900, p. 5, 'Noble and Ignoble Loyalties'.
31   *United Irishman*, 19 Jan. 1901, p. 3, 'Cuguan'.
32   Ryan, *Fenian Memories*, p. 184.
33   Yeats, *Collected Letters of W.B. Yeats*, vol. 2, pp. 669–83
34   *Freeman's Journal*, 1 April 1899.
35   Yeats, *Autobiographies*, pp. 308–09.
36   *Freeman's Journal*, 10 May 1899.
37   Yeats, *Plays*, p. 679.
38   Yeats, *Collected Letters*, vol. 2, p. 672.
39   Yeats, *Letters*, p. 319 (published 13 May 1899).
40   *Cork Examiner*, 13 May 1899.
41   *United Irishman*, 26 Jan 1901, by 'Shanganagh'.
42   *United Irishman*, 19 and 26 Jan. and 9 and 16 Feb. 1901.
43   NLI Ó Lúing Papers, MS 12,038, box 4, Dan McCarthy interview notes, pp. 1–2; Ibid., box 3, for another reference to this chair.

44   *United Irishman*, 23 Feb. and 27 April 1901.

45   *United Irishman*, 6 May and 26 Oct. 1901; Yeats, *Letters*, pp. 352–3 (1 Aug. 1901).

46   Yeats, *Letters*, p. 350 (21 May 1901).

47   Yeats, *Collected Letters*, vol. 3, 94 (July 1901); Yeats, *Letters*, p. 365.

48   *United Irishman*, 26 Oct. 1901 and 9 July 1904.

49   Yeats, *Collected Letters of W.B. Yeats*, vol. 3, pp. 187–9 (23 May 1902).

50   'MacBride, (Edith) Maud Gonne', in *DIB*, by Margaret O'Callaghan and Caoimhe Nic Dháibhéid.

51   Yeats, *Collected Letters*, vol. 3 (19–20 May. 1902). He consulted Lady Gregory about the spelling of the surname – was it correct as Ni or Ny, upper or lower case 'n' and Houlihan or Hoolihan (Ibid., p. 185, 23 May. 1902)? Later, he would change the first name to 'Cathleen'.

52   *Freeman's Journal*, 31 March and 3 April 1902.

53   O'Sullivan, *The Rose and the Bottle*, p. 120.

54   Tóibín, *Lady Gregory's Toothbrush*, pp. 45–49.

55   Yeats, *Letters*, pp. 365–8.

56   *Sinn Féin*, 14 February 1914, 'The Origin of the Abbey Theatre'.

57   Brennan, *Allegiance*, p. 204.

58   Murphy, 'Dark Liturgy, Bloody Praxis', p. 13.

59   Interviewed by Mary Kenny, *The Spectator*, 8 Nov. 1997.

60   *United Irishman*, 5 and 12 April 1902.

61   *The Echo*, 25 April 1902.

62   *United Irishman*, 10, 17 and 24 Oct. 1903.

63   Yeats, *Essays*, p. 312.

64   Yeats, *Letters*, p. 416, to 'Æ', 18 Dec. 1903, and to Lady Gregory, 2 Jan. 1904.

65   Gonne, *Servant of the Queen*, p. 321.

66   *United Irishman*, 17 and 24 Dec. 1904; Yeats, *Collected Letters*, vol. 3, to Gregory, 22 Dec. 1904; ibid., pp. 688n, 709n.

67   *United Irishman*, 28 Jan., 4 and 11 Feb 1905; *Sinn Féin*, 3 April 1909.

68   Yeats, *Autobiographies*, p. 309.

69   Yeats, *Letters*, p. 448, 15 March 1905.

70   Yeats, *Autobiographies*, pp. 308–09.

71   *Sinn Féin*, 2 Feb. 1907.

72   *Sinn Féin*, 2 and 9 Feb. 1907, 3 April 1909.

73   Maye, *Griffith*, pp. 286–92.

74   Yeats, 'J.M. Synge and the Ireland of his Time' in Yeats, *Essays and Introductions*, pp. 311–42.

75   *United Irishman*, 9 July 1904.

76   *United Irishman*, 4 March 1899, 'The Dublin Stage'.

77   *United Irishman*, 9 July 1904.

78 Elvery, 'Today We Will Only Gossip', p. 91.
79 Jones, 'The Island of Ireland, pp. 402–3.
80 Maye, *Griffith*, pp. 281–93.
81 Ellmann, *James Joyce*, p. 248 citing letters to S. Joyce, 6 and 11 Feb. 1907.
82 UCD MacWhite Papers, P194/657.
83 Tóibín, *Lady Gregory's Toothbrush*, pp. 65–9, 88–101.
84 Morash, *Irish Theatre*, p. 152.
85 *Freeman's Journal*, 15 April 1910.
86 Yeats, *Letters*, pp. 612–13.
87 *Nationality*, 29 Jan. 1916. See also Michael Orkney (Thomas Keohler?), 'William Butler Yeats: A Character Sketch' in *Sinn Féin*, 6 Nov. 1909.
88 Foster, *Yeats*, vol. 2, pp. 206–08.
89 Ó Lúing, *Ó Gríofa*, p. 149.
90 Foster, *Yeats*, vol. 2, pp. 50, 133, 165, 170, 207.
91 Cited at Foster, *Yeats*, vol. 2, p. 206.
92 NLI Ó Lúing Papers, MS 12,038, box 3, MacManus to Seán Ó Lúing (undated).
93 Yeats, *Poems*, pp. 601, 838–40.
94 Childe, *Modernism and Eugenics*, pp. 210–11; Yeats, 'J.M. Synge and the Ireland of his Time' in Yeats, *Essays and Introductions*, p. 314.
95 Harris, 'Blow the Witches Out', p. 487.
96 Harris, *Gender and Modern Irish Drama*, p. 102.
97 Yeats, *Poems*, p. 601, pp. 838–40.
98 Foster, *Yeats*, vol. 2, p. 598.
99 Wade, *Letters*, p. 525 (8 March 1909).
100 Chapman, *Yeats and English Renaissance Literature*, pp. 26–7.
101 *Irish Nation*, 23 Jan. 1909.
102 Mansergh, *Ireland in the Age of Reform and Revolution*, pp. 204–13; Maye, *Griffith*, pp. 303–16.
103 O'Connor, 'James Larkin in the United States', pp. 183–96.
104 BMH WS 193, pp. 2, 4.
105 *Sinn Féin*, 25 Oct. 1913; *Irish Times*, 19 Aug. 1922; Brennan, *Allegiance*, pp. 218–19; McCarthy, *Labour v. Sinn Féin*, pp. 19–20.
106 *Sinn Féin*, 6 Sept., 4, 11 and 25 Oct., 1 Nov.1913 (for example); BMH WS 707 (Noyk), p. 3; Davis, *Griffith*, p. 15; Yeates, *Lockout*, pp. 132–4, 352–7.
107 Lyons, *Griffith*, pp. 12–14.
108 H.E. Kenny, 'Griffith'.
109 BMH WS 384 (O'Kelly, also known as 'Sceilg'), p. 20.
110 Davis, *Arthur Griffith and Non-Violent Sinn Féin*, pp. 139–44,
111 Colum, *Griffith*, p. 163.
112 'Croker, Richard Welsted ("Boss")', in *DIB*, by William Murphy.

Chapter 10
Journalist, Editor and Crusader

1   *Sinn Féin* 2 Sept. 1911; Joyce, *Letters*, vol. 2, pp. 291–3, 315. 336, 339, 340; Ellmann, *Joyce*, p. 346.
2   *United Irishman*, 2 Nov. 1901; Joyce, *Occasional Writing*, p. 295.
3   BMH WS 687 (Monsignor Michael Curran), part 1, p. 12. Curran was Walsh's secretary 1906–19.
4   Kelly, *The Fenian Ideal*, p. 176.
5   NLI Ó Lúing, Album of Cuttings, for William M. Kenealy, 'Arthur Griffith As Editor' (unidentified publication); *Irish Times*, 'Funerals', 7 Jan. 1942.
6   Colum, *Griffith*, pp 18–19.
7   Glandon, *Griffith*, p. 37, citing a letter from Griffith's fellow-worker P.D. O'Lenihan dated 1949. Actors Barry Fitzgerald and Arthur Shields were sons of Adolphus.
8   Rouse, 'Popular Culture in Ireland', p. 582.
9   Colum, *Griffith*, p. 22; Shuman, *Practical Journalism*, p. 25.
10 *Evening Herald* (*Saturday Herald* from 28 May) for Charles Lucas (13 Feb.), Jonathan Swift (5 March), Patrick Delany (19 March), Lord Edward FitzGerald (2 April), The Sheares brothers (23 April), John FitzGibbon, Lord Clare (14 May), John Philpot Curran (4 June), Charles Hendal Bushe (16 July).
11 Glandon, *Griffith*, p. 66, citing a letter of 1951 from Griffith's neighbour and co-worker Joseph Hammond.
12 *Daily Independent*, 31 Dec. 1896.
13 Colum, *Griffith*, pp. 33–4, but as usual giving no source; Glandon, *Griffith*, p. 12, p. 30, n. 47.
14 McCracken, 'Arthur Griffith' and 'The Quest for the *Middelburg Courant*'; O'Sullivan, *Essays*, p. 106, pp. 108–11; 'At the Poets' Agency', *United Irishman*, 21 Dec. 1901, by 'Shanganagh'.
15 NLI Ó Lúing Papers, MS 12,038, box 3, Maud Griffith to Ó Lúing, 23 March 1949; Colum, *Griffith*, p. 8.
16 *United Irishman*, 22 April 1899; *Shan Van Vocht*, 3(8), pp. 146–9 and 3(9), pp. 163–4; Gonne, *Servant of the Queen*, p. 176; Colum, *Griffith*, p. 45.
17 NAI CBS Précis, box 6, for 14 Aug. 1898.
18 NAI CBS Précis, box 6, for May 1898.
19 UCD MacWhite Papers, P194/663, p. 10.
20 *United Irishman*, 26 Aug. 1899.
21 Stephens, *Arthur Griffith*, pp. 18–19.
22 *United Irishman*, 24 June 1899.
23 MacBride, *Servant of the Queen*, pp. 94–5, 266, 306, 312–3.
24 *United Irishman* 28 July 1900 for letter from Yeats. See also 24 Feb., 14 April, 2 June, 8 and 15 Sept., 10 Nov., 1 Dec. 1900, 18 May 1901 for seizures.

25   Gonne, *Servant of the Queen*, p. 239.
26   *Freeman's Journal*, 7 April 1900 and 8 Oct. 1901 (citing *Morning Leader*); Gonne, *Servant of the Queen*, pp. 198–9, p. 324.
27   Steele, *Women, Press and Politics*, pp. 73–4.
28   NAI CO 904, MFA 54/122.
29   O'Sullivan, *Essays and Recollections*, p. 104; Horgan, *Parnell to Pearse*, p. 94.
30   Birmingham, *Pleasant Places*, p. 190.
31   Kenny, 'Arthur Griffith as I Knew Him', part 2.
32   For example, NLI Ó Lúing Papers, MS 12,038, box 4, Dan McCarthy interview notes (1946), p. 3; The Griffith Settlement Bill second stage, *Seanad Éireann Reports*, vol. 1, no. 13 (14 March 1923).
33   Lyons, *Griffith*, p. 62; Horgan, *Parnell to Pearse*, pp. 94–5; Brennan, *Allegiance*, p. 94.
34   Lyons, *Ireland since the Famine*, p. 248.
35   Brennan, *Allegiance*, p. 207.
36   BMH WS 1765, pt. 1, p. 90.
37   NLI O'Brien Papers MS 13,975 for the prospectus, and MS 35,262/1 (22) for a list of 64 shareholders [1904].
38   Stephens, *Griffith*, p. 18; Lyons, *Griffith*, pp. 45, 47, 49, 58; Brown, *Press in Ireland*, p. 41; Colum, *Griffith*, pp. 46–7; BMH WS 1,698 (de Róiste), pt. 1, p. 78.
39   *United Irishman*, 27 Jan. and 7 Feb. 1903; Callinan, 'Joyce and the *United Irishman*', p. 91; 'Kelleher, Joyce's "The Dead"', pp. 419–22.
40   Joyce, *My Brother's Keeper*, pp. 173–4; Manganiello, *Joyce's Politics*, pp. 118–47; Tymoczko, *The Irish Ulysses*, pp. 229–37 ('The *United Irishman*'); Mecsnóber, 'James Joyce, Arthur Griffith, Trieste and the Hungarian national character', pp. 341–59; O'Riordan, 'A Citizen's Defence for Bloomsday'; Callinan, 'James Joyce and the *United Irishman*', pp. 51–103.
41   McCracken, 'Arthur Griffith', pp. 246–9.
42   *Freeman's Journal*, 12 March 1906; *Irish Times*, 12 March and 22 Feb. 1906 (includes offending text), 13 and 20 July 1907; *Sunday Independent*, 11 March 1906; Lyons, *Griffith*, p. 69; BMH WS 1,698 (de Róiste), pp. 78–9.
43   *Il Piccolo della Sera* (Trieste), 22 March and 19 May, 16 Sept. 1907 and 22 Dec. 1910 ("La Cometa dell' "Home Rule"'); *Sinn Féin*, 26 May, 9 and 16 June, 15 Sept. 1906, 11 May, 16 Sept. 1907; 8 Jan and 11 June 1910 ('Comet' cartoon), 16 May 1912, etc.; Joyce, *Occasional Writings*, pp. 138–59, 322–8; Manganiello, *Joyce's Politics*, pp. 139–40 (re another cartoon at *Sinn Féin*, 15 Jan. 1910, 'The Shade of Parnell').
44   Ellmann, *Joyce*, pp. 310–18, 320–1.
45   Lyons, *Recollections*, p. 70.
46   *United Irishman*, 24 Aug. 1901.

47   Staunton, 'The Nation Speaking to Itself', pp. 228–45.

48   Davis, *Griffith*, p. 7.

49   Bulfin, 'Rambles in Eirinn', *Sinn Féin*, 18 Aug. 1906; W.E. Fay, 'A Sunday Special', *Sinn Féin*, 8 Dec. 1906.

50   Anon., '*Cork Examiner*', in *Sinn* Féin, 8 Dec. 1906; *Sinn Féin*, 22 and 29 Sept. 1906.

51   Joyce, *Letters*, vol. 2, p. 147 (August 1906).

52   Lyons, *Griffith*, p. 48; Gonne, *Servant of the Queen*, p. 291, p. 306; Colum, *Griffith*, p. 46; NLI Lennon Papers, MS 22,289 for typescripts of *Courant* articles by 'Shanganagh'; NLI Ó Lúing Papers, MS 12,038, box 3, Seán Milroy to Seán Long (4 Sept. 1944) and Francis Griffith interview notes, no. 2 (29 Aug. 1945); Yeates, *Lockout*, p. 133.

53   Glandon, *Arthur Griffith*, p. 67, n. 30; *United Irishman*, 2 March 1901; *Capuchin Annual* 1938, p. 21 for note and photo of Power; Yeats, *Collected Letters*, vol. 1, p. 81 (19 March 1901) and vol. 3, p. 23 n.22 (Jan. 1901).

54   *United Irishman* 11 May 1901 (editorial) and Rooney, *Poems and Ballads*, p. xxxiv.

55   *Irish Press*, 4 July 1961, article by S.T. O'Kelly; NLI Lennon Papers, MS 22288 (3).

56   Joyce, *Letters*, vol. 2, p. 198; *Sinn Féin*, 10 Nov. 1906.

57   *United Irishman*, 19 Jan. 1901; NLI Ó Lúing Papers, MS 12,038, box 3, Interview notes Chrissie Doyle; Staunton, 'The Nation Speaking to Itself', p. 242.

58   *Sinn Féin*, 4 Jan. 1908.

59   Seanad Éireann, 14 March 1923.

60   *The Irish Nation and The Peasant*, 15 Jan. 1910.

61   NLI MacColuim Papers; *Evening Telegraph*, 15 March to 23 Aug. 1913 on Saturdays, for Vallancey, Halliday, O'Reilly, Barron, Petrie, O'Donovan, O'Curry, Hudson, Pigot, Dodd, Ferguson, MacHale, Reeves, Gilbert, O'Growney, Wilde, Cleaver (in that order).

62   Lyons, *Griffith*, p. 69; Béaslaí, *Griffith*, p. 16; Kenny, *Irish Patriot, Publisher and Advertising Agent*, pp. 22–3.

63   BMH WS 391 (Helena Molony), pp. 9–10.

64   *United Irishman*, 29 July, 16, 23 and 30 Sept. 1899; Matthews, *Renegades*, pp. 54–6; Davison, *James Joyce*, pp. 68–72.

65   *United Irishman*, 26 August and 9 Sept. 1899; 24 April, 26 Aug. and 28 May 1904, 16 March 1912, etc.

66   *United Irishman*, 23 Jan, 23 April, 14 and 28 May 1904; 'Griffith, Arthur', in *DIB*, by Michael Laffan.

67   Cheyette, *Between Race and Culture*, p. 105.

68   Joyce, *Letters*, vol. 2, p. 167, to Stanislaus Joyce, 25 Sept. 1906.

69   Sinn Féin, part 1 (18 Sept.), part 2 (24 Nov.) and part 3 (1 Dec.); Manganiello,
     Joyce's Politics, pp. 129–36.
70   Joyce, Letters, vol. 2, 167, 187, to Stanislaus Joyce, 6 Nov. 1906.
71   Ellmann, James Joyce, p. 346, Joyce, Letters, vol. 2, pp. 291–3, 315, 336, 339,
     340. Joyce in 1915 refers to Griffith's paper as 'Sinn Féin' but by then that title
     had been superseded by Griffith's next paper.
72   Kenner, Ulysses, p. 133. Sometimes misquoted and truncated as 'the idea for
     Sinn Féin'.
73   Éire-Ireland, 10 and 12 Nov. 1914, for example.
74   National Library of Ireland, for this letter at the end of the complete run of
     Éire-Ireland on microfilm.
75   Kenny, 'Scissors and Paste', pp. 335–49.
76   Irish Times and Freeman's Journal, 3 March 1915.
77   NLI Ó Lúing Papers, MS 12,039, box 1, Seán Doyle (Seán Ó Dubhghaill to Ó
     Lúing (May 1952), identifies the pieces by Griffith.
78   United Irishman, 21 Sept. 1901.
79   Brennan, Allegiance, p. 204.
80   Béaslaí, 'Arthur Griffith'.
81   Catholic Bulletin, 7 (Feb. 1917), p. 85; Béaslaí, 'Griffith'; Cathal O'Shannon,
     'Nationality Born 40 Years Ago', Evening Press, 17 June 1955; Ó Bróin,
     Augustine Birrell, p. 120; Davis, Arthur Griffith, pp. 18, 20, 22.
82   NLI Arthur Griffith Letters.
83   Colum, Griffith, p. 190; BMH WS 939 (Blythe), p. 66.
84   Davis, Arthur Griffith, p. 24; Glandon, Advanced-Nationalist Press, p. 282;
     Novick, 'Propaganda'.
85   O'Hegarty, Sinn Féin: an Illumination, pp. 15–16, 38, 29–33.

Chapter 11
1902–1916: Sinn Féin and the Rising

1   Lyons, Recollections, p. 17.
2   Ibid., pp. 13–14, 17–20.
3   Brennan, Allegiance, pp. 210–11, 287.
4   United Irishman, 4 August and 8 Sept. 1900, by 'Shanganagh'.
5   United Irishman, 6 Oct. 1900, p. 6 for a report of its first meeting
    ('Confederation of the Gaels'); BMH WS 317 (Gonne), p. 13.
6   Cumann na nGaedheal, Convention and Ceilidh Handbill [1902], NLI
    Ephemera EPHE46; NAI CBS Précis, box 15, 4 and 6 Nov. 1902.
7   NAI CBS Précis, box 6, 18 May 1903.
8   NAI CO 904 MFA 54/123, 19 May 1903; Irish Independent, 19 May 1903.

9   *Irish Independent* and *Freeman's Journal*, 29 Nov. 1905.

10   *Irish Independent*, 29 Nov. 1905; *The 'Sinn Fein' Policy*, pp. 2–4. The author of the pamphlet identifies himself as having written *The Resurrection of Hungary*, 'published fifteen months ago'.

11   Talbot, *Collins*, p. 48.

12   NLI Griffith to Mère Columba S. Butler.

13   *United Irishman*, 17 August – 24 Sept. 1901 for Rooney's address.

14   *Shan Van Vocht* 12 March and 5 Feb. 1897.

15   Murphy, *Catholic Bulletin*, pp. 49–51.

16   *United Irishman*, 26 May 1900, by 'Celt'.

17   *Sinn Féin: The Oldcastle Monthly Review*, Aug. 1902.

18   De Blacam, *What Sinn Féin Stands For*, p. 45.

19   Kelly, 'Radical Nationalisms, 1882–1916', p. 49.

20   *United Irishman*, 24 June 1899.

21   Birmingham, *Pleasant Places*, p. 188.

22   McCartney, 'The Political Use of History', pp. 3–19.

23   Ibid., p. 9; Kabdebó, *Ireland and Hungary*, *passim*.

24   Brennan, *Allegiance*, p. 13.

25   Ellman, *James Joyce*, p. 246.

26   Joyce, *Letters*, vol. 2, p. 187, to Stanislaus Joyce, 6 November 1906.

27   Maume, *Long Gestation*, pp. 86–8.

28   *Sinn Féin*, 10 June 1911, and 28 September to 26 October 1912.

29   *Sunday Independent*, 11 Sept. 1949, pen name 'Luke the Listener' whom Ó Lúing, *Griffith*, p. 237 identifies as Aodh de Blacam.

30   Joyce, *Occasional Writings*, pp. xii–xiv, 140, 322–42, including the translation from *Il Piccolo della Sera*, 22 March 1907.

31   BMH WS 1574.

32   NLI Ó Lúing Papers, MS 12,038, box 3, Bulmer Hobson to Seán Ó Lúing (May 1965).

33   BMH WS 111, p. 2.

34   UCD F.X. Martin Papers, P189/212, Pat McCartan to Prof. Martin, 5 Dec. 1962.

35   Henry, *Evolution of Sinn Féin*, p. 88.

36   Griffith, 'Bringing in the Guns', *The Southern Cross* (Buenos Aires), 28 Aug. 1914; BMH WS 307 (Thomas MacCarthy), p. 4; BMH WS 220 (Patrick O'Daly).

37   NLI Ó Lúing Papers, MS 12,038, box 4, Dan McCarthy interview notes (1946).

38   *Sunday Independent*, 11 Sept. 1949, pen name 'Luke the Listener' whom Ó Lúing, *Griffith*, p. 237 thought was Aodh de Blacam.

39   BMH WS 384, p. 24.

40 *Southern Cross*, 28 Aug. 1914.
41 Horgan, *Parnell to Pearse*, p. 97.
42 De Blacam, *What Sinn Féin Stands For*, p. 48,
43 BMH WS 104, pp. 4–6 for George Lyons' opinion on Griffith's membership.
44 BMH WS 1,765 (Seán T. Ó Ceallaigh), vol. 2, p. 156; O'Brien, 'Introduction', pp. 3–4.
45 NLI Ó Ceallaigh Papers, pp. 25–6.
46 O'Brien, 'Introduction', pp. 3–4.
47 *Irish Press*, 4 July 1961; BMH WS 1,765, pt. 2, p. 156.
48 BMH WS 1,765, pt. 2, p. 231.
49 BMH WS 205 (Gonne).
50 BMH WS 707 pp. 10–11 (4 July 1952).
51 NLI Ó Lúing Papers, MS 12,038, box 3, Bulmer Hobson to Seán Ó Lúing.
52 Liam O'Brien, 'The Historic Rising' (written in 1922); BMH WS 707 pp. 10–11.
53 BMH WS 3 (Ó Briain), p. 3.
54 Clery, 'Pearse, MacDonagh, and Plunkett', p. 221.
55 Heaney, 'On W.B. Yeats's "The Man and the Echo"', p. 98.
56 Piaras Béaslaí, 'Arthur Griffith'.
57 NLI O'Connell Papers, Prison Album, 'Book of Cells'.
58 NLI, Reading Gaol autograph book of Irish prisoners, December 1916.
59 NLI Lennon Papers, 29 Nov. 1916.
60 Hackett, *Ireland*, pp. 326–9.
61 Joyce, *Letters*, vol. 3, 22 (14 Sept. 1920); Foster, *Yeats*, vol. 2, p. 708 n56.

Chapter 12
Irish and Jewish

1 *Nationality*, 25 December 1915.
2 *Hansard*, House of Commons, 8 July 1920, vol. 131, col. 1719; Gilbert, *Churchill*, p. 364.
3 O'Riordan, 'Anti-Semitism in Irish Politics', pp. 15–27.
4 O'Connell, *Correspondence*, vol. 4, pp. 95, 277–8.
5 Fagan, *O'Connell*, pp. 388–98.
6 *Irish Times*, 2 Sept. 1881.
7 *Cork Examiner*, 15 March 1888.
8 *Irish Times*, 5 Dec. 1892.
9 Ben Pinchas, *Two Prize Essays*, pp. v, 82.
10 Moore, *Poetical Works*, vol. 2, pp. 205–6.
11 *The Pilot*, 23 August 1873.

12   *Freeman's Journal*, 13 July 1893.

13   Ibid.; Finlay, 'The Jew', p. 251.

14   Cheyette, *Construction of 'the Jew'* and *Between Race and Culture, passim*.

15   Bender, *Israelites in Erin*, pp. 51–6; Waterman, 'Changing Residential Patterns', pp. 41–50; Ó Gráda, *Jewish Ireland*, pp. 9–11; Reizbaum, *James Joyce's Judaic Other*, p. 60.

16   *Irish Times*, October 11, 1895, January 28, 1896, August 26, 1907; *Freeman's Journal*, 23 June 1896, 2 September 1908.

17   Michael, *Catholic Anti-Semitism*, pp. 198–201; Birnbaum, *The Anti-Semitic Moment, passim*.

18   Joyce, *Occasional Writing*, pp. x, 17–22, 291.

19   *Leader*, July 16, 1904, 323; *Evening Telegraph*, 24, 25 and 29 Sept. 1915; McIntosh, 'Ireland's First Jewish Lord Mayor'.

20   *Freeman's Journal*, 23 June 1896 and *Irish Times*, 11 July 1896, for example.

21   Kearns, *Dublin Tenement Life*, pp. 196–7.

22   Glandon, *Griffith*, p. 9; *The Leader*, 4 June 1904, pp. 228, 234–5.

23   Birnbaum, *Anti-Semitic Moment*, p. 385.

24   Barrett, 'Dreyfus Affair'; *United Irishman*, 4 March, 29 July, 16, 23 and 30 Sept. 1899, 14 Oct. and 11 Nov. 1899; Davison *James Joyce*, pp. 68–72.

25   *United Irishman*, 29 July, 19 August, 16, 23 and 30 Sept. 1899, 24 February 1900; Maume, 'Young Ireland', pp. 50–1; McGee, *Griffith*, p. 42.

26   *United Irishman*, 30 Sept. 1899, 3 and 31 March and 30 June 1900.

27   Kenny, 'F.H. O'Donnell: a Virulent Anti-Semite'.

28   *United Irishman*, 16 Sept. 1899; Hadel, *Joyce and the Jews*, p. 66.

29   Cheyette, 'Construction of 'the Jew', pp. 14–23, 43.

30   *United Irishman*, 27 July 1901 citing Hobson.

31   O'Toole, 'Provincial Thinking'; Lentin and McVeigh, 'After Optimism?', p. 116.

32   Hyman, *Jews*, pp. 213, 341; Maye, *Griffith*, pp. 362–72; Kenny, 'Arthur Griffith: More Zionist than Anti-Semite', pp. 38–41.

33   Judge, *Easter in Kishinev*, p. 88; Zipperstein, 'Inside Kishinev's Pogrom', p. 368; Sheehy-Skeffington, *Michael Davitt*, pp. 230–2, 268.

34   Davitt, *Within the Pale*, p. ix; Davitt, *Boer Fight for Freedom*, pp. 28, 42, 76 (citing the *Newcastle Chronicle*); King, *Davitt*, pp. 494–505; Zipperstein, 'Inside Kishinev's Pogrom', p. 371.

35   Kenny, 'Michael Davitt's Journalism for William Randolph Hearst'.

36   Keogh and McCarthy, *Limerick Boycott*.

37   *Leader*, 4 and 25 June 1904; Barrett, 'The Dreyfus Affair', p. 87; *New York Times*, 16 Sept. 1899.

38   Hyman, *The Jews*, p. 216.

39   *United Irishman*, 26 Aug. and 9 Sept. 1899, 28 May 1904; *Dana*, 1 (May 1904), pp. 27–8; Potts, *Joyce*, pp. 28–47, 150.

40 *United Irishman*, 23 January, 23 April and 14 May 1904.

41 Socialist Federation 1902, Handbill; *United Irishman*, 17, 24 and 31 January, 1903; *Freeman's Journal* and *Irish Times*, 24 Jan. 1903; Davison, O'Connor and O'Connor, "'Altman the Saltman'", pp. 46, 53, 56.

42 *Sinn Féin*, 18 Sept., 24 Nov. and 1 Dec. 1906; Joyce, *Letters*, vol. 2, pp. 164–8, 170–1, 200.

43 *United Irishman*, 23 Sept. 1899; Maume, 'Young Ireland', pp. 50–1; Keogh, *Jews*, p. 22.

44 *United Irishman*, 10, 17 and 24 Feb., 3 and 10 March, 7 April 1906; Stradling, *Cheap John's Auction*; Davison, *James Joyce*, pp. 17, 29–33, 70, 257.

45 Kenny, 'James Larkin and the Jew's Shilling', pp. 66–84.

46 Goldberg, 'Joyce and the Jewish Dimension', p. 5.

47 Kenny, 'William Bulfin's Rambles in Literary Journalism', *passim*; Bulfin, *Rambles in Eirinn*, pp. 307–09; *Sinn Féin*, 4 and 8 August 1906; *United Irishman*, 30 April 1904; *Southern Cross*, 3 February 1897.

48 O'Casey, *Autobiographies*, vol. 1, pp. 123–4.

49 Rivlin, *Shalom Ireland*; E.R.L., 'The Jewish Community in Dublin'.

50 *Lepracaun*, April 1906, p. 139; Rivlin, *Shalom Ireland*, p. 74; Kearns, *Dublin Tenement Life*, pp. 196–7; E.R.L., 'The Jewish Community in Dublin'.

51 Lipsett, 'Jews in Ireland', p. 31; Leventhal, 'What It Means To Be A Jew', p. 209; Kearns, *Dublin Tenement Life*, pp. 31–2, 205, 215.

52 Ibid.; Ó Gráda, *Jewish Ireland*, pp. 47–9, 188, 212.

53 *Lepracaun*, April 1908 and February 1909; Ó Gráda, *Jewish Ireland*, p. 65; Hyman. *Jews*, p. 168; Harfield, *Commercial Directory*, pp. 230–41.

54 Edelstein, *Moneylender*, pp. 53, 63, 99–100; Ó Gráda, *Jewish Ireland*, pp. 66–7.

55 BMH WS 707 (Noyk), pp. 1, 13; Maye, *Griffith*, p. 370; 'Noyek (Noyk), Michael', in *DIB*, by Paul Rouse.

56 Colum, *Griffith*, p. 173; Hyman, *Jews*, pp. 176, 202, 212–3, 333; 'Griffith' in *DIB*, by Michael Laffan.

57 De Blacam, Aodh, in *DIB*, by Patrick Maume.

58 *Sinn Féin*, 16 March 1912; *Sunday Independent*, 15 Jan. 1922; 'De Blacam, Aodh', in *DIB*, by Patrick Maume.

59 *Scissors and Paste*, 23 and 27 Jan. and 20 Feb. 1915; Kenny, '*Scissors and Paste*', pp. 339–40; *Nationality*, 25 Sept. 1915.

60 *Nationality*, 25 Dec. 1915; Maume, 'Young Ireland', p. 156.

61 O'Hegarty, *History of Ireland*, p. 636; Kenny, '"An Extraordinarily Clever Journalist"', p. 30.

62 Larkin, *James Larkin*, p. 78; *Irish Times*, 27 Aug. 1913; *Irish Worker*, 21 Oct. 1911.

63 Kenny, 'James Larkin and the Jew's Shilling', pp. 66–84; Maye, *Griffith*, pp. 362–72.

64   Larkin, *James Larkin*, p. 77; *Irish Worker*, 21 Oct. 1911.
65   Felsenstein, *Anti-Semitic Stereotypes*, pp. 53, 79–80; Yeates, *Lockout*, p. 547.
66   *Irish Worker*, 17 July and 5 August 1911; Pindar, *The Works*, vol. 2, pp. 297–8.
67   O'Sullivan, *Essays and Recollections*, pp. 104–11, 114–15.
68   Regan, *Irish Counter-Revolution*, pp. 333–6.
69   UCD Aiken Papers, Devoy to Jeremiah J. Lynch, Butte, Montana, 20 January 1921.
70   McCarthy, *Briscoe*, *passim*.
71   Wynn, 'Jews, Anti-Semitism and Irish Politics', pp. 51–66.
72   *Irish Times*, 18 August 1922.
73   Cheyette, 'Neither Excuse nor Accuse', p. 432.

Chapter 13
1917–1920: Griffith and de Valera

1   See http://www.decadeofcentenaries.com/ (at 25 November 2019); Laffan, *Resurrection of Ireland*, p. 114.
2   'On the One Road', by Frank O'Donovan.
3   Maye, *Griffith*, pp. 83–93.
4   *Catholic Bulletin* 12 (Nov. 1922), p. 690, letter from H.E. Kenny ('Sean-Ghall').
5   Laffan, *Resurrection of Ireland*, pp. 77–83, 96.
6   Ibid., pp. 107–08.
7   Bowman, 'Éamon de Valera: Seven Lives', pp. 191, 198.
8   Pakenham and O'Neill, *De Valera*, p. 71.
9   *Nationality*, 21 July 1917.
10   Pakenham and O'Neill, *De Valera*, p. 17; Dwyer, *De Valera*, p. 11; Fanning, *De Valera*, pp. 60–1.
11   Fitzpatrick, 'De Valera in 1917', in O'Carroll and Murphy, *De Valera*, p. 103.
12   Pakenham and O'Neill, *De Valera*, p. 66.
13   Dwyer, *De Valera*, pp. 12, 18; Thomas Dillon's memoir, cited in Coogan, *De Valera*, pp. 95–6.
14   Laffan, *Resurrection of Ireland*, pp. 122–8.
15   Dwane, *Early Life of Éamonn* [sic] *de Valera*, p. 53.
16   BMH WS 687 (Monsignor Michael Curran), pt. 1, p. 203.
17   Pakenham and O'Neill, *De Valera*, pp. 7–8, 10, 14–15.
18   Dwyer, *De Valera*, p. 2; Pakenham and O'Neill, *De Valera*, p. 8; Coogan, *De Valera*, pp. 34–5; Dwane, *De Valera*, pp. 25–6.
19   McMahon, *Republicans and Imperialists*, p. 42, citing National Archives Washington, State Department Records RG59/84ID.001/3 and .00/1125.
20   'De Valera, Éamon ("Dev")', in *DIB*, by Ronan Fanning.

21 Dwane, *De Valera*, pp. 25–6.
22 Pakenham and O'Neill, *De Valera*, pp. 67–8; *Evening Herald*, 25 Oct. 1917.
23 BMH WS 767 (Patrick Moylett), pp. 12–13.
24 BMH WS 722 (Dan MacCarthy), p. 18.
25 BMH WS 1,766 (William O'Brien), p. 135.
26 Ibid.; Miller, *Church, State, and Nation*, pp. 398–9.
27 BMH WS 1,765 (Seán T. O'Kelly), pp. 92–3.
28 *Cork Examiner*, 27 Oct. 1917.
29 Ibid.; Pakenham and O'Neill, *De Valera*, p. 68.
30 TCD MS, Report of the Proceedings of the Sinn Féin Convention, 1917.
31 Ibid., p. 29.
32 Ibid., pp. 47–9.
33 Dáil Éireann, 6 Jan. 1922.
34 TCD MS, Report of the Proceedings of the Sinn Féin Convention, 1917, p. 38.
35 Laffan, *Resurrection of Ireland*, pp. 128–35.
36 BMH WS 687 (Monsignor Michael Curran), pt. 1, p. 288. Curran did not say what the 'vile stories' were; BMH WS 1,770 (Kevin O'Sheil), pt. 6, pp. 786–7.
37 NAI CO 904, MFA 54/123, Maud Griffith to Edward Shortt, 3 Feb. 1919.
38 Dáil Éireann, 17 June 1919.
39 BMH WS 804 (Mortimer O'Connell), p. 29.
40 Lyons, *Recollections*, p. 74.
41 Jones, 'Hamlet's Mystery'.
42 Tóibín, *Mad, Bad, Dangerous*, pp. 135–74; Ellmann, *James Joyce*, p. 830.
43 NAI, CO 904, MFA 54/123, 'Griffith'. UCD MacWhite Papers, P194/22 has what appears to be a contemporary typed copy of this handwritten cable but with the typed date '19 January 1919' – which ostensibly is a typo given that de Valera was not then in America and relevant elections were not pending.
44 McCullagh, *De Valera*, vol. 1, p. 174.
45 UCD MacWhite Papers, P194/29, for example.
46 Fitzpatrick, 'De Valera in 1917', pp. 101–12.
47 NAI TSCH/3/S9995.
48 BMH WS 687 (Monsignor Michael Curran), pt. 1, p. 559.

Chapter 14
A Fateful Weekend

1 NLI Plunkett Diary, at 12–13 July 1921.
2 *Freeman's Journal*, 13 July 1921.
3 Ibid.
4 *Irish Times*, 23 July 1921; Téry, *En Irlande*, p. 156.

5   McGee, *Griffith*, pp. 241–304.

6   Murray, 'Obsessive Historian', pp. 50–2; Ferriter, *Judging Dev*, pp. 64–6.

7   Brennan, *Allegiance*, p. 245.

8   Pakenham, *Peace by Ordeal*, pp. 103–4, 118.

9   *Cork Examiner* and *Irish Times*, 10 Oct. 1921.

10   Ibid.

11   See, for example, Maye, *Griffith*, pp. 226–8.

12   *Irish Times*, 10 Oct. 1921.

13   Taylor, *Michael Collins*, pp. 161–7, citing Collins to John O'Kane, 17 Nov. 1921; Maye, *Griffith*, pp. 73–5.

14   Ó Broin, *In Great Haste*, pp. 25–74; McGee, *Griffith*, p. 480 n94; Kenny, 'Michael Collins' Religious Faith'.

15   O'Malley, 'Military Aviation in Ireland 1921–1945', pp. 25–32.

16   NLI Arthur Griffith Papers, 49,530/8/1 and 3 (Nevin Griffith to his father, 29 Oct. 1921 and Arthur Griffith to his wife, 22 Nov. 1921).

17   Taylor, *Michael Collins*, p. 165, citing Collins to John O'Kane, 4 Nov. 1921.

18   Ibid., p. 170, citing Collins to John O'Kane, undated.

19   *Irish Times*, 2 Dec. 1921.

20   Jones. *Whitehall Diary*, vol. 3, pp. 130–1 (14 Oct. 1921); Pakenham, *Peace by Ordeal*, pp. 236–7, citing a British document used in the negotiations.

21   Jones, *Whitehall Diary*, vol. 3, 157 (9 Nov. 1921).

22   *Irish Independent*, 3 Dec. 1921.

23   *Irish Times*, 3 Dec. 1921.

24   *Freeman's Journal*, 3 Dec. 1921.

25   Colum, *Griffith*, p. 296.

26   Ó Broin, *In Great Haste*, pp. 62, 71.

27   UCD De Valera Papers, P150/1560, De Valera to Joseph McGarrity, 27 Dec. 1921.

28   *Irish Independent*, 5 Dec. 1921.

29   *Irish Times*, 5 Dec. 1921.

30   *Irish Independent* and *Irish Times*, 5 Dec. 1921.

31   Ford, 'John Ford's arrival in Hollywood', p. 101.

32   NLI Plunkett Diary, at 3 Dec. 1921.

33   *Irish Bulletin*, quoted at *Cork Examiner*, 5 Dec. 1921.

34   NAI DE 2/304/1, Notes of Meeting of the Cabinet.

35   Pakenham, *Peace by Ordeal*, pp. 208, 298–301; Jones, *Whitehall Diary*, vol. 3, p. 179 (3 Dec. 1921).

36   McMahon, *British Intelligence and Ireland*, p. 57.

37   Pakenham, *Peace by Ordeal*, pp. 206–12.

38   McCullagh, *De Valera*, vol. 1, p. 240.

39   *Cork Examiner* and *Irish Independent*, 5 Dec. 1921.

40   Jones, *Whitehall Diary*, vol. 3, p. 180 (4 Dec. 1921); NAI DE 2/304/1, Memorandum of an interview between Michael Collins and David Lloyd George, 5 Dec. 1921.
41   Ó Broin, *In Great Haste*, p. 72.
42   Jones, *Whitehall Diary*, vol. 3, p. 132 (14 Oct. 1921).
43   UCD De Valera Papers, P150/1523, 1559. Also see https://www.difp.ie/viewdoc.asp?DocID=211.
44   *Freeman's Journal*, 5 Dec. 1921.
45   Jones, *Whitehall Diary*, vol. 3, pp. 180–1 (5 Dec. 1921); Pakenham, *Peace by Ordeal*, p. 220.
46   McGee, *Griffith*, p. 269 for Thomas Jones to the Prime Minister (Westminster Parliamentary Archives, Lloyd George Papers, F/25/2/51).
47   Jones, *Whitehall Diary*, vol. 3, pp. 180–81 (5 Dec. 1921).
48   *Freeman's Journal*, 25 Nov. 1921.
49   Ó Broin, *In Great Haste*, pp. 30–77.
50   NLI, Griffith Papers 49530/8, Griffith to his wife in Dublin, 17 and 22 Nov. 1921; *Irish Independent*, 8 Dec. 1921 for a photograph of the couple 'after the Peace Treaty was signed'; *Freeman's Journal*, 9 Dec. 1921; *Illustrated London News*, 19 Aug. 1922; Kenny, 'Arthur Griffith's Broken Column', p. 27.
51   BMH WS 1,280 (Broy), pp. 141–2 (31 Oct. 1955).
52   *Cork Examiner* and *Freeman's Journal*, 6 Dec. 1921; NAI DE 2/304/1, Memorandum of an interview.
53   Jones, *Diary*, vol. 2, p. 184; Crosby, *Lloyd George*, pp. 307–8.
54   For recent perspectives on the Anglo-Irish Treaty see M. Kennedy and B. Kissane in Crowley *et. al.*, *Atlas of the Irish Revolution*, section viii, pp. 642–59.
55   NAI DE 2/304/1, Memo of interview; Packenham, *Peace by Ordeal*, p. 258.
56   For a useful overview of historical perspectives see Maye, *Griffith*, pp. 191–219.
57   Taylor, *Michael Collins*, p. 189, citing a 'private source'; McKenna, 'In London with the Treaty Delegates', p. 331.

Chapter 15
1921: 'He Signed the Treaty'

1   UCD Hayes Papers, P52/222 (10–11), Notes of an interview with Mrs A. Griffith, August 1950.
2   Doherty and Keogh, *Michael Collins*, p. 134; DE 2/304/1: Final Text of the Articles of Agreement for a Treaty. Also see http://www.difp.ie/docs/volume/1/1921/214.htm.

3   Fanning, *De Valera*, pp. 122–7. De Valera was chancellor of that university for 54 years, from 1921 to 1976.
4   Fanning *et al.*, *Documents on Irish Foreign Policy*, vol. 1, pp. 307–8; Griffith to de Valera, 12 Nov. 1921. See https://www.difp.ie/viewdoc.asp?DocID=194.
5   NAI DE 2/304/1, Notes by Robert Barton of two sub-conferences held on 5/6 December 1921 at 10 Downing St. See https://www.difp.ie/viewdoc.asp?DocID=213.
6   Pakenham, *Peace by Ordeal*, pp. 217, pp. 293–5.
7   NAI DE 2/304/1, Final text of the Articles of Agreement for a Treaty between Great Britain and Ireland as signed, London, 6 December 1921. See https://www.difp.ie/docs/1921/Anglo-Irish-Treaty/214.htm.
8   Jones, *Whitehall Diary*, vol. 3, p. 183.
9   Miller, *Church, State and Nation*, pp. 393–4.
10 Maher, *The Oath*, pp. 213–29.
11 Murray, *Irish Boundary Commission*, *passim*.
12 UCD De Valera Papers, P150/1560 (27 Dec. 1921).
13 Napoli-McKenna, 'In London', p. 332.
14 BMH WS 1,770 (Kevin O'Shiel), pt. 6, pp. 847–9 discusses this exchange.
15 Napoli-McKenna, 'In London', p. 327.

Chapter 16
1922: Destruction and Death

1   McKenna, 'In London', p. 323.
2   Moody, *Ezra Pound*, p. 407; Ezra Pound, *ABC of Economics* (London, 1933), p. 35.
3   Moody, *Ezra Pound*, p. 407.
4   Pound, *Cantos*, pp. 84–5 (canto xix), 698.
5   Pound, *ABC of Economics*, p. 35.
6   Pound, *Cantos*, p. 501.
7   Cromwell, 'Oscar Wilde's Tomb'.
8   *Cork Examiner* and *Irish Times*, 10 Oct. 1921.
9   Martin, 'Jacob Epstein, Lady Gregory and the Irish Question', pp. 161–3.
10 Epstein, *Let There Be Sculpture*, pp. 37, 254, 357–8.
11 Brennan, *Allegiance*, p. 288.
12 McGee, *Griffith*, pp. 186, 189; O'Sullivan, *Essays and Recollections*, pp. 121–2; *Nationality*, 23 Nov. 1918.
13 BMH WS 826 (Maeve MacGarry), p. 27.
14 Colum, *Griffith*, p. 333.
15 Ó Lúing, *Ó Gríofa*, plate of letter facing p. 385.
16 UCD Desmond and Mabel FitzGerald Papers, P80/675 (23 and 24 March 1922).
17 *Irish Independent*, 17, 18 and 20 March 1922; Taylor, *Michael Collins*, pp. 221–2.

18   *Irish Times*, 26 August 1922.
19   UCD MacWhite Papers, P194/83–4.
20   O'Brien, *Forth the Banners Go*, pp. 219–20.
21   UCD De Valera Papers, P150/1428, Transcript of Folklore Commission recordings of January 1951.
22   BMH WS 939 (Blythe), p. 140.
23   Mitchell, *Jail Journal*, preface by Griffith, p. xv.
24   NLI Ó Lúing Papers, MS 12,038, box 3 for this anonymous note.
25   BMH WS 939 (Blythe), p. 145.
26   Ibid., p. 153.
27   Gogarty, *Sackville Street*, p. 185.
28   Statement by Oliver St John Gogarty, *Irish Times*, 14 Aug. 1922.
29   Phelan, *Travel and Comment*, p. 244; Walsh, 'Arthur Griffith, Michael Collins and James D. Phelan of San Francisco', pp. 81–94; UCD MacWhite Papers, P194/85, 29 July 1922 for sniping.
30   NLI Lennon Papers, MS 22,288 (3), Letter from Sister M. Loyola, Sisters of Charity, St Vincent's Hospital to Lennon, 28 August 1953.
31   NLI Ó Lúing Papers, MS 12,038, box 3, Patrick Carey interview notes, 31 March 1966, p. 5.
32   Gogarty, *Sackville Street*, pp. 188–9.
33   UCD Hayes Papers, P53/208, letter from Maud Griffith, 15 Oct. 1922.
34   Taylor, *Michael Collins*, p. 164.
35   Jones, *Whitehall Diary*, vol. 3, pp. 214–5 (17 Aug. 1922).
36   NLI Griffith Papers, MS 49,530/20, front and back.
37   *United Ireland*, 10 Oct. 1891; *Young Ireland*, 19 Aug. 1922; *Scéala Chatha* [South-West Command War News], 21 Aug. 1922; *Irish Press*, 11, 12, 18 and 24 June 1965; *Irish Press*, 23 June 1965 (letter from Eoin Ó Mathghamhna); NLI Arthur Griffith Papers MS L336, commemorative poster, [1922]; UCD Mulcahy Papers, P7/74–5; Alexander, 'Mourn and Then Onward'; O'Brien, 'Passion and Cunning', pp. 217–19.
38   *Cork Examiner*, 23 Aug. 1922; Hugh Martin, *Ireland in Insurrection*.
39   Téry, *En Irlande*, p. 167, translated by the present author.
40   Jones, *Whitehall Diary*, vol. 3, p. 219; Dolan, 'The Forgotten President', p. 103.
41   The Griffith Settlement Bill second stage, *Seanad Éireann Reports*, vol. 1, no. 13 (14 March 1923).

Chapter 17
Arthur Griffith and Joyce's *Ulysses*

1   Joyce, *Letters*, vol. 3, p. 51.
2   Ellmann, *Consciousness of James Joyce*, pp. 88–9.

3   Budgen, *Joyce*, p. 156.

4   Joyce, *James Joyce Archive*, pp. 402–11 (Buffalo IX.A.3-10) for a cutting from *The Freeman's Journal* (9 Jan. 1901) of 'Miss Margaret Sheehy's Recital. Antient Concert Rooms' that Joyce kept.

5   Kelleher, 'Irish History and Mythology', p. 421.

6   *New Republic*, 24 Oct. 1923 (p. 233); Colum, *Poems*, pp. 205–6, 'Odysseus: In Memory of Arthur Griffith'. Colum's variant, 'The Statesman', is shorter.

7   Tymocsko, *The Irish Ulysses*, pp. 231–4.

8   Ungar, 'Among the Hapsburgs: Arthur Griffith, Stephen Dedalus, and the Myth of Bloom', *passim*.

9   Tymocsko, *The Irish Ulysses*, p. 54.

10   Joyce, *Letters*, vol. 3, p. 61 (20 March 1922).

11   Ibid., p. 78 (23 Feb. 1923).

12   Fitzpatrick, *Ireland and the Making of Britain*, pp. 127–8.

13   Joyce, *Letters*, vol. 3, pp. 78 (1922), 108 (1924).

14   Ibid., pp. 65–7.

15   Bhreathnach-Lynch, *Albert G. Power*, pp. 71–3, p. 135.

16   Dolan, *Commemorating the Irish Civil War*, pp. 100–20; Sheehan, *Arthur Griffith*, pp. 2–3.

17   UCD De Valera Papers, P150/579 and 1,113.

18   BMH WS 1041 (Thomas Doyle); Kenny, 'Arthur Griffith's Broken Column'.

19   *Freeman's Journal*, 24 August 1922; Larkin, *Terror and Discord*, pp. 46–7.

20   Dolan, *Commemorating the Irish Civil War*, pp. 100–20.

Chapter 18
2022: Commemorating Griffith

1   *United Irishman*, 21 Sept. 1901, under his pen name 'Cuguan'.

2   Joyce, *My Brother's Keeper*, pp, 173–4.

3   Horgan, *Parnell to Pearse*, p. 97.

4   Lentin and McVeigh, *After optimism?*, p. 116.

5   Horgan, *Parnell to Pearse*, p. 331.

6   Maume, 'Young Ireland', p. 165.

7   *Irish Independent*, 18 August 1922; O'Kelly, 'Arthur Griffith', pp. 149–50.

8   Stephens, *Arthur Griffith*, p. 26.

9   NLI Lennon Papers, MS 22,293.

10   McGee, *Griffith*, pp. 344–93.

11   http://leovaradkar.ie/2016/08/varadkar-addresses-collins-griffith-commemoration/ (at 5 November 2019).

BIBLIOGRAPHY

Manuscripts
Bureau of Military History (BMH)
Witness Statements – including especially Liam Ó Briain (3), George Lyons (104), Denis McCullagh (111), Seamus O'Farrell (193), Maud Griffith (205), Maire O'Brolchain (302), Thomas MacCarthy (307), Maud Gonne McBride (317), J.J. O'Kelly (384), Helena Molony (391), Muriel Murphy (637), Msgr Michael Curran (687), Michael Noyk (707), Dan MacCarthy (722), Patrick McCartan (766), Patrick Moylett (767), Robert Brennan (779), Mortimer O'Connell (804), Maeve MacGarry (826), Sidney (Gifford) Czira (902), Ernest Blythe (939), Thomas Doyle (1,041), Eamon Broy (1,280), Bulmer Hobson (1,365), Seumas Mac a Muilleora (1,574), Liam de Róiste (1,698), Seumas Robinson (1,721), Seán T. Ó Ceallaigh (O'Kelly) (1,765), William O'Brien (1,766), Kevin O'Shiel (1,770).

IG (IrishGenealogy.ie)
Civil and church records of births, marriages and deaths online.

National Archives of Ireland (NAI)
CBS Précis, Box 6: Crime Branch Reports on Secret Societies. Dublin Metropolitan Police.
CO 904, Boxes 159–178, MFA 54/122-3: Colonial Office, Sinn Féin and republican suspects.
DE 2/304/1: Memorandum of an interview between Michael Collins and David Lloyd George, 5 Dec. 1921 (Documents on Irish Foreign Policy no. 212).
DE 2/304/1: Copy of Secretary's Notes of Meeting of the Cabinet and Delegation, 3 December 1921 (DIFP no. 209).

DE 2/304/1: Notes by Robert Barton of Two Sub-Conferences Held on December 5/6, 1921 at 10 Downing St (DIFP no. 213).

DE 2/304/1: Final Text of the Articles of Agreement for a Treaty Between Great Britain and Ireland As Signed (DIFP no. 21).

DFA/5/316/27/485: Arthur Griffith, First President of Ireland, Information Concerning (1952).

TSCH/3/S55983/1: William T. Cosgrave's Oration at Graveside of Griffith.

TSCH/3/S5739: Portraits of Griffith and Collins by John Lavery: Offer of Artist's Proofs (actually of a photo signed by sitter[s] and artist).

TSCH/3/S9190: Arthur Griffith: Personal papers (Merely refers in 1928 to six boxes of unidentified Griffith papers).

TSCH/3/S9995: Ministerial Appointments: Arthur Griffith.

2016/51/229: Arthur Griffith: Personal Papers (September 1972–July 1986).

National Library of Ireland (NLI)

Arthur Griffith Papers, 1894–1966. MSS 49,530/1–31 and LO 334–49, 12348.

Arthur Griffith Additional Papers, 1909–52, MSS 49,666 and L 353.

Arthur Griffith Letters re *Nationality*, etc., MSS 35,262/1 (2), 46,060.

Arthur Griffith to Mère Columba S. Butler on the death of her sister Mary Butler, from Mountjoy Prison, 12 May 1921, MS 4577.

Arthur Griffith to Lily Williams (Lily Williams Papers, 19 items), MS 5,943.

Celtic Literary Society Minute Books, MSS 19,934–5 (1–2).

Collins Papers, Copy typescript essay 'Ireland, Mother Ireland' by Michael [O'C], undated, MS 40,430/11.

Collins Papers, Print from transparency of cover of *The Beggar's Opera* with related print from flyleaf with signatures of General Michael Collins, Arthur Griffith, Éamon Duggan, Kitty Kiernan, etc., London, undated, MS 40,432/2.

Eblana: The Official Journal of the Leinster Literary Society, vol. 1, nos 1–7, February–May 1889, MS 3493.

Irish Transvaal Committee Minute Book, 1899–1900, MS 19,933.

Johnson (Thomas) Papers, Letters re *Irish Opinion*, Cathal O'Shannon to Johnson, 14 Dec. 1917, MS 17,239.

Kenny (H.E., 'Sean-Ghall') Papers. MS 15,082.

Leinster Debating/Literary Club/Society Minute Book 1888–92, MS 19,935.

Lennon (Michael) Papers, MSS 6957, 22,288–9, 22,293.

MacColuim (Fionán) Papers, Letter from Arthur Griffith to holders of debentures in the newspaper *Sinn Féin* referring to the financial position, 12 May 1910, MS 24,442.

McKenna Napoli, (Kathleen) Papers, including Griffith letters, MSS 22,736–22,814.

O'Brien (William) Papers, MSS 13,975 and 35,262/1 (22).

Ó Ceallaigh (Seán T. O'Kelly) Papers, MSS 27, 697, 27,700.

O'Connell (J.J.) Papers, Prison Album, 'Book of Cells', MS 19,924.

Ó Lúing (Seán) Album of Cuttings re Arthur Griffith, Ms 23,516.

Ó Lúing (Seán) Papers, MS 12,038–9.

Plunkett (Sir H.C.) Diary 1921, MS 42,222/41.

Reading Gaol autograph book of Irish prisoners, 1916, MS 46,585.

Sheehy-Skeffington Papers, MS 33,617.

Socialist Federation, Handbill (appealing to poor Jews to vote for James Connolly in Dublin in 1902). Copies at National Library of Ireland EPH C511 in English, and ILB 300 p 11 (items 80–81) in Yiddish.

National Museum of Ireland

HE:EW.5832: Frank Flood, message to on the eve of his execution signed Arthur Griffith, M.J. Staines, Eoin MacNeill and G.J. Duggan on behalf of his 'fellow prisoners'.

HE:EWL.207: Last Will and Testament of Arthur Griffith, dated April 27th 1916, the Thursday of the Easter Week rebellion.

Trinity College Dublin (TCD)

Report of the Proceedings of the Sinn Féin Convention Held in the Round Room, Mansion House, Dublin, on Thursday and Friday, 25th and 26th October 1917, Typescript, Early Printed Books, *OLS Samuels*, Box 103:5, p. 27, Samuels Collection of Printed Ephemera.

University College Dublin

Aiken Papers, John Devoy to Jeremiah J. Lynch, Butte, Montana, 20 Jan. 1921, MS P104/2592, p. 4.

Cole (Walter) Papers, MS P134.
De Valera (Éamon) Papers, MS P150.
FitzGerald (Desmond and Mabel) Papers, MS P80, 675 (24 March 1922).
Hayes (Michael) Papers, MS P53
Humphreys (Sighle) Papers, MS P106, 184/1/1 (13 Sept. 1916).
MacWhite (Michael) Papers, MS P194.
Martin (F.X.) Papers, MS P189.
Mulcahy (Richard) Papers, MS P7.

Parliamentary Reports

Report of the Departmental Committee Appointed by the Local Government Board for Ireland to Inquire into the Housing Conditions of the Working Class in the City of Dublin (London: HMSO, 1914). Cd. 7273. Includes two photographs of Cook Street area and a statement on p. 15 that Cook Street is 'almost surrounded by insanitary property'.

Books, Articles and Essays

Alexander, Sam, 'Mourn and Then Onward', *Modernism Lab*, at https://modernism.coursepress.yale.edu/mourn-and-then-onward/ (on 2 August 2019).

Bagwell, Richard, *Ireland Under the Stuarts and During the Interregnum*, 3 vols (London: Longmans, Green & Co., 1909–16).

Balliet, Conrad, 'The Lives – and Lies – of Maud Gonne', *Éire-Ireland*, 14, no. 3 (1979), 17–44.

Barr, Rebecca, Buckley, A. and M. O'Conneide, *Literacy, Language and Reading in Nineteenth-Century Ireland* (Liverpool: Liverpool University Press, 2019).

Barrett, Richard, 'The Dreyfus Affair in the Irish Nationalist Press, 1898–1899', *Études Irlandaises*, 32, no. 1 (2007), 77–89.

Barry, M.J. (ed.), *The Songs of Ireland* (Dublin: Duffy, 1845).

Béaslaí, Piaras, 'Arthur Griffith', *The Leader*, 16 Dec. 1944.

Beatty, Aidan and D. O'Brien (eds), *Irish Questions and Jewish Questions* (Syracuse, NY: Syracuse University Press, 2018).

Bender, Abby, *Israelites in Erin: Exodus, Revolution and the Irish Revival* (Syracuse, NY: Syracuse University Press, 2015).

Ben Pinchas, Hertz, *Two Prize Essays on the Post-Biblical History of the Jews* (London: Jewish Chronicle Office, 1852).

Benson, Asher, *Jewish Dublin: Portraits of Life by the Liffey* (Dublin: A. & A. Farmer, 2007).

Bhreathnach-Lynch, Sighle, *Expressions of Nationhood in Bronze & Stone: Albert G. Power, RHA* (Dublin: Irish Academic Press, 2019).

Birnbaum, Pierre, *The Anti-Semitic Moment: A Tour of France in 1898* (Chicago: University of Chicago Press, 2011).

Bobotis, Andrea, 'Rival Maternities: Maud Gonne, Queen Victoria, and the Reign of the Political Mother', *Victorian Studies*, 49, no. 1 (2006), 63–83.

Bowman, John, 'Éamon de Valera: Seven Lives', in O'Carroll and Murphy (eds), *De Valera and His Times*, pp. 182–95.

Brennan, Robert, *Allegiance* (Dublin: Browne and Nolan, 1950).

Briscoe, Robert, with Alden Hatch, *For the Life of Me* (Boston: Little, Brown, 1958).

Brown, Ivor, *The Way of My World* (London: Collins, 1954).

Brown, M.J., *Historical Ballad Poetry of Ireland* (Dublin and Belfast: Educational Co., 1912).

Brown, Stephen, *The Press in Ireland: A Survey and Guide* (Dublin: Brown and Nolan, 1937).

Budgen, Frank, *James Joyce and the Making of* Ulysses (New York: Smith & Hass, 1934).

Bulfin, William, *Rambles in Eirinn* (Dublin: Gill, 1907).

Callinan, Frank, 'James Joyce and the *United Irishman*, Paris 1902–3', *Dublin James Joyce Journal*, 3 (2010), 51–103.

Cambridge History of Ireland, vol. 4: 1880 to the Present, ed. Thomas Bartlett (Cambridge: Cambridge University Press, 2018).

Chapmann, W.K., *Yeats and English Renaissance Literature* (Basingstoke: Macmillan, 1991).

Cheyette, Bryan, *Construction of 'the Jew' in English Literature and Society: Racial Representations 1875–1945* (Cambridge: Cambridge University Press, 1993).

Cheyette, Bryan, *Between Race and Culture: Representations of the Jew in English* [and Irish] *and American Literature* (Stanford, CA: Stanford University Press, 1996).

Cheyette, Bryan, 'Neither Excuse nor Accuse: T.S. Eliot's Semitic Discourse', *Modernism/Modernity*, 10, no. 3 (2003), 431–7.

Childe, D.J., *Modernism and Eugenics: Wolfe, Eliot, Yeats, and the Culture of Degeneration* (Cambridge: Cambridge University Press, 2001).

Clery, Arthur E., 'Pearse, MacDonagh, and Plunkett. An Appreciation', *Studies*, 6, no. 22 (1917), 212–21.

Collins, Michael, *Path to Freedom* (Dublin: Talbot Press, 1922).

Colum, Mary, *Life and the Dream: An Autobiography* (Dublin: Dolmen, revised ed. 1966).

Colum, Padraic, *Arthur Griffith* (Dublin: Brown and Nolan, 1959).

Colum, Padraic, *Poems* (New York: Macmillan, 1932).

Colum, Padraic, *The Road Round Ireland* (New York: Robert McBride, [1926–30]).

Coogan, Tim Pat, *De Valera: Long Fellow, Long Shadow* (London: Hutchinson, 1993).

Crosby, T.L., *The Unknown Lloyd George: A Statesman in Conflict* (London and New York: Tauris, 2014).

Crowell, Ellen, 'Oscar Wilde's Tomb: Silence and the Aesthetics of Queer Memorial', at Dino Franco Felluga (ed.), *BRANCH: Britain, Representation and Nineteenth-Century History. Extension of Romanticism and Victorianism on the Net* (on 5 July 2019).

Crowley, J., Ó Drisceoil, D., Murphy, M. and J. Borgonovo (eds), *Atlas of the Irish Revolution* (Cork: Cork University Press, 2017).

Curry, James, and Ciarán Wallace, *Thomas Fitzpatrick and the* Lepracaun *Cartoon Monthly, 1905–1915* (Dublin: Four Courts, 2015).

Curtis, L.P., *Apes and Angels: The Irishman in Victorian Caricature*, rev. ed. (Washington and London: Smithsonian Institution, 1971).

Daly, M.E., *Industrial Development and Irish National Identity, 1922–1939* (Syracuse, NY: Syracuse University Press, 1992).

Davis, R.P., *Arthur Griffith and Non-Violent Sinn Féin* (Dublin: Anvil, 1974).

Davison, Neil, '"Cyclops", Sinn Féin, and "the Jew": An Historical Reconsideration', *Journal of Modern Literature*, 19, no. 2 (1995), 245–57.

Davison, Neil, *James Joyce,* Ulysses, *and the Construction of Jewish Identity: Culture, Biography, and 'The Jew' in Modernist Europe* (Cambridge: Cambridge University Press, 1998).

Davison, Neil, Vincent Altman O'Connor and Yvonne Altman O'Connor, "'Altman the Saltman" and Joyce's Dublin: New Research on Irish-Jewish Influences in Ulysses', *Dublin James Joyce Journal*, 6/7 (2013–2014), 44–72.

Davitt, Michael, *The Boer Fight for Freedom* (New York: Funk & Wagnalls, 1902).

Davitt, Michael, *Within the Pale: The True Story of Anti-Semitic Persecution in Russia* (New York: Barnes and Noble, 1903).

De Blacam, Aodh, *What Sinn Féin Stands For: The Irish Republican Movement; Its History, Aims and Ideals, Examined as to Their Significance to the World* (Dublin and London: Mellifont, 1921).

De Brún, Fionntán, *Revivalism and Modern Irish Literature: The Anxiety of Transmission and the Dynamics of Renewal* (Cork: Cork University Press, 2019).

De Valera, Eamonn [sic], *Ireland's Case Against Conscription* (Dublin and London: Maunsel, 1918).

DIB. Dictionary of Irish Biography from the Earliest Times to 2002, ed. James McGuire and James Quinn, 9 vols (Cambridge University Press, 2009), and online for additions.

Dillon, Thomas, 'Birth of the New Sinn Féin and the Ard Fheis 1917', *Capuchin Annual* (1967), 394–9.

Doherty, G. and D. Keogh (eds), *Michael Collins and the Making of the Irish State* (Cork: Mercier, 2006).

Dolan, Anne. 'The Forgotten President: the Awkward Memory of Arthur Griffith', in Dolan, Anne, *Commemorating the Irish Civil War: History and Memory, 1923–2000* (Cambridge: Cambridge University Press, 2003), pp. 100–20.

Doorly, Mary Rose, *Hidden Memories: The Personal Recollections of Survivors and Witnesses to the Holocaust Living in Ireland* (Dublin: Blackwater Press, 1994).

Dugger, J.M., 'Black Ireland's Race: Thomas Carlyle and the Young Ireland movement', *Victorian Studies*, 48, no. 3 (2006), 461–85.

Duncathail [sic], *Street Ballads, Popular Poetry and Household Songs* (Dublin: McGlashan & Gill, 2nd ed. 1865).

Dunleavy, Gareth and Janet, *Douglas Hyde: A Maker of Modern Ireland* (Berkeley: University of California Press, 1991).

Dwane, D.T., *Early Life of Éamonn [sic] de Valera* (Dublin: Talbot Press, 1922).

Dwyer, T. Ryle, *De Valera: The Man and His Myths* (Dublin: Poolbeg Press, 1991).

Edelstein, Joseph, *The Moneylender* (Dublin: Dollard, 1908).

Ellmann, Richard, *Oscar Wilde* (London: Hamish Hamilton, 1987).

Ellmann, Richard, *James Joyce* (Oxford: Oxford University Press, 1982).

Ellmann, Richard, *The Consciousness of James Joyce* (London: Faber, 1977).

Ellmann, Richard, *Ulysses on the Liffey* (Oxford: Oxford University Press, 1972).

Elvery, Beatrice (Lady Glenavy), *'Today We Will Only Gossip'* (London: Constable, 1964).

Epstein, Jacob, *Let There Be Sculpture: An Autobiography* (London, Michael Joseph, 1940).

E.R.L. [sic], 'The Jewish Community in Dublin', *Weekly Irish Times*, 8 January 1893.

Fagan, William, *The Life and Times of Daniel O'Connell*, 2 vols (Cork: John O'Brien and London: Simpkin, Marshall, 1847–8).

Fallon, Donal, *John MacBride* (Dublin: O'Brien, 2015).

Fanning, Ronan, *Éamon de Valera: A Will to Power* (London: Faber, 2015).

Fanning, Ronan, Michael Kennedy, Dermot Keogh and Eunan O'Halpin (eds), *Documents on Irish Foreign Policy*, Volume 1, 1919–1922 (Dublin: Royal Irish Academy, 1998), pp. 307–8.

Felsenstein, Frank, *Anti-Semitic Stereotypes: A Paradigm of Otherness in English Popular Culture, 1660–1830* (Baltimore, MD: John Hopkins University Press, 1995).

Fennessy, Ignatius, 'Father Peter Bradley and Irish Franciscan Chaplains in World Wars I and II', *Irish Sword*, 23, no. 94 (2003), 448–67.

Ferguson, Trish, *Maud Gonne* (Dublin: UCD Press, 2019).

Ferriter, Diarmaid, *A Nation and Not a Rabble* (London: Profile, 2015).

Ferriter, Diarmaid, *Judging Dev: A Reassessment of the Life and Legacy of Éamon de Valera* (Dublin: Royal Irish Academy, 2007).

Finlay, Thomas, 'The Jew in Ireland' and 'The Jew amongst us', *Lyceum*, vi, 70 (1893), 71, 215–18, 235–8, 251–5.

Fitzpatrick, Benedict, *Ireland and the Making of Britain* (New York and London: Funk & Wagnalls, 1922).

Fitzpatrick, David, 'De Valera in 1917: The Undoing of the Easter Rising', in O'Carroll and Murphy (eds), *De Valera and His Times*, pp. 101–12.

[Flood, Robert] R.F., 'Arthur Griffith: Some Early Memories', *Irish Times*, 26 August 1922.

Ford, Dan, 'John Ford's Arrival in Hollywood', in K.L. Stoehr and M.C. Connolly (eds), *John Ford in Focus: Essays on the Filmmaker's Life and Work* (Jefferson and London: McFarland, 2008), pp. 93–101.

Foster, R.F., *W.B. Yeats: A Life*, 2 vols (Oxford: Oxford University Press, 1997–2003).

Frazer, Adrian, *The Adulterous Muse: Maud Gonne, Lucien Millevoye and W.B. Yeats* (Dublin: Lilliput Press, 2016).

Gaeul, Liam, *Glory O! Glory O! The Life of P.J. McCall* (Dublin: The History Press, 2011).

Gallagher, Cormac, 'Ireland, Mother Ireland–An Essay in Psychoanalytic Symbolism', *The Letter* 12 (1998), 1–13.

Gibson, Andrew, *The Strong Spirit: History, Politics and Aesthetics in the Writings of James Joyce, 1898–1915* (Oxford: Oxford University Press, 2013).

Gilbert, Martin, *Winston S. Churchill, Volume IV: World in Torment, 1916–1922* (London: Heinemann and Boston: Houghton Mifflin, 1975).

Glandon, V.E., *Arthur Griffith and the Advanced-Nationalist Press in Ireland 1900–22* (Frankfurt am Main: Peter Lang, 1985).

Gogarty, Oliver, *As I Was Going Down Sackville Street* (London: Rich & Cowan, 1937).

Goldberg, Gerald Y., '"Ireland is the Only Country ...": Joyce and the Jewish Dimension', *The Crane Bag*, 6, no. 1 (1982), 5–12.

Gonne MacBride, Maud, *The Gonne-Yeats Letters, 1893–1938: Always Your Friend*, ed. Anna MacBride White and A. Norman Jeffares (London: Pimlico, 1993).

Gonne MacBride, Maud, *A Servant of the Queen*, ed. A. Norman Jeffares and Anna MacBride White (Bucks: Colin Smythe, 1994).

Griffith, Arthur, *Songs, Ballads and Recitations*, ed. Piaras Béaslaí (Dublin: Walton's, [1926]).

Griffith, Arthur, *The Finance of the Home Rule Bill: An Examination* (Dublin: National Council, 1921).

Griffith, Arthur, 'Preface', in Mitchel, *Jail Journal* (*infra*).

Griffith, Arthur. 'Speech to the First Annual Convention of the National Council, 28 November 1905', in *The 'Sinn Fein' Policy* (Dublin: Duffy, [1906]).

Griffith, Arthur, *The Resurrection of Hungary: A Parallel for Ireland* (Dublin: Duffy, Gill, Sealy, Bryers & Walker, 1904).

Hackett, Francis, *Ireland: A Study in Nationalism* (New York: Huebsch, 1918).

Hadel, Ira B., *Joyce and the Jews: Culture and Texts* (London: Macmillan, 1989).

Hannay, James Owen ('George A. Birmingham'), *Pleasant Places* (London and Toronto: Heinemann, 1934).

Harfield, G. E., *A Commercial Directory of the Jews of the United Kingdom* (London: Hewlett & Pierce, 1894).

Harris, Susan C., *Gender and Modern Irish Drama* (Bloomington: Indiana University Press, 2002).

Harris, Susan C., 'Blow the Witches Out: Gender Construction and the Subversion of Nationalism in Yeats's *Cathleen Ni Houlihan* and *On Baile's Strand*', *Modern Drama*, 39, no. 3 (1996), 475–89.

Heaney, Seamus, 'On W.B. Yeats's "The Man and the Echo"', *Harvard Review*, 4 (1993), 96–9.

Henry, Robert M., *The Evolution of Sinn Féin* (Dublin: Talbot, 1920).

Horgan, J.J., *Parnell to Pearse: Some Recollections and Reflections* (Dublin: Browne and Nolan, 1948).

Hutchinson, John, *The Dynamics of Cultural Nationalism: The Gaelic Revival and the Creation of an Irish Nation State* (London: Allen and Unwin, 1987).

Hyman, Louis, *The Jews of Ireland from Earliest Times to the Year 1910* (Shannon: Irish University Press, 1972).

Inghinidhe na h-Éireann, *First Annual Report, Session 1900–1901* (Dublin: O'Brien and Ards, 1901).

Jeffares, A.N., *W.B. Yeats: A New Biography* (London: Hutchinson, 1988).

Jones, Ernest, 'The Island of Ireland: A Psycho-Analytical Contribution to Political Psychology', in Jones, *Essays in Applied Psycho-Analysis* (London and Vienna: International Psycho-Analytical Press, 1923), pp. 398–414.

Jones, Ernest, 'The Oedipus-Complex as an Explanation of Hamlet's Mystery: A Study in Motive', *American Journal of Psychology*, 21, no. 1 (1910), 72–113.

Jones, Thomas, *Thomas Jones: Whitehall Diary*, ed. Keith Middlemas, 3 vols (London: Oxford University Press, 1969–1971).

Jordan, Anthony J., *Arthur Griffith with James Joyce & W.B. Yeats: Liberating Ireland* (Dublin: Westport Books, 2013).

Joyce, James, *Occasional, Critical and Political Writing*, ed. Kevin Barry (Oxford: Oxford University Press, 2000).

Joyce, James, *The James Joyce Archive [3]: Notes, Criticism, Translations and Miscellaneous Writings, vol. 2*, ed. Michael Groden (New York and London: Garland, 1979).

Joyce, James, *Letters*, ed. Stuart Gilbert and Richard Ellmann, 3 vols (New York: Viking, 1966).

Joyce, James, *Dubliners* (London: Grant Richards, 1914).

Joyce, James, *Chamber Music* (London: Elkin Mathews, 1907).

Joyce, P.W., *The Origin and History of Irish Names of Places*, 3 vols (Dublin: McGlashan, 1869).

Joyce, Stanislaus, *My Brother's Keeper: James Joyce's Early Years*, ed. Richard Ellmann (London: Faber, 1982).

Judge, Edward H., *Easter in Kishinev: Anatomy of a Pogrom* (New York: New York University Press, 1995).

Jung, Carl, 'The Significance of the Father in the Destiny of the Individual', in Carl Jung, *Collected Papers and Analytical Psychology* (London: Baillière, Tindall and Cox, 1916), pp. 156–75.

Kabdebó, Thomas, *Ireland and Hungary: A Study in Parallels, with an Arthur Griffith Bibliography* (Dublin: Four Courts, 2001).

Kearns, Kevin C., *Dublin Tenement Life: An Oral History* (Dublin: Gill & Macmillan, 1994).

Kelleher, John V., 'Irish History and Mythology in James Joyce's "The Dead"', *The Review of Politics*, 27, no. 3 (1965), 414–33.

Kelly, Matthew, 'Radical Nationalisms, 1882–1916', in *Cambridge History of Ireland*, pp. 33–61.

Kelly, Matthew, ' … and William Rooney spoke in Irish', *History Ireland*, 15, no. 1 (2007).

Kelly, M.J. *The Fenian Ideal and Irish Nationalism, 1882–1916* (Woodbridge, UK and Rochester, NY: Boydell, 2006).

Kenner, Hugh, *Ulysses* (Baltimore, MD: John Hopkins, 1987).

Kenny, Colum, '"Manufactured News" and Michael Davitt's Journalism for William Randolph Hearst in South Africa and Russia', in Van Tuyll *et al.*, *Irish Diaspora Press in America* (*infra*).

Kenny, Colum, 'F.H. O'Donnell: a Virulent Anti-Semite', *History Ireland*, (Jan/Feb 2020).

Kenny, Colum, 'A Fateful Weekend in 1921: At the Crux of Negotiations for an Anglo-Irish Treaty and an Independent Irish Parliament', *Parliaments, Estates and Representation*, 39, no. 1 (2019), 42–46.

Kenny, Colum, '*Scissors and Paste*: Arthur Griffith's Use of British and Other Media to Circumvent Censorship in Ireland, 1914–15', *Media History* 24, nos 3–4 (2018), 335–49 (www.tandfonlinc.com/loi/cmeh20).

Kenny, Colum, 'James Larkin and the Jew's Shilling: Irish Workers, Activists and anti-Semitism Before Independence', *Irish Economic and Social History*, 44, no. 1 (2017), 66–84.

Kenny, Colum, '"As If By Magic"? Arthur Griffith's "Surrender" of the Presidency of Sinn Féin to Éamon de Valera in 1917', *Éire-Ireland*, no. 52 (2017), 190–215.

Kenny, Colum, 'Sinn Féin, Socialists and "McSheeneys": Representations of Jews in Early Twentieth-Century Ireland', *Journal of Modern Jewish Studies*, 16, no. 2 (2017), 198–218 (https://www.tandfonline.com/loi/cmjs20).

Kenny, Colum. 'Arthur Griffith's Broken Column', *History Ireland*, 25 (2017), 27.

Kenny, Colum, 'Arthur Griffith: More Zionist than Anti-Semite', *History Ireland*, 24, no. 3 (2016), 38–41.

Kenny, Colum, 'From Buenos Aires to Belfast to Brooklyn: William Bulfin's Rambles in Literary Journalism,' *Irish Migration Studies in Latin America*, 8, no. 4 (2015), 10–26.

Kenny, Colum, '"An Extraordinarily Clever Journalist": Arthur Griffith's

Editorships, 1899–1919', in O'Brien and Larkin (*infra*, 2014), pp. 16–30.

Kenny, Colum, '"The Advertising Problem": an Irish Solution of 1910', *Journal of Historical Research in Marketing*, 6, no. 1 (2014), 116–30.

Kenny, Colum, *Irish Patriot, Publisher and Advertising Agent: Kevin J. Kenny (1881–1954)* (Ox Prints: Bray, 2011).

Kenny, Colum, 'Not So Quaint: Early Irish Reflections on Advertising', *Irish Marketing Review*, 21 (2011), 12–22.

Kenny, Colum, '"God Help Us!": The Media and Irish Catholicism', in Louise Fuller, John Littleton and Eamon Maher (eds), *Irish and Catholic? Towards an Understanding of Identity* (Dublin: Columba, 2006), pp. 90–102.

Kenny, H.E. ('Sean-Ghall') *et al.*, *Arthur Griffith: Michael Collins* (Dublin: Lester, 1922).

Kenny, H.E. ('Sean-Ghall'), 'Arthur Griffith As I Knew Him', *Young Ireland*, August-September 1922.

Kenny, H.E. ('Sean-Ghall'), 'William Rooney As I Knew Him'. *United Irishman*, 1 June 1902.

Kenny, Mary, 'Michael Collins's Religious Faith', *Studies*, 96 (2007), 425–8.

Keogh, Dermot, *Jews in Twentieth-Century Ireland: Refugees, Anti-Semitism and the Holocaust* (Cork University Press: Cork, 1998).

Keogh, Dermot, 'Irish Refugee Policy, Anti-Semitism and Nazism at the Approach of World War II', in Gisela Holfter (ed.), *German-Speaking Exiles in Ireland 1933–45* (Amsterdam and New York: Rodopi, 2006), pp. 37–73.

Keogh, Dermot, and Andrew McCarthy, *Limerick Boycott 1904: Anti-Semitism in Ireland* (Mercier Press, 2005).

King, Carla, *Michael Davitt After the Land League, 1882–1906* (Dublin: UCD Press, 2016).

Laffan, Michael, *The Resurrection of Ireland: The Sinn Féin Party 1916–1923* (Cambridge: Cambridge University Press, 1999).

Larkin, Emmet, *James Larkin: Irish Labour Leader 1876–1947* (London: Pluto Press, 1989).

Larkin, Felix M., *Terror and Discord: The Shemus Cartoons in the Freeman's Journal, 1920–1924* (Dublin: A. & A. Farmar, 2009).

Lentin, Ronit, and Robbie McVeigh, *After Optimism? Ireland, Racism and Globalisation* (Dublin: Metro Éireann Publications, 2006).

Levenson, Samuel, *Maud Gonne* (London: Cassell, 1976).

Leventhal, Abraham J. ('Con'), 'What It Means To Be A Jew', *The Bell*, 10, no. 3 (1945), 207–16.

Lipsett, Edward R. ('Halitvack'), 'Jews in Ireland: Some Impressions', *Jewish Chronicle*, 21 December 1906.

Lynch, Patrick, 'The Irish Free State and the Republic of Ireland, 1921–66', in T.W. Moody and F. X. Martin (eds), *The Course of Irish History* (Cork: Mercier Press, 1994), pp. 324–41.

Lyons, F.S.L., *Ireland Since the Famine* (London: Fontana, 1973).

Lyons, George A., *Some Recollections of Griffith and His Times* (Dublin: Talbot Press, 1923).

Lloyd George, David, *Where Are We Going* (New York: Doran, 1923).

Magee, G.M., *Productivity and Performance in the Paper Industry: Labour, Capital and Technology in Britain and America, 1860–1914* (Cambridge: Cambridge University Press, 1997).

Maguire, J.R., 'Oscar Wilde and the Dreyfus affair', *Victorian Studies*, 41, no. 1 (1997), 1–29.

Maher, Jim, *The Oath is Dead and Gone* (Dublin: Londubh, 2011).

Manganiello, Dominic, *Joyce's Politics* (London: Routledge & Kegan Paul, 1980).

Mansergh, Nicholas, *Ireland in the Age of Reform and Revolution: A Commentary on Anglo-Irish Relations and on Political Forces in Ireland, 1840–1921* (London: Allen & Unwin, 1940).

Martin, Eoin, 'Jacob Epstein, Lady Gregory and the Irish Question', *Sculpture Journal*, 26, no. 2 (2017), 159–74.

Martin, Hugh, *Ireland in Insurrection: An Englishman's Record of Fact*, with an introduction by Sir Philip Gibbs KBE (London: O'Connor, 1921).

Martin, Stoddard, 'Review' (of Frazer, *The Adulterous Muse (infra)*), with an afterword by Deirdre Toomey, *Yeats Annual*, 21 (2018), pp. 589–98.

Marx, Karl, 'The Excitement in Ireland', *New York Daily Tribune*, 11 January 1859.

Mathews, P.J., *Revival: The Abbey Theatre, Sinn Féin, the Gaelic League and the Co-operative Movement* (Cork: Cork University Press, 2003).

Mathews, P.J., 'Stirring Up Disloyalty: The Boer War, the Irish Literary Theatre and the Emergence of a New Separatism', *Irish University Review*, 33, no. 1 (2003), 99–116.

Mathews, P.J., 'A Battle of Two Civilizations? D.P. Moran and William Rooney', in *The Irish Review*, 29 (2002), 22–37.

Matthews, Ann, *Renegades: Irish Republican Women 1900–1922* (Cork: Mercier Press, 2010).

Maume, Patrick, *The Long Gestation: Irish Nationalist Life 1891–1918* (Dublin: Gill & Macmillan, 1999).

Maume, Patrick. 'Young Ireland, Arthur Griffith and Republican Ideology: the Question of Continuity', *Éire-Ireland*, 34, no. 2 (1999), 155–74.

Maume, Patrick. 'The Ancient Constitution: Arthur Griffith and his Ideological Legacy to Sinn Féin', *Irish Political Studies* (1995), 123–37.

Maye, Brian, *Arthur Griffith* (Dublin: Griffith College, 1997).

McAuliffe, Mary, 'An Idea Has Gone Abroad that All the Women Were Against the Treaty': Cumann na Saoirse and Pro-Treaty Women, 1922–3', in *Weeks and Fathartaigh (infra)*, pp. 161–82.

McCarthy, Kevin, *Robert Briscoe: Sinn Féin Revolutionary, Fianna Fáil Nationalist and Revisionist Zionist* (Frankfurt am Main: Peter Lang, 2016).

McCarthy, Michael, *Priests and People in Ireland* (Dublin: Hodges Figgis & London: Simpkin, Marshall, Hamilton, Kent, 1902).

McCarthy, Terry, *Labour v. Sinn Féin: the Dublin General Strike 1913/1914: the Lost Revolution* (London: *s.n.*, 3rd. ed., 2008).

McCartney, Donal, 'The Political Use of History in the Work of Arthur Griffith', *Journal of Contemporary History*, 8, no. 1 (1973), 3–19.

McCracken, 'The Irish Literary Movement, Irish Doggerel and the Boer War', in *Études Irlandaises*, 20, no. 2 (1995), 97–115.

McCracken, Donal, *The Irish Pro-Boers 1877–1902* (Johannesburg and Cape Town: Perskor, 1989).

McCracken, Donal B., *Forgotten Protest: Ireland and the Anglo-Boer War* (Belfast: Ulster Historical Foundation, 2003).

McCracken, P.A., 'Arthur Griffith's South African Sabbatical' and 'The Quest for the *Middelburg Courant*', in *Ireland and South Africa in Modern Times: Southern African–Irish Studies*, 3 (1996), 227–62, 282–9.

McCullagh, David, *De Valera*, 2 vols (Dublin: Gill, 2017–18).

McGee, Owen, *Arthur Griffith* (Newbridge: Merrion Press, 2015).

McGee, Owen, *The IRB: The Irish Republican Brotherhood, from the Land League to Sinn Féin* (Dublin: Four Courts, 2nd. ed., 2007).

McIntosh, Gillian, 'Ireland's First Jewish Lord Mayor: Sir Otto Jaffé and Edwardian Belfast's Civic Sphere', *Jewish Culture and History*, 11, no. 3 (2009), 1–20.

McKenna, Bernard, *James Joyce's* Ulysses: *A Reference Guide* (Westport, CT: Greenwood Press, 2002).

McKenna, K. Napoli, 'In London with the Treaty Delegates: Personal Recollections', *Capuchin Annual* (1971), 313–32.

McMahon, Deirdre, *Republicans and Imperialists: Anglo-Irish Relations in the 1930s* (New Haven and London: Yale University press, 1984).

McMahon, Paul, *British Spies and Irish Rebels: British Intelligence and Ireland, 1916–1945* (Woodbridge: Boydell, 2008).

Mecsnóber, Tekla, 'James Joyce, Arthur Griffith, Trieste and the Hungarian National Character', *James Joyce Quarterly*, 38, nos 3–4 (2001), 341–59.

Michael, Robert, *A History of Catholic Anti-Semitism: The Dark Side of the Church* (New York: Palgrave Macmillan, 2008).

Miller, David, *Church, State, and Nation in Ireland, 1898–1921* (Dublin: Gill and Macmillan, 1973).

Mitchel, John, *Jail Journal*, with a preface by Arthur Griffith (Dublin: Gill, 1914).

Moody, A. David, *Ezra Pound: Poet: A Portrait of the Man and his Work, Volume I: The Young Genius 1885-1920* (Oxford: Oxford University Press, 2009).

Moore, Thomas, *The Poetical Works of Thomas Moore: Collected by Himself*, 5 vols (Leipzig: Tauchnitz, 1842).

Moran, D.P., 'The Jew Question in Ireland', *The Leader*, 4 June 1904.

Morash, Chris, *A History of the Irish Theatre, 1601–2000* (Cambridge: Cambridge University Press, 2002).

Morrow, John, 'Thomas Carlyle, "Young Ireland" and the "Condition of Ireland Question"', *Historical Journal*, 51, no. 3 (2008), 643–7.

Mulhall, M.G., *Dictionary of Statistics* (London: Routledge, 1892).

Murphy, Brian P., *The Catholic Bulletin and Republican Ireland, with special reference to J.J. O'Kelly ('Sceilg')* (Belfast: Athol, 2005).

Murphy, Séamus, 'Dark Liturgy, Bloody Praxis: the 1916 Rising', *Studies*, 105, no. 417 (2016), 12–23.

Murray, P., 'Obsessive Historian: Éamon de Valera and the Policing of His Reputation', *Proceedings of the Royal Irish Academy: Archaeology, Culture, History, Literature*, 101C, no. 2 (2001), 37–65.

Murray, Paul, *The Irish Boundary Commission and its Origins 1886–1925* (Dublin: UCD Press, 2011).

Nadel, I.B., *Joyce and the Jews: Culture and Texts* (London: Macmillan, 1989).

Nagy, Joseph F., *Conversing with Angels and Ancients: Literary Myths of Medieval Ireland* (Ithaca and London: Cornell University Press, 1997).

Nelson, Bruce, *Irish Nationalists and the Making of the Irish Race* (Princeton: Princeton University Press, 2012).

Nicholson, Asenath, *Annals of the Famine in Ireland 1847, 1848 and 1849* (New York: French, 1851).

Novick, Ben, 'Propaganda I: Advanced Nationalist Propaganda and Moralistic Revolution, 1914–18', in T*he Irish Revolution, 1913–1923*, ed. Joost Augusteijn (Basingstoke and New York: Palgrave, 2002), pp. 34–52.

O'Brien, Conor Cruise, 'Passion and Cunning: An Essay on the Politics of W.B. Yeats', in Norman Jeffares and K.G.W. Cross (eds), *Excited Reverie: A Centenary Tribute to William Butler Yeats, 1865–1939* (New York: MacMillan, 1965), pp. 207–78.

O'Brien, Liam, 'The Historic Rising of Easter Week, 1916', in William G. FitzGerald (ed.), *The Voice of Ireland* (Dublin: Virtue, 1924), pp. 132–9.

O'Brien, Mark and Felix Larkin (eds), *Writing Against the Grain: Journalism and Periodicals in Twentieth-Century Ireland* (Dublin: Four Courts, 2014).

O'Brien, William, *Forth The Banners Go*, ed. Edward MacLysaght (Dublin: Three Candles, 1969).

O'Brien, William, 'Introduction', in Desmond Ryan (ed.), *Labour and Easter Week: A Selection from the Writings of James Connolly* (Dublin: Three Candles, 1949), pp. 1–21.

Ó Broin, León, *In Great Haste: The Letters of Michael Collins and Kitty Kiernan*, revised and extended by Cian Ó hÉigeartaigh (Dublin: Gill and Macmillan, 1996).

Ó Broin, León, *The Chief Secretary: Augustine Birrell in Ireland* (London: Chatto & Windus, 1969).

Ó Buachalla, Breandán, 'Lillibulero: the new Irish song,' *Familia: Ulster Genealogical Review*, 2, no. 7 (1991), 47–59.

O'Carroll, J.P. and John A. Murphy (eds), *De Valera and His Times* (Cork: Cork University Press, 1983).

O'Casey, Sean, *Autobiographies*, 2 vols (London: Macmillan, 1981).

O'Casey, Sean, *Drums Under the Window* (London: Macmillan, 1945).

Ó Ceallaigh, Seán T., 'Arthur Griffith', *Capuchin Annual* 1966, 132–50.

O'Connell, Daniel, *The Correspondence of Daniel O'Connell*, ed. Maurice O'Connell, 8 vols (Dublin: Irish Manuscript Commission, 1972–80).

O'Connell, Daniel, *Correspondence of Daniel O'Connell, the Liberator*, ed. W.J. Fitzpatrick, 2 vols (New York: Longmans Green, 1888).

O'Connor, Emmet, 'James Larkin in the United States, 1914–23', *Journal of Contemporary History*, 37, no. 2 (2002), 183–96.

O'Donoghue, D.J., 'The Literature of '67', *The Shamrock*, January–April 1893.

Ó Duibhir, Ciarán, *Sinn Féin: The First Election, 1908* (Manorhamilton: Drumlin, 1993).

Ó Gráda, Cormac, *Jewish Ireland in the Age of Joyce: A Socioeconomic History* (Princeton: Princeton University Press, 2006).

O'Hegarty, P.S., *History of Ireland under the Union, 1801 to 1922* (London: Methuen, 1952).

O'Hegarty, P.S., *The Victory of Sinn Féin: How it Won it and How it Used it* (Dublin: Talbot Press, 1924 and UCD Press, new ed. 1998).

O'Hegarty, P.S., *Sinn Féin: An Illumination* (Dublin and London: Maunsel, 1919).

O'Kelly, Seán T. (see Ó Ceallaigh).

Ó Lúing, Seán, 'Arthur Griffith and Sinn Féin', in *Leaders and Men of the Easter Rising: Dublin 1916*, ed. F.X. Martin (London, 1967), pp. 55–66.

Ó Lúing, Seán, *Art Gríofa* (Dublin: Sáirséal agus Dill, 1953).

O'Malley, M., *Military Aviation in Ireland 1921–1945* (National University of Ireland, Maynooth, Ph.D thesis, 2007).

O'Riordan, Alison, 'It Was Part of Life Then to Be Called a Dirty Jew', *Irish Independent*, 6 July 2008.

O'Riordan, Manus, 'Connolly, Socialism and the Jewish Worker', *Saothar* 13 (1988), 120–30.

O'Riordan, Manus, 'A Citizen's Defence for Bloomsday', *History Ireland*, 16, no. 3 (2008), 10–11.

O'Riordan, Manus, 'Anti-Semitism in Irish Politics – the Sinn Féin Tradition', *Irish Jewish Yearbook 1984–85*, 15–27.

O'Shea, Katharine, *Charles Stewart Parnell: His Love Story and Political Life*, 2 vols (New York: Doran, 1914).

O'Sullivan, Seumas, *The Rose and the Bottle* (Dublin, 1946).

O'Sullivan, Seumas, *Essays and Recollections* (Dublin and Cork: Talbot Press, 1944).

O'Toole, Fintan, 'Provincial Thinking and the Holocaust', *Irish Times*, 2 September 1992.

Pearse, Padraic, *Collected Works of P. H. Pearse*, 5 vols (Dublin: Phoenix, 1924).

Pakenham, Frank (Earl of Longford) and T. P. O'Neill, *Éamon de Valera* (London: Gill and Macmillan, 1970).

Pakenham, Frank (Earl of Longford), *Peace by Ordeal: An Account from First-Hand Sources of the Negotiation and Signature of the Anglo-Irish Treaty of 1921* (London: Sidgwick & Jackson, 1972. First published 1935).

Phelan, James Duval, *Travel and Comment* (San Francisco: Robertson, 1923).

Pindar, Peter, *The Works of Peter Pindar*, 3 vols (London: John Walker, 1794).

Potts, Willard, *Joyce and the Two Irelands* (Austin: University of Texas Press, 2000).

Pound, Ezra, *The Cantos of Ezra Pound* (New York: New Directions, 1970).

Pound, Ezra, *ABC of Economics* (London: Faber, 1933).

Pratt, L.R., 'Maud Gonne: "Strange Harmonies and Discord"', *Biography*, 6, no. 3 (1983), 189–208.

Quinn, James, 'History and the Making of National Citizens', in Barr, *Literacy* (*infra*), pp. 53–65.

Quinn, James, *Young Ireland and the Writing of History* (Dublin: UCD, 2015).

Rafter, Kevin, *Sinn Féin 1905–2005: In the Shadow of the Gunmen* (Dublin: Gill and Macmillan, 2005).

Regan, John M., *The Irish Counter-Revolution 1921–1936* (Dublin: Gill & Macmillan, 1999).

Reizbaum, Marilyn, *James Joyce's Judaic Other* (Stanford, CA: Stanford University Press, 1999).

Rivlin, Ray, *Shalom Ireland: A Social History of the Jews in Modern Ireland* (Dublin: Gill & Macmillan, 2003).

Rooney, William ('Fear na Muinntire' [Man of the People]), *Prose Writings* (Dublin and Waterford: Gill [1909]).

Rooney, William ('Fear na Muinntire' ['Man of the People']), *Poems and Ballads* (Dublin: *United Irishman* with Gill and O'Donoghue, [1902]).

Rouse, Paul, 'Popular Culture in Ireland', in *Cambridge History of Ireland*, pp. 577–603.

Ryan, Fred ('Irial'), 'Philosophies in Little: Men, Women and Morals', *United Irishman*, 26 January 1901.

Ryan, Mark, *Fenian Memories* (Dublin: Gill, 1946).

Sadlier, J., 'The Fate of Fr Sheehy: a Tale of County Tipperary', in *Young Ireland*, January–February 1885.

Schuchard, Ronald, '"An Attendant Lord": H.W. Nevinson's Friendship with W.B. Yeats', *Yeats Annual*, 7 (1990), 90–130.

Sheehan, Conn, *Arthur Griffith: 'None But Himself Can Parallel'* (s.l., 1992).

Sheehy-Skeffington, Francis, *Michael Davitt: Revolutionary, Agitator and Labour Leader* (Boston: Dana Estes, 1909).

Sheehy-Skeffington, Hanna, *British Militarism as I Have Known It* (New York: Donnelly Press, [1917]).

Shovlin, Frank, 'Who Was Father Conroy? James Joyce, William Rooney, and "The Priest of Adergool"', *James Joyce Quarterly*, 47, 2 (2010), 255–65.

Shuman, E.L., *Practical Journalism: A Complete Manual of the Best Newspaper Methods* (New York: Appleton, 1903).

Sinn Féin, *The Ethics of Sinn Féin* (by Riobard Ua Fhloinn?) (Dublin: Sinn Féin National Council, 1917).

Spurr, David, *The Rhetoric of Empire: Colonial Discourse in Journalism, Travel Writing and Imperial Administration* (Durham and London: Duke University Press, 1993).

St John Gogarty, Oliver, *As I Was Going Down Sackville Street: A Phantasy in Fact* (London: Rich and Cowan, 1937).

St John Gogarty, Oliver, 'The Passing of Arthur Griffith', in *Arthur Griffith: Michael Collins* (Dublin: Martin Lester, [1922]), pp. 52–4.

Staunton, Mathew D., 'The Nation Speaking to Itself: a History of the Sinn Féin Printing and Publishing Co. Ltd., 1906–1914', in J. Genet, S. Mikowski and F. Garcier (eds), *The Book in Ireland* (Newcastle Upon Tyne: Cambridge Scholars, 2008), pp. 228–45.

Steele, K.M., *Women, Press and Politics During the National Revival* (Syracuse, NY: Syracuse University Press, 2007).

Steele, K.M., 'Biography as Promotional Discourse: The Case of Maud Gonne', *Cultural Studies*, 15, no. 1 (2001), 138–60.

Stephens, James, *Arthur Griffith, Journalist and Statesman* (Dublin: Wilson, Hartnell & Co., [1922]).

Stradling, Matthew [Martin Mahony], *Cheap John's Auction* (London: Simpkin, Marshall and Dublin: Hodges, Foster, 1871).

Takagami, S., 'The Fenian Rising in Dublin, March 1867', *Irish Historical Studies*, 39, no. 115 (1995), 340–62.

Talbot, Hayden, *Michael Collins' Own Story* (London: Hutchinson, 1923).

Taylor, Rex, *Michael Collins* (London: Hutchinson, 1958).

Téry, Simone, *En Irlande: De la Guerre d'Indépendance à la Guerre Civile (1914–1923)* (Paris: Flammarion, [1923]).

Thornton, Weldon, *Allusions in* Ulysses: *An Annotated List* (Chapel Hill: University of North Carolina Hill, 1968).

Tóibín, Colm, *Mad, Bad, Dangerous to Know: The Fathers of Wilde, Yeats and Joyce* (London: Viking, 2018).

Tóibín, Colm, *Lady Gregory's Toothbrush* (Dublin: Lilliput, 2002).

Tymoczko, Maria, *The Irish Ulysses* (Berkeley: University of California Press, 1994).

Ungar, Andras, 'Among the Hapsburgs: Arthur Griffith, Stephen Dedalus, and the Myth of Bloom', *Twentieth Century Literature*, 35, no. 4 (1989), 480–510.

Van Tuyll, D.R, Mark O'Brien and Marcel Broersma (eds), *Other Voices: The Irish Diaspora Press in America* (Syracuse, NY: Syracuse University Press, forthcoming).

Walsh, J.P., 'Arthur Griffith, Michael Collins and James D. Phelan of San Francisco', *Éire-Ireland*, 23, no. 4 (1988), 81–94.

Ward, Margaret, *Maud Gonne, Ireland's Joan of Arc* (London: Pandora, 1990).

Waterman, Stanley, 'Changing Residential Patterns of the Dublin Jewish Community', *Irish Geography*, 14 (1981), 41–50.

Weeks, Liam and Mícheál Fathartaigh (eds), *The Treaty: Debating and Establishing the Irish State* (Dublin: Irish Academic Press, 2018).

Whelan, J.R., 'Literature and Nationality', *Shan Van Vocht*, 8 January 1897 and 5 February 1897.

Whelan, Kevin, 'The Memories of "The Dead,"' *Yale Journal of Criticism* 15 (2002), 59–97.

White, J.R., *The Significance of Sinn Féin: Psychological, Political and Economic* (Dublin: Lester, 1919).

Worthington, M.P., 'Folk songs in Joyce's *Ulysses*', *PMLA*, 71, no. 3 (1956), 321–39.

Wynn, Natalie, 'Jews, Antisemitism and Irish Politics: A Tale of Two Narratives', *PaRDeS; Zeitschrift der Vereinigung für Jüdische Studien*, e. V 18, Einblicke in die [insights into] 'British Jewish Studies' (University of Potsdam, 2012), 51–66.

Yeates, Padraig, *Lockout: Dublin 1913* (Dublin: Gill & Macmillan, 2000).

Yeats, W.B., *The Collected Letters of W.B. Yeats*, ed. John Kelly *et al.*, 4 vols (Oxford: Clarendon/Oxford University Press, 1986–2005).

Yeats, W.B., *The Plays, Volume II: The Collected Works of W.B. Yeats*, ed. David and Rosalind Clarke (New York and London: Palgrave, 2001).

Yeats, W.B. *Autobiographies*, ed. W.H. O'Donnell and Douglas Archibald (New York: New York, 1999).

Yeats, W.B., *The Countess Cathleen: Manuscript Materials*, ed. M.J. Sidnell and W.K. Chapman (Ithaca, NY: Cornell University Press, 1999).

Yeats, W.B., *The Variorum Edition of the Poems of W.B. Yeats*, ed. Peter Allt and R.K. Alspach (New York: Macmillan, 1977).

Yeats, W.B., *Uncollected Prose, Vol. 2: Articles and Miscellaneous Prose 1897–1939*, ed. J.P. Frayne and Colton Johnson (New York, 1976).

Yeats, W.B., *Memoirs*, ed. Denis Donoghue (London: Macmillan, 1972).

Yeats, W.B., *Essays and Introductions* (New York and London: Macmillan, 1961).

Yeats, W.B., *The Letters of W.B. Yeats*, ed. Allan Wade (London: Rupert Hart-Davis, 1954).

Yeats, W.B., *Where There Is Nothing*, a play in five acts, *United Irishman* special supplement, Samhain (November) 1902.

Yeats, W.B., *Cathleen ni Hoolihan; A Play in One Act and in Prose* (London: A.H. Bullen, 1902).

Zipperstein, Steven J., 'Inside Kishinev's Pogrom: Hayyim Nahman Bialik, Michael Davitt and the Burden of Truth', in Y. ChaeRan Freeze, Sylvia Fuks Fried, and Eugene R. Sheppard (eds), *The Individual in History: Essays in Honor of Jehuda Reinharz* (Waltham, MA: Brandeis University Press, 2015), pp. 365–83.

Newspapers, Periodicals and Annuals

An t-Óglách; Bell; Capuchin Annual; Catholic Bulletin; Cork Examiner; Dana; Daily Mirror; Éire-Ireland; Evening Herald; Evening Press; Evening Telegraph; Express (Dublin); *Fortnightly Review; Freeman's Journal; The Guardian* (Manchester); *Illustrated London News; Irish Bulletin; Irish Press; The Irish Times; Il Piccolo della Sera* (Trieste); *Irish Worker; Kilkenny People; Lepracaun; Nationality; The New York Times; Observer; Penny Magazine; Pilot (Boston); Scissors & Paste; Shan Van Vocht; Sinn Féin; Sinn Féin: The Oldcastle Monthly Review; Southern Cross* (Buenos Aires); *Spectator; Sunday Independent; Times* (London); *Sun* (New York); *United Irishman; Young Ireland.*

GRIFFITH'S TIMELINE

1871.   March 31: Arthur Joseph Griffith born in Dublin.

1885.   June 20: Receives Young Ireland book prizes from Fenian veteran John O'Leary.

1890.   Oct. 3: Elected president of the Leinster Debating/Literary Club.

1894.   Jan. 18: Invites his future wife Maud ('Mollie') Sheehan to *The Lily of Killarney*.

1897.   January: Goes to South Africa until 1898.

1898.   Oct. 24: Elected on his return to Ireland an honorary member of the Celtic Literary Society.

1899.   March 4: First issue of the weekly *United Irishman*, edited by Griffith.

1899.   Maud Gonne will write in 1938 that she got to know Griffith well during 1899.

1899.   Oct. 11: Boer War begins. Griffith secretary of the pro-Boer Irish Transvaal Committee.

1899.   Dec. 17: Griffith, Gonne and James Connolly clash with police when the colonial secretary Joseph Chamberlain MP visits Ireland.

1900.   Feb. 28: John MacBride, backed by Griffith, fails to be elected to parliament for South Mayo.

1900.   April: Queen Victoria visits Ireland. Gonne and Griffith protest.

1900.   April 9: Griffith jailed for two weeks after assaulting an editor who insulted Gonne.

1900.   April 15 (Easter Sunday): Maud Gonne founds Inghinidhe na hÉireann, women's group. Griffith helps it.

1900.   Sept. 30: First meeting of Griffith's Cumann na nGaedheal.

1901.   May 6: Death of Griffith's best friend William Rooney.

1902.	April 2: First production of Yeats' *Kathleen Ni Houlihan*. Griffith said his advice was taken on this play.
1902.	Oct. 26: Griffith first proposes that Irish MPs withdraw permanently from Westminster to set up an Irish assembly.
1904.	Griffith's *The Resurrection of Hungary* published as a long series of articles and also as a best-selling book.
1905.	Nov. 28: First annual conference of the 'National Council' endorses Griffith's policy of national self-reliance ('Sinn Féin').
1906.	March: *The 'Sinn Fein' Policy*, by Arthur Griffith, published.
1906.	May 5: First issue of Griffith's weekly *Sinn Féin*.
1907.	Jan. 26: First production of J.M. Synge's *Playboy of the Western World*. Griffith objects.
1909.	Aug. 23: First issue of daily *Sinn Féin*. Daily for five months.
1910.	Nov. 24: Arthur Griffith marries 'Mollie' Sheehan.
1911.	Sept. 2: Griffith the only editor to print in full James Joyce's letter about *Dubliners*.
1911.	Sept. 7: Birth of Arthur and Mollie's son.
1912.	Dec. 31: Birth of Arthur and Mollie's daughter.
1914.	July 26: Griffith takes part in Howth gun-running. Gets a rifle.
1914.	August 4: Britain declares war on Germany (First World War).
1914.	Sept. 9: Griffith meets future leaders of the 1916 Rising and agrees a strategy.
1914.	Oct. 26: First issue of Griffith's weekly *Éire-Ireland*. Soon suppressed.
1914.	Dec. 12: First issue of Griffith's weekly *Scissors and Paste*. Soon suppressed.
1915.	June 19: First issue of Griffith's weekly *Nationality*.
1916.	April 24: The Easter Rising begins. Rebels surrender 29 April.
1916.	April 27: Griffith makes his last will.
1916.	May 3: Griffith arrested (interned in England).
1916.	Dec. 23: Griffith released, after eight months, from Reading Gaol.

1917.   April 21: First issue of *Young Ireland: Éire Óg*, helped by Griffith.

1917.   May 9: Victory in the South Longford by-election sees a Sinn Féin candidate elected MP for the first time.

1917.   Oct. 25: De Valera replaces Griffith as president of Sinn Féin. Griffith elected vice-president.

1918.   May 17: Griffith and others arrested (a 'German Plot' is alleged), and interned in Gloucester.

1918.   June 20: While still interned, Griffith is elected MP for the first time, for Cavan East.

1918.   Nov. 11. First World War ends. Armistice Day.

1918.   Dec. 14–28: Sinn Féin's Irish landslide in UK general election. Still interned, Griffith returned again as MP for Cavan East.

1919.   Jan. 21: Dáil Éireann (an Irish parliament) convenes for the first time and declares Ireland a republic. Griffith and some other MPs absent due to their internment.

1919.   Jan. 21: Soloheadbeg ambush. Irish War of Independence begins. It will continue until July 1921.

1919.   March 6: Griffith released, after ten months, from Gloucester Prison.

1919.   April 1: De Valera elected president of Dáil Éireann. Appoints a cabinet. Griffith is made minister for home affairs.

1919.   June 17: Griffith is appointed president-substitute of Dáil Éireann, after de Valera goes to the USA.

1920.   Nov. 21: 'Bloody Sunday' killings. 'Black and Tans' active.

1920.   Nov. 26: Griffith arrested and interned in Mountjoy Prison.

1920.   Dec. 23: Government of Ireland Act (UK) becomes law, dividing Ireland and enabling a parliament in Northern Ireland.

1920.   Dec. 23: De Valera returns from the USA to Ireland after eighteen months. Griffith still in Mountjoy.

1921.   May 19–24: General election throughout Ireland. By agreement, all candidates outside Northern Ireland are returned unopposed.

1921.	June 22: King George V opens the parliament of Northern Ireland.
1921.	June 30: Griffith released from Mountjoy Prison.
1921.	July 10: Truce in War of Independence.
1921.	July 14–21: Four meetings in London between de Valera and Lloyd George to arrange negotiations for a possible treaty. Griffith in London as back-up.
1921.	Oct. 8–Dec. 6: Griffith heads treaty negotiations in London.
1921.	Dec. 2–4: Griffith rushes to Dublin to meet de Valera. Returns to London.
1921.	Dec. 6: Articles of Agreement for the Anglo-Irish Treaty signed by Griffith and others at 2.20 a.m. in Downing Street. De Valera will oppose them.
1922.	Jan. 7: Dáil Éireann approves the proposed treaty by 64 votes to 57.
1922.	Jan. 10: Griffith elected president of Dáil Éireann. De Valera and anti-treaty deputies walk out.
1922.	Feb. 2: James Joyce's *Ulysses* is published.
1922.	June 16: General Election for Dáil returns a pro-treaty majority.
1922.	June 28: Civil War begins. Will last eleven months. Four Courts destroyed 30 June.
1922.	Aug. 2: Harry Boland dies of gunshot wounds.
1922.	Aug. 12: Arthur Griffith collapses and dies.
1922.	Aug. 22: Michael Collins shot dead in Co. Cork.
1922.	October 25: Dáil approves the Constitution of the Irish Free State.
1923.	May: Civil War ends. State joins League of Nations in September.
1949.	April 18: Irish Free State becomes the Republic of Ireland.
1955.	December 14: Ireland joins the United Nations.
1973.	Jan. 1: Ireland joins the EEC (later the EU).
1998.	April 10: The Good Friday Agreement is signed.
2022.	Centenary of the foundation of the Irish state.

INDEX